Use these handy Zagat bookmarks to mark your favorites and the places you'd like to try. Plus, we've included re-useable blank book-marks for you to write on (and wipe off). Browsing through your Zagat guide has never been easier!

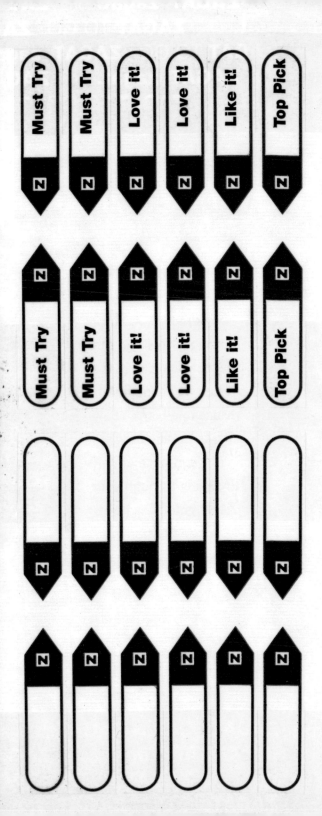

# ZAGAT®

# Atlanta
# Restaurants
# 2008/09

**LOCAL EDITOR**
Shelley Skiles Sawyer
**STAFF EDITOR**
Yoji Yamaguchi

Published and distributed by
Zagat Survey, LLC
4 Columbus Circle
New York, NY 10019
T: 212.977.6000
E: atlanta@zagat.com
www.zagat.com

## ACKNOWLEDGMENTS

We thank The Atlanta Chapter of Les Dames d'Escoffier, The Cook's Warehouse, *flavors – The Forum for Atlanta Food Culture and Dining* magazine, Gena Berry, Helen Cauley, Gina Christman, Diane Flannery, Jan Greene, Valerie Hoff, Carolyn O'Neil, Adair, Samuel and Cole Sawyer, Mr. and Mrs. Blair Skiles, Steven Shukow and Harrison Von Steiff, as well as the following members of our staff: Josh Rogers (associate editor), Amy Cao (editorial assistant), Sean Beachell, Maryanne Bertollo, Sandy Cheng, Reni Chin, Larry Cohn, Deirdre Donovan, Alison Flick, Jeff Freier, Roy Jacob, Natalie Lebert, Mike Liao, Dave Makulec, Andre Pilette, Kimberly Rosado, Becky Ruthenburg, Liz Borod Wright, Sharon Yates, Anna Zappia and Kyle Zolner.

# Contents

# About This Survey

Here are the results of our **2008/09 Atlanta Restaurants Survey,** covering 828 eateries in greater Atlanta, Savannah and other outlying areas. Like all of our guides, this one is based on the collective opinions of thousands of local consumers who have been there before you. Ratings have been updated throughout. We have retained a prior year's review for some places that have had no significant factual or ratings changes.

**WHO PARTICIPATED:** Input from 3,287 frequent diners forms the basis for the ratings and reviews in this guide (their comments are shown in quotation marks within the reviews). Of these surveyors, 50% are women, 50% men; the breakdown by age is 8% in their 20s; 25%, 30s; 25%, 40s; 24%, 50s; and 18%, 60s or above. Collectively they bring roughly 629,000 annual meals worth of experience to this Survey. We sincerely thank each of these participants – this book is really "theirs."

**HELPFUL LISTS:** Whether you're looking for a celebratory meal, a hot scene or a bargain bite, our top lists and indexes can help you find exactly the right place. See Most Popular (page 7), Key Newcomers (page 7), Top Ratings (pages 9-15) and Best Buys (page 16). We've also provided 45 handy indexes.

**OUR EDITOR:** Special thanks go to our local editor, Shelley Skiles Sawyer, a freelance food and travel writer and managing food editor for *flavors - The Forum for Atlanta Food Culture and Dining* magazine, based in Atlanta.

**ABOUT ZAGAT:** This marks our 29th year reporting on the shared experiences of consumers like you. What started in 1979 as a hobby involving 200 of our friends has come a long way. Today we have well over 300,000 surveyors and now cover dining, entertaining, golf, hotels, movies, music, nightlife, resorts, shopping, spas, theater and tourist attractions worldwide.

**SHARE YOUR OPINION:** We invite you to join any of our upcoming surveys – just register at **ZAGAT.com,** where you can rate and review establishments year-round. Each participant will receive a free copy of the resulting guide when published.

**AVAILABILITY:** Zagat guides are available in all major bookstores as well as on **ZAGAT.com, ZAGAT.mobi** (for web-enabled mobile phones) and **ZAGAT TO GO** (for smartphones). The latter two products allow you to contact many thousands of establishments with just one click.

**FEEDBACK:** There is always room for improvement, thus we invite your comments and suggestions about any aspect of our performance. Just contact us at **atlanta@zagat.com.**

New York, NY
June 18, 2008

Nina and Tim Zagat

# What's New

At the risk of repeating ourselves, we're happy to report that things have never been better for Atlanta diners. Restaurateurs are upbeat and coming up with new ideas to serve a hungry public undaunted by the sluggish national economy – witness the 84% of surveyors who say they are dining out more than or as much as they were two years ago.

**LOCAL $OURCERY:** Even if 62% of surveyors are willing to pay a premium for sustainably raised fare (and 58% would pay more for organic), some important newcomers are managing to offer affordably priced menus that emphasize locally sourced produce, meats and other goods. In Buckhead, Tom Catherall's Home (formerly Posh) is where celeb chef Richard Blais is dishing out his farm-to-table New American cuisine. At Holeman and Finch in South Buckhead, Linton Hopkins gets back to basics with everything from his handmade charcuterie to head-to-tail BBQ. Meanwhile, Chez Panisse alum Billy Allin and wife Kristin deliver sustainable American eats at their Decatur gastropub Cakes & Ale. These restaurants are making it possible to go green gastronomically without spending all the green in your wallet.

★ **HOT'LANTA:** Atlanta's explosive development has made it a magnet for major players from all over the country. The hub of recent activity is Midtown, where Jean-Georges Vongerichten is duplicating his Manhattan Spice Market in the new W Atlanta-Midtown hotel, Bay Area chef Chris Yeo and recording artist Ludacris (aka Chris Bridges) have steered their Singaporean spot Straits and Dallas-based Steel is showing the mettle of its Indochine cuisine. Over in Buckhead, seafooder AquaKnox from Las Vegas is betting on its 'global water cuisine' to hit the jackpot, and NYC's Tom Colicchio is gearing up to open an outpost of Craft this summer in the new Rosewood hotel, The Mansion on Peachtree.

**WALK IN THE PARK:** Historic intown neighborhoods have never been so busy. Inman Park newcomer Zaya zings with Mediterranean flavors worthy of the warm, patio-fronted space. Just down the street, in a superbly restored circa-1890 space, Parish ushers in the sights, sounds and tastes of New Orleans, while in nearby Grant Park, Stella offers moderately priced Italian *cucina* in a drop-dead setting next to bucolic Oakland Cemetery.

 **PAYIN' RELIEF:** With the price of virtually everything (except our homes) skyrocketing, it's no surprise that 67% of surveyors are spending more than they were in 2006. Still, the average cost of a meal in Atlanta has risen a modest 2.5% annually since our last survey, to $27.53, which remains well below the national average of $33.80.

Atlanta, GA
June 18, 2008

Shelley Skiles Sawyer

**GEORGIA**

Roswell

Stoney River Steaks*
Duluth

Berkeley Lake

Dobbins Air Force Base

Marietta

Norcross

La Grotta Ravinia

Seasons 52 Dunwoody

Doraville

Carrabba's Italian Grill*

Chamblee

LongHorn Steakhouse*

Smyrna

South City Kitchen ★

Canoe

JOEL

Detail below

Clarkson

Stone Mountain

Blue Ridge Grill
Pano's & Paul's

Decatur

Pine Lake

**Atlanta**

Watershed

Avondale Estates

---

*Check for other locations

Ritz-Carlton Buckhead Dining Room

BluePointe

Maggiano's Little Italy*

Capital Grille

Fogo de Chão

Bone's

Chops/Lobster Bar

Aria

Kyma

Nava

Buckhead Diner

Seasons 52

Antica Posta

Cheesecake Factory

Atlanta Fish Market

La Grotta ★

Five Guys*

Restaurant Eugene

Houston's ★

Ted's Montana Grill*

**Atlanta**

Floataway Cafe

Bacchanalia
Taqueria del Sol*

Nan Thai Fine Dining

PIEDMONT PARK

South City Kitchen

The Oceanaire

14th St.

10th St.

Ecco

Murphy's

**DOWNTOWN ATLANTA**

Sotto Sotto

Flying Biscuit*

CANDLER PARK

Georgia World Congress Center

Kevin Rathbun Steak

Rathbun's

---

# Most Popular

1. Bone's | *Steak*
2. Bacchanalia | *American*
3. Rathbun's | *American*
4. Chops/Lobster | *Seafood/Steak*
5. Aria | *American*
6. Buckhead Diner | *American*
7. Atlanta Fish | *Seafood*
8. Seasons 52 | *American*
9. Canoe | *American*
10. Kyma | *Greek/Seafood*
11. Houston's | *American*
12. JOËL | *French*
13. Cheesecake Fac. | *American*
14. Sotto Sotto | *Italian*
15. Ecco | *Continental*
16. Pano's & Paul's | *Continental*
17. BluePointe | *American*
18. Ritz/Buck. Din. | *French/Med.*
19. Nan Thai | *Thai*
20. La Grotta | *Italian*
21. Watershed | *Southern*
22. Maggiano's | *Italian*
23. Kevin Rathbun Steak | *Steak*
24. Capital Grille | *Steak*
25. Fogo de Chão | *Brazilian/Steak*
26. Murphy's* | *American*
27. Blue Ridge | *Southern*
28. South City Kitchen | *Southern*
29. Flying Biscuit | *Southern*
30. Floataway Cafe | *French/Italian*
31. Restaurant Eugene | *American*
32. Five Guys | *Burgers*
33. Ted's Montana* | *American*
34. Stoney River | *Steak*
35. Carrabba's | *Italian*
36. Nava | *Southwestern*
37. Taqueria/Sol | *Mex./Southwest*
38. Antica Posta | *Italian*
39. LongHorn Steak | *Steak*
40. Oceanaire | *Seafood*

It's obvious that many of the above restaurants are among the Atlanta area's most expensive, but if popularity were calibrated to price, we suspect that a number of other restaurants would join their ranks. Thus, we have added a list of 68 Best Buys on page 16.

## KEY NEWCOMERS

Our editors' take on some of the year's main arrivals. See page 171 for a full list.

Allegro | *Italian*

AquaKnox | *Seafood*

Beleza | *Brazilian*

Bluefin | *Asian Fusion/Japanese*

BrickTop's | *American*

Cuerno | *Spanish*

Hil, The | *American/French*

Holeman and Finch | *American*

Home | *Southern*

Lola | *Italian*

MF Buckhead | *Japanese*

Peasant Bistro | *French/Med.*

Room at 12 | *American/Steak*

Spice Market | *SE Asian*

Stella | *Italian*

Top Flr | *American*

Valenza | *Italian*

Zaya | *Mediterranean*

---

\* Indicates a tie with restaurant above

# Ratings & Symbols

| Zagat Top Spot | Name | Symbols | Cuisine | Zagat Ratings | | | |
|---|---|---|---|---|---|---|---|
| | | | | FOOD | DECOR | SERVICE | COST |

| Area, Address & Contact | **Ⓩ Tim & Nina's** ◑ *Southern* | | | ▽ 23 | 9 | 13 | $15 |
| | Buckhead \| 3000 Peach Branch Blvd. (Peach Pit Dr.) \| 404-555-6700 \| www.zagat.com | | | | | | |

**Review, surveyor comments in quotes**

"When the little ones howl with hunger", bring 'em to this Buckhead "feedfest", where "from beets to sweets, it's a feat to eat" it all; the Southern spread is known as "the heart of heartburn", the staff is "on permanent cigarette break" and the "plywood-and-staple" interior "wasn't designed by the Johnson Studio", but "who cares" when you "shovel it in" for "practically a plug nickel"?

---

**Ratings**

**Food, Decor** and **Service** are rated on the Zagat 0 to 30 scale.

| 0 | – | 9 | poor to fair |
| 10 | – | 15 | fair to good |
| 16 | – | 19 | good to very good |
| 20 | – | 25 | very good to excellent |
| 26 | – | 30 | extraordinary to perfection |
| | ▽ | | low response \| less reliable |

**Cost** reflects our surveyors' average estimate of the price of a dinner with one drink and tip and is a benchmark only. Lunch is usually 25% less.

For **newcomers** or survey **write-ins** listed without ratings, the price range is indicated as follows:

| I | $25 and below |
| M | $26 to $40 |
| E | $41 to $65 |
| VE | $66 or more |

---

**Symbols**

| Ⓩ | Zagat Top Spot (highest ratings, popularity and importance) |
| ◑ | serves after 11 PM |
| Ⓢ | closed on Sunday |
| Ⓜ | closed on Monday |
| ⊄ | no credit cards accepted |

# Top Food Ratings

Excludes places with low votes and those in Savannah and Other Outlying Areas.

29 | Bacchanalia | *American*

28 | Quinones Room | *American*
Rathbun's | *American*
Restaurant Eugene | *American*

27 | Aria | *American*
Ritz/Buck. Din. | *French/Med.*
Bone's | *Steak*
Park 75 | *American*
MF Sushibar | *Japanese*
Tamarind Seed | *Thai*
di Paolo | *Italian*
Nan Thai | *Thai*
Taka | *Japanese*
Sotto Sotto | *Italian*
Chops/Lobster | *Seafood/Steak*

26 | Alon's | *Bakery*
MF Buckhead | *Japanese*
Pano's & Paul's | *Continental*
Sam & Dave's | *BBQ*
JOËL | *French*

Pampas | *Argentinean/Steak*
Haru Ichiban | *Japanese*
Kevin Rathbun Steak | *Steak*
Rice Thai | *Thai*
La Grotta | *Italian*
Ritz/Atlanta | *Southern*
Canoe | *American*
Tierra | *Pan-Latin*
Little Alley | *Mediterranean*

25 | Nikolai's | *Continental/French*
Kyma | *Greek/Seafood*
Floataway Cafe | *French/Italian*
Sushi Huku | *Japanese*
Paolo's Gelato | *Ice Cream*
Chocolate Pink | *Dessert*
Watershed | *Southern*
Atmosphere | *French*
Souper Jenny | *Soup*
Eurasia Bistro | *Pan-Asian*
New York Prime | *Steak*

## BY CUISINE

### AMERICAN (NEW)
29 | Bacchanalia
28 | Quinones Room
Rathbun's
Restaurant Eugene
27 | Aria

### AMERICAN (TRAD.)
24 | Murphy's
Sun in Belly
23 | Paul's
Greenwoods
22 | George's

### ASIAN/PAN-ASIAN
25 | Eurasia Bistro
Sia's
21 | Pacific Rim Bistro
Aqua Blue
20 | Silk

### BAKERY
26 | Alon's
23 | Joli Kobe
20 | Corner Cafe
19 | La Madeleine

### BARBECUE
26 | Sam & Dave's
23 | Fat Matt's Rib
Harold's
Swallow at Hollow
22 | Jim N' Nick's

### BURGERS
22 | Vortex B&G
21 | Five Guys
18 | Universal Joint
16 | Zesto
Johnny Rockets

### CAJUN/CREOLE
25 | Hal's on Old Ivy
22 | Redfish
Tasting Room
21 | Pappadeaux
19 | Atkins Park

### CARIBBEAN/CUBAN
22 | Havana Sandwich
Las Palmeras
20 | Fuego
19 | Coco Loco's Cafe

## CHINESE

- 23 Chopstix
- Canton Cooks
- 21 Little Szechuan
- Hsu's Gourmet
- 20 Canton House

## COFFEE SHOP/DINER

- 24 Sun in Belly
- 23 Thumbs Up
- Ria's
- 21 Original Pancake House
- 20 Crescent Moon

## CONTINENTAL

- 26 Pano's & Paul's
- 25 Nikolai's Roof
- Ecco
- 24 Clark & Schwenk's
- Ritz/Buckhead Café

## DELIS/SANDWICHES

- 25 Muss & Turner's
- 23 Fickle Pickle
- 22 Havana Sandwich
- Metrofresh
- New Yorker Marketpl.

## DESSERT

- 27 Aria
- 26 Alon's
- 25 Paolo's Gelato
- Chocolate Pink
- 21 Dailey's

## ECLECTIC

- 22 Metrofresh
- SoHo
- 19 Vickery's
- 18 Eats
- 17 Luckie

## FRENCH

- 26 JOËL
- 25 Nikolai's Roof
- Floataway Cafe
- Atmosphere
- 22 Trois

## GREEK/MID EAST

- 25 Kyma
- 24 Rumi's
- Mezza
- 21 Persepolis
- Sultan's

## INDIAN

- 24 Madras Saravana
- 23 Zyka
- 22 Bhojanic
- Udipi Cafe
- 21 Himalayas

## ITALIAN

- 27 di Paolo
- Sotto Sotto
- 26 La Grotta
- 25 Floataway Cafe
- 24 La Tavola

## JAPANESE

- 27 MF Sushibar
- Taka
- 26 MF Buckhead
- Haru Ichiban
- 25 Sushi Huku

## MEDITERRANEAN

- 27 Ritz/Buckhead Din. Rm.
- 26 Little Alley
- 23 Eno
- Café Lily
- Krog Bar

## MEXICAN/TEX-MEX

- 24 Nuevo Laredo
- Taqueria del Sol
- 23 Pure Taqueria
- Pappasito's
- 22 Zapata

## PIZZA

- 24 Cameli's Pizza
- Shorty's
- 23 Fritti
- Baraonda
- 21 Osteria 832

## PUB FOOD

- 21 Brick Store
- 20 Marlow's Tavern
- 18 Meehan's Public
- Universal Joint
- 17 Manuel's Tavern

## SEAFOOD

- 27 Chops/Lobster Bar
- 25 Kyma
- 24 Clark & Schwenk's
- Cabernet
- 23 Atlanta Fish Market

## SOUL FOOD

| 24 | Fat Matt's Chicken |
| 23 | Fat Matt's Rib |
| 22 | Horseradish |

## SOUTHERN

| 26 | Ritz/Atlanta |
| 25 | Watershed |
| 24 | Wisteria |
|    | JCT. Kitchen |

## STEAKHOUSES

| 27 | Bone's |
|    | Chops/Lobster Bar |
| 26 | Pampas Steak |

|    | Kevin Rathbun Steak |
| 25 | New York Prime |

## THAI

| 27 | Tamarind Seed |
|    | Nan Thai |
| 26 | Rice Thai |
| 24 | Little Bangkok |
| 23 | Mali |

## VEGETARIAN

| 24 | Madras Saravana |
| 22 | Cafe Sunflower |
|    | Udipi Cafe |
| 19 | Flying Biscuit |
|    | R. Thomas Deluxe |

# BY SPECIAL FEATURE

## BRUNCH

| 27 | Park 75 |
| 26 | Canoe |
| 25 | Watershed |
|    | Atmosphere |
|    | Babette's Cafe |

## BUSINESS DINING

| 29 | Bacchanalia |
| 28 | Restaurant Eugene |
| 27 | Aria |
|    | Bone's |
|    | Chops/Lobster Bar |

## CELEBRITY CHEFS

| 29 | Bacchanalia |
|    | (Anne Quatrano, Clifford Harrison) |
| 28 | Rathbun's |
|    | (Kevin Rathbun) |
|    | Restaurant Eugene |
|    | (Linton Hopkins) |
| 27 | Aria |
|    | (Gerry Klaskala) |
|    | Ritz/Buckhead Din. Rm. |
|    | (Arnaud Berthelier) |

## CHILD-FRIENDLY

| 25 | Watershed |
|    | Souper Jenny |
| 24 | Wisteria |
|    | Murphy's |
|    | Madras Saravana |

## HOTEL DINING

| 27 | Ritz/Buckhead Din. Rm. |
|    | Park 75 (Four Seasons) |
| 26 | La Grotta (Crowne Plaza) |

|    | Ritz/Atlanta |
| 25 | Nikolai's Roof (Hilton) |

## NEWCOMERS (RATED)

| 26 | MF Buckhead |
| 23 | Beleza |
|    | Relish |
| 22 | Valenza |
| 19 | BrickTop's |

## PEOPLE-WATCHING

| 28 | Rathbun's |
| 27 | Aria |
|    | Nan Thai |
| 26 | MF Buckhead |
| 25 | Kyma |

## PRIX FIXE/ TASTING MENUS

| 29 | Bacchanalia |
| 28 | Quinones Room |
|    | Restaurant Eugene |
| 27 | Ritz/Buckhead Din. Rm. |
|    | Park 75 |

## QUICK BITES

| 26 | Alon's |
| 25 | Chocolate Pink |
|    | Souper Jenny |
| 24 | Shorty's |
|    | Nuevo Laredo |

## QUIET DINING

| 28 | Quinones Room |
|    | Restaurant Eugene |
| 27 | Ritz/Buckhead Din. Rm. |
| 26 | Pano's & Paul's |
|    | La Grotta |

## ROMANTIC

- 29 Bacchanalia
- 28 Quinones Room
-    Restaurant Eugene
- 27 Ritz/Buckhead Din. Rm.
-    Sotto Sotto

## SINGLES SCENES

- 25 Hal's on Old Ivy
- 24 Repast
-    Capital Grille
-    Shaun's
-    Pricci

# BY LOCATION

## ALPHARETTA

- 27 di Paolo
- 26 Pampas Steak
- 24 Cabernet
- 23 Pure Taqueria
-    Bonefish Grill

## ATLANTIC STATION

- 20 Willy's Mexicana
-    Lobby at 12
- 19 Rosa Mexicano
- 18 Dolce Enoteca
- 17 Strip

## BROOKHAVEN

- 23 Haven
- 22 Valenza
- 19 Terra Terroir
-    Chin Chin
- 18 Pub 71

## BUCKHEAD

- 27 Aria
-    Ritz/Buckhead Din. Rm.
-    Bone's
-    Taka
-    Chops/Lobster Bar

## CHAMBLEE

- 21 Five Guys
-    Himalayas
- 20 El Taco Veloz
-    Athens Pizza
- 19 Pig-N-Chik

## CHESHIRE BRIDGE

- 25 Woodfire Grill
- 24 Little Bangkok
-    Taqueria del Sol
- 22 Alfredo's
-    Nino's

## COBB

- 24 Stoney River
- 22 Houston's
- 21 Sal Grosso
- 20 Maggiano's
- 19 La Madeleine

## DECATUR

- 25 Watershed
-    Eurasia Bistro
- 24 Madras Saravana
-    Mezza
-    Sushi Avenue

## DOWNTOWN

- 26 Ritz/Atlanta
- 25 Nikolai's Roof
-    Morton's
- 24 French Am. Brasserie
- 23 Ruth's Chris

## DULUTH

- 26 Haru Ichiban
- 25 Sia's
- 24 Stoney River
- 22 Melting Pot
-    Kurt's

## DUNWOODY

- 26 La Grotta
- 25 McKendrick's Steak
- 24 Com
- 23 Fleming's/Steak
- 22 Chequers

## EAST ATLANTA

- 22 Earl, The
- 21 Figo Pasta
-    Five Guys
- 20 Grant Pizza
- 18 Azio

## EMORY

- 25 Floataway Cafe
- 22 Thai Chili
- 21 Top Spice
-    Mellow Mushroom
- 20 Le Giverny

## INMAN PARK

- 28 Rathbun's
- 27 Sotto Sotto
- 26 Kevin Rathbun Steak
- 24 Shaun's
-    Wisteria

## KENNESAW

- 22 Melting Pot
- 21 Zucca
- 20 Carrabba's
- 19 Ted's Montana
- Chin Chin

## MARIETTA

- 26 Sam & Dave's
- 24 Hashiguchi
- 23 Aspens/Steak
- Pappasito's
- 22 La Parrilla

## MIDTOWN

- 27 Park 75
- MF Sushibar
- Tamarind Seed
- Nan Thai
- 26 Tierra

## NORCROSS

- 25 Grace 17.20
- 23 Hi Life
- Dominick's
- 22 Zapata
- 21 Pappadeaux

## OUTLYING AREAS

- 28 Five & Ten
- 24 Last Resort
- 22 Blue Willow
- Basil Press
- La Parrilla

## PONCEY-HIGHLAND

- 25 Babette's Cafe
- Pura Vida
- 23 TWO urban licks
- 22 Java Jive
- 20 Fellini's Pizza

## ROSWELL

- 26 Rice Thai
- Little Alley
- 24 Nagoya
- Stoney River
- 23 Fickle Pickle

## SANDY SPRINGS

- 25 Sushi Huku
- 24 Rumi's

- 23 Joli Kobe
- Canton Cooks
- Ruth's Chris

## SAVANNAH

- 25 Elizabeth on 37th
- Sapphire Grill
- Garibaldi's
- 23 Bonefish Grill
- 22 Il Pasticcio

## SMYRNA

- 25 Muss & Turner's
- 23 South City Kitchen
- Blackstone
- 22 Jim N' Nick's
- 21 Zucca

## SOUTH BUCKHEAD

- 28 Restaurant Eugene
- 23 Paul's
- Taurus
- 22 Houston's
- Cafe Sunflower

## TUCKER

- 24 Shorty's
- 20 Crescent Moon
- Blue Ribbon
- Matthews
- 19 Bambinelli's

## VININGS

- 26 Canoe
- 24 Clark & Schwenk's
- 22 SoHo
- 21 Mellow Mushroom
- River Room

## VIRGINIA-HIGHLAND

- 26 Alon's
- 25 Paolo's Gelato
- 24 La Tavola
- Murphy's
- Fat Matt's Chicken

## WESTSIDE

- 29 Bacchanalia
- 28 Quinones Room
- 24 JCT. Kitchen
- Food Studio
- Nuevo Laredo

# Top Decor Ratings

**27**
Nan Thai
Quinones Room

**26**
Ritz/Buckhead Din. Rm.
Canoe
Restaurant Eugene
Kevin Rathbun Steak
MF Buckhead
Nikolai's Roof
Bacchanalia

**25**
BluePointe
JOËL
Aria
Park 75
Trois
Food Studio
Grace 17.20
Krog Bar
TWO urban licks
Rathbun's
ONE. midtown

Ecco

**24**
Chops/Lobster Bar
Kyma
Sun Dial
Capital Grille
Ritz/Buckhead Café
Ritz/Atlanta
Imperial Fez
Pampas Steak
Eurasia Bistro
City Grill
Blue Ridge
Dolce Enoteca
Au Pied
French Am. Brasserie

**23**
Nam
Aspens/Steak
Ray's on the River
Luckie
Beleza

## OUTDOORS

Food 101
Horseradish Grill
Ibiza
Mosaic
Portofino

Rice Thai
Ritz/Atlanta
Shaun's
Six Feet Under
TAP

## ROMANCE

Beleza
Clark & Schwenck's
Cuerno
Feast
Food Studio

Quinones Room
Repast
Ritz/Buckhead Din. Rm.
Room at 12
Sia's

## ROOMS

AquaKnox
Bistro VG
Kevin Rathbun Steak
Lola
MF Buckhead

Oceanaire
ONE. midtown
Peasant Bistro
Spice Market
TWO urban licks

## VIEWS

Canoe
Capital Grille
French Am. Brasserie
JCT. Kitchen
Nikolai's Roof

Ray's on the River
Stats
Sun Dial
Taurus
Top Flr

# Top Service Ratings

| | |
|---|---|
| **29** Quinones Room | **24** Morton's |
| **28** Bacchanalia | New York Prime |
| Ritz/Buckhead Din. Rm. | Kyma |
| **27** Bone's | Fogo de Chão |
| Park 75 | McKendrick's Steak |
| **26** Restaurant Eugene | Hal's on Old Ivy |
| La Grotta | Sotto Sotto |
| Nan Thai | Blue Ridge |
| Aria | Sia's |
| Chops/Lobster Bar | Rice Thai |
| Nikolai's Roof | di Paolo |
| Ritz/Atlanta | Food Studio |
| **25** Pano's & Paul's | Pampas Steak |
| Clark & Schwenk's | Wisteria |
| Rathbun's | Floataway Cafe |
| Capital Grille | Ritz/Buckhead Café |
| JOËL | **23** Eurasia Bistro |
| Canoe | Alfredo's |
| Kevin Rathbun Steak | Babette's Cafe |
| MF Buckhead | Tierra |

# Best Buys

In order of Bang for the Buck rating.

1. Paolo's Gelato
2. Belly General
3. Souper Jenny
4. Five Guys
5. Chocolate Pink
6. Varsity
7. Java Jive
8. Bobby & June's
9. Willy's Mexicana
10. George's
11. Rising Roll Sandwich
12. Thumbs Up
13. Oak Grove Market
14. Chipotle
15. Zesto
16. Fickle Pickle
17. Cameli's Pizza
18. Alon's
19. Dressed Salads
20. Metrofresh
21. Sam & Dave's
22. Slope's BBQ
23. New Yorker Marketpl.
24. Ria's
25. Silver Skillet
26. Matthews
27. Fellini's Pizza
28. El Taco Veloz
29. Grant Pizza
30. Crescent Moon
31. Havana Sandwich
32. La Parrilla
33. White House
34. Fresh to Order
35. Nirvana Café
36. Jalisco
37. Harold's BBQ
38. Fat Matt's Chicken
39. Taqueria del Sol
40. Eats

## OTHER GOOD VALUES

Ann's Snack Bar
Barbecue Kitchen
Blue Eyed Daisy
Brake Pad
Bread Garden
Busy Bee
Caribe Café
Carver's Country Kitchen
88 Tofu House
El Rey de Taco
Gumbeaux's
Hometown BBQ
Jake's
Madras Chettinaad
Mexico City
Old South BBQ
Pho 79
Pho Dai Loi
Pho Hoa
Provisions to Go
Pung Mie
Rexall Grill
Rib Ranch
Salsa
Silver Midtown Grill
Son's Place
Stella
Thelma's Kitchen

# RESTAURANT
# DIRECTORY

# Atlanta

|  | FOOD | DECOR | SERVICE | COST |

**Agave**  *Southwestern*                                  | 22 | 20 | 22 | $30 |

**Cabbagetown** | 242 Boulevard SE (Carroll St.) | 404-588-0006 |
www.agaverestaurant.com

A "hip intown crowd" gravitates to this "slice of New Mexico" in
Cabbagetown for "top-notch" Southwestern cuisine with some
"new twists", which can be "well lubricated" by an "impressive margarita selection"; the "caring owner" and his "awesome" staff aim to
please, and the "stylish" space boasts two fireplaces and an "attractive" enclosed patio; though it's "on the pricey side", most consider
it a "class act" all around.

**Agnes & Muriel's**  *Southern*                         | 18 | 19 | 19 | $22 |

**Midtown** | 1514 Monroe Dr. NE (Piedmont Ave.) | 404-885-1000 |
www.mominthekitchen.com

Fans find this "charming" Midtown Southerner a "hoot" as they
"carb it up" on "yummy-in-the-tummy" 1950s "housewife cuisine"
that matches the "campy" "retro" digs complete with "Barbie dolls"
and "happy aqua walls"; the service is "attentive", with a "sense of
humor", but to detractors dismayed by "mediocre" eats and "freakish" decor, what "used to be hip is now past its sell-by date."

**Alfredo's**  *Italian*                                  | 22 | 13 | 23 | $31 |

**Cheshire Bridge** | 1989 Cheshire Bridge Rd. NE (bet. Lavista &
Piedmont Rds.) | 404-876-1380 | www.alfredositalianrestaurant.com

It's "all about nostalgia" at this Cheshire Bridge "institution" that
"seems like its been there forever", dishing out "solid interpretations" of "old-time" Italian-American "comfort food" since the days
of "telephones with dials"; it's "still charming", thanks to "low-key,
attentive" waiters who "really care" and the "kitsch" of the "timewarp" decor, complete with "dim lighting", "fake '70s paneling" and
"red leather" booths.

**NEW Allegro**  *Italian*                          ▽ | 20 | 22 | 22 | $42 |

**Midtown** | The Belvedere | 560 Dutch Valley Rd. (Monroe Dr.) |
404-888-1890 | www.allegroatlanta.com

Midtowners are "impressed" by this Italian newcomer, a "solid addition" to the city's dining scene showcasing the "marvelous" cuisine
of chef Jose Rego (ex Sotto Sotto), which is served by a "young" staff
in a "lovely" space highlighted by a pleasant wraparound patio; critics are less upbeat about "inconsistent" fare and service, but most
agree it "shows great promise" and "can't wait to go back."

**Z Alon's**  *Bakery*                                    | 26 | 16 | 19 | $15 |

**NEW Dunwoody** | Park Pl. | 4505 Ashford Dunwoody Rd.
(Perimeter Ctr.) | 678-397-1781
**Virginia-Highland** | 1394 N. Highland Ave. (Morningside Dr.) |
404-872-6000
www.alons.com

"Neighbors from six zip codes" "line up" at this "unbelievable"
Virginia-Highland bakery for "exceptional bread and pastries" (a

"sin worth committing") and "phenomenal" prepared foods, including "fantastic" sandwiches and "fabulous" salads; service ranges from "sharp" to "spotty", there's "limited seating", which is "primarily for takeout", and you'll need to "keep your wits about you as you fight" the "crowds", which is why many are "jumping for joy" at the opening of the larger, "snazzy" Dunwoody sibling in 2008.

### Amalfi ⊠ *Italian*  ▽ 23 | 14 | 19 | $30

**Roswell** | 292 S. Atlanta St. (½ mi. south of Marietta Hwy.) | 770-645-9983 | www.amalfiatlanta.com

"*Bellissima*" bray boosters of this midpriced, "real-deal" Italian located in a Roswell strip mall that's "all about its freshly prepared", "authentic" dishes and service that keeps "getting better"; the atmosphere is "quiet" in the "simple" environs that are ideal for "marathon dinners" and intimate "talk-a-thons."

### **NEW** American Girl Place  *American*  - | - | - | I

**Alpharetta** | North Point Mall | 1202 N. Point Circle (N. Point Pkwy.) | 770-625-5222 | www.americangirl.com

Treat the apple of your eye to brunch, lunch, dinner or the ever popular dessert bar at this casual American bistro in the Alpharetta outpost of the toy store chain, where the bright, confectionlike setting is all about the eponymous doll – i.e. special high chairs for 'Felicity' or 'Samantha', plus a huge loaner stash if you forgot your own or it needs some company; just no Barbies please.

### American Roadhouse  *Diner*  18 | 13 | 18 | $14

**Virginia-Highland** | 842 N. Highland Ave. (bet. Drewry St. & Greenwood Ave.) | 404-872-2822 | www.american-roadhouse.com

"They actually care about toast" at this "reliable", "no-nonsense" American on the main drag in Virginia-Highland, where "long lines of people" file in the doors to "dig into" "outrageous" portions of "tasty" "traditional breakfast food prepared just the way you want it"; the "casual" digs are "nothing fancy", but the "surroundings are lovely", the prices are "reasonable" and the setting is "kid-friendly."

### Anis Bistro  *French*  22 | 20 | 18 | $33

**Buckhead** | 2974 Grandview Ave. (Pharr Rd.) | 404-233-9889 | www.anisbistro.com

This "laid-back" Buckhead boîte "takes ooh-la-la to a new level" with its "authentic" and "reasonably priced" Gallic cuisine, which is brought to table by "delightful" "French-accented" servers; alfresco dining on the "special" year-round patio is a "close-your-eyes-and-you're-in-Provence" experience that's "perfect for a date", but detractors fret over an occasionally "absent" staff that seems to be "daydreaming of France."

### Annie's Thai Castle ⓜ *Thai*  22 | 15 | 18 | $27

**Buckhead** | 3195 Roswell Rd. NE (Peachtree Rd.) | 404-264-9546

For "several years running" this "dependable" Buckhead Thai has been serving "straightforward" "favorites to please all palates"; the "dimly lit" interior "leaves a lot to be desired" and frugal foes fume it's "expensive", but "consistent" cooking and "friendly" service keep loyal subjects coming back.

**Ann's Snack Bar** *American*  ▽ 23 | 5 | 13 | $10

**Downtown** | 1615 Memorial Dr. (Wyman St.) | 404-687-9207

Fans learn how to "mind the rules" at this "American treasure" in Downtown ("Atlanta's version of the 'Soup Nazi'") for Miss Ann's "legendary" "handmade" ghetto burger, which many deem the "best you'll ever put in your mouth" and, some claim, could "knock a man down with its weight alone"; be prepared to "brave her attitude" as well as the "two-hour waits" at this "small dive" that's short on seats (only eight) but "full of character."

**Anthony's** 🅂 *American*  19 | 23 | 21 | $52

**Buckhead** | 3109 Piedmont Rd. (bet. E. Paces Ferry & Peachtree Rds.) | 404-262-7379 | www.anthonysfinedining.com

Like "Tara revisited", this New American housed in an "elegant", "historic" Southern mansion "nestled" on three wooded acres within "the congestion of Buckhead" is an "impressive" locale "ideal" for "tourists", corporate events and special occasions; the Southern-accented fare is "well prepared" and the staff "anticipates your needs", and while some find the victuals "overpriced", others frankly don't give a damn thanks to the "lovely romantic setting."

**🆉 Antica Posta** *Italian*  24 | 20 | 22 | $46

**Buckhead** | 519 E. Paces Ferry Rd. (Piedmont Rd. NE) | 404-262-7112 | www.anticaposta.com

"They get it" at this "exceptional" (but "expensive") Northern Italian "in the heart of Buckhead", where "superb" "Tuscan classics" "with a creative flair" "melt in your mouth"; owner Marco Betti is a "real pro" who "makes you feel like family" in the "quaint", "cozy" setting of a remodeled house, and while the tables may be "so tight you could marry your neighbor", you can always catch your breath in the "spacious" downstairs bar.

**Après Diem** *Continental*  17 | 19 | 16 | $22

**Midtown** | Midtown Promenade | 931 Monroe Dr. NE (Virginia Ave.) | 404-872-3333 | www.apresdiem.com

"Feel hip lounging in a chaise" "surrounded by deep people" at this "bohemian" Midtown Continental offering "affordable bites", an "amazing dessert case" and an "extensive drink menu" in an "eclectic", "candlelit" space that becomes a "twentysomething heaven" when the "very late-night crowd" rolls in; "down-to-earth" servers are "friendly" but "be prepared to wait (and wait and wait) for your check"; N.B. there's live jazz on Wednesdays.

**Aqua Blue** *Eclectic/Pan-Asian*  21 | 21 | 21 | $37

**Roswell** | 1564 Holcomb Bridge Rd. (Old Alabama Rd.) | 770-643-8886 | www.aquablueatl.com

At this "familiar, upscale" Roswell spot, "unique combinations" of Asian-accented Eclectic fare, "out-of-this-world sushi" and "stellar martinis" are served in a "trendy" space, with a "beautiful bar scene" that may "not be for those with heart conditions"; though some grouse the "sexy" scene is cooled by "mediocre" service and "overpriced" eats, others insist it's "the place to take a date" for a "big city experience in the 'burbs."

### NEW AquaKnox  *Seafood*   `- | - | - | E`
**Buckhead** | Terminus Bldg. | 3280 Peachtree Rd. NE (Piedmont Rd.) | 404-477-5600 | www.aquaknox.net

Pros predict that this "excellent" upscale seafooder in Buckhead is "destined to become an Atlanta favorite" thanks to chef William Sigley's "spectacular" 'global water cuisine', and service "as good as you'll find in any place"; the "fabulous" space awash with shades of blue, wave patterns and crystal bubbles is highlighted by an open kitchen and "cool waterfall wine cellar", which are nearly overshadowed by a bar scene attracting some of the "city's prettiest people."

### Z Aria ⊠ *American*   `27 | 25 | 26 | $56`
**Buckhead** | 490 E. Paces Ferry Rd. NE (Maple Dr.) | 404-233-7673 | www.aria-atl.com

Gerry Klaskala's "destination restaurant" in Buckhead "never misses", offering "sublime", "slow-cooked" New American cuisine, "fabulous" desserts, "killer wines" and "splendid", "knowledgeable" service in a "refined", "minimalist" space with a "secret romantic table in the wine cellar"; critics complain of a "noisy" scene, a "slightly superior attitude" from the staff and "very, very high prices", but most agree it's "worth a splurge for that special occasion."

### Aspens Signature Steak  *Steak*   `23 | 23 | 22 | $38`
**Marietta** | Kroger Shopping Ctr. | 2942 Shallowford Rd. (Sandy Plains Rd.) | 678-236-1400
**Marietta** | Avenues Shopping Ctr. | 3625 Dallas Hwy. SW (1 mi. west of Barrett Pkwy.) | 770-419-1744
www.knowwheretogogh.com

The "awesome" steaks and "melt-in-your-mouth" prime rib could "turn a vegetarian into a meat eater" at this "upscale", yet "comfortable" Marietta pair from the Sedgwick Group (Bistro VG and Pure), where the "early-bird specials are worth dining early for"; "cozy" lodge decor matches the "warm" ambiance and "exceedingly polite" service, and while critics claim "consistency is often an issue", others consider them some of the "best dining in the area."

### Athens Pizza House  *Pizza*   `20 | 12 | 18 | $14`
**Chamblee** | Chamblee Plaza | 5550 Peachtree Industrial Blvd. (Longview Dr.) | 770-452-8282
**Decatur** | Athens Plaza | 1341 Clairmont Rd. (N. Decatur Rd.) | 404-636-1100
www.athenspizzaatlanta.com

Families and students "on a budget" flock to this duo of independently owned Greek pizzerias in Chamblee and Decatur, which are "highly recommended" for "fresh" pies ("feta makes it a standout") and "reliable" "authentic" Hellenic eats, served by a "friendly" staff in "comfortable" digs that are "nothing fancy"; naysayers

| | FOOD | DECOR | SERVICE | COST |

nix the "salty" fare and service that's "hit-or-miss", but for others it's a "no-brainer."

## Atkins Park ◐ *American*  | 19 | 18 | 18 | $23 |

**Smyrna** | Shops at Village Green | 2840 Atlanta Rd. (Spring St.) | 770-435-1887
**Cumming** | Vickery Vill. | 5820 S. Vickery St. (Post Rd.) | 678-513-2333
**Virginia-Highland** | 794 N. Highland Ave. NE (St. Charles Ave.) | 404-876-7249
www.atkinspark.com

Whether you come for the "reliable" brunch or "pub grub" during a bit of "late boozing", these "affordable", "kid-friendly" Americans "do not disappoint" with "well-executed" Cajun-accented fare and "bend-over-backwards" service that makes up somewhat for the "second-hand smoke" from the bar; the Virginia-Highland sibling is "filled with local history", the "quaint" Smyrna location has a "delightful" patio that's usually crowded with "singles" and "soccer moms", and the newest spot in Cumming boasts "cozy fireplaces inside and out."

## Atlanta Bread Co. *Deli*  | 17 | 13 | 15 | $12 |

**Marietta** | Merchant's Walk | 1255 Johnson Ferry Rd. NE (E. Cobb Dr.) | 770-509-3838
**Smyrna** | 4490-B S. Cobb Dr. (Cumberland Pkwy.) | 770-438-6800
**Cumming** | 908 E. Buford Hwy. (Market Place Blvd.) | 770-888-9921
**Douglasville** | Desktop Plaza | 6875-A Douglas Blvd. (Bill Arp Rd.) | 678-715-5481
**Suwanee** | 3320 Lawrenceville Suwanee Rd. (Satellite Blvd.) | 678-541-0320
**Morrow** | 1943 Mt. Zion Rd. (Mt. Zion Blvd.) | 770-472-1997
**Peachtree City** | 401 City Circle (I-74) | 770-486-1330
**Snellville** | Presidential Commons Shopping Ctr. | 1708 Scenic Hwy. (bet. Janmar Rd. SW & Tree Ln. SW) | 678-344-9099
**Woodstock** | 180 Woodstock Square Ave. (I-92) | 678-445-2794
www.atlantabread.com

A "somewhat healthy alternative to fast food", this "bustling" deli chain dishes out a "broad variety" of "delicious hot soups", "wonderful" sandwiches and "tempting" desserts in a "family-friendly" setting that offsets the generic "cookie-cutter" digs and "lackadaisical" service; foes find the branches "maddeningly inconsistent" and feel the fare "has gone downhill over the years."

## ☑ Atlanta Fish Market *Seafood*  | 23 | 19 | 21 | $40 |

**Buckhead** | 265 Pharr Rd. NE (Peachtree Rd.) | 404-262-3165 | www.buckheadrestaurants.com

The Buckhead Life Group's "piscine standard bearer" "amazes" afishionados with what seems like a "zillion choices" of "freshly caught fish from around the world" that's "reliably well prepared"; service is "friendly" and "helpful", but it can be "uneven", and while some say the "cavernous" "bustling" dining room is "what a great fish house ought to look like", to others it "feels more like a Sam's Club"; P.S. the "waits can be insane", so regulars "make a point to have reservations" or "eat at the bar."

|  | FOOD | DECOR | SERVICE | COST |
|--|------|-------|---------|------|

### Atlantic Seafood Company  *Seafood*   | 22 | 21 | 20 | $40 |

**Alpharetta** | 2345 Mansell Rd. (N. Point Pkwy.) | 770-640-0488 |
www.atlanticseafoodco.com

"A definite keeper", this Alpharetta seafood spot nets diners in the
mood for "totally fresh" fin fare from a "solid menu of diverse
choices", served by a "chirpy" staff in a cavernous "warehouse"
space with "dockside decor" and "great ambiance"; despite "deafening" noise levels, many find it a "superb spot for entertaining", but
others sniff "you can do better" at these "prices."

### Atmosphere  Ⓜ *French*   | 25 | 21 | 21 | $38 |

**Midtown** | 1620 Piedmont Ave. (E. Morningside Dr. NE) | 678-702-1620 |
www.atmospherebistro.com

Francophiles fawn over this "*magnifique*" Midtown boîte for its "impressive", "authentic" modern French cuisine, including the "best
duck confit" "on this side of the pond", and "terrific" service; housed
in a "charming cottage" with a "perfect" patio, it's a "superb alternative" for an "intimate evening with your sweetie", or a "hassle-free"
"dinner with friends"; P.S. "live jazz is a plus."

### Au Pied de Cochon  ◑ *French*   | 19 | 24 | 19 | $49 |

**Buckhead** | InterContinental Buckhead | 3315 Peachtree Rd. NE
(Piedmont Rd. NE) | 404-946-9070 | www.aupieddecochonatlanta.com

For a "three-course meal at 3AM", this 24/7 "sister of the Parisian
landmark" in Buckhead's InterContinental Hotel is a "favorite" of
many, thanks to its "lush surroundings" and "posh" "art nouveau design" that attracts a "high bling factor" clientele; the French fare is
"tasty" ("superb" signature pig trotters) and the Sunday brunch is
"out of this world", although purists sniff "it may look like Paris, but
does not taste like it", and the service, while "friendly", can be
"spotty" at times.

### Au Rendez Vous  Ⓩ⏛ *French*   | 21 | 7 | 17 | $21 |

**Sandy Springs** | 1328 Windsor Pkwy. (Osborne Rd. NE) |
404-303-1968

"If cassoulet is your thing", *amis* endorse this family-owned, "blink-
or-you'll-miss-it" Sandy Springs French and its "extremely reasonable" slow-cooked "comfort" cuisine, served in a "cozy" (read:
"ridiculously small"), "no-frills" space – be prepared to eat "with a
refrigerator in your face"; they now serve beer and wine, but it's still
"cash only", and skeptics are "not that impressed" by what they call
"just ok" fare and "slow" service.

### Avra Greek Tavern  *Greek*   | 20 | 18 | 20 | $32 |

**Midtown** | 794 Juniper St. NE (5th St.) | 404-892-8890 |
www.avragreektavern.com

A "spirited experience" awaits at this "festive" Midtown Greek serving "decent", "relatively inexpensive" taverna fare ("flaming cheese
is better than it sounds") with "great panache" but "without pretension", although some hecklers raise hellenic about "uninspired"
eats; diners are "welcomed warmly" in a "gracious old bungalow"
with "ornate Victorian" decor and a "perfect" wraparound porch.

| | FOOD | DECOR | SERVICE | COST |

**Azio Downtown** *Italian*    18 | 15 | 16 | $16

**Downtown** | Peachtree Ctr. | 229 Peachtree St. NE
(Andrew Young Int'l Blvd.) | 404-222-0808 | www.aziodowntown.com
Additional locations throughout the Atlanta area

**Little Azio** *Italian*

**Smyrna** | Ivy Walk | 1675 Cumberland Pkwy. (Atlanta Rd. SE) |
678-426-0333
**NEW Kennesaw** | 600 Chastain Rd., Ste. 210 (Townpark Dr. NW) |
678-213-1200
**Alpharetta** | 12635 Crabapple Rd. (Birmingham Hwy./Rte. 372) |
678-366-3636
**NEW Alpharetta** | 3719 Old Alabama Rd. (Jones Bridge Rd.) |
678-205-5800
**Midtown** | 903 Peachtree St. NE (8th St.) | 404-876-7711
**Westside** | 1700 Northside Dr. (I-75) | 404-917-1717
**Decatur** | 340 W. Ponce de Leon Ave. (bet. Fairview Ave. &
Ponce de Leon Pl.) | 404-373-4225
**NEW Norcross** | 3975 Holcomb Bridge Rd. (bet. Deerings Ln. &
Wetherburn Way) | 678-206-0220
**East Atlanta** | 749 Moreland Ave. SE (Ormewood Ave.) | 404-624-0440
www.littleazio.com
Additional locations throughout the Atlanta area

"Eclectic but inexpensive" is how boosters describe this Downtown
Italian and its more casual *bambini*; "fresh" *cucina* and a "beautiful cathedral"-like space make the original location a popular
option for the convention and business set, while the smaller,
counter-service spin-offs are "pleasant pit stops" for a "hip lunch"
with "great people-watching"; skeptics, though, find them "uninspired" and "nothing special."

**Babette's Cafe** Ⓜ *European*    25 | 20 | 23 | $35

**Poncey-Highland** | 573 N. Highland Ave. (Freedom Pkwy.) |
404-523-9121 | www.babettescafe.com
It's "like wrapping yourself in an old blanket" at this "jewel in
Poncey-Highland", where "soul-warming" European cuisine and a
"superb" Sunday brunch come courtesy of a chef-owner who "really
cares about her customers"; a "long-time" staff provides "impeccable" service in the "charming", "rustic" house with a patio overlooking Freedom Trail, and even though there's "nothing hip or trendy
here", pros ponder "what's not to love?"

**Ⓩ Bacchanalia** Ⓢ *American*    29 | 26 | 28 | $85

**Westside** | Westside Mktpl. | 1198 Howell Mill Rd. (bet. 14th St. &
Huff Rd.) | 404-365-0410 | www.starprovisions.com
The "French Laundry of the South" is what devotees dub this Westside
New American, Atlanta's perennial No. 1 for Food that "lives up to
its amazing reputation" with a prix fixe menu of "superb" cuisine
crafted from the "freshest local ingredients", "right-on" "wine pairings" and "excellent", "personalized" service; the "industrial" space
is "elegant without being stuffy" (a few find it "drafty"), but be prepared for tabs so "steep" that cronies quip "taking a date here says
'you are the one – because I can't afford anyone else.'"

### Bambinelli's *Italian*   19 | 13 | 19 | $18

**Tucker** | Sports Authority Vill. | 3202 Northlake Pkwy. NE
(Henderson Mill Rd.) | 770-493-1311 | www.bambinellispizza.com
"Be prepared to look at pics of the grandkids" at this "family-run",
"kid-friendly" Tucker Italian where "mama greets you at the door"
and "gramps" is often "playing the piano"; "plenty of red-sauce
dishes" and "heavenly garlic knots" make for a "nice" "homestyle"
meal or "casual lunch" in a "comfortable" strip-mall space.

### Bamboo Garden *Chinese*   ∇ 19 | 18 | 20 | $17

**Decatur** | 1707 Church St. (Decatur Rd.) | 404-294-6160
**Duluth** | 3925 Pleasant Hill Rd. (Peachtree Industrial Blvd.) | 770-622-1445
www.bamboo-gardens.com
The "weird mix" of Chinese cooking and Indian spices "works" for
devotees of this "inexpensive" Decatur-Duluth duo that "never disappoints" thanks to "reliable" eats and "good" service; detractors,
though, demur at the "same old" fare that "can be found in any
American strip mall – and nowhere in China."

### Bangkok Thai ⊠ *Thai*   ∇ 21 | 13 | 20 | $19

**Midtown** | Ansley Sq. | 1492 Piedmont Ave. (Monroe Dr.) | 404-874-2514
A "hip crowd" with a "taste for Thai" heads over to this Midtown
stalwart that's "been a favorite for years and years" for "yummy-in-
my-tummy" "standards" at "bargain" prices and "friendly, caring"
service; the "tired" digs notwithstanding, loyalists insist "if it's not
your neighborhood place, it should be."

### Baraonda *Italian*   23 | 19 | 19 | $24

**Midtown** | 710 Peachtree St. (3rd St.) | 404-879-9962 |
www.baraondaatlanta.com
"Wood-fired pizzas with real personality", "tasty pastas" and "killer
entrees" attract fans to this Midtown Italian that's "perfect" for a
"convenient" "work lunch" or "pre-theater" bite, but for a "relaxed
dinner" it's advisable to "avoid Fox start times"; the "cool" and "casual" "European" scene is "always hopping", and while the "hot
waiters" can provide "super-fast service" "when you're running late for
a show", others gripe they're often "too busy posing to serve you."

### Barbecue Kitchen ⊄ *Southern*   ∇ 18 | 8 | 21 | $12

**Airport (Atlanta)** | 1437 Virginia Ave. (Harrison Rd.) | 404-766-9906
Hey, "all the cops can't be wrong" about this "reliable" meat-and-three
"in the shadow of Hartsfield" Airport that also attracts "Downtown
bankers", folks with "long layovers" and Southsiders hankerin' for
"huge portions" of "homestyle" Southern cooking; "mothering" waitresses "with plenty of sugar and spice" (though some "not so nice")
and '60s-esque wood paneling complete the nostalgic scene.

### Basil's *Mediterranean*   20 | 17 | 19 | $32

**Buckhead** | 2985 Grandview Ave. (Pharr Rd.) | 404-233-9755 |
www.basils.net
"Charming outdoor dining" on the "tree-covered deck" is a "big draw"
at this "quaint" Mediterranean in a renovated house in Buckhead,

where a "delightful" menu of "reasonably priced" fare also keeps loyalists "coming back"; "no one hurries you for the table" – a "rare treat" in Atlanta – and while some gripe about "uneven" cooking and service, for others it remains a "solid" option.

**NEW Beleza** M _Brazilian_                     | 23 | 23 | 20 | $37 |

**Midtown** | 905 Juniper St. (8th St.) | 678-904-4582 | www.belezalounge.com

"Euro vibe meets spa food" at this "innovative" new Midtown Brazilian from Riccardo Ullio (of Sotto Sotto and Fritti fame) serving up "creative" "killer" cocktails and "terrific", "super-fresh" ("that scallop was alive 30 minutes ago") small plates with a "healthy flair" in a "simple" space with a "clean, refreshing design" and a "growing wall" of flora; the staff is "knowledgeable" and the buzz is "hip", but just be warned – the "prices add up fast."

**Z Belly General Store** _American_        | 19 | 21 | 19 | $11 |

**Virginia-Highland** | 772 N. Highland Ave. (St. Charles Pl.) | 404-872-1003 | www.bellystore.com

Located in a "landmark" Virginia-Highland building, this "eclectic" American with a "familiar general store feel" provides locals with "tasty" "quick bites" including bagels that "wow" and "excellent" cupcakes; bashers bellyache about the staff's "attitude" and the "pricey" fare when there's "better to be had elsewhere", but the "fabulous" setting complete with a "sunny farm table" perfect for "wonderful" people-watching outside makes it a "fun place to visit."

**Benihana** _Japanese_                         | 19 | 17 | 20 | $34 |

**Alpharetta** | 2365 Mansell Rd. (N. Point Pkwy.) | 678-461-8440
**Downtown** | Peachtree Ctr. | 229 Peachtree St. NE (Andrew Young Int'l Blvd.) | 404-522-9627
**South Buckhead** | 2143 Peachtree Rd. (Bennett St.) | 404-355-8565
www.benihana.com

"Dinner and a show" take on new meaning at this "entertaining" Japanese steakhouse chain, the "original teppanyaki experience" complete with "acrobatic", "knife-flipping" chefs who "slice and dice" your meal tableside; party-poopers pooh-pooh the "bland" grub, "hokey" theatrics and "chop-chop" service, and crack that "if you go without kids", it helps to "drink a lot."

**Bhojanic Homestyle Indian** S _Indian_  | 22 | 16 | 19 | $20 |

**Decatur** | 1363 Clairmont Rd. (N. Decatur Rd.) | 404-633-9233 | www.bhojanic.com

"Those who like it hot" will find "lots of options" at this "inventive" family-owned Indian in Decatur, an "incredible value" for its "superb" fare, including "outstanding" tapas and vegetarian selections "savory enough to convert carnivores"; service is "quick" and "friendly" in the "casual", yet "hip" strip-mall space near Emory that's usually packed with "university and intown folks who like real ethnic food"; P.S. live music Wednesdays and Fridays is a "real treat."

|  | FOOD | DECOR | SERVICE | COST |
|---|---|---|---|---|

### Bistro VG ⊠ *French* 
(fka Van Gogh's)

| 22 | 22 | 21 | $39 |
|---|---|---|---|

**Roswell** | 70 W. Crossville Rd. (Crabapple Rd.) | 770-993-1156 | www.knowwheretogogh.com

The Sedgwick family has "done the seemingly impossible" and "improved on a classic", the former Van Gogh's in Roswell that now sports a "cool new look" and an "enticing" contemporary French menu that's "more casual" and "more affordable" than the previous incarnation; a "younger crowd" and "mature adults" alike convene in the "fabulously hip", "white-on-white" space, where "cheery" service adds to the "airy" ambiance.

### Blackstone *Seafood/Steak*

| 23 | 21 | 22 | $42 |
|---|---|---|---|

**Smyrna** | Vinings West | 4686 S. Atlanta Rd. (Log Cabin Dr.) | 404-794-6100 | www.blackstoneatlanta.com

"No need to travel" to "stuffy Buckhead" sniff Smyrna surveyors, thanks to this "neighborly" steakhouse that's "just what this developing area needs", serving "excellent" beef and seafood in a "friendly" setting with a "great bar" and working fireplace; critics quibble over "pricey" fare and "spotty" service, but others are "never disappointed"; N.B. live music Tuesdays–Saturdays.

### Blue Eyed Daisy *Southern*

| ▽ 21 | 23 | 19 | $17 |
|---|---|---|---|

**Palmetto** | Serenbe | 9065 Selborne Ln. (Atlanta-Newnan Rd.) | 770-463-8379 | www.blueeyeddaisy.com

For "pure serenity at the Serenbe" community in Palmetto, fans tout this "dream" of a Southern bakeshop for its "quaint, new-looks-old", "good-for-the-earth" space with a "relaxed", "welcoming vibe, as well as "fantastic" baked goods and Southern offerings that are "worth the splurge"; the service can be "uneven" at times, but the "young" staff is "eager and friendly."

### NEW Bluefin ☻ *Asian Fusion/Japanese*

| - | - | - | M |
|---|---|---|---|

**South Buckhead** | 1829 Peachtree Rd. NE (Palisades Rd. NE) | 404-963-5291 | www.bluefinatlanta.com

South Buckhead gets an infusion of glam with this midpriced LA-based Asian fusion – Japanese beauty where East meets West on the contemporary menu that includes sashimi, sushi and a premium sake selection (it also offers takeout); creamy white banquettes, throw pillows, mod light fixtures and wavy accents highlight the space, which includes an expansive sushi bar in the back.

### Z BluePointe *American*

| 24 | 25 | 22 | $51 |
|---|---|---|---|

**Buckhead** | 3455 Peachtree Rd. (Lenox Rd.) | 404-237-9070 | www.buckheadrestaurants.com

"Paris Hilton would fit right in" to the "see-and-be-seen" scene of this "slick" Buckhead Life New American where the "dramatic", high-ceilinged room with "beautiful humans draped over the bar" sipping "pool-size martinis" provides "lesser mortals" with something to "check out"; "superb" Pan-Asian–inspired flavors and "pristine" sushi highlight the "mouthwatering" menu, which is served by an "impeccable" staff, and while the tragically hip find it so "last year", it remains a "hit" with "expense-account" diners, "ce-lebrities" and rich "old men" carrying on "affairs."

### Blue Ribbon Grill  *American*
20 | 16 | 21 | $21

Tucker | 4006 Lavista Rd. (Briarclifff Rd.) | 770-491-1570

"You'll want to become a regular" at this "neighborhood joint" in Tucker promise pros who "love" the "personal" service and "huge portions" of "tasty" American eats, including "wonderful burgers" and "great" homemade chips; though it "could use a slight upgrade", the "cozy" "lodge-type" space is "inviting."

### ☑ Blue Ridge Grill  *Southern*
23 | 24 | 24 | $45

Buckhead | 1261 W. Paces Ferry Rd. (Northside Pkwy.) | 404-233-5030 | www.blueridgegrill.com

"Well-heeled" locals and "corporate" "bigwigs" "escape to a gourmet Appalachian getaway" "right in the heart of Buckhead" at this "trendy" "log cabin fantasy" with a "romantic" stone fireplace and "delight-ful" porch off the bar; "fantastic" "repeat-your-name" service and "divinely delicious" Southern cuisine make it a popular option for those "need-to-impress" occasions, and while some find it "preten-tious" and "overpriced", regulars insist "you get what you pay for."

### Blu Greek Taverna  *Greek*
20 | 17 | 18 | $26

Marietta | 26 Mill St. (Marietta Pkwy.) | 770-429-4096 | www.blugreektaverna.com

"When they say portions are big enough for two, believe them" ad-vise aficionados of this "good-value" Greek, a "surprising find just off Marietta Square" serving "hearty", "fresh and modern" Hellenic fare; the "lovely" blue-hued space is a "pleasant" setting for "relax-ing and enjoying the company of friends."

### Bobby & June's
### Kountry Kitchen ☑ *Southern*
20 | 12 | 20 | $11

Midtown | 375 14th St. (State St.) | 404-876-3872

"Like it or not", "you're in and out in 20 minutes" at this "classic" Midtown meat-and-three, even though there's "always a crowd" of "students", "suits and servicemen" angling to get their "kountry fix" of "damn good" "down-home Southern cooking and BBQ", including "breakfasts worth clogging your arteries"; "joint" sums up the digs, but for a "taste of the old South", it's the "real deal."

### Bombay Grill  *Indian*
∇ 17 | 14 | 16 | $23

Chamblee | 2165 Savoy Dr. (bet. Peachtree & Shallowford Rds.) | 678-530-9555

For an "excellent" lunch buffet of "no-nonsense" Indian cuisine, this cheap Chamblee choice right off the highway is the "favorite" option of a devoted clientele; the "gardenlike" setting, which includes a "large banquet hall", is "surprisingly upscale", but detractors demur at "poor" service and food they say has "gone downhill."

### Bonefish Grill  *Seafood*
23 | 21 | 21 | $31

Alpharetta | 11705C Jones Bridge Rd. (Abbotts Bridge Rd.) | 770-475-6668
**NEW** Buford | 3420 Buford Dr. (Gravel Springs Rd.) | 678-546-8240

(continued)

## Bonefish Grill

**NEW** Snellville | The Avenue | 1350 Scenic Hwy. 124, Ste. 200 (Webb Gin House Rd.) | 678-344-8945
www.bonefishgrill.com

"Anything but fishy", these national seafood chain links are "much needed in the 'burbs", which explains why they're "always packed" to the gills with finatics hooked on "fresh-as-fresh-can-be bounty", "innovative drinks" and "excellent service"; "quality linens, silverware and wine glasses" enhance a setting with "much more ambiance than you'd expect", appealing to couples angling for a "romantic night out", and making them a "great value."

## ☑ Bone's Restaurant  *Steak*

| 27 | 22 | 27 | $62 |

**Buckhead** | 3130 Piedmont Rd. (Peachtree Rd.) | 404-237-2663 | www.bonesrestaurant.com

Voted Atlanta's Most Popular, this Buckhead "bastion of big beef and business" "knows how to do cow", offering "peerless", "melt-in-your-mouth" steaks as well as a "phenomenal" wine list and "service out the wazoo" to a local "who's who" that gravitates here for "deals or romantic meals"; you can dine at the "power bar" or in the warren of "comfy" rooms where an "old boys' club" atmosphere rules, and while the "check can cause a coronary", bullish backers snort "prices be damned."

## Brake Pad ◑  *American*

| ▽ 18 | 16 | 18 | $15 |

**Airport (College Park)** | 3403 Main St. (Rugby Ave.) | College Park | 404-766-1515 | www.brakepadatlanta.com

"Woodward kids, Delta lunchers and locals" in College Park flock to this "casual" American that's "close enough to the airport" for a "layover" meal, serving "great hamburgers" as well as "fresh surprises" such as the "*muy bueno*" tilapia tacos; while it can get "noisy" inside the converted "gas station", the seasonal patio is "the place to be on a sunny day", offering "good people- and train-watching" opportunities.

## Bread Garden  ☒⇄  *Bakery/Sandwiches*

| ▽ 26 | 3 | 10 | $8 |

**Midtown** | 549 Amsterdam Ave. (Monroe Dr.) | 404-875-1166

Loafers "could live on" the "amazing" bread and rolls from this Midtown bakery that's also known for its "divine" cookies and muffins, making it a "favorite" provisioner for "picnics" in nearby Piedmont Park; cognoscenti just "ignore" the "grumpy" owner's crusty "attitude", as well as decor that consists of one "small table."

## Brickery Grill & Bar  *American*

| 18 | 13 | 18 | $21 |

**Sandy Springs** | Hilderbrand Ct. | 6125 Roswell Rd. (Hilderbrand Dr.) | 404-843-8002 | www.thebrickery.com

"They don't know everyone's name, but treat you like they do" at this "*Cheers* of Sandy Springs", a "reliable" venue for "basic" American "comfort food" at a "reasonable price" that attracts a "loyal pack of regulars", including families, seniors and those "grabbing a bite before heading over to the Punchline"; while there's "nothing fancy" about it, most agree it's as "solid as a brick."

| | FOOD | DECOR | SERVICE | COST |
|---|---|---|---|---|

**Brick Store Pub** ◐ *Pub Food*  | 21 | 23 | 21 | $18 |

**Decatur** | 125 E. Court Sq. (E. Ponce de Leon Ave.) | 404-687-0990 |
www.brickstorepub.com

"Get your pint on" at this "cozy brewhouse" in Decatur that's "absolutely the best" in the minds of many thanks to its "lengthy list of spirits" and "superb suds" that are paired with pub fare that goes "beyond decent into wondrous"; brick walls, wooden tables and a "top-notch" Belgian bar make up the "charming" space that's often "super-crowded", which is why service can be "as slow as a semester in school", the staff's "impressive knowledge" notwithstanding.

**NEW BrickTop's** *American*  | 19 | 19 | 20 | $31 |

**Buckhead** | Terminus Bldg. | 3280 Peachtree Rd. NE (Piedmont Rd.) |
404-841-2212 | www.bricktops.com

"When you want to go somewhere nicer with the kids", this "shiny" link of a Nashville-based chain in a "hot location" in Buckhead's Terminus Building is a "reliable" option, offering "amazingly friendly" service and "hearty" American fare in an "upscale" atmosphere, as well as a "nice outdoor patio" and "great bar" that attract an "after-work" crowd; critics, though, throw bricks at what they consider nothing more than an "overpriced" "Houston's 2.0."

**Brio Tuscan Grille** *Italian*  | 19 | 19 | 18 | $30 |

**Buckhead** | 2964 Peachtree Rd. (Pharr Rd.) | 404-601-5555
**Dunwoody** | 700 Ashwood Pkwy. (Ashford Dunwoody Rd.) | 678-587-0017
www.brioitalian.com

"Surprisingly good" "for a chain", this "popular" pair is a "safe bet" for a "casual", "reasonably priced" experience featuring an "extensive" menu of "flavorful" Northern Italian fare and "fast" service in a "beautiful" "open" dining room, and "sun dress season" on the patio "can't be beat", especially at the Dunwoody branch overlooking a lake with swans; detractors deplore the "high-decibel dining", "average" food and "uneven" service, but most agree "you could do much worse."

**Brooklyn Cafe** *American*  | 18 | 14 | 19 | $32 |

**Sandy Springs** | Springs Landing | 220 Sandy Springs Circle
(bet. Johnson Ferry Rd. & Mt. Vernon Hwy.) | 404-843-8377 |
www.brooklyncafe.com

As "comfortable" as an "old shoe", this "friendly" strip-mall American in Sandy Springs is generally viewed as a "good go-to selection" for "unpretentious" dining in an "informal" setting where you can show up "in a suit or sweat suit" with equal aplomb; while some are still "not sure" about the new ownership, others applaud it for the "revamped" menu and "ambitious" wine list.

**Brookwood Grill** *American*  | 20 | 19 | 21 | $28 |

**Roswell** | 880 Holcomb Bridge Rd. (Warsaw Rd.) | 770-587-0102 |
www.brookwoodgrill.com

The service is a "cut above" most at this moderately priced Roswell American offering "good-size portions" of "solid standards" from a "varied menu that appeals to adults and teenagers" alike; critics, though, clamor that it "needs a makeover" – "starting in the kitchen" and moving on to the "stuffy" digs with the "80s fern bar" aesthetic.

**Buca di Beppo**  *Italian*  | 17 | 19 | 20 | $25 |

**Alpharetta** | 2335 Mansell Rd. (N. Point Pkwy.) | 770-643-9463 | www.bucadibeppo.com

Alpharettans "can't help but like" this local link of a national chain known for "lots of rooms crammed" with "over-the-top" decor (e.g. "the Pope's head on a lazy Susan") and "humongous" family-style portions, served by a "witty" staff in a "group-friendly" setting that's a hit with parents "who want to drown out the sound of their own children"; "needa di Pepto!" cry critics put off by "ginormous" helpings, dismissing it as "Olive Garden on steroids."

**Z Buckhead Diner ●**  *American*  | 23 | 20 | 22 | $35 |

**Buckhead** | 3073 Piedmont Rd. NE (E. Paces Ferry Rd.) | 404-262-3336 | www.buckheadrestaurants.com

Though it's "constantly reinventing itself", this "favorite" from the Buckhead Life Group is as "reliable" as "Old Yeller", delivering "terrific" "unique" "twists" on New American "comfort food" and "snappy" service from a "witty" staff in a "lively", "charmingly retro '50s setting"; the "wide-ranging clientele" makes for some "bizarre people-watching", but for an "upscale family gathering" or "late" "after-the-show" dining, "it works"; P.S. "no reservations means long waits", so it's best to "call ahead to get on the list."

**Busy Bee Cafe**  *Soul Food*  | ∇ 27 | 10 | 22 | $13 |

**Downtown** | 810 Martin Luther King Jr. Dr. SW (Joseph E. Lowry Blvd.) | 404-525-9212 | www.thebusybeecafe.com

Those in search of some of the "best soul food in Atlanta" can stop right here at this Downtown "institution" "with rich history and desserts to match" declare devotees who "go out of their way" for the "real thing", including the signature "Beelicious" fried chicken and "fantastic" greens; it's "always packed" with "locals and tourists" alike, who don't "mind standing in line for an hour" in the "small", "no-frills" space where you can "sit and soak up Southern comfort."

**Byblos M**  *Lebanese/Mediterranean*  | ∇ 21 | 15 | 18 | $23 |

**Roswell** | 10684 Alpharetta Hwy. (bet. Houze & Mansell Rds.) | 678-352-0321 | www.byblos-atlanta.com

A "great change of pace", this Roswell Lebanese-Med serves up "authentic", "beautifully presented" cuisine, including "bargain" weekday lunch and Thursday-night dinner buffets, as well as a Sunday brunch spread, all with plenty of options for the "undecided diner"; the staff "exudes warmth and hospitality", and weekend belly dancers add to the "interesting" experience.

**Cabernet ⊠**  *Steak*  | 24 | 23 | 23 | $48 |

**Alpharetta** | 5575 Windward Pkwy. (Westside Pkwy.) | 770-777-5955 | www.cabernetsteakhouse.com

"Life is a Cabernet" at this "underrated", "upscale" Alpharetta chophouse where chef Richard Holley is a "genius at both meat and seafood" and the "old-fashioned" service is "on par" with the "outstanding" steaks; an "über-masculine" color scheme, "quiet booths" in the back and a "terrific bar scene" with live music on weekends make it "worth the drive" for "special events" or "business" meals, albeit at "expense-account" tabs.

### Cafe Alsace Ⓜ *French*  22 | 20 | 21 | $27

**Decatur** | 121 E. Ponce de Leon Ave. (Church St.) | 404-373-5622 | www.cafealsace.net

For a "romantic getaway any night of the week", fans tout this "intimate" Decatur Gallic serving "mouthwatering" cuisine with a "*très unique*" Alsatian accent, including arguably the "richest spaetzle found anywhere" and an "excellent" Sunday brunch; "top-notch" service by "pleasant", "French-speaking waiters" adds to the "charm" and makes up for the "tight fit" in the "tiny" bistro digs.

### Café di Sol *American*  20 | 18 | 18 | $24

**Poncey-Highland** | 640 N. Highland Ave. (North Ave.) | 404-724-0711

"Watch the people pass by" from the "divine" patio of this "cozy neighborhood" haunt in Poncey-Highland offering a menu of "delicious" New American fare with "something for every mood"; the atmosphere is "pleasant" in the "European cafe" setting where there's occasional live music, and while some suspect the cooking "lacks a je ne sais quoi", sunny supporters say "this place is a steal."

### Cafe Intermezzo ⓓ *Coffeehouse*  21 | 19 | 15 | $21

**Dunwoody** | Park Place Shopping Ctr. | 4505 Ashford Dunwoody Rd. (Perimeter Ctr. E.) | 770-396-1344
**South Buckhead** | 1845 Peachtree Rd. NE (Collier Rd.) | 404-355-0411 www.cafeintermezzo.com

Satisfy your "sweet tooth" at this coffee-and-dessert duo in Dunwoody and South Buckhead offering a "never-ending display" of "sinfully delicious" treats and one of the "largest drink menus in town", with "every type" of java "you can imagine"; "always crowded" with "beautiful" people, they're "perfect" for a "girls' get-together", après-theater or an "I-don't-want-the-date-to-end drink", even though "laughable" service makes many "wish they'd stayed home."

### Café Lily *Mediterranean*  23 | 19 | 22 | $31

**Decatur** | Shops of W. Ponce de Leon Pl. | 308 W. Ponce de Leon Ave. (Ponce de Leon Pl.) | 404-371-9119 | www.cafelily.com

This "marvelous" Med bistro "never fails to please" Decatur denizens with the "consistently fantastic" creations of "clever" chefowner Anthony Pitillo, paired with a "sophisticated" wine list that includes a "full page of Zins", all at an "affordable price point"; while regulars "mourn the loss" of papa Angelo Pitillo, the ambiance remains "happy and warm" and the service is "upbeat" but "not obtrusive" in the "cozy", "candlelit" space.

### Cafe Prego Ⓢ *Italian*  19 | 14 | 21 | $28

**Buckhead** | Chastain Sq. | 4279 Roswell Rd. (bet. Midvale & Rickenbacker Drs.) | 404-252-0032

"Come once" and you'll be "welcomed", "come twice and they make you part of the family" at this "quintessential neighborhood" Italian in Buckhead that's "not your average strip-mall eatery"; while the ambiance is "lacking", the fare is "consistently good", so it's usually "stuffed with" a "clubby" bunch of regulars, including an "over-60" contingent, giving the word "'cozy' a whole new definition."

## Cafe Sunflower ⑤ *Vegetarian* | 22 | 16 | 20 | $20 |

**Sandy Springs** | Hammond Springs Ctr. | 5975 Roswell Rd. (Hammond Dr.) | 404-256-1675
**South Buckhead** | Brookwood Square Ctr. | 2140 Peachtree Rd. NW (Colonial Homes Dr.) | 404-352-8859
www.cafesunflower.com

"Who needs meat?" ponder proponents of these "casual", "inexpensive" vegetarian specialists in South Buckhead and Sandy Springs where the "Birkenstock crowd" and other fans always "feel healthy" dining on "creative", "surprisingly good" meatless offerings (including "unbelievable" vegan desserts) that could "convert even the most die-hard carnivore"; "friendly" service keeps things warm and fuzzy.

## **NEW** Cakes & Ale *American* | - | - | - | I |

**Decatur** | 254 W. Ponce de Leon Ave. (bet. Commerce Dr. & Ponce de Leon Pl.) | 404-377-7994 | www.cakesandalerestaurant.com

At their new Dectaur gastropub, chef-owner Billy Allin (ex Berkeley's Chez Panisse, Watershed) and his wife, Kristin, serve up unassuming American cuisine with a light Italian accent made from locally sourced seasonal ingredients and humanely raised meats, while pastry chef Cynthia Wong provides sustainable sweet endings; the simple space awash in warm colors sports brown leather benches and a small bar.

## Cameli's Gourmet Pizza Joint *Pizza* | 24 | 10 | 19 | $13 |

**Midtown** | Ford Factory Sq. | 699 Ponce de Leon Ave. (Ponce de Leon Pl.) | 404-249-9020 | www.camelispizza.com

"Even Northerners" applaud the "terrific", "creative" pizzas at this "fantastic local" Midtown pizzeria where the "monster" slices are "remarkably cheap", and served up by "friendly" "pierced and tattooed alts"; what "used to be a complete hole-in-the-wall" now sports a "slick look" with an "expanded" space that includes a new bar.

## ☑ Canoe *American* | 26 | 26 | 25 | $49 |

**Vinings** | Vinings on the River | 4199 Paces Ferry Rd. NW (Chattahoochee River) | 770-432-2663 | www.canoeatl.com

"All grown up and going strong", this "solid performer" "nestled on the banks of the Chattahoochee" delivers "superb" New American cuisine (featuring "all sorts of mammals") that "hits all of your taste buds", including a "festive brunch" that's "well worth the trip"; the "stunning" riverside setting is "charming no matter what time of year" (and despite the "severe drought"), and combined with "your-wish-is-my-command" service, pros promise it'll "never fail" to "impress your clients, friends and paramours."

| | FOOD | DECOR | SERVICE | COST |
|---|---|---|---|---|

**Canton Cooks** ◗ *Chinese*                    | 23 | 8 | 17 | $19 |

**Sandy Springs** | Office Depot Shopping Ctr. | 5984 Roswell Rd. NE (Hammond Dr.) | 404-250-0515

"You don't have to travel to Buford Highway" for "outstanding" Cantonese say fans of this Sandy Springs Sino spot serving "authentic", "interesting dishes not seen on most Chinese menus"; the strip-mall digs are "not much to look at" and the "service leaves something to be desired", but it's always "crowded" and night owls "love that it's open until 2 AM."

**Canton House** *Chinese*                    | 20 | 13 | 18 | $16 |

**Buford Hwy. (Chamblee)** | 4825 Buford Hwy. (Chamblee Tucker Rd.) | Chamblee | 770-936-9030 | www.cantonhouserestaurant.com

Fans laud this Chamblee Cantonese that serves some of the "best dim sum in Atlanta" from a "seemingly endless conga line" of "authentic" "Chinese delights" that are "worth the patience needed" to countenance the "wait" and occasionally "confused" service; the space boasts large "airy" rooms with "bright" chandeliers, but diners are virtually "hanging from the rafters on weekends", when the "crowds are fierce."

**Ⓩ Capital Grille** *Steak*                    | 24 | 24 | 25 | $58 |

**Buckhead** | Capital Bldg. | 255 E. Paces Ferry Rd. (Bolling Way) | 404-262-1162 | www.thecapitalgrille.com

"You'll be pampered from beginning to end" at this "ritzy" Buckhead link in a "damn fine" chain of steakhouses, where "exceptional" steaks "with all the fixings" and "spectacular" "skyline views" make it a "solid choice" to "impress" a "date, spouse or business client"; a "happening bar scene" attracts plenty of "movers and shakers" as well as a "post-surgery see-and-be-seen crowd", and while wallet-watchers wince at "pork barrel price tags", those with sufficient "capital" cash in on "one of the best experiences in the city."

**Caramba Cafe** *Tex-Mex*                    | 15 | 11 | 13 | $17 |

**Virginia-Highland** | 1409-D N. Highland Ave. (bet. Lanier Pl. NE & University Dr. NE) | 404-874-1343 | www.carambacafe.com

A "huge margarita list" and "decent" "old-school" Tex-Mex fare at "terrific" prices make this family-owned spot in the heart of the action in Virginia-Highland "popular" with the locals; it "doesn't look like much" and the service ranges from "surly" to downright "zany", but fans "keep coming back."

**Caribe Café** Ⓩ *Caribbean*                    | - | - | - | I |

**Marietta** | 45 N. Fairground St. (Washington Ave.) | 678-213-1434 | www.tasteofthewestindies.com

Cognoscenti call this Marietta Caribbean a "find in the truest sense of the word", serving up "interesting" "island fusion" fare that "sings", including "very spicy" jerk chicken that'll "knock your socks off" and "divine" passion fruit mousse; the mood is casual in the decidedly "no-frills" setting.

| | FOOD | DECOR | SERVICE | COST |
|---|---|---|---|---|

## Carpe Diem  *Mediterranean*    20 | 22 | 18 | $26

**Decatur** | Ice House Lofts | 105 Sycamore Pl. (Commerce Dr.) | 404-687-9696 | www.apresdiem.com

Housed in a "rehabbed" loft space "big enough to land a small airplane", with "artful" decor, a "stylish lounge area" and a "relaxed" patio and fountain, this Decatur Med is a "comfy place" to "linger" over "delicious" eats or a "wonderful array" of "yummy" desserts with the "artsy schmartsy crowd"; while critics fault the fare as "inconsistent", others insist there's enough "good karma" around to make up for it.

## ⊠ Carrabba's Italian Grill  *Italian*    20 | 17 | 19 | $24

**Kennesaw** | 1160 Ernest Barrett Pkwy. (Roberts Blvd.) | 770-499-0338
**Smyrna** | 2999 Cumberland Blvd. (Cobb Pkwy.) | 770-437-1444
**Douglasville** | 2700 Chapel Hill Rd. (Tom Murphy Frwy./I-20) | 770-947-0330
**Duluth** | 2030 Sugarloaf Circle (Satellite Blvd.) | 770-497-4959
**Dunwoody** | 1210 Ashford Crossing (Old Perimeter Way) | 770-804-0467
**Morrow** | 1887 Mt. Zion Rd. (Mt. Zion Blvd.) | 770-968-3233
**Peachtree City** | W. Park Plaza | 500 Commerce Dr. (Hwys. 54 & 74) | 770-631-1057
www.carrabbas.com

The "next best thing to a 'real' Italian restaurant", these suburban links of a "reliable" chain feature "large portions" of "fairly inexpensive", "not watered-down" grub served in "homey" digs; while some report "inconsistent" service and quality that "varies from franchise to franchise", the overall word here is "satisfying."

## Carver's Country Kitchen  ⊠⇄ *Soul Food/Southern*    ▽ 26 | 6 | 14 | $11

**Westside** | 1118 W. Marietta St. NW (Longley Ave.) | 404-794-4410 | www.carverscountrycooking.com

"Off the beaten path but worth the adventure", this Westside ma-and-pa Southerner is the "last bastion of perfectly executed soul food in Atlanta" according to fans familiar with its "stick-to-your-bones", "good-as-it-gets" victuals all made from scratch and "tea so sweet it makes your teeth hurt"; expect "lines out the door" of the "old" building, cafeteria-style service and "tight" seating that you "share with your neighbors", who run the gamut from the business set to students.

## ⊠ Cheesecake Factory  *American*    19 | 19 | 18 | $27

**Marietta** | Cumberland Mall | 1609 Cumberland Mall (Cobb Pkwy.) | 770-319-5515
**Alpharetta** | North Point Mall | 2075 N. Point Circle (N. Point Pkwy.) | 770-751-7011
**Buckhead** | 3024 Peachtree Rd. NW (Pharr Rd.) | 404-816-2555
**Dunwoody** | Perimeter Mall | 4400 Ashford Dunwoody Rd. (Hammond Dr.) | 678-320-0201
www.thecheesecakefactory.com

The menu's "mammoth" – and "so are the crowds" – at this "family-pleasing" chain where the "endless" American options arrive in equally "colossal" portions (ironically, "they give you so much there's no room" for their "heavenly" namesake desserts); despite "ordinary" settings, "spotty" staffing and "lots of commotion", these "well-oiled machines" are so "busy, busy, busy" that they're best accessed "off-hours" to avoid a "long wait."

**Chequers Seafood Grill** *Seafood*   22 | 20 | 21 | $36
**Dunwoody** | 236 Perimeter Center Pkwy. (Hammond Dr.) | 770-391-9383 | www.chequersseafood.com
This "longtime" maritimer near Perimeter Mall in Dunwoody has "been a favorite" "for years" among business types and hungry shoppers angling for "reasonably priced" seafood "prepared any way you like", while brunchers report the "fabulous" Sunday spread is "like being at a fancy hotel breakfast without having to stay"; "responsive" servers are "eager to please", and while some feel it's "showing its age" in both the menu and decor, others find the experience "lovely."

**Chicago's Steak, Seafood & Pasta** *Steak*   18 | 16 | 19 | $27
**Marietta** | 990 Whitlock Ave. (Burnt Hickory Rd.) | 770-590-1500
**Roswell** | Shallowford Corners | 4401 Shallowford Rd. (Johnson Ferry Rd.) | 770-993-7464
www.chicagosrestaurant.com
This "convenient" suburban steakhouse duo in Marietta and Roswell offers a "solid lineup" of "proven American favorites", "awesome" martinis and "down-home" service in a "friendly" environment; detractors dub the digs "fern bar central" and demur at the "uninteresting" fare and "erratic" service, but "fair" prices keep it "crowded" with a "faithful" clientele.

**NEW Chima Brazilian**   - | - | - | E
**Steakhouse** *Brazilian*
**Buckhead** | 3215 Peachtree Rd. NE (W. Shadowlawn Ave.) | 404-424-8281 | www.chimasteakhouse.com
Buckhead business types, beef eaters and buffet buffs bent on a bottomless moo-vable feast now have this upscale, all-you-can-eat Brazilian steakhouse named after a regional drink that represents hospitality; a searing array of traditional meats and seafood is complemented by a specialty salad bar, and gauchos deliver the skewered goods in a warmly accented, rustic space accented with rich woods.

**China Cooks** *Chinese*   ∇ 22 | 7 | 16 | $19
**Sandy Springs** | 215 Northwood Dr. NE (Roswell Rd.) | 404-252-6611
"Don't let the location scare you" reassure regulars of this "authentic" Chinese on a Sandy Springs side street that's "worth" the jaunt for "some of the best" "traditional" offerings in town, "served piping hot"; night owls appreciate the "late eats" (it's open until 2 AM), and those put off by the strip-mall digs have it "delivered" or get it "to go."

**China Delight** *Chinese*   ∇ 21 | 15 | 18 | $15
**Chamblee** | 2390 Chamblee Tucker Rd. (Cumberland Dr.) | 770-986-0898
The ingredients are "always fresh" at this Chamblee Cantonese that appeals to "rookies and veterans alike" with its roster of

"unique" Hong Kong–style dim sum selections that are "served daily", along with an "excellent" "seafood"-centric menu of à la carte offerings; fans consider it the "best spot" in the area to celebrate the "Chinese New Year."

## Chin Chin  *Chinese*                           19 | 15 | 19 | $19

**Kennesaw** | Barrett Parkway Shopping Ctr. | 1635 Old 41 Hwy. NW (Barrett Pkwy.) | 770-218-3993

**Smyrna** | 2800 Spring Rd. SE (Cobb Pkwy.) | 770-319-8331

**Alpharetta** | 3070 Windward Plaza (Windward Pkwy.) | 770-569-7565

**Midtown** | Ford Factory Sq. | 699 Ponce de Leon Ave. (Ponce de Leon Pl.) | 404-881-1556

**Brookhaven** | Cherokee Plaza | 3887 Peachtree Rd. (N. Druid Hills Rd.) | 404-816-2229

**Duluth** | 6575 Sugarloaf Pkwy. (Satellite Blvd.) | 770-813-1319

**Dunwoody** | Perimeter Ctr. | 1100 Hammond Dr. (Peachtree Dunwoody Rd.) | 770-913-0266

**South Buckhead** | Kroger Shopping Ctr. | 1715 Howell Mill Rd. NW (Bellemeade Ave.) | 404-609-5618

**Peachtree City** | 2100 Hwy. 54 E. (Peachtree Pkwy.) | 770-487-9188

**Woodstock** | Woodstock Ctr. | 9820 Hwy. 92 (I-575) | 770-928-3896
www.chinchinonline.com
Additional locations throughout the Atlanta area

"Reliable" but "not run-of-the-mill", this chain-chain doles out "delicious" Chinese, served by a "witty" staff in "subtle" interiors with exhibition kitchens that are "never garish"; while some feel it's "not what it was some years ago" due to excessive "growth", homebodies still "adore" the "quick and easy" takeout and delivery so fast "you need to have the table set before you call."

## Chipotle  *Mexican*                           18 | 13 | 15 | $10

**Cobb** | 2973 Cobb Pkwy. (Spring Hill Pkwy.) | 770-916-0788

**Roswell** | 10800 Alpharetta Hwy. (Mansell Rd.) | 770-642-0710

**Alpharetta** | 5250 Windward Pkwy. (Main St.) | 678-867-9459

**Midtown** | 718 Ponce de Leon Ave. NE (Ponce de Leon Pl.) | 404-685-3531

**Buckhead** | 3424 Piedmont Rd. (Lenox Rd.) | 404-869-7921

**DeKalb** | Toco Hills Shopping Ctr. | 2963 N. Druid Hills Rd. NE (bet. Clairmont & Lavista Rds.) | 404-929-9907

**Duluth** | John's Creek Vill. | 11720 Medlock Bridge Rd. (McGinnis Ferry Rd.) | 770-623-1724

**Duluth** | 2040 Pleasant Hill Rd. (I-85 N, exit 104) | 678-584-0011

**Dunwoody** | 123 W. Perimeter Ctr. (bet. Ashford Dunwoody Rd. & Perimeter Center Pkwy.) | 770-677-5542

**Sandy Springs** | 5920 Roswell Rd. (bet. Cliffwood & Hammond Drs.) | 404-252-2998
www.chipotle.com
Additional locations throughout the Atlanta area

Amigos applaud this "addictive" Mexican chain serving "gigantic" burritos and other "fresh" "better-than-fast-food fast food" in "large portions" that "ensure a full belly", all at prices that "can't be beat"; "high-tech", if somewhat "sterile", digs with big patios match the "clean" flavors in a "family-oriented" scene, and the staff delivers counter service with "a smile."

| | FOOD | DECOR | SERVICE | COST |
|---|---|---|---|---|

**Chocolate Bar** Ⓜ *Dessert*    20 | 19 | 19 | $22

**Decatur** | Artisan Bldg. | 201 W. Ponce de Leon Ave. (Commerce Dr.) | 404-378-0630 | www.thechocolatebardecatur.com

Surveyors report a "luscious experience" at this "flirty" Decatur dessert specialist and wine bar offering an "innovative selection of sweets", including a "fantastic" three-course sweet plate meal that's "better than sex"; the "sexy" warm-toned space "will surely please" for "after-dinner treats" or "rekindling with a loved one", in spite of "snooty" service and prices that lead some to quip that "everything here is bite-size, except for the check."

**Ⓩ Chocolate Pink Pastry Café** Ⓜ *Dessert*   25 | 22 | 20 | $14

**Midtown** | 905 Juniper St. NE, Unit 108 (bet. 7th & 8th Sts.) | 404-745-9292 | www.chocolatepinkcafe.com

It's "almost a shame to eat" the "delectable" dessert "delights" that "look more like art than food" at this Midtown sweet spot, but aficionados assure us they "taste as wow as they look" and come in "all shapes, sizes and flavors"; "friendly" service and a "welcoming" pink-and-brown decor add to the "nirvana" experience, and while it's a bit "on the expensive side", chocoholics agree it's "worth the splurge"; P.S. you can "host your own chocolate-filled events" in the private room upstairs.

**Ⓩ Chops/Lobster Bar** *Seafood/Steak*   27 | 24 | 26 | $60

**Buckhead** | Buckhead Plaza | 70 W. Paces Ferry Rd. (Peachtree Rd.) | 404-262-2675 | www.buckheadrestaurants.com

A "magnificent venue", this Buckhead Life Group "staple" is a "classic carnivore's" and "seafood lover's delight", serving "mind-blowingly good" "beach-and-beast" fare with a "first-rate wine list" to match, at "expense-account" prices; the service is "phenomenal" in the "clubby" upstairs steakhouse and the "more intimate" downstairs piscatorium, and there's "great people-watching" on both floors and a "hopping bar scene at happy hour"; while a few feel it's "hyped out of reality", others insist it "never fails" for a "special evening" or "high-powered business" dining.

**Chopstix** *Chinese*   23 | 17 | 22 | $37

**Buckhead** | Chastain Sq. | 4279 Roswell Rd. (Wieuca Rd.) | 404-255-4868 | www.chopstixatlanta.net

Popular with the Buckhead "establishment", including a sizable "blue-haired" contingent, this "high-end" purveyor of Middle Kingdom cuisine serves "superb", "imaginative" dishes crafted from "top-quality ingredients" (definitely "not your delivery Chinese"); "courtly" service from "waiters in tuxedos", "elegant" decor ("without those hanging red lanterns") and an "upscale piano bar" all belie the strip-mall location; cognoscenti caution "it'll cost you."

**Chosun OK** *Korean*   - | - | - | I

**Doraville** | 5865 Buford Hwy. NE (Oakcliff Rd.) | 770-452-1821

While this Buford Highway Korean "won't win any awards for looks", "the food is mighty tasty" according to cognoscenti who commend the "kalbi" and other BBQ fare that "faithfully represent" the traditional cuisine; the staff "makes an effort to speak English", making this a "pleasing" experience for "small- to medium-sized groups of meat eaters."

**City Grill** 🅱 *American*　　　| 22 | 24 | 22 | $43 |

**Downtown** | 50 Hurt Plaza (Edgewood Ave.) | 404-524-2489 | www.citygrillatlanta.com

Its location in a "gorgeous" former Fed building, complete with sweeping staircases and "marble everywhere", and "stunning" decor are why many dub this New American the "grande dame of Downtown dining"; chef Sean Holler's "outstanding" menu "will have you oohing and aahing" as well, while "top-level" service and an "elegant" setting also make it an "excellent choice for an expense account meal."

**Ⓩ Clark & Schwenk's**　　　| 24 | 23 | 25 | $47 |
**Seafood & Oyster Bar** *Continental/Seafood*

**Vinings** | Riverview Vill. | 3300 Cobb Pkwy. (Cumberland Blvd.) | 770-272-0999 | www.candsoysterbar.com

"Impeccable" service and "delectable" "fresh" fin fare, "expertly prepared" by chef Jon Schwenk, make this "special" Continental seafooder seem "like NYC", even if it is in a Vinings strip mall; fans "can't get enough" of the "wonderful" raw bar or "well-thought-out" wine list, either, served in an "old-school" "mahogany-and-mirrors" space with a "lively" atmosphere, and while some complain about how "pricey" it is, most agree this newcomer is "always happening."

**Clubhouse, The** *American*　　　| 17 | 18 | 18 | $32 |

**Buckhead** | Lenox Sq. | 3393 Peachtree Rd. NE (Lenox Rd.) | 404-442-8891 | www.theclubhouse.com

Fans of this "lively" New American chain link in Buckhead's Lenox Square "never would've guessed it's in a mall" from the "over-the-top" decor featuring "arched ceilings" and a "mahogany" bar; still, it's a "favorite" "after-shopping" stop of many, with an "extensive menu" of "basic clubhouse fare" served in "huge portions" and "desserts bigger than the hips they eventually end up on."

**Coco Loco's Cafe** *Caribbean/Cuban*　　　| 19 | 11 | 17 | $18 |

**Buckhead** | Buckhead Crossing Shopping Ctr. | 2625 Piedmont Rd., Ste. G40 (Sydney Marcus Blvd.) | 404-364-0212 | www.cocolocoatlanta.com

"Eat till you burst" at this "little slice of Havana" near the Lindbergh MARTA station in Buckhead serving "wonderful" Cuban and Caribbean grub, including "outstanding" tres leches; the "lack of exterior appeal" is "easily overlooked" thanks to "reasonable" prices and a "friendly" staff; it also "works great for takeout."

**Colonnade** ⌀ *Southern*　　　| 20 | 10 | 20 | $20 |

**Cheshire Bridge** | 1879 Cheshire Bridge Rd. NE (bet. Lavista Rd. & Piedmont Ave.) | 404-874-5642

A true "throwback", this "beloved" Cheshire Bridge "charmer" has been around "since snakes had legs" and it's still "busting at the seams" with "trendy gay" men and "every octogenarian within 30 miles" in for dinners (and weekend lunches) of "lovingly prepared" "Southern comfort food", including its "legendary" fried chicken;

|  | FOOD | DECOR | SERVICE | COST |
|---|---|---|---|---|

"beehived waitresses" work the "large" space that "fills up fast", but "strong drinks" and "people-watching" make the "inevitable waits" "go down easy"; P.S. remember: no "shorts", tank tops or credit cards accepted.

## Com Dunwoody ☒ *Vietnamese* — 24 | 16 | 21 | $21
**Dunwoody** | 5486 Chamblee Dunwoody Rd. (Mt. Vernon Rd.) | 770-512-7410

## Com Vietnamese Grill *Vietnamese*
**Dunwoody** | 4005 Buford Hwy. (Clairmont Rd.) | 404-320-0405 | www.comgrill.com

"Long waits" are the norm at this "awesome" Vietnamese duo in Dunwoody that's a "cut above" the competition, but "worth it" according to insiders who laud its "boldly flavorful" dishes "not found anywhere else in the city"; "helpful" servers, a "hip vibe" and "dressed-up" "contemporary" decor add to the "festive" scene, and the fact that it's a "real bargain" makes it even more "delightful."

## Corner Cafe *American* — 20 | 14 | 17 | $21
**Buckhead** | 3070 Piedmont Rd. NE (E. Paces Ferry Rd.) | 404-240-1978 | www.buckheadrestaurants.com

Noshers who "need more than a deli sandwich" head for this "bright, cheery" New American from the Buckhead Life Group for its "creative" breakfasts, "tasty" sandwiches and "super brunches" with a "Southern flair", as well as "fantastic" goods from the attached bakery that are "worth the trip alone"; while contrarians feel it "should be more impressive than it is", it's usually "crowded" nonetheless, especially on weekends.

## Cowtippers *Steak* — 15 | 13 | 18 | $22
**Midtown** | 1600 Piedmont Ave. (Monroe Dr.) | 404-874-3751 | www.cowtippersatlanta.com

Midtowners in the mood for "reasonably priced" meat and a "festive atmosphere" mosey over to this "country-meets-city", "Western-style" steakhouse near Ansley Mall, where a Texas-sized patio is "always lively" with families and a "cruisey gay clientele" that goes there to "sweat and be seen"; service ranges from "friendly" to "iffy", but many prefer to "skip" the merely "decent" eats and just "mix and mingle over drinks."

## Crescent Moon *Diner* — 20 | 16 | 18 | $14
**Decatur** | 174 W. Ponce de Leon Ave. (Commerce Dr.) | 404-377-5623
**Tucker** | Northlake Mall | 4800 Briarcliff Rd. NE (Henderson Mill Rd.) | 678-937-9020
www.crescentmooneatery.com

"Long lines" are "proof enough" that there's "no finer diner" than these "meccas of breakfasts" in Decatur and Tucker where "mouthwateringly good" "down-home" morning fare is served "all day", as well as "amazing" brunch and "huge" lunch and dinner offerings, in "shiny" "retro" digs; hecklers "hate the uneven service" and "hit-or-miss" food, but others are happy to "wait", "enjoy and waddle home"; the newer Tucker location has a soda fountain.

| | FOOD | DECOR | SERVICE | COST |
|---|---|---|---|---|

**NEW Cuerno** ◗ *Spanish* | - | - | - | M

**Midtown** | 905 Juniper St. NE (8th St.) | 678-904-4584 |
www.sottosottorestaurant.com

Riccardo Ullio (Beleza, Fritti and Sotto Sotto) takes the bull by the
horns and places him at the entrance of his newest venture, this
Midtown Spanish showcasing chef Ken Bouche's authentic tapas,
paellas and entrees, with a black-hoofed leg of *jamon iberico,* the
world's most prized pig, making the rounds; layers of dark slate, antique tiles and curtains evoking Spanish lace make for a moody setting suitable for dates or nibbles with friends at the bar.

**Daddy D'z** *BBQ* | 20 | 9 | 16 | $14

**Southside (Atlanta)** | 264 Memorial Dr. SE (Hill St.) | 404-222-0206 |
www.daddydz.com

"It's a hole-in-the-wall" "like a BBQ joint should be", so 'cuennoisseurs' "take the plunge" and ignore the "sketchy neighborhood"
around this Southside smoke spot, "a stone's throw" from Turner
Field, for "blow-your-mind" ribs, "yummy" pulled pork, "solid" sides
and "ice-cold" beer; sports fans and workers from nearby
Downtown also groove on live blues on weekends and "friendly"
service – "just be sure to park your car where you can see it."

**Dailey's** *American* | 21 | 18 | 20 | $36

**Downtown** | 17 Andrew Young Int'l Blvd. NE (bet. Peachtree Center Ave. &
Peachtree St.) | 404-681-3303 | www.daileysrestaurant.com

A "long-standing" choice of business diners for "basic" American
eats, this Downtown sibling of City Grill is "divine" in the eyes of
fans mainly for its "incredible" dessert bar, a "feast for the eyes as
well as the taste buds", in addition to "consistently wonderful" entrees and "always pleasant" service; the "lovely" upstairs dining
room evokes a "New Orleans garden room", while the "swank"
downstairs bar mixes "knockout" martinis to the strains of live
music at night.

**Dantanna's** ◗ *Seafood/Steak* | 19 | 17 | 17 | $30

**Buckhead** | Shops Around Lenox | 3400 Around Lenox Dr. (Peachtree Rd.) |
404-760-8873 | www.dantannas.com

"Yuppie bar meets sports bar" at this Buckhead surf 'n' turf near
Lenox Square, where "SEC darlin's support their 'Dawgs" over "surprising" steaks, "above-average" burgers and "super" seafood (it's
"not just wings") in "dark and cozy" digs with "plenty of TVs" and a
cigar room with a "great smoke filtration system"; sensitive sorts report the "friendly" waitresses are "very easy on the eyes."

**Dante's Down the Hatch** *Fondue* | 18 | 23 | 19 | $38

**Buckhead** | 3380 Peachtree Rd. NE (opp. Lenox Sq.) | 404-266-1600 |
www.dantesdownthehatch.com

For a "touristy night out" or a "different" kind of "romantic evening",
this "gimmicky" Buckhead "fixture" is "as fun as a fondue restaurant
can get", where you can dine in a "pirate ship" surrounded by "live
gators" in a moat, with live jazz, "tasty adult beverages" and "peppy"
service adding to the "adventure"; critics keelhaul the eats as "me-

| | FOOD | DECOR | SERVICE | COST |
|---|---|---|---|---|

diocre" and decor as "dated" "*Inferno* redux", but for many it's a "must-see" at least "once in a life."

### ☑ di Paolo Ⓜ *Italian*    27 | 20 | 24 | $41

**Alpharetta** | Rivermont Sq. | 8560 Holcomb Bridge Rd. (Nesbit Ferry Rd.) | 770-587-1051 | www.dipaolorestaurant.com

A "suburban wonder" "with big-city flair" in Alpharetta, Atlanta's No. 1 Italian is "one of the few real gastronomic delights north of the perimeter", thanks to "superb" cuisine and "fantastic wine list"; "impeccable" service, "low lights" and "cool yet homey" decor set the stage, but critics admonish the staff to "lose the attitude", and since the "small" space "can get busy" and "loud", insiders advise "make a reservation or go on a Sunday"; N.B. chef Darin Hiebel and his wife assumed ownership post-Survey.

### Doc Chey's Asian Kitchen *Noodle Shop*    19 | 12 | 17 | $13

**Emory** | 1556 N. Decatur Rd. (Clifton Rd.) | 404-378-8188
**Virginia-Highland** | Highland Walk | 1424 N. Highland Ave. (University Ave.) | 404-888-0777
www.doccheys.com

The "good karma" of this "ever expanding" noodle chain keeps "carb lovers" "coming back" for "top-notch low-priced meals" that are "creative" and "healthy", though purists find the "pseudo-Asian" eats "overrated"; the "casual" decor "doesn't impress", nor does the "hit-or-miss" service, but the "delightful" patio and "atmosphere" "make up" for many glitches, and did we mention that it's "cheap"?

### Dolce Enoteca Ⓢ *Italian*    18 | 24 | 17 | $44

**Atlantic Station** | Atlantic Station | 261 19th St. NW (State St.) | 404-872-3902 | www.dolcegroup.com

"If you want to be a part of the hip scene in Atlantic Station", this "showcase" Italian "funded by absentee Hollywood owners" is "popular with the young crowd" for its "chic" setting that includes "floor-to-ceiling curtains", "fireplace TV screens" and an overall "trendy" vibe; detractors, though, find the "pricey" fare "spectacularly ordinary" and the service "not very accommodating" – unless you're "dressed like a model."

### Dominick's *Italian*    23 | 18 | 23 | $25

**Lawrenceville** | 197 W. Crogan St. (S. Perry St.) | 770-277-8477
**Norcross** | 95 S. Peachtree St. NW (Holcomb Bridge Rd.) | 770-449-1611

"Go hungry" to this pair of Italian "favorites" in Lawrenceville and Norcross known for "family-style platings" of "delicious pastas" and "potent" garlic bread – and "be prepared to share" or "take home leftovers"; even though the "cramped" quarters are usually packed with "happy, noisy clients", the service is "impeccable."

### Downwind Ⓢ *American*    18 | 16 | 15 | $15

**DeKalb** | Peachtree-DeKalb Airport | 2000 Airport Rd., 2nd fl. (Clairmont Rd.) | 770-452-0973 | www.downwindrestaurant.com

"Hamburger lovers will flip over" the "delicious" "handmade" burgers at this "laid-back" American located right "on the tarmac" of PDK airport, with an "awesome" outdoor deck "overlooking the runway", where you can watch everything from "corporate jets to biplanes" take off and land; the owner's a "character", and though the staffers appear "overworked", they "sure are glad you came."

### Dreamland Bar-B-Que *BBQ*

| 17 | 10 | 17 | $16 |

**Roswell** | 10730 Alpharetta Hwy. (Mansell Rd.) | 678-352-7999
**Norcross** | 5250 Peachtree Pkwy. (Peachtree Corners Circle) |
770-446-6969
www.dreamlandbbq.com

"Get good and messy" at these Norcross and Roswell outposts of the "famous" Tuscaloosa-based BBQ that serve up "h-u-uge portions" of "fall-off-the-bone ribs" and "even better" sides in "fairly typical" digs complete with "license plates on the wall"; for critics who find them "overrated" and "more about the name than the food", it's like a "bad dream."

### Dressed - Salads with Style ⊠ *American*

| 19 | 16 | 17 | $13 |

**Midtown** | Plaza Midtown | 950 W. Peachtree St. NW, Ste. 240
(Peachtree Pl.) | 404-347-3434 | www.dressedsalads.com

An "impressive variety" of "high-quality ingredients" and "phenomenal" selection of "divine" dressings allow one to "make the salad of your dreams" at this Midtown American that also serves "can't-go-wrong" soups from Souper Jenny; the "sleek" space has a "New Yorky" feel and the delivery service is "reliable" and "speedy", but some find it a bit "pricey for what you get."

### Dusty's Barbecue *BBQ*

| 16 | 8 | 16 | $13 |

**Emory** | 1815 Briarcliff Rd. NE (Clifton Rd.) | 404-320-6264 |
www.dustys.com

For "quick, tasty" eats that are "not fast food", this BBQ near Emory, "one of the few inside the perimeter", is a "longtime favorite", dishing out "damn good" NC-style pit offerings and other "good grub"; frankly, it's a "dump", but the service is "friendly", and while some find the fare merely "serviceable", fans insist the "'cue is true."

### Earl, The ◑ *American*

| 22 | 13 | 14 | $15 |

**East Atlanta** | 488 Flat Shoals Ave. SE (Glenwood Ave.) | 404-522-3950 |
www.badearl.com

"Take in the urban" scene along with some of the "city's best burgers" and "divine" "skinny fries" at this East Atlanta American, a "good ol' hangout joint" and a "great music venue" as well, where you'll find lots of the "alternative set", as well as plenty of "hungover people" during brunch; just be "prepared for a side of tobacco with your meal", for it's "very smoky in there."

### East Pearl ◑ *Chinese*

| - | - | - | I |

**Duluth** | 1810 Liddell Ln. (Crestwood Pkwy.) | 678-380-0899

"The dim sum is the star" at this hard-to-find Chinese in Duluth, a "locals' favorite" offering a "wide selection" of Cantonese small bites to those who have taken the dive; "don't let the service or decor deter you" – and don't forget the GPS – because the "food is fabulous" according to aficionados.

| | FOOD | DECOR | SERVICE | COST |
|---|---|---|---|---|

**Eats**  *Eclectic*  | 18 | 7 | 13 | $10 |

**Midtown** | 600 Ponce de Leon Ave. NE (bet. Glen Iris Dr. & Lakeview Ave.) | 404-888-9149 | www.eatsonponce.net

"Rastas, punks" and "policemen" alike "crowd" into the booths at this Midtown "dive" for "cheap" Eclectic offerings such as "amazing" jerk chicken, "tasty" vegetables and "build-your-own" pasta; though it reminds some of a "soup kitchen" where you basically "wait on yourself", even the "penurious find value" in this "joint" with a mysterious "magnetic pull."

**Z Ecco**  *Continental*  | 25 | 25 | 23 | $40 |

**Midtown** | 40 Seventh St. NE (Cypress St.) | 404-347-9555 | www.fifthgroup.com

An "instant favorite" of many, this Midtown Continental from the Fifth Group "stands out" with chef Micah Willix's "flexible", "taste-and-share" menu of "exceptional" fare (e.g. "divine" fried goat cheese balls) paired with a "deep wine list"; a "vaulted glass lobby" and "captivating" open kitchen highlight the "gorgeous" Johnson Studio–designed space, where the staff is "on top of things" and "fantastic bartenders" mix "innovative" cocktails in the "lively" bar full of "beautiful people"; while "noise" and "attitude" can be issues, most agree it "lives up to the hype."

**Eclipse di Luna**  *Spanish*  | 21 | 18 | 18 | $27 |

**Buckhead** | 764 Miami Circle NE (Piedmont Rd.) | 404-846-0449 | www.eclipsediluna.com

A "festive alternative" in Buckhead for the "young and beautiful", this Spanish tapastry serves up small plates with "big flavors" and "reasonable prices" that you can wash down with "marvelous mojitos" and "sangria that'll knock your *zapatos* off"; live Latin bands "keep the place groovin'" and the staff delivers "service with a smile", but it almost gets "so loud your ears will bleed", so many opt for the patio, where you "can hear."

**Edo**  *Japanese*  | ▽ 19 | 17 | 18 | $24 |

**Decatur** | Toco Hills Shopping Ctr. | 2945 N. Druid Hills Rd. (Lavista Rd.) | 404-728-0228 | www.edo-atlanta.com

A "lovely surprise" in a somewhat "ugly" shopping center, this Toco Hills Japanese delivers "worthy" sushi and "huge portions" of "surprisingly good" teppanyaki eats that are sliced, diced and served by "animated", "super-friendly" grill chefs (a "must for kids' birthdays"), although purists find the fare "sadly ordinary"; the space is "big and "comfortable", and the "private" tatami rooms have *horigotatsu* tables with "holes in the floor for your legs" to spare you from sitting "Japanese-style."

**NEW VIII fifty**  🗷 *American*  | - | - | - | M |

**Roswell** | Holcomb Woods | 1570 Holcomb Bridge Rd., Ste. 850 (Old Alabama Rd.) | 678-206-0850 | www.850atlanta.com

A former Mexican restaurant is now the site of this snazzy Roswell New American where chef Daniel Massie's cosmopolitan small and large plates and specially priced bar bites, live music and wine tastings

| | FOOD | DECOR | SERVICE | COST |
|---|---|---|---|---|

attract a varied crowd; rich copper and warm woods accent the sophisticated and sprawling space that includes a dance floor and an outdoor patio with big-time views and Miami Beach–inspired cabanas.

### 88 Tofu House ● *Korean*

▽ | 21 | 9 | 14 | $13

**Buford Hwy. (Atlanta)** | 5490 Buford Hwy. (Rte. 285) | 770-457-8811
"When you need that spicy soup fix", fans tout this "fab" 24/7 Buford Highway Korean for its "reasonably priced", "seething cauldrons" of broth, "soft tofu" and "your choice of ingredients", served with a "table full of yummy" accompaniments; service can vary from "helpful" to "rude", and the "unassuming" digs resemble a "cafeteria", but most "just ignore" both, since the "consistently good" fare is the "best cure for what ails you."

### Einstein's *American*

18 | 18 | 17 | $24

**Midtown** | 1077 Juniper St. NE (12th St.) | 404-876-7925 |
www.einsteinsatlanta.com
"The people-watching keeps people coming back" to this Midtown stalwart popular for its "incredible patio" "under really big trees", where a "gay-centric crowd" mingles with "urban hipsters" and area workers for a "happy hour" of "stiff drinks" (though ongoing construction nearby may drive some indoors to the "trendy bar"); there's a "wide choice" of "decent" New American fare, including "massive desserts" that "make you swoon" and a "fantastic" brunch, but for critics the equation involves "slow" service and "unspectacular" food.

### El Azteca *Mexican*

16 | 11 | 17 | $16

**Alpharetta** | 13800 Hwy. 9 N. (Bethany Bend) | 678-867-9950
**Alpharetta** | 9925 Haynes Bridge Rd. (Old Alabama Rd.) |
770-569-5234
**Midtown** | 939 Ponce de Leon Ave. (Freedom Pkwy.) |
404-881-6040
**Dunwoody** | 1412 Dunwoody Village Pkwy. (off Mt. Vernon Rd.) |
770-399-7757
**Sandy Springs** | 5925 Roswell Rd. (Hammond Dr.) | 404-252-7347
**South Buckhead** | 1784 Peachtree St. NE (Palisades Rd.) |
404-249-1522
www.elaztecaatlanta.com
"Far from gourmet" but "still a top choice" of many for "dependable" "standard" Mexican, this "family-friendly" south-of-the-border chain offers "amazing value", and "people-watching" over "killer" margaritas on its "large" patios remains a popular pastime; many concede, however, that the "social scene" is "better than the food" or "dismal dining rooms."

### El Rey de Taco ● *Mexican*

▽ | 24 | 12 | 14 | $12

**Buford Hwy. (Doraville)** | Pinetree West Shopping Ctr. |
5288 Buford Hwy. NE (Oakmont Ave.) | Doraville | 770-986-0032
You can "take in a soccer game from Mexico on TV" at this "modest little cantina" in Doraville serving "authentic", "home-cooked" south-of-the-border "street food" that's definitely "not American-Mexican"; it may be a "dive" but "happy" amigos "can't say enough" about this "real deal" that never closes.

| | FOOD | DECOR | SERVICE | COST |
|---|---|---|---|---|

### El Taco Veloz  *Mexican*  
20 | 3 | 13 | $9

**Smyrna** | 925 Windy Hill Rd. (Atlanta Rd.) | 770-432-8800
**Chamblee** | Chamblee Commercial Ctr. | 3245 Chamblee Dunwoody Rd.
(bet. Buford Hwy. & New Peachtree Rd.) | 770-458-7779
**Buford Hwy. (Doraville)** | 5084 Buford Hwy. (Chamblee Dunwoody Rd.) |
Doraville | 770-936-9094 ●
**Norcross** | 2077 Beaver Ruin Rd. (I-85) | 770-849-0025
**Duluth** | 2700 Buford Hwy. (Old Peachtree Rd.) | 770-622-0138
**Sandy Springs** | 5670 Roswell Rd. NE (I-285) | 404-252-5100
Though these Mexican "stands" are no more than "a few tables" and
a "drive-thru window", *fanáticos* fawn over their "delicious" tacos
made with ingredients ranging from "run-of-the-mill" to "more exotic"
(tongue, anyone?), and insist you "won't find more authentic" eats
"unless you cross the border" – and they're *muy "el cheapo"*; service
is "friendly", and "may be better if you speak Spanish."

### Eno  ⊠ *Mediterranean*  
23 | 21 | 21 | $44

**Midtown** | 800 Peachtree St. (5th St.) | 404-685-3191 |
www.enorestaurant.com
"Local foodies", oenophiles and the "pre-theater" crowd "love" this
"cozy" Midtowner for its "well-prepared" Med fare and "top-notch"
wine list, including 120 by the glass; a connected retail shop, a wine
bar and patio overlooking Peachtree and "helpful" service from an
"educated" staff add to the "wonderful" experience; N.B. a late-
Survey chef change may not be reflected in the above Food score.

### Enoteca Carbonari  ⊠ *Italian*  
22 | 21 | 20 | $36

**Midtown** | 710 Peachtree St. NE (3rd St.) | 404-810-9110 |
www.enotecacarbonari.com
"Flavorful, well-presented" Italian small plates, "excellent" house-
made charcuterie, a "nice selection" of cheeses and an "amazing"
Boot-centric wine list "covering a wide range of prices" attract fans
to this Midtown *fratello* of Baraonda; a "well trained staff" provides
"careful" service in the "flawless", "wonderfully comfortable" space
boasting stone columns, wrought iron and a wall of *vino*.

### ESPN Zone  *American*  
10 | 18 | 13 | $25

**Buckhead** | 3030 Peachtree Rd. NW (Buckhead Ave.) | 404-682-3776 |
www.espnzone.com
"If massive portions, chaos and testosterone" are "your dining
preferences", this Buckhead American is the "next best place to
Turner Field" since the "TVs all over the place" (including the downstairs men's room) ensure "you'll never miss a play", and the game
room is "awesome"; the service is "slow" and the "bar" fare is "mediocre", but for "kids" and "sports nuts" who "don't go for the food",
it's "a blast."

### Eurasia Bistro  ⊠ *Pan-Asian*  
25 | 24 | 23 | $31

**Decatur** | 129 E. Ponce de Leon Ave. (bet. Church St. & Clairmont Ave.) |
404-687-8822
A "favorite" "go-to place" of many for "special events", "perfect
date nights" or just a "late lunch" in Decatur, this "romantic" spot is

the showcase for chef Wendy Chang's "excellent", "artfully presented" Pan-Asian cuisine; a "gracious", "unobtrusive" staff "aims to please" amid "elegant", "quiet" surroundings that are "good for entertaining when you want to hear your dining partner's conversation."

## Everybody's Pizza *Pizza* | 20 | 14 | 16 | $16 |
|---|---|---|---|---|

**Decatur** | Emory Vill. | 1593 N. Decatur Rd. (Oxford Rd.) | 404-377-7766
**Virginia-Highland** | 1040 N. Highland Ave. (Virginia Ave.) | 404-873-4545
www.everybodyspizza.com

"Everybody loves" this "popular" pizza pair in Decatur and Virginia-Highland for their "incredibly tasty" pies that "make you feel righteous" ("and your pocketbook says amen"), "huge build-your-own salads" and a "vast selection of beers on tap"; the decor is "minimal" but both have "great decks" where a "mixed" crowd of "yuppies", "students, profs and locals" hangs, but "make sure you have a lot of time" since service can be "slow."

## NEW Fadó Irish | - | - | - | I |
|---|---|---|---|---|
## Pub & Restaurant *Pub Food*

**Buckhead** | 279 Buckhead Ave. (Bolling Way) | 404-841-0066 | www.fadoirishpub.com

This popular Emerald Isle haunt in Buckhead has been resurrected blarney stone by blarney stone in a newly erected multi-level building located right around the corner from its previous site, with a stronger emphasis on the Irish and American fusion pub fare to go with all that Guinness; the various vignettes (Victorian room, grand room, old-fashioned shop, iron-clad cellar, etc.) from the old space remain the same, while a rooftop bar and a full-service patio with fireplace and heated floors offer promising views through most of the year.

## Farmhouse Restaurant Ⓜ *American* | ▽ 25 | 22 | 21 | $36 |
|---|---|---|---|---|

**Palmetto** | Inn at Serenbe | 10950 Hutcheson Ferry Rd. (off South Fulton Pkwy.) | 770-463-2610 | www.serenbe.com

Many feel the drive through the "beautiful hill country" to this "charmer" at Serenbe alone is "worth it", but for foodies the "icing on the cake" is chef Nicholas Bour's "excellent" "home-cooked" American with Southern accents made from local "farm-fresh ingredients", served on a "limited" prix fixe menu; guests "love" the grounds of the "cute small community" and the "delightful" porch, and the "reasonable" $10 BYO corkage fee gives it added "value."

## Fat Matt's Chicken Shack *Southern* | 24 | 9 | 14 | $13 |
|---|---|---|---|---|

**Virginia-Highland** | 1821 Piedmont Ave. NE (Rock Springs Rd.) | 404-875-2722

"Delightfully dumpy and well worn" ("it's the food version of the sweatshirt my wife wants to throw out"), this inexpensive Virginia-Highland Southerner sizzles with the "hands-down best chicken" and "absolutely great" catfish, served with a "dash of sass" to a mess of folks who "don't care how the place looks"; "come empty" and "leave full" – just "wash your hands" (and that sweatshirt) "afterwards."

| | FOOD | DECOR | SERVICE | COST |
|---|---|---|---|---|

### Fat Matt's Rib Shack ● *BBQ/Southern*    | 23 | 10 | 14 | $15 |

**Virginia-Highland** | 1811 Piedmont Ave. NE (Rock Springs Rd.) | 404-607-1622

"Finger-lickin'" fans flock to the "granddaddy of Atlanta's rib shacks" in Virginia-Highland for a "messy and simple" "feast for a king" of "succulent" ribs "to die for (and we probably will)"; add "ice cold beer", "great" live blues and cheap prices and you'll know why there are "lines out the door"; "no frills – no problem", for while "it ain't much to look at", it "delivers with a vengeance."

### Feast *American*    | 22 | 23 | 21 | $29 |

**Decatur** | 314 E. Howard Ave. (E. Trinity Pl.) | 404-377-2000 | www.feastatlanta.com

A "charming" "find" (though locating it can be "hard"), this "delightful" Decatur destination delivers "terrific small plates" and other "amazing", "affordable" New American fare in a "cozy", "romantic" space that's "gorgeous without an ounce of pretension", with a wood-burning oven to "keep things warm" and a "new patio"; "helpful", "accommodating" service is another plus, and despite a few grumblings over "inconsistent" eats, most agree it's "worth the trip."

### Feed Store ☒ *Southern*    ▽ | 19 | 18 | 17 | $32 |

**Airport (College Park)** | 3841 Main St. (bet. John Wesley & Yale Aves.) | College Park | 404-209-7979 | www.thefeedstorerestaurant.com

"Luckily, forks and knives are provided" instead of "nosebags" at this "unfortunately named" "surprise find" in College Park, where "trendy and down-home-style" Southern eats and a "chic" renovation of a former feed store make it a "good choice" for "entertaining clients near the airport"; "poor" service, though, goes against the grain of this otherwise "bright spot" in the neighborhood.

### Fellini's Pizza ● *Pizza*    | 20 | 12 | 15 | $12 |

**Buckhead** | 2809 Peachtree Rd. NE (Rumson Rd.) | 404-266-0082
**Buckhead** | 4429 Roswell Rd. NE (Wieuca Rd.) | 404-303-8248
**Candler Park** | 1634 McLendon Ave. NE (Clifton Rd.) | 404-687-9190
**Decatur** | Vista Grove Plaza | 2820 Lavista Rd. (Oak Grove Rd.) | 404-633-6016
**Decatur** | 333 Commerce Dr. (bet. Hillyer & Sycamore Pls.) | 404-370-0551
**South Buckhead** | 1991 Howell Mill Rd. NW (Collier Rd.) | 404-352-0799
**Poncey-Highland** | 909 Ponce de Leon Ave. (Linwood Ave.) | 404-873-3088

Piezani "dream about" this "fabulous", "family-friendly" pizzeria chain "slinging slices topped to your liking" that "hit the spot" and, best of all, it "doesn't rob your pocket"; "colorful" "tattooed" characters deliver the goods (though some appear to "wish they were somewhere else") in "shabby-chic" settings highlighted by "diverse people-watching" and "fountain-side" "patio dining."

### Fickle Pickle ☒ *American*    | 23 | 19 | 19 | $14 |

**Roswell** | 1085 Canton St. (Woodstock St.) | 770-650-9838 | www.ficklepicklecafe.com

At his Roswell New American, chef Andy Badgett's "awesome" fried pickles are "not to be missed" and the rest of the "casual" bill of fare,

| | FOOD | DECOR | SERVICE | COST |
|---|---|---|---|---|

including "wonderful" "gourmet sandwiches", is "consistently good"; the service is "friendly", and the "desirable" location "close to the town square" makes it a "great place" to "sit outside" "with a friend", especially when it's "crowded in that little house."

### Figo Pasta/Osteria del Figo *Italian*    21 | 15 | 17 | $16

**Westside** | 1210 Howell Mill Rd. (Huff Rd.) | 404-351-3700
**Decatur** | 627 E. College Ave. (Weekes St.) | 404-377-2121
**East Atlanta** | Edgewood Retail Shopping Plaza | 1220 Caroline St. (Moreland Ave.) | 404-586-9250
**South Buckhead** | 1170B Collier Rd. (Defoors Ferry Rd.) | 404-351-9667
www.figopasta.com

"You get wa-a-y more than you expect" at this "tasty" Italian quartet that's "heaven" for pastafarians with its "fabulous" pick-your-pasta-and-sauce combinations; "easy in-and-out" semi-"self-service" can be a bit "sporadic", but "the price is right" for "foodies on a budget", the "simple" digs are "inviting", and it's "convenient" and "kid-friendly"; critics may find the sauces "bland" and noodles "over-cooked", but most feel it's "ok in a pinch."

### Fire of Brazil Churrascaria *Brazilian/Steak*    21 | 20 | 22 | $42

**Alpharetta** | 5304 Windward Pkwy. (Westside Pkwy.) | 678-366-2411
**Downtown** | 218 Peachtree St. NW (Andrew Young Int'l Blvd.) | 404-525-5255
**Dunwoody** | 118 Perimeter Ctr. W. (Hammond Dr.) | 770-551-4367
www.fireofbrazil.com

These upscale Brazilian "meatfests" are "just what the doctor (Atkins) ordered" according to carnivores and even "vegetarians" who go "wild" over the "unlimited quantities" of "addictive" meats, a "surprisingly good salad bar" and "attentive" service in a warm setting; they're "favorites" of many for a "work meeting", "special occasion" or "large party on an expense account", and while foes find them "overpriced" for "just ok" eats, others deem them a "good value."

### 🅉 Five Guys *Burgers*    21 | 11 | 17 | $10

**Acworth** | Shoppes of Acworth | 3450 Cobb Pkwy. NW (Dogwood Ln. NW) | 770-917-9377
**Alpharetta** | Center Stage at Winward Pkwy. | 5230 Windward Pkwy. (bet. Ashleigh Ln. & Jordan Ct.) | 678-867-7930
**Roswell** | Mansell Vill. | 580 E. Crossville Rd. (Alpharetta Hwy.) | 770-649-1818
**Alpharetta** | 6410 N. Point Pkwy. (N. Point Ct.) | 770-346-0366
**Austell** | 1757 East-West Connector (Austell Rd. SW) | 770-944-7308
**Chamblee** | 1891 Chamblee Tucker Rd. (bet. Peachtree Industrial Blvd. & Peachtree Rd.) | 770-220-0992
**Suwanee** | 340 Town Center Ave., Ste. A1 (bet. Buford Hwy. & Lawrenceville Suwanee Rd.) | 770-945-4670
**East Atlanta** | The Edgewood Retail District | 1253 Caroline St. (bet. Marion Pl. & Moreland Ave. NE) | 404-688-6474
**Gainesville** | 658 Dawsonville Hwy. (Shallowford Rd.) | 678-450-9496

*(continued)*

*(continued)*

## Five Guys

**South Buckhead** | Lindbergh City Ctr. | 558 Main St. NE (Lindbergh Dr.) | 404-848-9119
www.fiveguys.com
Additional locations throughout the Atlanta area

Though they're "five to seven napkins on the messy scale", the "better-than-homemade" burgers at these links in a "welcome" Virginia-based chain "make any bad day better", "cooked fresh to order" with "all the fixings you want at no added cost" and complemented by "phenomenal" fries "made daily from fresh potatoes"; you "serve yourself" with the help of a "cheerful" counter staff in "clean" spaces channeling a "'50s malt shop", and while some "don't understand the buzz", for most "these guys fit the bill."

## Five Seasons Brewing Co. *American*   22 | 17 | 19 | $27

**Alpharetta** | 3655 Old Milton Pkwy. (Brookside Pkwy.) | 770-521-5551
**Sandy Springs** | Prado Shopping Ctr. | 5600 Roswell Rd. (I-285) | 404-255-5911
www.5seasonsbrewing.com

"Don't let the 'brewery' tag fool you" advise fans of this "depend-able" duo in Alpharetta and Sandy Springs where the "tantalizing" New American cuisine emphasizing "fresh" "local and organic" in-gredients is "not at all pub fare" and "can steal the spotlight" from the "awesome" beers; co-owner Dennis Lange, the "host with the most", and a "friendly" staff make you "comfortable" in the "lodge-like" surroundings with "on-site breweries" in "full view."

## Fleming's Prime Steakhouse & Wine Bar *Steak*   23 | 23 | 23 | $53

**Dunwoody** | 4501 Olde Perimeter Way (Ashford Dunwoody Rd.) | 770-698-8112 | www.flemingssteakhouse.com

"All you need is a sharp knife and a big appetite" at this "upscale" chain link in Dunwoody where "fantastic" steaks and a "world-class" wine list (including a "large" by-the-glass program) give locals "an alternative to driving to Buckhead"; an "upbeat" staff delivers "top-notch" service in the "relaxed", "clubby setting", and while some critics find it merely "average", others "highly recommend" it when you have a jones for a "tasty slab of meat."

## Z Floataway Cafe 🅂🅼 *French/Italian*   25 | 22 | 24 | $43

**Emory** | Floataway Bldg. | 1123 Zonolite Rd. NE (bet. Briarcliff & Johnson Rds.) | 404-892-1414 | www.starprovisions.com

For a "top-notch" dinner "without emptying the piggy bank", afi-cionados recommend this "less formal" Emory sibling of Quinones and Bacchanalia, where chef Drew Belline incorporates "amaz-ingly fresh local" produce into his "fabulous" "casual" French-Italian fare, paired with "one of the most interesting wine lists in town"; the service is "attentive" and "unpretentious", and recent renovations "reduced" the "noise", making it even easier to "float away from reality" here.

| | FOOD | DECOR | SERVICE | COST |
|---|---|---|---|---|

## ☒ Flying Biscuit  *Southern*

**19** | **15** | **17** | **$16**

**NEW** **Marietta** | 1084 E. Johnson Ferry Rd. (Little Willeo Rd.) | 770-321-4445
**Midtown** | 1001 Piedmont Ave. NE (10th St.) | 404-874-8887
**Buckhead** | 3515 Northside Pkwy. NW (bet. Beechwood Dr. & Paces Ferry Rd.) | 404-816-3152
**Candler Park** | 1655 McLendon Ave. NE (Clifton Rd.) | 404-687-8888
www.flyingbiscuit.com

"You can't call yourself a true Atlanta resident" unless you've "swooped on in" to this "lighthearted" Southern "legend" that's "blossomed" into a chain, serving fans far and wide "delish" "all-day breakfast", "addictive biscuits" and other "filling" "comfort food"; "sunny, happy people" in "eclectic early hippie" digs manage the "cattle call" of "Sunday morning brunch-goers", and while some critics snort that "franchising" has caused it to "fall like a bad soufflé", for others it remains an "old stand-by."

## ☒ Fogo de Chão  *Brazilian/Steak*

**24** | **20** | **24** | **$55**

**Buckhead** | 3101 Piedmont Rd. NE (bet. E. Paces Ferry & Peachtree Rds.) | 404-995-9982 | www.fogodechao.com

"Bring out your inner wolf" to the "Lipitor capital of Georgia", this Brazilian "beeffest" in Buckhead that's a "dream come true" for "carnivores" and "PETA's nightmare", where fans partake of "unlimited" helpings of "perfectly prepared" meat "served tableside on skewers", as well as offerings from a "gorgeous" "Las Vegas buffet–style" salad bar; "efficient" "gauchos" "dressed in native costumes" deliver the "nonstop array" of flesh in a "fancy" setting with "enormous fire pits", and while it's "not cheap", most agree it's "worth every penny."

## Fontaine's Oyster House ● *Seafood*

**16** | **16** | **16** | **$22**

**Virginia-Highland** | 1026½ N. Highland Ave. NE (Virginia Ave.) | 404-872-0869

"Feel like you just walked off Bourbon Street" in this "old-fashioned bar" in Virginia-Highland that reels in finatics with "tasty" oysters, the "best lobster bisque in town" and other seafood that "tastes like it came straight off the boat"; an "awesome" deck "any time of year", "fantastic jukebox" and "amazing chandelier" add to the "cool" scene, and while purists consider it "more of a bar than a restaurant", most agree the weekly "food-drink" specials are a "steal."

## Food 101  *American*

**20** | **19** | **20** | **$30**

**Sandy Springs** | 4969 Roswell Rd. NE (Belle Isle Rd.) | 404-497-9700
**Virginia-Highland** | 1397 N. Highland Ave. NE (E. Rock Springs Rd.) | 404-347-9747
www.101concepts.com

If you're "jonesin' for home cooking", this New American duo delivers a "melt-in-your-mouth" "intro to how dining should be done", with "reliable" comfort food "favorites with a slight twist", "inventive theme dinners" and "yummy brunch"; in contrast to the "energetic" service, the decor is "calming" and there's a "good vibe at the bar"; Virginia-Highland gets extra credit for its "inviting" patio.

|  | FOOD | DECOR | SERVICE | COST |
|---|---|---|---|---|

### ☑ Food Studio ☒ *American* | 24 | 25 | 24 | $48

**Westside** | King Plow Art Ctr. | 887 W. Marietta St. NW (Brady St.) | 404-815-6677 | www.thefoodstudio.com

"The gods must have blessed" the entire cast at this "stylish" "special-occasion" destination "in the King Plow art district" on the Westside, where "exposed brick" and "intimate lighting" highlight the "cool" decor of the former "plow factory", setting the scene for chef Mark Alba's "fabulous", "inventive" New American cuisine; "spotless" service makes "you feel like one of the family" and contributes to a "wonderful dining experience."

### NEW Fox Bros. Barbecue *BBQ* | - | - | - | I

**Candler Park** | 1238 Dekalb Ave. (bet. Candler & Jospehine Sts.) | 404-577-4030 | www.foxbrosbbq.com

"Just follow the smoke signals from" the "massive pits" of this "hopping" new BBQ in Candler Park and "you won't be sorry" attest aficionados of its "outrageously good" "slow cooked meats" doused with "inspired" sauce and served up in "overwhelming" portions; the no-frills digs overlook MARTA tracks but fans aren't there for the views.

### Fratelli di Napoli *Italian* | 18 | 18 | 18 | $30

**Roswell** | 928 Canton St. (Atlanta St.) | 770-642-9917 | www.fratelli.net

"*Molto bene*" boast boosters of this midpriced Southern Italian in Roswell where "family-style" platters full of "rich and tasty" "standard" red-sauce dishes "make you wish you'd been born into that *famiglia*"; while a few find the experience "very up and down", many others feel the "accommodating" service, "convivial" atmosphere that's "kid-friendly without being over-casual" and "big round tables" make it "great for groups" or a "girls' night out."

### French American | 24 | 24 | 23 | $42
### Brasserie ☒ *American/French*
### (aka F.A.B.)

**Downtown** | Southern Company | 30 Ivan Allen Jr. Blvd. (W. Peachtree St.) | 404-266-1440 | www.fabatlanta.com

This "beautiful" "reincarnation" of the "late, lamented Brasserie Le Coze" is a "worthy successor" and the "best thing to come into Downtown in ages" say fans who fawn over its "superb" French brasserie fare (with New American dishes adding "variety"), "cavernous", yet "gorgeous", "four-level" interior (a rooftop area is in the works) and "wonderful" service; cronies confirm "they still have the touch."

### Fresh to Order *American* | 21 | 15 | 17 | $14
### (aka F2O)

**Midtown** | 860 Peachtree St. NE (bet. 6th & 7th Sts.) | 404-593-2333
**Duluth** | 10900 Medlock Bridge Rd. (Abbotts Bridge Rd.) | 678-720-9333
**Sandy Springs** | 6125 Roswell Rd. (Hilderbrand Dr.) | 404-567-8646
www.f2ofresh.com

At this "clever" and "well-named" New American chain, "wholesome" "high-class food for a working-class price" is "prepared quickly" and "ready for takeout or eat-in" by an "energetic" staff; you order at the counter in what's basically a "self-serve" arrangement, in "cool" digs that match the "fast, casual" environment; as pros point out, the "crowds speak for themselves."

### Fritti  *Pizza*   23 | 19 | 19 | $25

**Inman Park** | 309 N. Highland Ave. NE (Elizabeth St.) | 404-880-9559 | www.frittirestaurant.com

"When your stomach says Sotto Sotto, but your wallet says no go", fans recommend its pizzeria spin-off next door in Inman Park, serving pizzas ranging "from the everyday to the exotic" from its wood-burning oven, as well as "sinfully delicious" Italian dishes such as "truffle oil mushrooms"; a "nice" wine selection and "killer $2 Bloody Marys" at Sunday brunch lubricate the "see-and-be-seen" scene of "yuppies", and despite all the development in the neighborhood, the patio still offers a "nice view of Downtown."

### Fuego Spanish Grill  *Spanish*   20 | 17 | 18 | $24
### (fka Fuego Cafe & Tapas Bar)

**Midtown** | 1136 Crescent Ave. NE (bet. 13th & 14th Sts.) | 404-389-0660 | www.fuegocafe.com

"*Olé*" cry amigos of this small-plates specialist in Midtown that has fans fired up over "amazing" tapas, "authentic" Spanish and Latin entrees and some of the "best sangria in town"; it's "lots of fun for a big group", with "pleasant" service, a "great happy hour" and live flamenco music Thursdays–Saturdays – and, it's "not too pricey."

### Gabriel's ⊠ *Bakery*   ∇ 24 | 13 | 18 | $15

**Marietta** | 800 Whitlock Ave. (Burnt Hickory Rd.) | 770-427-9007 | www.gabrielsdesserts.com

"Politics, gossip and Southern staples" are on the bill of fare at this "sweet" "neighborhood hangout" in Marietta, where Ms. Johnnie Gabriel (aka Paula Deen's cousin) also whips up "splendid desserts" and "beautiful special-occasion cakes"; there's "no decor" to speak of in the "shopping center" spot but there's "none needed", thanks to the "friendly" atmosphere and some of the "best homemade food in all of metro Atlanta", at prices that "won't burn a hole in the pocketbook."

### Garrison's Broiler & Tap  *American*   19 | 19 | 18 | $33

**Duluth** | Medlock Crossing | 9700 Medlock Bridge Rd. (State Bridge Rd.) | 770-476-1962

**Vinings** | Vinings Jubilee Shopping Ctr. | 4300 Paces Ferry Rd. SE (Spring Hill Pkwy.) | 770-436-0102
www.garrisonsatlanta.com

This "solid" suburban duo earns a "thumbs-up" from fans for a "broad menu" of "consistently" "delicious" American fare, "effusive" service and a "prompt" kitchen, which make it a "favorite for lunch"; Duluth sports an "attractive" rooftop deck, and Vinings boasts "taproom" decor and a patio with a "great view of the village."

### Gasthaus Le Café ⊠Ⓜ *German*   - | - | - | M

**Cumming** | 310 Atlanta Rd. (bet. Maple St. & Veterans Memorial Blvd.) | 770-844-7244 | www.gasthauscumming.com

Insiders lament that the jig may be up for "Cumming's best-kept secret", citing "long waits on Saturday nights", thanks to chef Reinhold

Weger's "excellent" German cuisine (his "schnitzel can't be beat"), paired with an "exceptional" beer selection; a "knowledgeable" staff mans the "tiny space" with outdoor *biergarten*, creating a "welcoming" atmosphere at this "unexpected treasure in an unlikely location."

### Genki *Japanese* | 19 | 11 | 14 | $24 |

**Buckhead** | 3188 Roswell Rd. NW (Sardia Way) | 404-869-8319 | www.genki-inc.com

"Creative" sushi and "decent" noodle bowls from this "hip" Buckhead Japanese "hit the mark" for "young locals", especially on the patio, and valet parking is a "plus" in this "busy area"; service varies from "fast" and "helpful" to "horribly rude", and claustrophobes carp it's often "too crowded to enjoy" the experience.

### George's *American* | 22 | 12 | 20 | $12 |

**Virginia-Highland** | 1041 N. Highland Ave. NE (Virginia Ave.) | 404-892-3648 | www.georgesbarandrestaurant.com

"Every neighborhood needs" an "institution" like this "family-owned" American in Virginia-Highland with "character to spare", serving "hand-patted, addictive" burgers and "cheap" beer in a "laid-back dive" setting with a patio "for people-watching"; there's "nothing fancy here", just a "familiar feel", "friendly" folks and "one of the very best hamburgers in town."

### Georgia Grille Ⓜ *Southwestern* | 22 | 15 | 19 | $34 |

**South Buckhead** | Peachtree Sq. | 2290 Peachtree Rd. NE (bet. Peachtree Hills Ave. & Peachtree Memorial Dr.) | 404-352-3517 | www.georgiagrille.com

Fans tout this "longtime charmer" in South Buckhead as a "good value" for "terrific margaritas" and "outstanding" Southwestern cuisine, including "unreal lobster enchiladas"; chef-owner Karen Hilliard "always make patrons feel at home" in the "quaint", "intimate" space graced with paintings by namesake Georgia O'Keeffe and a "pleasant" outdoor patio, all of which make it a place "you can always count on."

### Gilbert's Mediterranean Cafe *Mediterranean* | ▽ 20 | 14 | 18 | $27 |

**Midtown** | 219 10th St. NE (Piedmont Ave.) | 404-872-8012 | www.gilbertscafe.com

Boosters of this "quaint" Mediterranean "in the heart of Midtown" "have never been disappointed" by the "nicely prepared" "low-fuss" food and wine, but most are "drawn in" by the "cozy" atmosphere and "consistently cool", "gay-friendly" "vibe" in the otherwise "claustrophobic" space; there's karaoke every Wednesday night, when the whole scene "turns from Greek to go-go", and pros promise the "shockingly strong drinks will have you singing and dancing in no time."

### Gladys Knight & Ron Winans' Chicken & Waffles *Southern* | 18 | 15 | 15 | $19 |

**Downtown** | 529 Peachtree St. NW (bet. North Ave. & Pine St.) | 404-874-9393

*(continued)*

## Gladys Knight & Ron Winans'
## Chicken & Waffles

**Lithonia** | Stonecrest | 7301 Stonecrest Concourse, Ste. 123
(Turner Hill Rd.) | 770-482-6766
www.gladysandron.com

"Who knew chicken and waffles worked so well together" ponder fans
of this Southern duo who are willing to brave "long waits" for its "simply delicious" signature duet and other "deep-fried delights" with
"catchy names"; critics complain of "slow" service and a "tourist-
trap" atmosphere, but it's a hit with many as a "late-night spot."

### NEW Glenwood, The  *Southern*                 - | - | - | I

**East Atlanta** | 1263 Glenwood Ave. (Flat Shoals Ave.) | 404-622-6066 |
www.theglenwood.net

A "great take on the gastropub concept", this East Atlanta newcomer offers "imaginative" New American bar food with a Southern
riff, not to mention "reasonable prices and portions"; a 15-ft.-high
ceiling, exposed brick and burnt orange tones highlight the space,
which is complemented by an outdoor deck.

### Globe, The  ☒ *American*                  20 | 23 | 19 | $32

**Midtown** | Technology Sq. | 75 Fifth St. NW (Spring St.) | 404-541-1487 |
www.globeatlanta.com

"Technology enabled for the inner-geek", this "happening" New
American at Georgia Tech's Technology Square attracts an "eclectic" crowd with its "sleek", "refreshing" "New Age decor", featuring a
"large, yet intimate" zinc-topped bar and an expansive patio, as well
as "creative" eats and "tasty libations" at "good prices"; some critics
lament that "something has slipped" since it "opened with a bang",
however, while others are "not sure what the initial fuss was about."

### Goldberg's Bagel Co. & Deli  *Deli*         20 | 11 | 17 | $14

**Midtown** | Colony Sq. | 1197 Peachtree St. NE (bet. 14th & 15th Sts.) |
404-888-0877
**Buckhead** | 1272 W. Paces Ferry Rd. NW (I-75) | 404-266-0123
**Buckhead** | Roswell Wieuca Shopping Ctr. | 4383 Roswell Rd. NE
(Wieuca Rd.) | 404-256-3751
**Dunwoody** | Georgetown Shopping Ctr. | 4520 Chamblee Dunwoody Rd.
(I-285) | 770-455-1119

Become an "honorary NYer" at this "favorite" deli quartet that sets
the "gold standard" for local nosh with "excellent" bagels and
"hearty" "overstuffed" sandwiches; "everyone knows everyone" at
these "power-breakfast headquarters" where the staff "does its
best to accommodate the masses", and though the decor could use
some "help", the Roswell Road original "includes more seating."

### Goldfish  *Seafood*                        21 | 21 | 19 | $33

**Dunwoody** | 4400 Ashford Dunwoody Rd. NE (Perimeter Ctr.) |
770-671-0100 | www.heretoserverestaurants.com

Waves of "suburbanites" come to this "hip" Dunwoody seafooder
(sibling of Prime, Shout, Strip and Twist) for "fabulous" sushi and
other "fresh" offerings, plus a "decent" wine list; the "slick" space is

"always packed to the gills", and the "happening" bar is a "popular" "happy-hour" venue; some critics carp about "awful acoustics", "poor service" and "overpriced" fare, but many others consider it "one of the best choices" around; N.B. a post-Survey chef change is not reflected in the above Food score.

### Gold Star Cafe & Bakery  American  ▽ 15 | 10 | 14 | $13

**Midtown** | 903 Peachtree St. NE, Ste. C (8th St.) | 404-870-0002 | www.goldstarcafe.com

"You can have your cake and eat it too" at this Midtown American serving up "tempting" baked goods, "varied" sandwiches and "breakfast all day long" in a space that's "a little like your friend's mom's kitchen"; the "waits can be long" in the AM while the "walk-up" service makes it a popular choice for a "quick lunch stop", the "unconcerned" service notwithstanding.

### Gordon Biersch Brewery  Pub Food  16 | 16 | 17 | $22

**Midtown** | 848 Peachtree St. NE (7th St.) | 404-870-0805 | www.gordonbiersch.com

A "solid choice" for "casual" "midpriced" American pub fare that's actually "decent" for a national "chain" and "rotating seasonal" brews that are "always interesting", this "casual" Midtown link is "popular" for a "quick lunch" or as an "after-work" "hangout"; critics are "blah"-sé to the "corporate" eats, and most agree that the "beer's the thing" here.

### ☑ Grace 17.20 ⓢ American  25 | 25 | 23 | $39

**Norcross** | The Forum | 5155 Peachtree Pkwy. NW (Jones Bridge Rd.) | 678-421-1720 | www.grace1720.com

"One of the few independent gems in the chain-cluttered suburbs", Barbara DiJames' "amazing" Norcross New American "makes you forget you're dining in a strip mall" with "outstanding", "elegantly presented" cuisine, a "beautiful" setting that evokes the wine country ("love sitting outside next to the fire in the fall") and "impeccable" service; whether for a "romantic excursion", "special occasion" or just a "quiet dinner", it's an "enjoyable experience."

### Grand China  Chinese  17 | 13 | 18 | $23

**Buckhead** | 2975 Peachtree Rd. NE (Pharr Rd.) | 404-231-8690 | www.grandchinaatl.com

A Buckhead "mainstay", this Chinese is "thoroughly up to date" when it comes to "reliable" cuisine of "exceptional" quality at "reasonable prices" and "friendly" service from the "lovely" owner who "personally greets each customer"; while the room may be "slightly dowdy", it's "well maintained", but still, many "enjoy it more" at home and rely on what some claim is the "fastest delivery in the South."

### Grant Central Pizza  Pizza  20 | 14 | 15 | $13

**Grant Park** | 451 Cherokee Ave. SE (Glenwood Ave.) | 404-523-8900
**East Atlanta** | 1279 Glenwood Ave. SE (Flat Shoals Ave.) | 404-627-0007

"Locals know" these "beloved" pizzeria twins in East Atlanta and Grant Park are the "places to go" for "consistently good" pies made with "hand-tossed dough" and "fresh toppings" that are "cheap, fast, hot and satisfying"; both of these "friendly" spots are located in "cool historic" areas, and fans insist their pies "transcend the standard neighborhood pizza joint fare."

### Grape at Atlantic Station  *Mediterranean*     16 | 18 | 18 | $27

**Atlantic Station** | Atlantic Station | 264 19th St. (W. District Ave.) | 404-815-0090

### Grape at Inman Park  *Mediterranean*

**Inman Park** | Inman Park | 300 N. Highland Ave. (Elizabeth St. NE) | 404-577-4662

### Grape at Phipps Plaza  *Mediterranean*

**Buckhead** | Phipps Plaza | 3500 Peachtree Rd. NE (Oak Valley Rd.) | 678-990-9463

### Grape at Sandy Springs  ⧉ *Mediterranean*

**Sandy Springs** | CityWalk at Sandy Springs | 227 Sandy Springs Pl. NE (Roswell Rd.) | 404-250-9463

### Grape at The Forum  ⧉ *Mediterranean*

**Norcross** | 5145 Peachtree Pkwy. NW (Medlock Bridge Rd.) | 770-447-1605

### Grape at Vinings  ⧉ *Mediterranean*

**Vinings** | Vinings Jubilee Shopping Ctr. | 4300 Paces Ferry Rd. SE (Paces Mill Rd.) | 770-803-9463
www.yourgrape.com

Oenophiles "love the idea" of this Mediterranean chain where a "dizzying array" of wines is "grouped" on an "educational" menu "especially suited" "for novices" and paired with "interesting" "small plates"; outdoor seating and a "relaxing" atmosphere make it a "wonderful" choice for a "quick dinner before a movie", a "date" or to "hang out" and "unwind after a tough day", although some sour grapes find the service "disappointing", the fare "mediocre" and "overpriced."

### Greenwoods on Green Street  Ⓜ *Southern*     23 | 17 | 20 | $23

**Roswell** | 1087 Green St. (bet. Canton & Woodstock Sts.) | 770-992-5383

"Be prepared to eat yourself into a food coma" at this "one-of-a-kind" Roswell regional American that "invented the term" "gourmet Southern" with "insanely huge" "family-style" portions of the "best fried chicken on the planet" and "fantastic" "veggies" – but "save room" for the "big and tasty" pies; a "laid-back" vibe and "'hi, honey'" service make a meal here "like Sunday dinner at grandma's", except for the "huge crowds", and fans insist it's "worth the wait."

### Gumbeaux's, A Cajun Cafe  ⧉Ⓜ *Cajun*     ▽ 24 | 17 | 18 | $22

**Douglasville** | 6712 E. Broad St. (Hwy. 92) | 770-947-8288 | www.gumbeauxs.com

"Cajun to a T" is how fans describe this Douglasville spot they declare one of the "best restaurants in the county" for its "many selections" of "tasty", "genuine" eats that "makes you feel like you're dining in the bayou" – including some that'll test whether you can "stand the heat"; the "interesting" setting is "always crowded" and "noisy", and for jambalayaholics "stuck in the middle of Georgia", it's "worth the trip."

## Hae Woon Dae Bar B Que ◑ *Korean* ▽ 22 | 10 | 17 | $22

**Buford Hwy. (Doraville)** | 5805 Buford Hwy. (Oakcliff Rd.) |
Doraville | 770-451-7957

Even if you "can't pronounce" the name, this Buford Highway Korean
is a "great find" for "huge portions" of "delicious" BBQ made with
"fresh ingredients" "on the tabletop grill", and a "helpful staff" that
"walks you through" the "do-it-yourself" "experience"; the strip mall
space "next to a gentleman's club" notwithstanding, pros promise
"you can't go wrong"; N.B. open until 6AM.

## Hal's on Old Ivy 🗷 *Steak* 25 | 18 | 24 | $50

**Buckhead** | 30 Old Ivy Rd. NE (Piedmont Rd.) | 404-261-0025 |
www.hals.net

"They put the 'cool' in 'old school'" at this "amazing" Buckhead
Creole-influenced steakhouse with a "clubby spirit" and a hint of
"Louisiana" "spice" that really "packs 'em in" thanks to "buttery" fi-
lets that are among the "best in town" and "career servers" who provide "impeccable" service; a "winner for dinner", it also boasts a
"smoky bar scene" "buzzing with energy" and "incredible" people-
watching among the "single (or soon-to-be-single) over-40" set.

## Happy Valley Seafood ◑ *Chinese* ▽ 18 | 9 | 14 | $16

**Buford Hwy. (Atlanta)** | Plaza Fiesta | 4166 Buford Hwy. NE
(bet. Dresden Dr. & Skyland Rd.) | 404-633-9383

It doesn't have to be a "lazy Sunday", or even a "weekend" to cruise
the "carts" filled with "some of the finest dim sum" in town at this
no-frills Buford Highway Chinese, for the "scrumptious goodies" are
served "all day"; a few critics find the fare "unimaginative" and the
service "rushed", but for many others it remains a "good choice."

## Harold's Barbecue 🗷 *BBQ* 23 | 10 | 17 | $13

**Southside (Atlanta)** | 171 McDonough Blvd. SE (Lakewood Ave.) |
404-627-9268
**Jonesboro** | 265 Hwy. 54 (Rte. 138) | 770-478-5880
www.haroldsbarbecue.com

The "BBQ couldn't be better" at this "no-frills" Southside "dive"
where "$15 gets you a heap of food", including "hand-sliced" pork
"straight from the smoker" and the "best Brunswick stew going",
served up by "waitresses who have been there forever"; "you
shouldn't even call the decor 'decor'", but, hey, you just "can't beat
the convenience to the Federal pen" located next door; N.B. the
Jonesboro location is independently owned and operated.

## Harry & Sons *Asian* 20 | 15 | 18 | $22

**Virginia-Highland** | 820 N. Highland Ave. NE (Greenwood Ave.) |
404-873-2009 | www.harryandsonsrestaurant.com

"When you can't decide" which Asian direction you want to take,
this "dependable", "unpretentious" sibling and neighbor of Surin in
Virginia-Highland answers the call with "solid" Thai fare and "melt-
in-your-mouth" sushi ("Harry Maki roll is da bomb"); it's "damn
cheap", and service comes "with a smile", so it's no wonder it's "always packed" with "trendy" locals.

|  | FOOD | DECOR | SERVICE | COST |
|---|---|---|---|---|

### ☑ Haru Ichiban  *Japanese*  `26` `14` `22` `$27`

**Duluth** | Mall Corner Shopping Ctr. | 3646 Satellite Blvd.
(Pleasant Hill Rd.) | 770-622-4060

"Worth the drive to the hinterlands" (aka Duluth), this Japanese "strip-mall place" earns accolades from intowners and suburbanites alike for its "excellent", "fresh" sushi and "tons of tasteful dishes without raw fishes"; "reasonable" prices and "outstanding" service help make up for the "drab" digs and "hard-to-find" location.

### Hashiguchi  ☒ *Japanese*  `24` `14` `19` `$30`

**Marietta** | The Terrace | 3000 Windy Hill Rd. SE (Powers Ferry Rd.) |
770-955-2337

**Buckhead** | Shops Around Lenox | 3400 Woodale Dr. NE (Peachtree St.) |
404-841-9229 ◑

"Countless regulars" count on these "consistent" Japanese twins in Buckhead and Marietta for "excellent" eats at "fair prices", including "quality" sushi and a "great variety" of "authentic cooked" offerings, served by a "friendly", "caring" staff; "not many know about" the "hidden" Lenox location, making it a more "intimate" setting, but either venue is a "wonderful" choice for a "quiet business gathering" or a "lively ladies' night."

### Havana Sandwich Shop  *Cuban/Sandwiches*  `22` `5` `14` `$11`

**Buford Hwy. (Atlanta)** | 2905 Buford Hwy. NE (N. Druid Hills Rd.) |
404-636-4094

This Buford Highway Cubano "has been around 31 years for a reason" – namely, the "quintessential Cuban sandwich" and other "inexpensive" "kick-ass" fare that "draws big lunch crowds"; "bare-bones" "early bus station lunchroom" decor "doesn't matter" to fans "blinded" by "authentic, flavorful" eats, and the "friendly" staff that's "brief on words" "could beat customers over the head with their sandwiches and people would still come back for more."

### Haveli Indian Cuisine  *Indian*  `16` `10` `13` `$20`

**Marietta** | 490 Franklin Rd. SE (Rte. 120) | 770-955-4525
**Downtown** | 225 Spring St. NW (bet. Andrew Young Int'l Blvd. &
Harris St.) | 404-522-4545

"Come hungry" and "close your eyes" to the spartan digs at these "reliable" Indian twins in Downtown and Marietta, where "convenient" "buffets" offer a "good selection" of "standard" offerings; critics who find the "just ok" fare "overpriced" and the service "slack" are "so sad" to see how they've "slipped."

### Haven  Ⓜ *American*  `23` `21` `21` `$38`

**Brookhaven** | 1441 Dresden Dr. NE (bet. Appalachee & Camille Drs.) |
404-969-0700 | www.havenrestaurant.com

At this "high-end" Brookhaven venue, "sophisticated" New American cuisine "appeals to a wide range" of tastes (albeit at "big price tags"), while "gracious hosts" and a "knowledgeable staff" "get the job done" in a "warm" space with "beautiful art" and a "stylish patio"; an "eclectic" crowd of "locals", "pretty people" and "nip-and-tuck" types makes for "lively" "people-watching" in spite of the "snob factor."

| | FOOD | DECOR | SERVICE | COST |
|---|---|---|---|---|

**Highland Tap** *Steak*  | 20 | 16 | 18 | $29 |

**Virginia-Highland** | 1026 N. Highland Ave. NE (Virginia Ave.) | 404-875-3673 | www.highlandtapatlanta.com

"Climb down steep stairs" to this reasonably priced "subterranean steakhouse" in Virginia-Highland where carnivores "buckle down (or unbuckle?)" for some "serious beef", including "burgers the way they're supposed to be", while gin-teel types anoint it the "martini champion of Atlanta"; the service is "solid", and the "sexy" "cellar setting" is ripe for "a rendezvous in a dark booth" or a "meeting with friends" in the "smoky" bar.

**NEW Hil, The** Ⓜ *American/French*  | - | - | - | M |

**Palmetto** | Serenbe | 9110 Selborne Ln., Ste. 110 (Hutcheson Ferry Rd.) | 770-463-6040 | www.the-hil.com

"Bring a designated driver and a GPS" to this French–New American in the heart of the "beautiful" "Serenbe settlement" that's "worth the drive" for "genius" chef-owner Hilary White's "creative", "wonderful" fare crafted from local ingredients; co-owner Jim White and the chef's mom oversee a "friendly staff", while the "lovely" Stan Topol–designed space includes a "good cocktail lounge" and wraparound balcony overlooking the main drag.

**Hi Life Kitchen & Cocktails** Ⓩ *American*  | 23 | 19 | 22 | $34 |

**Norcross** | 3380 Holcomb Bridge Rd. (Jimmy Carter Blvd.) | 770-409-0101

Even after a "recent ownership change", this Norcross New American is still "a nice night out" thanks to "outstanding" fare and "accommodating" service from an "ever-smiling" staff in a "small", yet "comfortable" space with a "neighborhood feel"; it's a "little pricey", but for an "intimate dinner for two" or a "business" meal "without having to head into Buckhead", most agree it "never disappoints."

**Himalayas Indian** *Indian*  | 21 | 14 | 17 | $18 |

**Chamblee** | Chamblee Plaza | 5520 Peachtree Industrial Blvd. (Longview Dr.) | 770-458-6557

Cognoscenti counsel "don't let the almost empty strip mall scare you away" from this Chamblee Indian, for the "consistently good" eats are some of the "best in the city", and its "affordability" "makes it a weekly" option for many locals; service from the "taciturn" staff can be "spotty" at times, but it's usually "fast", and sure, the "dingy" digs "could use a makeover", but the "food is what shines here."

**NEW Holeman and Finch** ☾ *American*  | - | - | - | I |

**South Buckhead** | 2277 Peachtree Rd. (Peachtree Memorial Dr.) | 404-948-1175 | www.holeman-finch.com

Simple food served public house–style is the hallmark of this nearby New American sibling of Restaurant Eugene in South Buckhead, where chef Linton Hopkins throws whole animal cooking into the pot with his trademark local ingredients (think house-made charcuterie, hearth-baked bread); low prices and late hours (the full menu is served until 1:30 AM) encourage laid-back loafing in the 60-seat space crafted from sustainable cork and reclaimed materials, and adorned with vintage Coca-Cola paraphernalia.

| | FOOD | DECOR | SERVICE | COST |
|---|---|---|---|---|

### NEW Home  *Southern*
(fka Posh)

| | - | - | - | M |
|---|---|---|---|---|

**Buckhead** | 111 W. Paces Ferry Rd. (E. Andrews Dr.) | 404-869-0777 |
www.heretoserverestaurants.com

Tom Catherall (Shout, Strip, Twist) rolls out the welcome mat at the
former Posh in Buckhead with a new, more casual concept featuring
star chef (and *Top Chef* contestant) Richard Blais' farm-to-table
New American fare with a modern Southern accent; artwork in the
cozy renovated house features chalk-and-slate sketches of pigs, a
nod to the menu's pork shoulder with local collards, with pictures of
the owner's children adding a touch of, well, home.

### Hometown Barbecue  M⇗ *BBQ*

| | - | - | - | I |
|---|---|---|---|---|

**Lawrenceville** | 1173 Hwy. 29 S. (Johnson Rd. SW) | 770-963-5383
Local 'cuennoisseurs who've "grown up eating" the BBQ at this
Lawrenceville smokehouse insist it's "always been great", while others praise the "consistent" quality of its "excellent ribs", Brunswick
stew and other "tasty" offerings; it's situated in a charming renovated house with an outdoor pavilion and deck.

### Hong Kong Harbour ● *Chinese*

| | 19 | 9 | 16 | $17 |
|---|---|---|---|---|

**Cheshire Bridge** | 2184 Cheshire Bridge Rd. NE (Lavista Rd.) |
404-325-7630
"If you get a sudden urge for Chinese in the middle of the night" this
"casual" Cheshire Bridge ethnic will "probably be open" (until 1 AM
Sundays–Thursdays and 3 AM on weekends) and wokking up "authentic" eats that are "beautifully" served; it's also a "dim sum habit
pleaser" since they offer it "every day" in the "tired", "tacky" interior, but there's a "friendly" vibe and hey, it "saves you a drive all the
way to Chamblee."

### Horseradish Grill  *Southern*

| | 22 | 23 | 22 | $40 |
|---|---|---|---|---|

**Buckhead** | 4320 Powers Ferry Rd. NW (Wieuca Rd.) | 404-255-7277 |
www.horseradishgrill.com
A "classic Buckhead well-heeled experience", this "tasteful"
"charmer" housed in a "cozy" "old horse barn" "just off Chastain Park"
"continues to please" with "exceptional", "sophisticated" Southern
fare and "outstanding" service; while some feel it's just "living off its
reputation", citing "uninspired" eats and "sporadically attentive"
service, it remains a "favorite" spot of many for "pre-concert" meals
or to impress "out-of-towners"; P.S. cognoscenti counsel arriving
early to "snatch a spot" on the "romantic" "patio" "under the oaks."

### House of Chan  *Chinese*

| | ∇ 24 | 11 | 21 | $17 |
|---|---|---|---|---|

**Smyrna** | Cumberland Square North Shopping Ctr. | 2469 Cobb Pkwy. SE
(Herodian Way) | 770-955-9444
"Tucked away" in an "unassuming" Smyrna strip mall, this "tiny"
Chinese is a "favorite stop" of those in-the-know for its "huge portions" of "fantastic food" "priced at a steal"; the dining room may
look as if it "hasn't been updated since the '70s", but "friendly" service and "incredible value" make it "worth the drive" – and besides,
there's always "takeout."

|  | FOOD | DECOR | SERVICE | COST |
|---|---|---|---|---|

## Houston Mill House ⊠ *American* — ▽ 18 | 23 | 20 | $22

**Emory** | 849 Houston Mill Rd. NE (Clifton Rd.) | 404-727-4033 |
www.houstonmillhouse.com

Housed in an "interesting" "historic" cottage on the Emory campus,
this American may be "the best-kept secret in Atlanta", but those
in-the-know tout its traditional offerings as some of the "best" "in
the area", served in "portions" that are "not too large" and "nicely
presented"; the "wonderful" setting with a "view of the woods" and
hefty hearthstone fireplace make it "great for work parties" or to
"celebrate a personal milestone."

## ⊠ Houston's *American* — 22 | 19 | 22 | $31

**Cobb** | 3050 Windy Hill Rd. SE (Powers Ferry Rd.) | 770-563-1180
**Buckhead** | 3321 Lenox Rd. NE (E. Paces Ferry Rd.) | 404-237-7534
**Buckhead** | 3539 Northside Pkwy. NW (W. Paces Ferry Rd.) |
404-262-7130
**South Buckhead** | 2166 Peachtree Rd. NW (Colonial Homes Dr.) |
404-351-2442
www.hillstone.com

A "chain that doesn't feel like one", this "reliable" national franchise
"clicks" thanks to a "pretty darn good" menu of "all-American comfort" items (including a notoriously "addicting spinach dip") and a
"modern metropolitan" ambiance that brings in "mingling singles"
after work; despite debate on the cost – "inexpensive" vs.
"overpriced" – most report "solid quality" here.

## Hsu's Gourmet *Chinese* — 21 | 17 | 20 | $32

**Downtown** | 192 Peachtree Center Ave. (Andrew Young Int'l Blvd.) |
404-659-2788 | www.hsus.com

Some of the "best Asian food in the Downtown area" can be found
at this "very satisfying" Chinese sibling of Pacific Rim and Silk, a "reliable" purveyor of "tasty, authentic" Sichuan cuisine, including
Peking duck that's "worth the trip to the obscure location"; some
feel the space is "getting worn", but "not the welcome" from a
"friendly" staff, making it a "treasure" for businesspeople and out-
of-towners "stuck" in the neighborhood.

## NEW Hudson Grille ● *American* — 14 | 18 | 15 | $20

**Brookhaven** | 4046 Peachtree Rd. NE (Dresden Dr. NE) | 404-233-0313 |
www.metrocafes.com

"Flat-screen TVs galore" "make sure you never miss the action"
from the "comfy leather booths" at this "upscale sports bar" in
Brookhaven from the Metrotainment Cafes group (Cowtippers,
Einstein's) that scores with its "extensive" "draft beer selection" and
"trendy" ambiance; "subpar" Traditional American eats and "ques-
tionable" service strike out in the eyes of some critics, though.

## Huey's *Cajun/Creole* — 18 | 11 | 16 | $20

**South Buckhead** | 1816 Peachtree Rd. (bet. Collier Rd. & 26th St.) |
404-873-2037 | www.hueysrestaurant.com

For an "awesome guilty treat", fans tout the "killer beignets" at this
South Buckhead Cajun-Creole stalwart as some of the "best outside

| | FOOD | DECOR | SERVICE | COST |

of New Orleans", which can be complemented with "awesome café au lait"; the all-season patio makes for an "interesting breakfast place", and while purists pan it as "mediocre relative to the Big Easy", others insist it's the "best local source" for a taste of the Crescent City.

## Huong Giang *Vietnamese*

| | - | - | - | I |

**Buford Hwy. (Atlanta)** | 4300 Buford Hwy. (Dresden Dr.) | 404-929-9838
The "banh mi can't be beat" at this "fancy" yet affordable Vietnamese on Buford Highway that aficionados insist is a "step up from others along this busy strip"; despite a bit of a language barrier, the service is "quick" and the casual surroundings are "spacious."

## Ibiza 🗷 M *Mediterranean*

| | ∇ 20 | 22 | 20 | $28 |

**South Buckhead** | 2285 Peachtree Rd. (Peachtree Hills Ave.) |
404-352-3081 | www.ibizarestaurantlounge.com
"Step back" to a "time when reclining while you ate was acceptable" at this midpriced South Buckhead Mediterranean from Rafih and Rita Benjelloun (of Imperial Fez fame), serving an "outstanding" menu featuring "yummy" tapas, with "awesome drinks" to match the mood; the atmosphere is "casual" in the "exotic" setting with semiprivate nooks and a lively outdoor patio redolent with the scent of flavored tobacco smoked from hookahs.

## Il Localino *Italian*

| | 21 | 18 | 20 | $46 |

**Inman Park** | 467 N. Highland Ave. NE (Albion Ave. NE) | 404-222-0650 |
www.localino.info
"If you want to dance with your server", this "festive" Inman Park spot comes highly "recommended" by revelers who've been "swept off their feet" by a "charming" yet "crazy" staff that transforms "good" "family" Italian fare into a "zoo" complete with "campy music", "disco balls" and "party hats"; it's best for "groups", but the "allure is over" for those who kvetch over the "hefty price tag for a lot of kitsch" and food that's "just ok."

## Imperial Fez *Moroccan*

| | 19 | 24 | 21 | $48 |

**South Buckhead** | 2285 Peachtree Rd. NE (Peachtree Hills Ave.) |
404-351-0870 | www.imperialfez.com
For a "different" dining experience, locals and "tourists" alike "take off" their "shoes", "sit on the floor" and dig into "authentic" fare "with their hands" at this South Buckhead Moroccan where "gorgeous belly dancers" highlight the "superb entertainment"; gracious "chefs Rafih and Rita do a great job", and while cynics dismiss it as "overpriced" and "gimmicky to the max", others recommend it as a "refreshing" option for "birthday dinners" or "bachelor parties."

## Ippolito's *Italian*

| | 19 | 14 | 18 | $21 |

**Kennesaw** | Town Center Plaza | 425 Barrett Pkwy. NW (I-75) |
770-514-8500
**Alpharetta** | 12850 Hwy. 9 N. (Windward Pkwy.) | 678-624-1900
**Roswell** | Centennial Shopping Ctr. | 2270 Holcomb Bridge Rd. (Eves Rd.) |
770-992-0781
**Suwanee** | 350 Town Center Ave., Ste. 103 (Buford Hwy.) | 678-985-4377
*(continued)*

*(continued)*

## Ippolito's

**Norcross** | 5277 Peachtree Pkwy. (Peachtree Corners Circle) |
770-663-0050
**Sandy Springs** | Abernathy Sq. | 6623 Roswell Rd. NE (Abernathy Rd.) |
404-256-3546
www.ippolitos.net

OTP "pasta lovers" say "*mangia*" at this local family-owned "saucy
Italian" chain where "free" "garlic rolls worth the trip" precede "huge
portions" of "decent" "typical Southern" fare; "service varies" and
it's "always busy" and usually "noisy", but "hey, it's a family place" –
and one "that won't break the bank."

## Jake's 🅜 *Dessert*　　　　　▽ 19 | 14 | 18 | $8

**Decatur** | 515 N. McDonough St. (Trinity Pl.) | 404-377-9300

Aficionados with the inside scoop "heart" this Decatur desserter for
its "unique selections" of "awesome" "homemade ice cream" that
are "quite pricey" but also "quite good"; some find the decor a "little
forlorn", but "you can't beat the cute location" inside a children's
bookstore; N.B. it no longer serves lunch.

## Jalisco 🅢 *Mexican/Tex-Mex*　　　21 | 11 | 20 | $14

**South Buckhead** | Peachtree Battle Shopping Ctr. | 2337 Peachtree Rd. NE
(bet. Lindbergh Dr. & Peachtree Hills Ave.) | 404-233-9244

An "old Atlanta favorite" that's been around since 1978, the Coronado
family's South Buckhead "institution" offers "hot and tasty" "old-
style" Tex-Mex and Mexican served up "almost too fast"; "Formica-
topped tables" highlight the plain room that's "always crowded"
with "professionals and housewives" at lunchtime and families at
night, but the "wonderful" staff "seats you in a snap."

## Jason's Deli *Deli*　　　　　　17 | 10 | 14 | $12

**Alpharetta** | 3070 Windward Plaza (Windward Pkwy.) | 770-619-2300
**Alpharetta** | 7300 N. Point Pkwy. (Mansell Rd.) | 770-664-5002
**Buckhead** | 3330 Piedmont Rd. NE (Peachtree Rd.) | 404-231-3333
**Norcross** | Forum Shopping Ctr. | 5131 Peachtree Pkwy.
(Medlock Bridge Rd.) | 770-368-9440
**Sandy Springs** | 5975 Roswell Rd. NE (Hammond Dr.) | 404-843-8212
**Tucker** | 4073 Lavista Rd. (I-285) | 770-493-4020
www.jasonsdeli.com

These "grab-and-go" delis are "busy" and they "deserve to be",
thanks to "obscenely generous" portions of nosh that "rocks", from
"fresh fixings" on the salad bar to "mile-high" sandwiches, and free
ice cream makes them a "parents' dream"; the "cafeteria-style" service is "efficient", and the "food makes up for any shortcomings" in
the "standard" digs with "zero ambiance" that are "noisy enough to
bring your loudest kids" without embarrassment.

## 🅩 Java Jive 🅜🖃 *American*　　　22 | 21 | 21 | $13

**Poncey-Highland** | 790 Ponce de Leon Ave. NE (Freedom Pkwy.) |
404-876-6161

A "favorite breakfast place" of many in Poncey-Highland, this
"quirky" American keeps fans "coming back" with "fresh, home-

| | FOOD | DECOR | SERVICE | COST |

made" treats such as "delish gingerbread waffles", "must-have" pancakes and some of the "best coffee in town", all served by a "charming" staff; present and past coexist in the space complete with "WiFi" and "WWII-vintage appliances."

### JCT. Kitchen & Bar 🗷 Southern   24 | 21 | 20 | $34

**Westside** | 1198 Howell Mill Rd. (bet. 14th St. & Huff Rd.) | 404-355-2252 | www.jctkitchen.com

Fans are making tracks to this eatery "tucked away" in the "increasingly popular" Westside for chef Ford Fry's "successful delivery" of "amazing" Southern eats with a "fresh spin", served in a "hip" spot that "overlooks the train tracks", with a "gorgeous, wide" bar offering "beautiful views of Midtown" and a dining room with "soul"; critics complain about "deafening" decibels and "iffy" service, but others declare it a "cool" concept "well executed by industry pros."

### Jim N' Nick's Bar-B-Q  BBQ   22 | 17 | 19 | $18

**Smyrna** | 4574 S. Cobb Dr. (East-West Connector SE) | 678-556-0011
**Conyers** | 2275 GA-20 SE (Stockbridge Hwy.) | 770-785-4453
www.jimnnicks.com

"Big eaters" with "small budgets" appreciate this 'Bama-based 'cue chain serving "huge portions" of "old-school" BBQ and "tasty" sides "created and served with care" that often add up to a "week's worth of leftovers"; "reasonable prices", "attentive" service and "dressy" decor make them "solid" choices for a "casual night out."

### Jitlada  Thai   ▽ 16 | 14 | 14 | $18

**Cheshire Bridge** | Cheshire Square Shopping Ctr. | 2329C Cheshire Bridge Rd. (Lavista Rd.) | 404-728-9040 | www.jitladacuisine.com

The "dishes are always fresh and delicious" at this "reasonably priced" Thai in a Cheshire Bridge strip mall, where pros promise you can get "in and out" of the "charming" room "in under 20 minutes", making it a popular "last-minute" option "before a movie" at the nearby cinema; during the day it attracts a "good business crowd."

### 🗷 JOËL 🗷 French   26 | 25 | 25 | $60

**Buckhead** | The Forum | 3290 Northside Pkwy. NW (W. Paces Ferry Rd.) | 404-233-3500 | www.joelrestaurant.com

After an "elegant renovation", this "reinvented" upscale Buckhead French is "much more inviting" and the "excellent" "bistro" menu "more user-friendly", but it still "knocks it out of the park" thanks to chef Joël Antunes' "fabulous" cuisine backed by a "phenomenal" wine list and "superior" service; a few foes frown at the "elf"-like portions while claustrophobes feel "cramped" in the "smaller" configuration, but for most it remains a "big-night" destination.

### Joey D's Oak Room  American   20 | 19 | 20 | $31

**Dunwoody** | 1015 Crown Pointe Pkwy. (Abernathy Rd.) | 770-512-7063
"You get what you expect" at this "popular oasis" in Dunwoody, in the form of "plentiful" American fare, including a corned beef sandwich that "has no equal", and "consistently good" service in a "clas-

sic heavy oak" setting; to many, though, the main draw is the "spectacular" bar manned by "knowledgeable" bartenders.

### Johnny Rockets  *Burgers*    | 16 | 15 | 16 | $14 |

**Marietta** | Avenue at East Cobb | 4475 Roswell Rd. (Johnson Ferry Rd.) | 770-509-0377
**Buckhead** | Phipps Plaza | 3500 Peachtree Rd. NE (Lenox Rd.) | 404-233-9867
**Buckhead** | 5 W. Paces Ferry Rd. NW (Peachtree St.) | 404-231-5555
**Douglasville** | Arbor Place Mall | 6700 Douglas Blvd. (Bright Star Rd.) | 770-577-2636
**Downtown** | Underground Atlanta | 50 Upper Alabama St. SW (Pryor St.) | 404-525-7117
**Lawrenceville** | Discover Mills Mall | 5900 Sugarloaf Pkwy. (I-85) | 678-847-5800
www.johnnyrockets.com

"If you love *American Bandstand*", this "old-fashioned" hamburger chain will have you hopping over "tasty" burgers, "addictive" fries and onion rings and "thick" shakes that are "worth every fat gram" and arrive "Johnny-on-the-spot" "quick"; "personal jukeboxes" at each table play "era-appropriate" tunes, accompanied by a "singing, dancing" staff, so "bring the kids" or anyone "from three to 103."

### Johnny's New York Style Pizza  *Pizza*    | 17 | 9 | 14 | $13 |

**Marietta** | Market Square Shopping Ctr. | 2970 Canton Rd. (bet. Chastain & E. Piedmont Rds.) | 678-797-0505
**Marietta** | 4880 Lower Roswell Rd. (Johnson Ferry Rd.) | 678-560-2228
**Alpharetta** | 2850D Holcomb Bridge Rd. (Steeple Chase Rd.) | 770-993-1455
**Alpharetta** | 869 N. Main St./Hwy. 9 (Windward Pkwy.) | 678-867-6773
**Cumming** | 911 Market Place Blvd. (Hwy. 20) | 770-205-9317
**Alpharetta** | 9950 Jones Bridge Rd. (Old Alabama Rd.) | 770-777-9799
**Inman Park** | 676 Highland Ave. (Sampson St.) | 404-523-6339 ●
**Cheshire Bridge** | 1810 Cheshire Bridge Rd. NE (bet. Manchester & Piedmont Rds.) | 404-874-8304
**Decatur** | 340B Church St. (Sycamore St.) | 404-373-8511
www.jnysp.com

"No frills, no hassle" and "kid-friendly" to boot, this pizzeria chain is a popular choice for "great" pies, and while "NY it's not", it's "as good as it's going to get this deep into Dixie" and it "keeps your wallet happy"; the "quality varies by location", while the "scruffy" interiors "don't encourage lingering", but "decor and service don't bring in the crowds" – the "pizza does."

### Joli Kobe Bakery  *Bakery/Continental*    | 23 | 19 | 20 | $22 |

**Sandy Springs** | The Prado Plaza | 5600 Roswell Rd. (I-285) | 404-843-3257 | www.jolikobe.com

"Don't let the word 'bakery' fool you" advise aficionados of this "unique" bakeshop "tucked away" in the Prado in Sandy Springs, where an "excellent" "attached restaurant" serves Continental offerings such as "perfect quiche, salads and soups", along with the "irresistible" desserts that make this spot the "real deal"; the "small", "sterile" space notwithstanding, "ladies who lunch" are there "en masse" for the "refreshing" change from the "ubiquitous chain" offerings in the area.

### ☑ Kevin Rathbun Steak 🖪 *Steak*  | 26 | 26 | 25 | $58 |

**Inman Park** | Inman Alley | 154 Krog St. (Lake Ave.) | 404-524-5600 | www.kevinrathbunsteak.com

"Peter Luger South" is what "beef lovers" dub Kevin Rathbun's "phenomenal", "expensive" steakhouse in Inman Park that's "every bit as good as the Buckhead competition", serving "exceptional" cuts and "unique" sides that "make you want to lick the plate"; the "magical interior" from the Johnson Studio is a "delicious update" (read: "not stuffy") of the "masculine" "shrine to meat" template (although some find the "oversized" portrait of the chef "distracting"), while the "knowledgeable" staff delivers "impeccable" service.

### King & I  *Thai*  | 19 | 11 | 21 | $18 |

**Midtown** | Ansley Sq. | 1510F Piedmont Ave. SE (Monroe Dr.) | 404-892-7743

The "friendly staff" "remembers what you like and how you like it" if you're a regular at this "old reliable" Thai in Midtown, where the "consistently good" eats "can be spiced up" to your preference; it's a "great value", and while some find the decor lacking, the ambiance is "comforting", and of course there's always "takeout."

### Kobe Steaks  *Japanese/Steak*  | ▽ 20 | 17 | 21 | $30 |

**Sandy Springs** | Prado Shopping Ctr. | 5600 Roswell Rd. NE (I-285) | 404-256-0810 | www.kobesteaks.net

"If you like hibachi", this Sandy Springs Japanese is one of the "best in town" swear "repeat customers" who applaud "amazing aged" beef and other "good" offerings; while the digs may "need a facelift", the "cook-it-in-front-of-you" show by "entertaining" chefs is an "added bonus" the "whole family can enjoy."

### ☑ Krog Bar ●🖪 *Mediterranean*  | 23 | 25 | 22 | $25 |

**Inman Park** | Stove Works | 112 Krog St. NE (bet. Edgewood Ave. NE & Irwin St. NE) | 404-524-1618 | www.krogbar.com

It may be roughly "the size of an NYC apartment", but Kevin Rathbun's petite Inman Park Mediterranean is big on "flair" with its "alfresco, communal setting" and "hip", "cozy" interior, where diners can "taste at will" a "wide array" of "light and simple tapas", and "mix it up" with "new" "discoveries" from the "superbly selected" "wine list"; "start a date", "meet friends" or simply "hang out" with the "helpful" staff that's "happy to talk vino" at this "welcome addition" to the local "late-night scene."

### Kurt's 🖪 *European*  | 22 | 17 | 21 | $35 |

**Duluth** | 4225 River Green Pkwy. (Peachtree Industrial Blvd.) | 770-623-4128 | www.kurtsrestaurant.com

The upscale *geschwister* of Vreny's Biergarten, this Duluth European is an "excellent value" for its "*wunderbar*" cuisine with a pronounced "German influence", "potent" beers and "friendly", "old-fashioned" service; while the setting is "formal", a "warm", "family atmosphere" prevails, and it boasts one of the "best outdoor patios" in town.

| | FOOD | DECOR | SERVICE | COST |
|---|---|---|---|---|

## 🛛 Kyma 🖺 *Greek/Seafood* | 25 | 24 | 24 | $51 |

**Buckhead** | 3085 Piedmont Rd. NE (E. Paces Ferry Rd.) | 404-262-0702 |
www.buckheadrestaurants.com

Serving "fish so fresh" you almost "expect to see a harbor out back",
this "superb" "haute Greek" from the Buckhead Life Group wins kudos for its "phenomenal" seafood-centric cuisine that's paired with
a "bountiful" wine list; "whitewashed walls" and "cool drapes" highlight the "stunning" room with a "festive", yet "relaxing", vibe, and
the service is "out of this world", which is why most agree this "truly
unique" experience is "worth every penny – and it costs a few."

## La Fonda Latina *Pan-Latin* | 20 | 12 | 15 | $15 |

**Buckhead** | 2813 Peachtree Rd. NE (Rumson Rd.) | 404-816-8311
**Buckhead** | 4427 Roswell Rd. NE (Wieuca Rd.) | 404-303-8201
**Candler Park** | 1639 McLendon Ave. NE (Page Ave.) | 404-378-5200
**Poncey-Highland** | 923 Ponce de Leon Ave. (Linwood Ave.) |
404-607-0665

For "all things Latin", fans flock to these "informal" "kid-friendly"
"mainstays", where they tuck into "amazing" fish tacos, "real" salsa
and "well-seasoned" paella ("is there any other in Atlanta?"), and
wash them down with "extraordinary margaritas"; "no-nonsense"
digs include "wildly colored rooms" and popular outdoor decks at
the Roswell Road and Poncey-Highland locations, and while "service
can be an issue", the menu still offers "great flavor for the price."

## 🛛 La Grotta 🖺 *Italian* | 26 | 21 | 26 | $52 |

**Buckhead** | 2637 Peachtree Rd. NE (bet. Lindbergh Dr. & Wesley Rd.) |
404-231-1368

## 🛛 La Grotta Ravinia 🖺 *Italian*

**Dunwoody** | Crowne Plaza Ravinia Hotel | 4355 Ashford Dunwoody Rd.
(Hammond Dr.) | 770-395-9925
www.lagrottaatlanta.com

"Oldies but goodies", this Italian duo is a "sentimental favorite"
venue for "celebrating the great moments of life", with "creative yet
familiar" fare that's "consistently excellent" and a "professional"
staff that "treats you like royalty" in an "elegant", "white-tablecloth"
setting; while some feel the Dunwoody sibling is "prettier", many
still prefer the "romantic" Buckhead original, but most agree they're
among "the best in the city."

## La Madeleine *Bakery/French* | 19 | 18 | 15 | $15 |

**Cobb** | 1931 Powers Ferry Rd. (Windy Hill Rd.) | 770-952-8426
**Marietta** | Providence Sq. | 4101 Roswell Rd. (Johnson Ferry Rd.) |
770-579-3040
**Duluth** | 2255 Pleasant Hill Rd. (Satellite Blvd.) | 770-814-0355
**Dunwoody** | Perimeter Sq. | 1165 Perimeter Ctr. W.
(Peachtree Dunwoody Rd.) | 770-392-0516
www.lamadeleine.com

For a "quick in-and-out meal" "without the fast-food feel", fans tout
these "convenient" "self-serve" links in a national chain for their
"accessible" French "comfort" fare, including soups "to die for" and
"heavenly" baked goods; the "brasserie" settings with "homey"

|  | FOOD | DECOR | SERVICE | COST |

brick fireplaces are "warm and cozy", but "unreliable" cooking and service "ranging from great to awful" lead some to conclude that they're "overpriced."

## La Parrilla *Mexican*

| 22 | 17 | 21 | $16 |

**Marietta** | 2500 Dallas Hwy. (Barrett Pkwy.) | 770-424-9500
**Marietta** | 29 S. Marietta Pkwy. (Whitlock Ave.) | 770-427-0055
**Acworth** | 6110 Cedar Crest Rd. (N. Cobb Pkwy.) | 770-974-4600
**Alpharetta** | 112460 Crabapple Rd. (Birmingham Hwy.) | 770-346-9902
**Alpharetta** | 865 N. Main St. (Windward Pkwy.) | 678-339-3888
**Westside** | 1801 Howell Mill Rd. (I-75) | 404-603-9091
**Newnan** | 222 Newnan Crossing Blvd. W. (Bullsboro Dr.) | 770-251-9081
**Woodstock** | 1065 Buckhead Crossing (Towne Lake Pkwy.) | 770-928-3606
www.laparrilla.com

The "*muy bueno*" Mexican made with "very fresh ingredients" at this sprawling, "midpriced" group is "better than most", which is why surveyors find it "hard to believe it's a chain"; live mariachi bands at some locations are "sure to lift your spirits" if the "friendly", "efficient" service and "generous" portions don't, and help you overlook how "crowded" and "hot" it is in the otherwise "pleasant" "cantina" setting.

## La Paz *Tex-Mex*

| 19 | 15 | 15 | $22 |

**Vinings** | Vinings Jubilee Shopping Ctr. | 2950 New Paces Ferry Rd. (Paces Ferry Rd.) | 770-801-0020 | www.lapaz.com

While it may "not be the most authentic", this Vinings Mexican remains a "favorite" of many for its "creative" dishes "you can't find elsewhere", "tasty" margaritas and sangria, and "reasonable prices"; the service is "efficient" and you'll find "all the usual Mexicana" in the "historic" "old church" where it's situated.

## NEW La Petite Maison 🗷 *French*

| - | - | - | M |

**Sandy Springs** | 6510 Roswell Rd. (bet. Abernathy Rd. & Chaseland Rd.) | 404-303-6600

"Two sisters from France" have transformed a "former Johnny Rockets" into this moderately priced, "*très formidable*" French in Sandy Springs where "marvelous" Gallic fare and "good wines" are delivered by "accented servers"; the old burger joint now boasts red velvet booths, an enclosed patio, "excellent (but loud) energy" and the "warm atmosphere of Nice."

## Las Palmeras 🗷🅜 *Cuban*

| 22 | 9 | 17 | $17 |

**Midtown** | 366 Fifth St. NE (Durant Pl.) | 404-872-0846

Fans shout "*fabuloso*" about the "lovingly prepared" Cuban cuisine at this "tiny" yet "comfortable" "hole-in-the-wall" "tucked away" "on a residential street in Midtown", where servers will "treat you like family, even if it's your first visit"; though the decor "ain't all that special", "don't be fooled by the appearance", for amigos insist it's a "delight."

## La Tavola *Italian*

| 24 | 20 | 22 | $33 |

**Virginia-Highland** | 992 Virginia Ave. NE (N. Highland Ave.) | 404-873-5430 | www.latavolatrattoria.com

Though it's often "crowded" and "noisy", the Fifth Group's "*molto bene*" Italian in Virginia-Highland is nonetheless a "transporting" experience thanks to "simple, elegant" dishes on a menu that "changes regularly", an "interesting" wine list and "impeccable" service; the "cozy" space has a "European feel", and while some feel "uncomfortable" in the "tight squeeze", the "back patio" is always an option.

## Lee's Golden Buddha & Mo Mo Ya *Asian*

| 19 | 17 | 18 | $24 |

**Buckhead** | 3861 Roswell Rd. (bet. Le Brun & Piedmont Rds.) | 404-261-3777 | www.momoyaga.com

A "two-fer that works", this Buckhead Chinese-Japanese "satisfies both kids and adults" with "terrific" (albeit "Americanized") Chinese, "fresh", "fairly priced" sushi and "yummy" teppanyaki prepared by "energetic" chefs; Japanese gardens and a waterfall create a "tranquil" tableau, although "lots of birthday parties" with "loud children" going on make some appreciate the "quick delivery service" all the more.

## Le Giverny *French*

| 20 | 15 | 20 | $33 |

**Emory** | Emory Inn | 1641 Clifton Rd. (bet. Briarcliff & N. Decatur Rds.) | 404-325-7252 | www.legiverny.net

When you want to "impress someone" "without breaking the bank", this Emory bistro near the CDC delivers with a "wonderful" selection of "good basic" French cuisine and "fine" service that make it a "favorite" of "doctors", "professors" and "ladies who lunch"; though the decor can be a "total buzzkill" for some, fans still recommend this spot "for a romantic evening" or "end-of-the-week cocktail."

## Les Fleurs De Lis Café *French*

| ∇ 27 | 17 | 16 | $31 |

**Downtown** | Healey Bldg. | 57 Forsyth St. NW (Walton St.) | 404-230-9151

The "food is better than the surroundings suggest" at this "amazing" French "sleeper" housed in a "classic" Downtown building, with "exquisite flavors and aromas" filling the "quaint", "tiny" space that'll remind you of "a bistro on the streets of Paris", and where you'll "become close friends with the table next to you"; regulars recommend it for a "romantic dinner" or "a long lunch on one's birthday", but perhaps not "if you're in a hurry", for the service, while "charming", can be "slow."

## NEW Lime Taqueria *Mexican*

| - | - | - | M |

**Smyrna** | West Vlg. | 4600 W. Village Pl., Ste. 3000 (Village Jct.) | 678-309-1113 | www.limetaqueria.com

Jessy and Renee Diaz's "elegant new" Smyrna Mexican is impressing fans with "inventive and delicious" "large plates and tapas" and "excellent margaritas" crafted from an array of top-shelf agave juice; the "beautifully done" space in a mixed-use building features candles, palm trees, whimsical lime wedges and South Beach-inspired colors, all of which "add to the great dining experience."

## Z Little Alley Z *Mediterranean*

| 26 | 19 | 23 | $30 |

**Roswell** | Crossing at Roswell | 690 Holcomb Bridge Rd. (Old Roswell Rd.) | 770-992-9198 | www.littlealley.com

It's "easy to keep coming back" to this Roswell Mediterranean where "outstanding tapas" tops the "interesting" menu of chef Richard Willt, and an "eager" staff and "solicitous owners" provide "top-rate" service; despite the "desolate shopping-center" location, the atmosphere is "fabulous", although some complain the "live entertainment" can be "ear-splitting"; N.B. a post-Survey renovation, which includes reclaimed pine walls and a sexy red bar, is not reflected in the above Decor score.

### Little Bangkok  *Thai*

| 24 | 12 | 20 | $17 |

**Cheshire Bridge** | 2225 Cheshire Bridge Rd. NE (Woodland Ave.) | 404-315-1530

There's "always a wait" at this Thai even though it's "easy to miss" at its strip-mall address on "gritty" Cheshire Bridge Road, a "favorite" stop for "locals" and even "chefs from other restaurants" for "awesome" eats, including vegetables "so fresh" they "crunch", and "attentive" servers who "guide you in the right direction" on the menu; aficionados advise "don't let the outside scare you", for inside there's some of the "best food for the price" "in the metro area."

### Little Szechuan  *Chinese*

| 21 | 10 | 21 | $17 |

**Buford Hwy. (Doraville)** | Northwood Plaza | 5091C Buford Hwy. (Shallowford Rd.) | Doraville | 770-451-0192

"Seek and ye shall be rewarded" at this "hidden gem" in Doraville showcasing the "consistently good" Chinese cuisine of "master chef" Kong Ko, who "has an amazing memory" for "customers' favorite dishes" and "always throws in" a little something "extra"; despite "poor decor" and a somewhat "seedy" location, it remains a "longtime favorite" of many.

### Lobby at Twelve  *American/Mediterranean*

| 20 | 22 | 19 | $36 |

**Atlantic Station** | Twelve Hotel | 361 17th St. NW (Atlantic Dr.) | 404-961-7370 | www.lobbyattwelve.com

"Surprisingly reasonable", this "trendy" spot in Atlantic Station's Twelve Hotel "appeals to locals" and visitors alike with "jazzy", "modern" decor, a "delightful" Med–New American menu and a "lively" bar scene complete with "awesome eye candy" and the "hip-hop elite"; cynics who "expected more" from restaurateur Bob Amick, however, find the service "spotty" and the fare "underwhelming."

### Loca Luna  *Pan-Latin*

| 19 | 21 | 16 | $24 |

**Midtown** | 550 Amsterdam Ave. NE (Monroe Dr.) | 404-875-4494 | www.loca-luna.com

"The music is always a-kickin'" at this "wild" Midtown Pan-Latin where "rowdy crowds" nibble on "surprisingly good tapas" and down "fabulous mojitos" when they're not "dancing" or joining in on the "party" action in the "spacious" dining room or on the "great" outdoor patio; critics feel the "food hasn't quite caught up" to the "lively", "clublike" scene.

### NEW Lola Bellini Bar & Restaurant  *Italian*

| - | - | - | M |

**Buckhead** | Terminus | 3280 Peachtree Rd. NW (bet. Piedmont Rd. & Turner McDonald Pkwy.) | 404-892-9292 | www.heretoserverestaurants.com

A first for the Here To Serve group (Twist, Shout, Prime, Posh and others), this Italian "winner" is all about the boot-shaped country's best, including signature Bellinis, a large antipasto bar, a fragrant rotisserie and pizza oven, and a gelato cart; the "prettiest girl in Buckhead" is what insiders call the "lovely" Johnson Studio-designed space, which features a huge fire pit and "great" bar.

**Z LongHorn Steakhouse** *Steak*          18 | 15 | 18 | $26

**Marietta** | 2636 Dallas Hwy. SW (Ridgeway Rd.) | 770-514-0245
**Kennesaw** | Esplanade | 2700 Town Center Dr. NW (Busbee Pkwy.) | 770-421-1101
**Cobb** | Akers Mill Sq. | 2973 Cobb Pkwy. SE (Akers Mill Rd. SE) | 770-859-0341
**Marietta** | 4721 Lower Roswell Rd. (Johnson Ferry Rd.) | 770-977-3045
**Buckhead** | 2430 Piedmont Rd. (Lindbergh Way) | 404-816-6338
**Emory** | 2892 N. Druid Hills Rd. (Lavista Rd.) | 404-636-3817
**Duluth** | 10845 Medlock Bridge Rd. (Abbotts Bridge Rd.) | 770-622-7087
**Lawrenceville** | 800 Lawrenceville Suwanee Rd. (Duluth Hwy. NW) | 770-338-0646
**Sandy Springs** | 6390 Roswell Rd. (Abernathy Rd.) | 404-843-1215
**East Point** | Camp Creek Mktpl. | 3840 Camp Creek Pkwy. (I-285) | 404-346-4110
www.longhornsteakhouse.com
Additional locations throughout the Atlanta area

You "can count on" this "consistent", "quality chain" steakhouse for a "reasonably priced" "good hunk o' beef" along with a "huge selection" of sides in a "laid-back" "cowboy" setting that's "always crowded and boisterous", and though the service is "spotty", "sometimes you luck out"; still, "horrendous" waits and an overall "corporate sameness" prompt some naysayers to "spend a few bucks more and go elsewhere."

**Lowcountry Barbecue Outpost** *BBQ*          ▽ 19 | 12 | 21 | $15

**Suwanee** | Stonebridge Promenade | 3455 Peachtree Pkwy., Ste. 201 (McGinnis Ferry Rd.) | 678-688-7678 | www.outpostbbq.com
The BBQ is "high-flying" at this Suwanee caterer-cum-restaurant specializing in "South Carolina–style" 'cue featuring dishes such as pulled pork, shrimp and grits and Lowcountry boils; you "order at the counter" from a "friendly" staff in the "very clean" digs, and whether "for eat-in or takeout", most agree it's a "good addition to the neighborhood."

**NEW Luckie Food**          17 | 23 | 17 | $28
**Lounge** ● *American/Eclectic*

**Downtown** | 375 Luckie St. (Ivan Allen Blvd.) | 404-525-5825 | www.luckiefoodlounge.com
While you're "right across the street from the Georgia Aquarium" "you may feel like you're in" one at this Downtown American-Eclectic that's "kid"-friendly by day, a "club scene" by night (with a cover on weekends); a sea of fish tanks surrounds the "impressive" "lounge" space that glows with LED lighting and plasma TVs, and the seafood-centric menu has "something for everyone", including a "great selection of sushi", although ordering can be "like rolling dice" say foes, who find the service "inconsistent" as well.

| | FOOD | DECOR | SERVICE | COST |
|---|---|---|---|---|

### Machu Picchu  *Peruvian*                     ▽ 18 | 11 | 16 | $16

**Buford Hwy. (Atlanta)** | Northeast Plaza Shopping Ctr. | 3375 Buford Hwy. (bet. Clairmont & N. Druid Hills Rds.) | 404-320-3226

A "good introduction" to "down-home" Peruvian fare for the "uninitiated", this affordable Buford Highway spot delivers "solid", "authentic" eats, including "great lunch specials", that are "worth the trip"; the strip-mall space is strictly no-frills, and the service sometimes seems a "little short-handed."

### Madras Chettinaad  *Indian*                  ▽ 23 | 15 | 18 | $18
### (fka Bollywood Masala Grill House)

**Decatur** | Center Point Plaza | 2201 Lawrenceville Hwy. (N. Druid Hills Rd.) | 404-636-6614 | www.madraschettinaad.com

"Don't let the exterior turn you off" of this "awesome" Indian located in a Decatur strip mall, for the fare, which includes lots of "vegetarian options" and a "fantastic lunch buffet", is "unbelievable"; the "lovely", "welcoming" staff is "extremely child-friendly", and the "Bollywood movies" shown on a "giant TV" are "kitschy", but "entertaining."

### Madras Saravana Bhavan  *Indian/Vegetarian*   24 | 12 | 15 | $15
### (nka Saravana Bhavan)

**Decatur** | North Dekalb Sq. | 2179 Lawrenceville Hwy. (N. Druid Hills Rd.) | 404-636-4400 | www.saravanabhavan.com

Even if you can't "pronounce the names" on the menu, it's all about the "big yum-m" at this "busy" Decatur spot, voted Atlanta's No. 1 Indian for its "amazing selection" of "authentic", "delicious" "vegetarian" eats, at "reasonable prices" that make it doubly "popular"; despite the "lack of ambiance" in the "loud, busy" setting and service that "leaves much to be desired", it's an "excellent value."

### ☑ Maggiano's Little Italy  *Italian*          20 | 19 | 20 | $30

**Cobb** | Cumberland Mall | 1601 Cumberland Mall, Ste. 200 (Cobb Pkwy.) | 770-799-1580
**Buckhead** | 3368 Peachtree Rd. NE (GA 400) | 404-816-9650
**Dunwoody** | Perimeter Mall | 4400 Ashford Dunwoody Rd. (I-285, exit 29) | 770-804-3313
www.maggianos.com

You almost "expect to see Sinatra walk in behind you" at this "1940s-esque", checkered-tablecloth chain where "monster portions" of "red-sauce" Italiana are dished out in "enjoyably hectic" surroundings; some dub it a "mixed bag", citing a "mass-production", "quantity-trumps-quality" approach, but fans tout this "crowd-pleaser" as a "big night out" for "not a lot of money."

### Majestic  ◑ *Diner*                          ▽ 12 | 9 | 14 | $11

**Poncey-Highland** | Plaza Shopping Ctr. | 1031 Ponce de Leon Ave. NE (N. Highland Ave.) | 404-875-0276

An "Atlanta institution" (circa 1929), this "awesome" 24/7 diner in Poncey-Highland is a "greasy spoon that lives up to its name" and is "always ready when you are", especially if "you're drunk" and need to "feed your pie hole" in the "middle of the night", or are just in the mood for some "ironic" "after-hours" "people-watching"; the "old-style" setting is "charming", but sober sorts sigh the "service and food don't match."

## Malaya  *Asian*                                    ▽ 17 | 11 | 15 | $19

**South Buckhead** | Howell Mill Vill. | 857 Collier Rd., Ste. 10 (Howell Mill Rd.) | 404-609-9991

While it gets props for "above-average Thai and Chinese", insiders insist the "yummy" "Malay is the way" at this South Buckhead Asian where the "owner will greet you like an old friend" and service comes "with a genuine smile"; "easy access" and a "pleasant atmosphere" overcome the "dingy strip-mall" location, while homebodies hail its "delivery" as among the "best in northwest Atlanta."

## Mali  *Thai*                                        23 | 17 | 19 | $22

**Virginia-Highland** | 961 Amsterdam Ave. NE (N. Highland Ave.) | 404-874-1411 | www.malirestaurant.com

"There's never a wait" at this "underrated", "hidden jewel" in Virginia-Highland, where you "can't go wrong" with the "delicious" Thai fare and "kick-ass sushi" that's "much better" than other, "better known" spots, at more "reasonable prices"; the "family crew" running the show is "delightful", and for those who feel "cramped" in the "cozy" interior, the "lovely patio" is "functional year-round."

## Manuel's Tavern ◑ *Pub Food*                        17 | 15 | 17 | $15

**Poncey-Highland** | 602 N. Highland Ave. NE (North Ave.) | 404-525-3447 | www.manuelstavern.com

Cognoscenti counsel newcomers "don't mind the awkward stares" at this "honest-to-goodness tavern" in Poncey-Highland, an "institution" that's always filled with "tons of regulars", ranging from "politicos" to "average Joes", all there for the "good conversation", "delicious" burgers and other "solid", "reasonably priced" pub grub; the "rude" staff and "beery", "smoky" digs are all part of the "appeal."

## Marlow's Tavern ◑ *Pub Food*                        20 | 19 | 20 | $23

**Alpharetta** | Camden Vill. | 3719 Old Alabama Rd. (Jones Bridge Rd.) | 770-475-1800

**NEW** **Midtown** | Plaza Midtown | 950 W. Peachtree St. NW, Ste. 215 (10th St. NE) | 404-815-0323

**Vinings** | 2355 Cumberland Pkwy. SE (Paces Ferry Rd.) | 770-432-2526 www.marlowstavern.com

This "urban" "sports bar" trio comes "highly recommended" for its "better-than-average", "reasonably priced" American bar fare, including "firecracker shrimp" that "makes every day feel like the Fourth of July" and a "delicious" brunch; the service is "friendly", and despite "close quarters", the interiors "do not feel cramped", and all three locations have alfresco seating.

## Mary Mac's Tea Room  *Southern*                     19 | 15 | 19 | $19

**Midtown** | 224 Ponce de Leon Ave. NE (Myrtle St. NE) | 404-876-1800 | www.marymacs.com

Everybody from "businesspeople" to "blue hairs", "aching" for some "down-home" Southern cooking, is drawn to this "sentimental favorite" in Midtown that "mentally whisks you back to grandma's kitchen"

| | FOOD | DECOR | SERVICE | COST |
|---|---|---|---|---|

with "Atlanta's best veggie plate" and "potent sweet tea"; "spunky waitresses with Southern drawls" "turn on the charm" in the "homespun" surroundings, and while a few skeptics feel it's merely "coasting on its reputation", to many others it simply "oozes comfort."

## Matthews Cafeteria ☒ *Southern*

| 20 | 7 | 15 | $11 |
|---|---|---|---|

**Tucker** | 2299 Main St. (north of Lawrenceville Hwy.) | 770-491-9577 | www.matthewscafeteria.com

You're apt to "see an Atlanta business mogul eating fried chicken with the guy who cuts his lawn" at this "landmark" "cafeteria-style" Southern in Tucker that's the "definition of a meat and three", where the "real down-home" fare "hasn't changed" in 50 years and the sweet tea will "keep you up at night"; while the "dingy" digs are in "need of some TLC" ("my elementary school cafeteria was more welcoming"), the place does have "character."

## NEW Maxim Prime *Steak*

| - | - | - | M |
|---|---|---|---|

**Downtown** | Glenn Hotel | 110 Marietta St. NW (Spring St.) | 404-469-0700 | www.maximprime.com

Flashing flesh of another sort, *Maxim* magazine has teamed up with culinary concept king Jeffrey Chodorow to create this splashy modern steakhouse in Downtown's sleek Glenn Hotel where the temptations include crudo and sushi, entrees designed to share and an array of small plates; the bi-level space glows with backlighting galore and modern, moving art installations, while the bar is decorated with the seven deadly sins and less-than-subtle depictions of the Garden of Eden greet you at the door.

## McCormick & Schmick's *Seafood*

| 20 | 19 | 19 | $38 |
|---|---|---|---|

**Downtown** | CNN Ctr. | 190 Marietta St. NW (Centennial Olympic Park Dr.) | 404-521-1236
**Dunwoody** | 600 Ashwood Pkwy. (bet. Ashford Dunwoody Rd. & Meadow Ln.) | 770-399-9900
www.mccormickandschmicks.com

An "endless menu" that "changes daily depending on what's freshly caught" reels folks into this "elevated seafood" duo in Downtown and Dunwoody, where the quality is "high", the fish "fresh" and the atmosphere "clubby" (with "scenic" outdoor seating at the Dunwoody location); some protest the "slow-as-molasses" service, not to mention "kind-of-costly" tabs, but so long as you have an "expense account" handy, the "unsurpassed variety" can't be beat.

## McKendrick's Steak House *Steak*

| 25 | 21 | 24 | $54 |
|---|---|---|---|

**Dunwoody** | Park Place Shopping Ctr. | 4505 Ashford Dunwoody Rd. NE (bet. Hammond Dr. & Perimeter Ctr.) | 770-512-8888 | www.mckendricks.com

Though it flies "under the radar" of many, loyalists insist this "exceptional" Dunwoody meatery "holds its own against all others" with "excellent" "brontosaurus-size" steaks, "seared to perfection", and "solid sides"; the service is "personal" and "attentive" in the "upscale", "guy-haven" room with "big booths" that belies the "shopping-center location", and while it's "pricey", many agree it's "worth it."

| | FOOD | DECOR | SERVICE | COST |
|---|---|---|---|---|

## McKinnon's Louisiane  *Cajun/Creole*   18 | 12 | 19 | $37

**Buckhead** | 3209 Maple Dr. NE (Peachtree Rd.) | 404-237-1313 |
www.mckinnons.com

"Don't judge a book by its cover" insist fans of this "divine" strip-
mall spot in Buckhead that's "been around forever" offering "old-
school" Cajun-Creole eats and "cosseting" service in a "comforting"
setting with a "hoot" of a piano bar; critics, though, find the fare
"bland" and "disappointing"; N.B. a post-Survey face-lift is not reflected in the Decor score.

## Meehan's Public House ⬤ *Pub Food*   18 | 16 | 17 | $21

**Sandy Springs** | 227 Sandy Springs Pl. NE (Roswell Rd.) | 404-843-8058
**Vinings** | 2810 Paces Ferry Rd. SE (Cumberland Pkwy.) | 770-433-1920
www.meehansalehouse.com

More than just "the place to be on St. Patty's day", these "lively
neighborhood pubs" in Sandy Springs and Vinings offer "surprisingly good" Irish "pub grub" that you can wash down with a "wide
variety of adult beverages"; the "dark, smoky" interiors are often
"crowded" and "noisy", which is why many "love the outdoor dining
areas", and while purists pan the "faux" Gaelic experience and service can be "pot luck", others find it "enjoyable" and "friendly" to
"kids" of "any age."

## Mellow Mushroom  *Pizza*   21 | 13 | 15 | $15

**Marietta** | 1690 Powder Springs Rd. SW (Macland Rd.) |
770-425-5511
**Marietta** | Shallowford Crossing | 2421 Shallowford Rd. NE (Trickum Rd.) |
770-516-1500
**Marietta** | Old Towne | 736 Johnson Ferry Rd. (Lower Roswell Rd.) |
770-579-3500
**Alpharetta** | 6000 Medlock Bridge Pkwy. (Medlock Bridge Rd.) |
770-813-0818
**Midtown** | 931 Monroe Dr. NE (bet. 8th & 10th Sts. NE) |
404-874-2291
**Emory** | 1679 Lavista Rd. NE (Briarcliff Rd.) | 404-325-0330
**Decatur** | Commerce Sq. | 265 Ponce de Leon Pl. (Commerce Dr.) |
404-370-0008
**Dunwoody** | 5575 Chamblee Dunwoody Rd. (Dunwoody Village Rd.) |
770-396-1696
**Sandy Springs** | 6218 Roswell Rd. NE (Johnson Ferry Rd. NE) |
404-252-5560
**Vinings** | Vinings Jubilee | 2950 New Paces Ferry Rd. SE (Paces Ferry Rd. SE) |
770-435-5949
www.mellowmushroom.com
Additional locations throughout the Atlanta area

"They take their time making each hand-tossed pie" at this "long-
standing" "local chain" where "high-quality ingredients" on "divine
crust" go into "creatively named", "irresistible" pizzas that "rock";
it's a "casual" "family favorite" where "there are always other kids
more wild than yours" in the "Grateful Dead meets 21st-century"
setting, resulting in an "incredible din", and critics complain that or-
ders often take a long, strange trip to your table, thanks to a staff
that's "as mellow as the name suggests."

|  | FOOD | DECOR | SERVICE | COST |
|--|------|-------|---------|------|

### Melting Pot  *Fondue*
22 | 19 | 21 | $40

**Kennesaw** | 2500 Cobb Place Ln. (Cobb Place Blvd.) | 770-425-1411
**Alpharetta** | Shoppes at Mansell | 1055 Mansell Rd. (GA 400) |
770-518-4100
🆕 **Midtown** | 754 Peachtree St. NE (4th St.) | 404-389-0099
**Duluth** | 3610 Satellite Blvd. NW (Pleasant Hill Rd.) | 770-623-1290
www.meltingpot.com

"For a classic taste of the '80s", this "cheese"-centric chain offers "all fondue, all the time" (including a "heavenly" dessert version) to those willing to "cook their own dinner"; "attentive" service in a "serene" setting also makes it a winner for a "date", "get-out-of-the-doghouse-with-the-wife" dinner or "special occasion", and while wallet-watchers see theirs get "thinner", for many it's a "relaxing" option.

### Metrofresh  *Sandwiches/Soup*
22 | 17 | 21 | $15

**Midtown** | Midtown Promenade | 931 Monroe Dr. NE (8th St.) |
404-724-0151 | www.metrofreshatl.com

A "fresh idea" that has many in Midtown "absolutely hooked", this Eclectic soup and salad specialist offers a "great mix of ever-changing items" that are "affordable, fresh and healthy"; "email subscribers" "eagerly anticipate" the "day's menu" and "witticisms" from the "helpful staff" that includes "Mr. *Party of Five* himself" (actor-cum-owner Mitchell Anderson), while the "clean, cheerful" space has a "neighborhoody" vibe, and whether you opt for a "quick sit-down" or "carryout", you "feel healthier just walking in the door."

### Mexico City Gourmet  *Mexican*
16 | 11 | 17 | $17

**Decatur** | North Decatur Plaza | 2134 N. Decatur Rd. (Clairmont Rd.) |
404-634-1128 | www.mexicocitygourmet.com

The "reliable" Mexican "standards" and other "higher brow" offerings at this Decatur "institution" make some want to "dance and cuss" (or it could be the "amazing margaritas"); while the some find the "Americanized" eats "interchangeable" with that of "10 other restaurants" and the decor "subpar", the "nice" staff "tries to please", and "for whatever reason", many find it "charming" and worth a "try."

### Mezza–A Lebanese Bistro 🈂️Ⓜ️  *Lebanese*
24 | 18 | 23 | $23

**Decatur** | Oak Grove Ctr. | 2751 Lavista Rd. (Oak Grove Rd.) |
404-633-8833 | www.mezzabistro.com

More than just a "novel concept", this Decatur Lebanese is a "destination-worthy restaurant" in an "unlikely location" that attracts "people from all over metro Atlanta" with its "many, many options" of "awesome" "small plates" that are "very well priced" and "good for sharing"; weekend "belly dancing" adds heat to an already "warm atmosphere", and "down-home service" from "folks who know what they're talking about" makes all "feel welcome."

### 🆉🆕 MF Buckhead  *Japanese*
26 | 26 | 25 | $58

**Buckhead** | 3280 Peachtree St., Ste. 110 (2nd St. NW) | 404-841-1192 |
www.mfbuckhead.com

The Kinjo brothers (MF Sushibar, Nam) inspire a collective "wow" with this "stunning" Japanese production "in the heart of Buckhead", where "fantastic grilled items" and "sublime" sushi crafted with "melt-in-your-mouth" seafood bring "tears" to the eyes of "overwhelmed" fanatics; "ultramodern" digs with "high ceilings" and "outstanding" art ooze "smart sophistication", and "gorgeous" "servers galore" deliver "impeccable service" – you can "expect to pay" for all this, but "it's well worth it."

### ☑ MF Sushibar  *Japanese*          27 | 22 | 21 | $46

**Midtown** | 265 Ponce de Leon Ave. (Penn Ave.) | 404-815-8844 | www.mfsushibar.com

Atlanta's No. 1 Japanese, the Kinjo brothers' "world-class" Midtown sushi establishment is "worth the trip from wherever" for "amazingly fresh", "artfully presented" fare in a "quintessentially West Coast" space, where you "feel cool walking in the door"; though the staff delivers "attentive" (if "snooty") service, it still "can take a while for your food to arrive", and it's so "expensive" you "may have to decide whether to buy that piece of furniture" or dine here, but most agree "you get what you pay for"; P.S. "reservations are a must."

### Mick's  *American*          16 | 15 | 17 | $21

**Midtown** | 557 Peachtree St. NE (North Ave.) | 404-875-6425 | www.thepeasantrestaurants.com

The "last one standing" of a former "classic" chain, this "old favorite" in Midtown dishes out "consistent basic American" fare, including "famous fried green tomatoes" that make many "smile" and desserts that are "better than sex" for some; the ambiance is "quaint" in the "'50s diner setting", and while some complain of "slow" service and "lackluster food", it will "always be an old standby" for many.

### Minerva Indian Cuisine  *Indian*          ∇ 22 | 6 | 11 | $17

**Alpharetta** | 4305 State Bridge Rd. (S. Bridge Pkwy.) | 678-566-7444 | www.minervacuisine.com

Fans who find "way too much to choose" from on the "dinner menu" of this Alpharetta Indian "go for lunch" instead, so they can "sample all" of the "fresh, tasty" offerings from the "incredible buffet" with enough meatless options to "satisfy a vegetarian diet"; "plastic tablecloths" define the "lackluster" "warehouse" digs, but those who "eat here weekly" obviously don't care.

### Mitra  ☒ *American*          20 | 19 | 19 | $35

**Midtown** | 818 Juniper St. (bet. 5th & 6th Sts.) | 404-875-5515 | www.mitrarestaurant.com

"Devoted" fans of this "clever" Midtown New American say "bravo" to chef Gerardo Ramos for his "mouthwatering" fare with a serious "Latin" accent that's both "reasonably priced and delicious"; "careful and attentive service" in the "quiet, quaint" environs of the "classic" rustic house where it's set make it an experience "not to be missed."

### Moe's & Joe's  ◑ *Pub Food*          13 | 11 | 15 | $12

**Virginia-Highland** | 1033 N. Highland Ave. (Virginia Ave.) | 404-873-6090 | www.moesandjoes.com

This Virginia-Highland "institution" "looks exactly like a dive bar should" and "hasn't changed one bit" since 1947, except for the

| | FOOD | DECOR | SERVICE | COST |
|---|---|---|---|---|

"ever-eclectic crowd" attracted by "cheap" "Pabst Blue Ribbon on draft" and "decent bar food"; if you "don't have high expectations", it's a "great place to relax with friends" "sitting under the trees" "on the sidewalk" or in "red vinyl booths."

## Moe's Southwest Grill  *Southwestern*    | 13 | 10 | 13 | $11 |

**Marietta** | 125 Barrett Pkwy. (Prado Ln.) | 678-581-0236
**Cobb** | 860 Johnson Ferry Rd. NE (Glenridge Dr. NE) | 404-303-0081
**Roswell** | 2354 Holcomb Bridge Rd. (Fouts Rd.) | 770-594-8050
**Midtown** | Colony Sq. | 1197 Peachtree St. NE (14th St.) | 404-870-8884 ⓢ
**Midtown** | Ansley Mall | 1544 Piedmont Ave. NE (Monroe Dr.) | 404-879-9663
**Buckhead** | 3722 Roswell Rd. NE (Piedmont Rd.) | 404-231-1690
**Emory** | Loehmann's Plaza | 2484 Briarcliff Rd. NE (Woodlake Dr. NE) | 404-248-9399
**Decatur** | 863 Ponce de Leon Ave. NE (Barnett St.) | 404-607-7892
**Dunwoody** | Northridge Sq. | 8290 Roswell Rd. (Northridge Rd.) | 678-585-7573
**South Buckhead** | 2915 Peachtree Rd. (Peachtree Ave.) | 404-442-8932
www.moes.com
Additional locations throughout the Atlanta area

This "fast-casual" Southwestern chain delivers "gut-busting burritos and tacos" "customized to order" with "assembly-line" efficiency in "crowded", "cafeteria"-like settings; while purists plead "no mo'" of its "bland", "Wonder Bread version of Latin cuisine", defenders tout it as a "good-value" option when you want to "feed the family" or "fill up in a tasty hurry."

## ☑ Morton's The Steakhouse  *Steak*    | 25 | 21 | 24 | $65 |

**Buckhead** | Peachtree Lenox Bldg. | 3379 Peachtree Rd. NE (Lenox Rd.) | 404-816-6535
**Downtown** | SunTrust Plaza Bldg. | 303 Peachtree Center Ave. NE (Baker St.) | 404-577-4366
www.mortons.com

"Consistency abounds" at these Buckhead and Downtown links of a "can't-go-wrong" steakhouse chain pairing "well-prepared" chops that "hang off the plate" with "seriously powerful martinis"; "arm-and-a-leg" pricing comes with the territory, along with a "Saran-wrapped presentation" of raw meats (accompanied by an instructional "recitation" by the waiter) – a "shtick" that many find "tired."

## Mosaic  *Eclectic*    | 22 | 19 | 23 | $38 |

**Buckhead** | 3097 Maple Dr. NE (Peachtree St.) | 404-846-5722 | www.mosaicatl.com

"Take a date today, you'll be married tomorrow" swear devotees of this "quaint" Buckhead Eclectic, a "favorite" of many for its "creative" cuisine (including an "excellent" brunch) and "gracious" staff that "goes out of its way to make you happy"; add a "lovely little cottage" "slightly off the beaten path" with a "beautiful" patio and "charming" ambiance – so "what wouldn't you love" about it?

|  | FOOD | DECOR | SERVICE | COST |
|---|---|---|---|---|

## Mt. Fuji
### Japanese Steakhouse  *Japanese/Steak*     ▽ 21 | 15 | 22 | $30
**Marietta** | 180 S. Cobb Pkwy., Ste. 26 (Gresham Ave. NE) |
770-428-0095 | www.mtfujimarietta.com
Surveyors who've scaled this Japanese in Marietta report "fresh",
"innovative" sushi and "wonderful" teppanyaki tables with knife action that's "always fun to watch"; the "cordial" owner is the "only
sushi chef", so things can "get busy" during "prime hours" but it's
"well worth the wait."

## Mu Lan  *Chinese*     ▽ 18 | 16 | 16 | $29
**Midtown** | 824 Juniper St. NE (bet. 5th & 6th Sts.) |
404-877-5797
For those who are tired of the "same old, same old", fans recommend this Midtown Chinese serving a "creative", "eclectic" menu of
"upscale" fare in "huge" portions; situated in a "quaint house on
Juniper", it offers a "very comfortable" setting, but most consider it
"better for delivery", thanks to "speedy" service.

## ☑ Murphy's  *American*     24 | 21 | 22 | $28
**Virginia-Highland** | 997 Virginia Ave. NE (N. Highland Ave.) |
404-872-0904 | www.murphysvh.com
At this Virginia-Highland "institution", everyone from "foodies" to
"picky eaters" can "find something to love" from the "reasonably"
priced, seasonally changing menu of "standard American fare with
flair", including "yummy baked goods", desserts "to die for" and an
"amazing wine list", while its "brunch fame is well deserved" ("if you
can get in"); "friendly" service helps foster a "warm feeling" in the
"charming", but always "crowded", space; N.B. the retail wine shop
on the premises offers weekly tastings and seminars.

## Muss & Turner's  ☒ *American/Deli*     25 | 18 | 19 | $23
**Smyrna** | 1675 Cumberland Pkwy. (S. Atlanta Rd.) | 770-434-1114 |
www.mussandturners.com
Enthusiasts exhort "you muss go" to this New American "culinary
delight" that "started the Smyrna dining revolution and still leads
the pack", a "killer deli" by day that morphs into a table service place
at night, all the while serving "divine sandwiches" and other "incredible" fare, along with an "almost unparalleled beer selection"; the
"personable" owners "really care", and despite the "classy" concept, the scene is so "unpretentious" many "would feel comfortable
in their PJs."

## Nagoya  *Japanese*     24 | 10 | 16 | $27
**Roswell** | 48 King St. (S. Atlanta St.) | 770-998-8899
Roswellians relish having some of the "best sushi in the suburbs" in
their backyard at this "outstanding" Japanese in a "nondescript
plaza" where "congenial" chefs craft "fresh", "innovative" fin fare,
and while the teppanyaki "tableside show" is "a little cheesy", it's always a "birthday favorite" of "families"; so what if the digs "could
use a face-lift" – it's a "respectable" operation that "never disappoints", and a "good value" as well.

|      | FOOD | DECOR | SERVICE | COST |
|------|------|-------|---------|------|

### Nakato  *Japanese*

21 | 20 | 21 | $35

**Cheshire Bridge** | 1776 Cheshire Bridge Rd. NE (Piedmont Rd.) |
404-873-6582 | www.nakatorestaurant.com

One of Atlanta's "first" Japanese, this Cheshire Bridge "treasure" is
the "real deal" say those who appreciate "artistry through sushi" as
well as "excellent" teppanyaki prepared by "personable table
chefs"; "gracious" service adds to the "serene" mood of the "sooth-
ing interior" that's a "quiet place for relaxing" or a "business" meal.

### Nam  ☒  *Vietnamese*

25 | 23 | 23 | $34

**Midtown** | Midtown Promenade | 931 Monroe Dr. NE (8th St. NE) |
404-541-9997 | www.namrestaurant.com

It's "hard not to love" the "superbly prepared" Vietnamese cuisine
(including the "delicious", "must-try" "shaking beef") at this "sexy",
"upscale" Midtown sibling of MF Sushibar and MF Buckhead; "beautifully dressed servers" in "red flowing silk gowns" attend the
"cozy", "romantic" room in the "tiny strip storefront" space, and
though parking is "tricky" and prices are "breathtaking", it's "highly
recommended" by fans who "could eat here every day of the week."

### ☒ Nan Thai Fine Dining  *Thai*

27 | 27 | 26 | $43

**Midtown** | 1350 Spring St. NW (17th St. NW) | 404-870-9933 |
www.nanfinedining.com

An "elegant place worthy of its stripes", Atlanta's No. 1 for Decor is
this "sophisticated" Midtown Thai in a "stunning", "sensual" Johnson
Studio–designed space that feels like "another universe", with "feng
shui"-friendly bathrooms that are "worth the trip" "whether or not
you have to use" them; "exquisite", "upscale" dishes come in "beautiful" presentations that rival the "gorgeous", "finely dressed" servers who make guests "feel like royalty", and while it's all predictably
"pricey", it's the "complete package."

### ☒ Nava  *Southwestern*

23 | 23 | 22 | $42

**Buckhead** | Buckhead Plaza | 3060 Peachtree Rd. NE (W. Paces Ferry Rd.) |
404-240-1984 | www.buckheadrestaurants.com

This "reliable" Southwest "standout" from the Buckhead Life Group is
"still a favorite after all these years" thanks to "imaginative" regional
fare "infused with new life by chef Jesse Perez", "killer margaritas"
and a "value-priced" "wine list", and "competent" service; the
"multilevel seating provides great people-watching", but "nothing
beats the outdoor patio", and while some foes feel it's "way past its
prime" ("hello, 1980s!"), amigos still find it "fresh and fashionable."

### New Yorker Marketplace & Delicatessen  ☒  *Deli*

22 | 9 | 17 | $12

**Buckhead** | 322 Pharr Rd. NE (Peachtree Rd.) | 404-240-0260

A "little place that delivers big", this Buckhead deli is an "absolute
favorite" of noshers for its "awesome" sandwiches, while "cook-at-
home" types value the "butcher counter" and its "delicious" "selection" of "prime" meats; the staff is "friendly" and the owner "treats you
like family", and while there's "no atmosphere" in the bodega-style
digs, for fans this "gem" is "as close as you can get to NY" in town.

| | FOOD | DECOR | SERVICE | COST |
|---|---|---|---|---|

### ☑ New York Prime  *Steak*   25 | 22 | 24 | $64

**Buckhead** | Monarch Tower | 3424 Peachtree Rd. NE (Lenox Rd.) |
404-846-0644 | www.newyorkprime.com

The "prime is divine" and the portions are "massive" at this "fantastic" Buckhead steakhouse where "unbelievable cuts" of beef and "delicious sides" are served with "crisp efficiency"; "dealmakers feel at home" in the "cool room" "dominated by an indoor palm tree" and hosting a "very active", "smoky" bar scene and "live music" that "makes table conversation challenging"; it's "crazy expensive", and some "disappointed" detractors "don't get" the attraction, but others (with "expense accounts") "can't wait to go back."

### Nickiemoto's  *Pan-Asian*   20 | 17 | 18 | $28

**Midtown** | 990 Piedmont Ave. NE (10th St.) | 404-253-2010 |
www.nickiemotosmidtown.com

"You can always count on a regular crowd" of "pretty people" to "keep the buzz going" at this "eclectic" "bait-and-booze joint" in Midtown that "pulls it all together" with "excellent" Pan-Asian eats and "creative" sushi; the "patio setting" is "wonderful", "and yes, big Southern boys in dresses" do come out for the "Monday night" "drag show", but "make reservations" because even "on a quiet night, this place is still hopping."

### Nicola's  Ⓜ *Lebanese*   ▽ 18 | 7 | 21 | $23

**Emory** | 1602 Lavista Rd. NE (bet. Briarcliff & Cheshire Bridge Rds.) |
404-325-2524 | www.nicolas-restaurant.com

The namesake of this Emory Lebanese is a "story unto himself", and while his "sons have taken over" the business, he can still be seen on the premises, and his "friendly spirit" lives on; "delicious" dishes are served by a "warm" staff in a "welcoming" environment, and though it may look like "Nicola hasn't spent two cents on the joint since he moved in", the "place really rocks" on weekends, when belly dancers "put on their show."

### ☑ Nikolai's Roof  ⓈⓂ *Continental/French*   25 | 26 | 26 | $73

**Downtown** | Hilton | 255 Courtland St. NE (bet. Baker & Harris Sts.) |
404-221-6362 | www.nikolaisroof.com

"Drink in" "magnificent 360-degree views" (and "flavored" house vodkas) at this "Atlanta classic" atop the Hilton in Downtown, "still a top-tier experience" "after over 30 years", and more "quiet" and "elegant" since it was "forgotten by the trendoids" "decades ago"; "waiters" with "European accents" "treat you like royalty" while serving "excellent" French cuisine with "Russian" "touches", and while some sniff it's "not what it used to be", it remains a "favorite" of many for "expense-account" dining and "special occasions."

### Nino's  *Italian*   22 | 17 | 22 | $33

**Cheshire Bridge** | 1931 Cheshire Bridge Rd. NE (Piedmont Ave.) |
404-874-6505 | www.ninosatlanta.com

The "old-world Italian" fare and "top-notch" service at this mid-priced "family-owned and -operated" Cheshire Bridge *cucina* "bring back regulars and entice newcomers", and while it's "not über-gourmet", it's "perfect" to fans (and besides, "who could say no to a dessert cart?"); the "small", "dark" space has a "romantic" air, but the scene can get "pretty festive", so a "relaxing date" might be out of the picture.

**Nirvana Café & Grill**  *American*          | 18 | 14 | 16 | $13 |

**Roswell** | Village Festival | 10930B Crabapple Rd., Ste. 120 (Crossville Rd.) | 678-277-2626
**Alpharetta** | Flynn Crossing Shopping Ctr. | 5192 McGinnis Ferry Rd. (Windward Pkwy.) | 678-893-9000
www.eatnirvana.com

For a "touch of hipster urbanity in suburbia", Alpharetta and Roswell diners descend on this "quirky" family-owned pair for "healthy" and "tasty" American fare "made from scratch", and many "gotta have that homemade ice cream"; "warm" service and a "casual", "family-oriented" atmosphere take some of the edge off the decor ("like eating a sandwich in my garage"); N.B. Alpharetta also serves dinner.

**Noche**  *Southwestern*          | 20 | 17 | 17 | $24 |

**Virginia-Highland** | 1000 Virginia Ave. NE (N. Highland Ave.) | 404-815-9155 | www.heretoserverestaurants.com

Pros promise an "all-around good time" at this Virginia-Highland Southwesterner by Tom Catherall (Twist, Shout, Prime, Strip, Goldfish) serving "fantastic" small plates that represent "excellent value", especially the "Monday all-you-can-eat" option; the servers are "friendly" and the bartenders "are not shy with their pours" when concocting some of the "best margaritas in Atlanta", which make for a "festive" "after-work" scene; when the "small" space gets too crowded, many head for the outdoor patio.

**Noodle**  *Noodle Shop*          | 19 | 16 | 18 | $16 |

**College Park** | 3693 Main St. (Princeton Dr.) | 404-767-5155 📧
**Midtown** | 903 Peachtree St. NE (8th St.) | 404-685-3010
**Decatur** | 205 E. Ponce de Leon Ave. (Church St.) | 404-378-8622
www.noodlehouse.net

Though the menu of noodles and rice is "simple", there's "enough variety to suit everyone" at this "affordable" trio serving "tasty" "neo-Asian food with flair" in "large bowls" "chock-full of yummy things"; the "sleek yet inviting" spaces are "kid-friendly" and "casual", and the locations are convenient enough to "calm the savage lunch crowds" of "young urban dwellers"; they're also "solid" "take-out" options.

**Norcross Station Cafe** 📧 *American*          | 19 | 19 | 17 | $19 |

**Norcross** | 40 S. Peachtree St. (Holcomb Bridge Rd. NW) | 770-409-9889 | www.norcrossstation.com

The "Amtrak Crescent blows by around 8:30 PM these days", passing this "good ol' standby" located in a "quaint" former Norcross train depot that's now "very much a family place" serving "solid", "wholesome" American fare "at a fair price"; the "nice" staff adds to the "charm", and "great decorations" keep the locomotive theme "alive."

| | FOOD | DECOR | SERVICE | COST |
|---|---|---|---|---|

### Northlake Thai Cuisine ☒ *Thai*   ▽ 24 | 21 | 24 | $28

**Tucker** | Kroger Shopping Ctr. | 3939 Lavista Rd. (Montreal Rd.) |
770-938-2223

"Head and shoulders above anything in the neighborhood" and
"worth the drive" from anywhere, this casual "fine-dining" Tucker
Thai is lauded for "fantastic" fare "seasoned to perfection" and
served with "style"; if "strip-mall chic" exists, it's alive and well in
the "elegant" space "hidden" in an "unlikely location" "behind a
Kroger"; while almost "nobody knows where it is", those who do
confirm it's truly a "real find in a sea of mediocrity."

### Nuevo Laredo Cantina ☒ *Mexican*   24 | 12 | 18 | $20

**Westside** | 1495 Chattahoochee Ave. NW (bet. Collier & Howell Mill Rds.) |
404-352-9009 | www.nuevolaredocantina.com

"Nothing comes close" to the "authentic" "border cuisine" at Atlanta's
No. 1 Mexican, located on an "industrial" stretch of Westside; "go
early" or "prepare to camp out" "on the porch" with the rest of the
"throngs" who come "from far and wide" for the "tremendous" *comida*,
though pitchers of "terrific margaritas" "help" ease the "brutal"
waits; "walls lined with snapshots" provide the only decoration in
the "down-to-earth" digs.

### Oak Grove Market ☒ *Deli*   21 | 11 | 19 | $11

**Decatur** | 2757 Lavista Rd. (Oak Grove Rd.) | 404-315-9831 |
www.oakgrovemarket.com

Relive the "days gone by" at this Decatur "butcher shop-cum-deli"
that resembles a "'50s diner" and "sets the standard" for a "neighborhood gathering spot", where the "friendliest people in town"
dole out prepared "homestyle comfort" foods, including "great
burgers" and "tasty" sandwiches, while "terrific butchers" cut up
"excellent meats"; "bargain" lunch specials are another reason this
"mainstay" has such a "loyal following."

### Oceanaire, The *Seafood*   23 | 23 | 23 | $48

**Midtown** | 1100 Peachtree St. (12th St.) | 404-475-2277 |
www.theoceanaire.com

"So good that it's hard to believe it's a chain", this "exceptional" seafood franchise in Midtown features "all the exuberance of a steakhouse in a fish house", starting with a "bountiful menu" and "fine
wine list"; "happening" bar scenes, "ocean liner"–like settings and
"big prices" reflect the overall "classy" mood.

### OK Cafe *Diner*   20 | 16 | 21 | $19

**Buckhead** | West Paces Ferry Shopping Ctr. | 1284 W. Paces Ferry Rd.
(Northside Pkwy.) | 404-233-2888 | www.okcafe.com

"Diner-style" "Southern fried bliss" is on the menu at this
"Buckhead breakfast haunt" offering "large helpings" of "real
country food", served "with a smile" by "perky waitresses"; it's a
popular spot for "power lunches" or "family" meals, where "you'll
see everyone from Ted Turner to the babysitter" "crammed" in the
space highlighted by neon and Formica, and those on the go "love"
the "takeaway" option.

| | FOOD | DECOR | SERVICE | COST |
|---|---|---|---|---|

### Old South Barbecue  *BBQ* ▽ 23 | 10 | 23 | $13

**Smyrna** | 601 Burbank Circle (Windy Hill Rd.) | 770-435-4215 | www.oldsouthbbq.com

The BBQ at this "longtime" Smyrna smokehouse is some of the "best this side of the Mississippi" according to fans who extol the "sweet-sticky-gooey-flavorsome" sauce and "succulent meats", served in "excellent-size portions"; "quick" and "super-friendly" service helps excuse the "log cabin" environs ("what atmosphere?") with a "'great view' of the highway", but most just focus on the 'cue and "forget the rest", anyway.

### ☒ ONE. midtown kitchen  *American* 22 | 25 | 21 | $38

**Midtown** | 559 Dutch Valley Rd. (Monroe Dr.) | 404-892-4111 | www.onemidtownkitchen.com

With its "impressive wine wall" and "hanging lamps" that resemble the "Hogwart School's" "candles", the "stylish" Midtown flagship of Todd Rushing and Bob Amick (TWO urban licks, Trois) is "perfect" for "business dinners", a "girls' night out", "dates" or "impressing out-of-towners"; amid a "boisterous" scene, the "innovative" New American eats and "amazing wine list" "can be heard loud and clear", and the staff is "knowledgeable", if sometimes "full of itself"; a few cynics sniff "it's all about the look, not the food", but others find it "delightful."

### One Star Ranch  *BBQ* 20 | 11 | 16 | $18

**Alpharetta** | 732 N. Main St. (bet. Henderson Village Pkwy. & Vaughn Dr.) | 770-475-6695
**Buckhead** | 25 Irby Ave. NW (Roswell Rd.) | 404-233-7644
www.onestarranch.com

"When you get a hankerin' for some" "Texas-style" BBQ, "git ur boots on" and two-step on over to these 'cue twins in Alpharetta and Buckhead for "fork-tender" "beef ribs", pulled pork that "rocks" and other smoked fare that's "light on sauce but big on taste"; while the intown location resembles a "run-down shack" and the suburban sibling is "nothing fancy", either, service does come "with a smile."

### Original Pancake House  *Diner* 21 | 10 | 16 | $14

**Alpharetta** | The Plaza at Windward | 5530 Windward Pkwy. (Westside Pkwy.) | 678-393-1355
**Cheshire Bridge** | Tara Shopping Ctr. | 2321 Cheshire Bridge Rd. (Lavista Rd. NE) | 404-633-5677
**Peachtree City** | Peachtree City Mktpl. | 239-243 Marketplace Connector (Hwy. 54) | 770-486-7634
**Stone Mountain** | 5099 Memorial Dr. (Memorial College Ave.) | 404-292-6914
www.originalpancakehouse.com

A "seemingly endless variety of pancakes" (especially the "don't-miss" apple and "unusual" Dutch Baby versions) makes fans flip for this "real-deal" chain that supplies "Sunday morning comfort" for many; service is "fast (if not so friendly)" and the price is right, but "better coffee would be an improvement."

| | FOOD | DECOR | SERVICE | COST |
|---|---|---|---|---|

### Oscar's Villa Capri ⑤ *Italian* ▽ 27 | 19 | 23 | $39

**Dunwoody** | Orchard Park Shopping Ctr. | 2090 Dunwoody Club Dr.
(Jett Ferry Rd.) | 770-392-7940 | www.oscarsvillacapri.com

"You can get lost" "for a few hours" at this "excellent" Dunwoody
Italian that "feels" "like Italy", if not "heaven", to fans for its "fantastic",
"upscale" cuisine, including "innovative nightly specials"; the
"shopping-center" space is "intimate" (read: "tables are a little
close together"), and the staff is "accommodating", although cognoscenti confide "it helps to be a regular."

### Osteria 832 *Italian* 21 | 16 | 18 | $18

**Virginia-Highland** | 832 Highland Ave. NE (Greenwood Ave.) |
404-897-1414 | www.osteria832.com

Maybe it "ain't haute cuisine", but the "simple" Italian fare from this
"family-friendly" sibling of Doc Chey "in the heart of Virginia-
Highland" is "delicious", "reliable" and "cheap" (even more so on
Tuesdays, when wines are "half-price"); the atmosphere is "pleasant" and you can "people-watch" from the "relaxing" patio, but unless you're a "boomer with a baby", "go late" "to avoid" the "crazy
early rush of families" with "wild" "little kiddies."

### Outback Steakhouse *Steak* 18 | 15 | 18 | $26

**Kennesaw** | Cobb Place Shopping Ctr. | 810 Ernest W. Barrett Pkwy. NW
(Home Center Dr. NW) | 770-795-0400
**Cumming** | Kohl's Shopping Ctr. | 1715 Market Place Blvd.
(Buford Dam Rd.) | 678-455-7225
**Roswell** | 655 W. Crossville Rd. (King Rd.) | 770-998-5630
**Buckhead** | Buckhead Court Shopping Ctr. | 3850 Roswell Rd. NE
(Piedmont Rd.) | 404-266-8000
**Emory** | Toco Hills | 2145 Lavista Rd. NE (N. Druid Hills Rd.) |
404-636-5110
**Douglasville** | 6331 Douglas Blvd. (Chapel Hill Rd.) |
770-949-7000
**Dunwoody** | Perimeter Pl. | 1220 Ashford Crossing (Crown Pointe Pkwy.) |
770-481-0491
**Peachtree City** | 995 N. Peachtree Pkwy. (Hwy. 74) | 770-486-9292
**Stone Mountain** | Park Place Shopping Ctr. | 1525 E. Park Place Blvd.
(Hwy. 78) | 770-498-5400
www.outback.com

For those who want "nothing unexpected", this "dependable"
steakhouse chain doles out "hearty", "well-seasoned" steaks at "decent" prices, which help explain the "two hour waits"; service is
"friendly" and "quick", and the call-in option, when they "bring your
order out to your car", is always popular, but jaded critics jeer at the
"bloomin' average" eats and "kitschy" "Aussie" theme.

### Oz Pizza *Pizza* 19 | 11 | 14 | $13

**East Point** | 2805 Main St. (White Way) | 404-761-7006
**Fairburn** | 5 Broad St. NW (Campbellton St.) | 770-306-0603 ⑤
www.ozpizza.net

The "delicious" pizzas at this homegrown pizzeria pair in East Point
and Fairburn are "as good as any in town", thanks to "almost unlimited
choices" of toppings, "over-the-top sauce" and "perfect crusts"; "ef-

"ficient" service and "outdoor patios" add to the "good vibe" and help make them a "nice local alternative" to the "national chains."

### Pacific Rim Bistro  *Pan-Asian*

| 21 | 17 | 19 | $31 |

**Downtown** | SunTrust Plaza Bldg. | 303 Peachtree Center Ave. (Baker St.) | 404-893-0018 | www.pacificrimbistro.com

This Downtown sibling of Hsu's and Silk provides an "excellent variety" of "above-average" Pan-Asian fare (at "above-average prices") including "fresh" and "varied" sushi; "convenient" for the lunch crowds and "business" set, it's a "comfortable" experience, though perhaps more so "for singles than families."

### Palace, The  *Indian*

| - | - | - | I |

**Norcross** | 6131 Peachtree Pkwy. (Holcomb Bridge Rd.) | 770-840-7770 | www.thepalaceatl.com

For a dhosa "authentic Indian", those in-the-know head to this Norcross naanery where the flatbread is "to die for" and the chicken tikka masala is "out of this world"; while impatient types gripe about "slow service", others appreciate the "unobtrusive" staff for "allowing you to enjoy" the "experience" – and besides, most agree the fare is "worth waiting for."

### Palm  *Steak*

| 23 | 20 | 22 | $59 |

**Buckhead** | Westin Buckhead | 3391 Peachtree Rd. NE (bet. GA 400 & Lenox Rd.) | 404-814-1955 | www.thepalm.com

"Old-school dining" is alive and well at this Buckhead hotel outpost of the "distinguished" chain carnivorium born in NYC in 1926, which draws "movers and shakers" with its "enormous" steaks and lobsters plated in "distinguished" settings adorned with celebrity "caricatures"; sure, the tabs are reminiscent of "mortgage payments" and service can career from "top-notch" to "surly", but ultimately they're "consistently good."

### Palomilla's Cuban Grill House   *Caribbean/Cuban*

| ∇ 23 | 10 | 20 | $18 |

**Norcross** | Spalding Plaza | 6470 Spalding Dr., Ste. B (Holcomb Bridge Rd.) | 770-242-0078 | www.palomillasatlanta.com

For those who "want to try" the "real taste of Cuba", this "popular" Norcross purveyor is "as good as it gets" according to fans who laud its "cheap", *"delicioso"* eats and "unbelievable" sangria, served by a "friendly" staff in a "casual" strip-mall space; amigos insist it's "well worth the drive."

### ⚡ Pampas Steakhouse  *Argentinean/Steak*

| 26 | 24 | 24 | $49 |

**Alpharetta** | 10970 State Bridge Rd. (Jones Bridge Rd.) | 678-339-0029 | www.pampassteakhouse.com

For a "grand experience" in the "suburbs", gauchos gallop to this "fantastic" Argentinean steakhouse in Alpharetta for "outstanding steaks" and other "top-notch food", and a "dulce de leche" "prepared tableside" for a finishing touch that's "special beyond words"; the service is usually "excellent", although it can be "inconsistent", while the "soft-glowing candlelit interior" gets "noisy when crowded"; it's "pricey", but still a "wonderful" choice for a "special occasion."

|  | FOOD | DECOR | SERVICE | COST |
|---|---|---|---|---|

### Panahar ⓜ *Bangladeshi*     23 | 10 | 21 | $19

**Buford Hwy. (Atlanta)** | Northeast Plaza Shopping Ctr. | 3375 Buford Hwy. NE, Ste. 1060 (N. Cliff Valley Way) | 404-633-6655

A "hidden gem" in a Buford Highway strip mall, this "charming" Bangladeshi is a "unique" find "in a sea of Hispanic eateries", offering "delicious", "vegetarian-friendly" fare, including a "lunch buffet that cannot be beat", at "low prices", and BYO with no corkage fee; the owner is "very accommodating" and servers "act as great guides" (albeit "slow" ones), all of which make it "worth the drive from anywhere in town."

### ⓩ Pano's & Paul's Ⓢ *Continental*     26 | 22 | 25 | $59

**Buckhead** | West Paces Ferry Shopping Ctr. | 1232 W. Paces Ferry Rd. (Northside Pkwy.) | 404-261-3662 | www.buckheadrestaurants.com

An Atlanta "landmark" and "flagship for the Buckhead Life" Group, this "grande dame" is "keeping pace" with newcomers, appealing to an "older", "glamorous" crowd with "sublime" Continental cuisine and an "extensive" wine list, served by a "highly trained" staff that makes "everyone feel welcome"; the "elegant" "Rat Pack"-inspired "honey-hideaway" setting belies its "strip-mall" location, and while some feel it's a "little frayed around the edges", others still regard it as an "amazing" "celebratory" "experience."

### ⓩ Paolo's Gelato Italiano ⓜ⇗ *Ice Cream*     25 | 14 | 19 | $6

**Virginia-Highland** | 1025 Virginia Ave. NE (N. Highland Ave.) | 404-607-0055 | www.paolosgelato.com

The "line outside the door says it all" at this "tiny storefront" gelateria (voted Atlanta's No. 1 Bang for the Buck), whose "decadent" gelato with "drop-dead flavors" make it the "perfect complement to the neighborhood restaurants" in Virginia-Highland; the "easy-on-the-eyes" owner serves you with "self-assured Italian flair" in a space that's "smaller than your closet" ("you have to go outside to change your mind"), and fans agree that anyone "should begin or end a visit" to the area here.

### Pappadeaux Seafood Kitchen *Cajun/Creole*     21 | 18 | 19 | $29

**Marietta** | 2830 Windy Hill Rd. (I-75) | 770-984-8899
**Alpharetta** | 10795 Davis Dr. (Mansell Rd.) | 770-992-5566
**Norcross** | 5635 Jimmy Carter Blvd. (I-85) | 770-849-0600
www.pappas.com

A must-"deaux" for OTPers "dying for Louisiana cuisine", this trio from the "prodigious Pappas organization" "never disappoints" fans with its "huge portions" of "awesome" seafood-centric "Cajun-Creole" fare, "best-value" lunch buffet and "top-notch" service – "for the price point"; still, "wait times" "can be a problem", while the "lively, upbeat" atmosphere can become "madcap", and some foes find it all "as authentic as the Blue Bayou at Disneyland."

### Pappasito's Cantina *Mexican*     23 | 19 | 20 | $24

**Marietta** | 2788 Windy Hill Rd. (I-75) | 770-541-6100 | www.pappas.com

Natch, it's "from Texas", this "warehouse of a restaurant" chain link in Marietta serving *"grande"* "margaritas" and "huge portions" of "delicious" Mexican "with a twist" in a "lively" "cantina" setting; it's "not inexpensive", though, and "long waits at peak times" are to be expected, but "attentive" servers have it under control, and children "love to watch tortillas being made" in the "kid-friendly" environment.

### NEW Parish ● *Cajun/Creole*                    - | - | - | M

**Inman Park** | 240 N. Highland Ave. (Inman Village Pkwy. NE) | 404-681-4434 | www.parishatl.com

The aura of New Orleans and the strains of live music spill onto the streets of Inman Park from this midpriced new venture by Concentrics Restaurants (of ONE, TWO and Trois fame), where chef Timothy Magee's Cajun-Creole concoctions are sure to cast a voodoo spell; the original tin ceiling and other details of the circa-1890 Atlanta Pipe and Foundry Company building have been lovingly restored and accented with zinc bar, wine barrel stave chandeliers and two patios (one dog-friendly) – all that's missing is the Spanish moss.

### ☑ Park 75 *American*                    27 | 25 | 27 | $70

**Midtown** | Four Seasons | 75 14th St. (bet. Peachtree & W. Peachtree Sts.) | 404-253-3840 | www.fourseasons.com

"Consistently excellent" in all respects, this "pleasure palace" in Midtown's Four Seasons hotel sets the "standard by which other high-end restaurants should be judged", with "divine" New American cuisine, including an "excellent brunch" and "outstanding" weekend chocolate bar ("break out the maternity pants"), service that almost "outshines the food" and an "elegant setting" that's "posh without feeling stuffy"; in sum, it's a "beautiful dining experience" that's "worth the bloated prices."

### Pasta da Pulcinella *Italian*                    23 | 18 | 21 | $27

**Midtown** | 1123 Peachtree Walk NE (bet. 12th & 13th Sts.) | 404-876-1114 | www.pastadapulcinella.com

"Pasta heaven" is what devotees dub this Midtown Northern Italian offering a "small but wonderful" menu of "amazing" dishes that "make hearts soar", including the signature apple and sausage ravioli that some pastafarians praise as "the best around"; it's set in a "pretty" "converted house" tucked away in a "puzzle of small streets" "behind mega towers" that makes for a "cozy" "romantic" setting, and it's a "good value" to boot.

### Pasta Vino *Italian*                    19 | 13 | 19 | $21

**Alpharetta** | 11130 State Bridge Rd. (Kimball Bridge Rd.) | 770-777-1213
**Buckhead** | Peachtree Battle Shopping Ctr. | 2391 Peachtree Rd. NE (Peachtree Battle Ave.) | 404-231-4946 | www.pvbuckhead.com

The "quintessential neighborhood Italian cafes", these "casual", independently owned spots in Alpharetta and Buckhead please patrons with "consistently yummy fare", including some of the "best pizza around", "huge" salads and "delicious" pasta dishes; a "kid-friendly" environment and "great outside seating" make up for "no-frills decor", and "new owners" of the intown spot have "made wonderful improvements to the ambiance."

| | FOOD | DECOR | SERVICE | COST |
|---|---|---|---|---|

**Pastis** *French*  21 | 20 | 18 | $31

**Roswell** | 936 Canton St. (Magnolia St.) | 770-640-3870 |
www.roswellpastis.com

Housed in a "charming" "two-story storefront" space in Roswell's
"quaint historic district", this "cute" French bistro is a "popular"
choice for a "date", thanks to "outstanding" fare at a "fair price", "alfresco dining" on the "wonderful" "balcony" and "accommodating"
service; the "lively bar" scene is an "upscale hangout" for "divorced
locals", while "live music" on "weekends" is a "nice touch" (albeit
"loud"), and though critics find the food "hit-or-miss", *amis* insist
"*c'est vaut le voyage.*"

**Paul's** *American*  23 | 20 | 22 | $48

**South Buckhead** | 10 Kings Circle (Virginia Pl.) | 404-231-4113 |
www.greatfoodinc.com

"Charming" chef Paul Albrecht brings a "personal touch" to his
"laid-back" "bistro" "hidden" in South Buckhead's "quaint"
"Peachtree Hills", the showcase for his "spot-on" American eats and
a "terrific wine program" that includes "half-price bottles on
Sundays"; the bar scene is "happening" and the "live music" is a "bonus" (those who prefer a "quieter" evening may want to head "upstairs"), and while some feel the food is "not consistent", for others
it remains a "special dining experience."

**NEW Peasant Bistro** *French/Mediterranean*  - | - | - | M

**Downtown** | 250 Park Ave. West NW (Marietta St. NW) | 404-230-1724 |
www.peasantatl.com

Veteran restaurateurs Maureen Kalmanson and Pamela Furr
(Mick's, Pleasant Peasant) bring this midpriced newcomer to a
Downtown location overlooking Centennial Park, where chef Shane
Devereux creates French- and Mediterranean-accented bistro fare;
an eclectic art collection pops on rich smoky walls in the new two-
story, made-to-look-old space with brick columns, a sweeping stair-
case and a main level bar.

**Penang** *Malaysian/Thai*  22 | 16 | 19 | $17

**Buford Hwy. (Chamblee)** | Orient Ctr. | 4897 Buford Hwy. NE
(Chamblee Tucker Rd.) | Chamblee | 770-220-0308 |
www.penangatlanta.com

Fans tout this Buford Highway "standout" as a "solid" choice delivering "consistently" "tasty" Malaysian and Thai fare that makes for
a "fine foreign feast" to "share" with "friends"; a "helpful" staff
guides you through dozens of "exotic specialties", including "exceptional dirt-cheap lunch options"; the "wonderfully tacky" "tropical"
decor may be "cartoon"-like, but everything else is the "real deal."

**Persepolis** *Persian*  21 | 14 | 16 | $24

**Sandy Springs** | 6435 E. Roswell Rd. (Abernathy Rd.) | 404-257-9090 |
www.persepoliscuisine.com

"The food will take you to another place and time" at this "delicious"
Sandy Springs Persian where "kebabs rule" but there are "lots" of
other "amazing" "taste sensations" that will "make you want more",

including an "ample" lunch buffet spread; sure, the strip-mall space "could do with a sprucing up", but the "quality" fare and "delightful" service make it "well worth a visit."

### Petite Auberge ☒ *Continental* | 19 | 14 | 19 | $33 |

**Emory** | Toco Hills Shopping Ctr. | 2935 N. Druid Hills Rd. (Lavista Rd.) | 404-634-6268 | www.petiteauberge.com

This Toco Hills Continental garners a "loyal following of Decatur matrons", "retirees" and others who appreciate the "consistent" "old-world" cuisine sans "experimental pretense" and the "old-fashioned formal service"; "yeah, the place looks a little dated", but "it still has heart", which "makes up for a lot of things."

### P.F. Chang's China Bistro *Chinese* | 20 | 21 | 19 | $26 |

**Marietta** | Cumberland Mall | 1624 Cumberland Mall SE (Cobb Pkwy.) | 770-803-5800
**Alpharetta** | 7925 N. Point Pkwy. (Mansell Rd.) | 770-992-3070
**Buford** | Mall of Georgia | 3333 Buford Dr. (Mall of Georgia Dr.) | 678-546-9005
**Dunwoody** | 500 Ashwood Pkwy. (Ashford Dunwoody Rd.) | 770-352-0500
www.pfchangs.com

Expect "major hustle-bustle" at these "noisy" links of the Chinese chain, where the "sanitized", "mass-produced" menus "aren't really authentic" yet do "appeal to most palates" (when in doubt, the "lettuce wraps rule"); no one minds the "spotty" service and "ersatz" Sino decor since they "have the formula down" – starting with "nothing-fancy" prices and an overall "fun" vibe.

### Pho Dai Loi *Vietnamese* | ∇ 22 | 10 | 16 | $10 |

**Forest Park** | 4061 Jonesboro Rd. (Conley Rd.) | 404-363-2423

Forest Park phonatics who "have the itch" for "excellent Vietnamese" head to this "wonderful" no-frills find that "rivals any place on Buford Highway" with its "sound", "authentic" fare, including "some of the best pho in town"; bargain prices and "clean" digs are other reasons it's "recommended" by regulars.

### Pho Hoa *Vietnamese* | ∇ 19 | 7 | 13 | $13 |

**Buford Hwy. (Doraville)** | Asian Sq. | 5150 Buford Hwy. (I-285) | Doraville | 770-455-8729 | www.phohoa.com

"Hot bowls" of "delicious pho" and other "spicy" "comfort food" "as spicy as you may want it" attracts phans to this Doraville Vietnamese where you can be "daring" and "try anything" on the menu according to insiders; the "mirrors-and-neon" decor notwithstanding ("didn't all the '70s casinos get imploded?"), many are willing to take the "dive into Vietnam."

### Pho 79 *Vietnamese* | ∇ 26 | 15 | 22 | $14 |

**Buford Hwy. (Doraville)** | 5000 Winters Chapel Rd. NW (Peeler Rd.) | Doraville | 404-728-9129

They "know pho" at this "hidden gem" on Buford Highway where neophytes can "discover the breadth and depth of Vietnamese cuisine" thanks to its "authentic" bill of fare, including "really good" and "warm" soups and "even warmer service"; the "updated set-

FOOD DECOR SERVICE COST

ting" is "surprisingly child-friendly", and the "cheap and satisfying" experience is "well worth the search."

**Phuket Thai** ⊠ *Thai*                    ▽ 19 | 15 | 20 | $18

**Buford Hwy. (Atlanta)** | 2839 Buford Hwy. NE (N. Druid Hills Rd.) | 404-325-4199

Fans "have fun" just "pronouncing the name" of this "often over-looked" Buford Highway Thai and "rave" about the "divine" cuisine that's both "plentiful" and "inexpensive", washed down with "their own" microbrew beer from Bangkok; "attentive" service makes it a "special dining treat" despite the "crummy strip-mall" space with "dingy Oriental" decor "circa 1950s."

**Pig-N-Chik** *BBQ*                          19 | 7 | 14 | $12

**Chamblee** | 5071 Peachtree Industrial Blvd. (Clairmont Rd.) | 770-451-1112
**Sandy Springs** | Fountain Oaks Shopping Ctr. | 4920 Roswell Rd. NE (Long Island Dr.) | 404-255-6368
www.pignchik.net

The pit masters at this smoky pair in Sandy Springs and Chamblee have "turned BBQ into a science", creating "pure pulled [pork] pleasure" that "lives up to the hype" and Brunswick stew "with a kick"; the "simple" decor isn't an "issue since you're in and out in no time", but if it is, "carryout" is "as good as dine in" – either way, it's "dependable and cheap."

**NEW Pisces** ● *Seafood*                     - | - | - | M

**Alpharetta** | 4120 Old Milton Pkwy. (Alexander Dr.) | 770-475-0057 | www.piscesseafoodandjazz.com

As well as fresh fin fare, steaks and a carefully chosen wine list, this Alpharetta seafooder offers brunch on Sundays and live jazz every night; the freestanding building sports cozy seating nooks, functional private dining and a lively bar, while stone fireplaces add a touch of warmth to the spacious dining room, where the music stage generates some heat of its own.

**Pittypat's Porch** *Southern*               15 | 17 | 17 | $35

**Downtown** | 25 Andrew Young Int'l Blvd. NW (Spring St.) | 404-525-8228 | www.pittypatsrestaurant.com

"Hoop skirts and magnolia blossoms will have you whistling Dixie" at this Downtown "institution" where "classic" Southern fare and an interior that "evokes images of *Gone With the Wind*" make it a "must-see" for "newbies to Atlanta"; skeptics dismiss it as a "tourist trap with all the trimmings" that "might have been good in Margaret Mitchell's day", but now "the bloom is off the mint julep."

**Pleasant Peasant** *American*               19 | 17 | 19 | $32

**Midtown** | 555 Peachtree St. NE (Linden Ave.) | 404-874-3223 | www.thepeasantrestaurants.com

While it may "not [be] edgy", for "consistency and value" this veteran Midtown American is "still a winner", and the "perfect choice" for "business" lunches and pre- and après-"Fox" or "symphony"; the "intimate" setting is "upscale" but "relaxed", and while a few feel it's getting "tired", for many others it remains a "nostalgic favorite."

| | FOOD | DECOR | SERVICE | COST |
|---|---|---|---|---|

### Portofino  *Italian*

| | 21 | 19 | 21 | $37 |
|---|---|---|---|---|

**Buckhead** | 3199 Paces Ferry Pl. NW (bet. E. Andrews Dr. & W. Paces Ferry Rd.) | 404-231-1136 | www.portofinobistro.com

A "well-rounded menu" of "dynamite" Italian fare, and "extensive wines by the glass" and flights from the "excellent" "but inexpensive" list are the "real attraction" of this "charming" Buckhead venue, although "'tis a dream to dine in the spring" on the "lovely" "brick" patio "under the trees" as well; the "splendid" staff "tries hard" to please, and prices that "won't break the bank" make it "a place to come back to again and again."

### Pricci  *Italian*

| | 24 | 21 | 23 | $47 |
|---|---|---|---|---|

**Buckhead** | 500 Pharr Rd. NE (Maple Dr.) | 404-237-2941 | www.buckheadrestaurants.com

The "open kitchen" at this "high-energy" Buckhead Life Group entry "helps whet the appetite" for the "first-rate", "upscale Italian" cuisine that "always seems to hit the target", while "cheerful" service from an "experienced" staff adds to the "great vibe"; the "lovely" (yet "dated") "'80s"-esque room is "comfortable" if "not memorable", and often "noisy" with a "lively crowd" of business types, theatergoers and "out-of-towners."

### Prime  *Seafood/Steak*

| | 23 | 19 | 21 | $44 |
|---|---|---|---|---|

**Buckhead** | Lenox Sq. | 3393 Peachtree Rd. NE (Lenox Rd.) | 404-812-0555 | www.heretoserverestaurants.com

An "enjoyable", "white-tablecloth" "retreat from the hustle" of the Lenox Square Mall can be found at this steakhouse-and-seafood sibling of Twist, Shout, Posh, Prime and Lola, where "standout" steaks and "well-presented sushi" make a fashion statement; "kid-friendly" service, "top-drawer people-watching" and one of the "best early-bird specials in town" are further reasons to "get away from the food court and let your dollars fly."

### Provisions to Go  ☒ *Deli*

| | ▽ 25 | 18 | 22 | $20 |
|---|---|---|---|---|

**Westside** | Westside Mktpl. | 1198 Howell Mill Rd. NW (Huff Rd.) | 404-365-0410 | www.starprovisions.com

Bacchanalia fans can get "a taste of the good life without breaking the bank" at this "superb" deli sibling located at the entrance of Star Provisions in the Westside, where "top-notch ingredients" go into "wonderful sandwiches", "scrumptious desserts" and "delicious" breads; the decor may be "off" but the shelves are crammed with lots of "visual eye candy", and while all this "fine dining on a sandwich budget" isn't cheap, "who said takeaway has to be pedestrian?"

### Pub 71  *Irish*

| | 18 | 17 | 18 | $19 |
|---|---|---|---|---|

**Brookhaven** | Brookhaven Station | 4058 Peachtree Rd. NE (Dresden Dr.) | 404-467-8271 | www.pub71.com

The "friendly" "staff always entertains" at this Brookhaven Irish public house serving pub grub staples such as fish-'n'-chips that are "worth the trip" as well as "cheap drinks" ("what more could a guy want?"); the *Cheers*-like setting "can be crowded on weekend nights" at this "neighborhood" "hangout spot."

|  | FOOD | DECOR | SERVICE | COST |
|---|---|---|---|---|

**Pung Mie** *Chinese*  ∇ 21 | 15 | 17 | $24

**Buford Hwy. (Doraville)** | 5145 Buford Hwy. NE (Shallowford Rd.) | Doraville | 770-455-0435

For "upscale Chinese" in an "elegant" setting "on Buford Highway" – no, "you didn't read wrong" – this "reliable" spot is singled out for its "many varieties" of "expertly prepared" dishes, including some "exotic" offerings, bolstered by "noodles and breads" that "make it worth" the trip; "helpful" servers navigate the "massive" space with "lots of private rooms" and "even a stage."

**Pura Vida** *Pan-Latin*  25 | 19 | 22 | $33

**Poncey-Highland** | 656 N. Highland Ave. NE (bet. North Ave. & Ponce de Leon Blvd.) | 404-870-9797 | www.puravidatapas.com

"Genius" chef Hector Santiago is a "master in taste" who "doesn't dumb down his dishes" at his "small-plates nirvana" in Poncey-Highland, where "amazingly original" Latin tapas are paired with "excellent mojitos" and "seemingly bottomless pitchers" of sangria; "good service", "cool surroundings" and choice "location" make it a "terrific date spot", although wallet-watchers warn the "creative bites can bite your pocketbook."

**Pure Taqueria** *Mexican*  23 | 19 | 18 | $21

**Alpharetta** | 103 Roswell St. (Old Milton Pkwy.) | 678-240-0023 | www.knowwheretogogh.com

One of the "hippest" spots on the north side, this "upscale" Alpharetta taqueria from the owners of Bistro VG, Aspens and Vinny's on Windward is dishing out "unique" Mexican cuisine full of "new and inventive flavors" in a "renovated" garage structure named after the old gas station next door; while some feel it "needs to work on staff training", pros promise a "magical" experience.

**⧫ Quinones Room** 28 | 27 | 29 | $114
**at Bacchanalia** ⧩Ⓜ *American*

**Westside** | Courtyard of Bacchanalia | 1198 Howell Mill Rd. (bet. 14th St. & Huff Rd.) | 404-365-0410 | www.starprovisions.com

"Worth the raid on the wallet", this Westside "stunner" from the owners of Bacchanalia is Atlanta's No. 1 for Service in this Survey thanks to an "extremely professional but friendly" staff that deftly delivers eight- to 10-course tasting menus of "inspired, world-class" American cuisine and "perfect" optional wine pairings; the "elegantly chic" room with "very few seats" is "like a jewel box", although the ambiance is "unpretentious" and the "antithesis of stuffy", all of which makes for an "exceptional dining experience" "from beginning to end."

**Raging Burrito** *Californian/Mexican*  18 | 14 | 16 | $14

**Decatur** | 141 Sycamore St. (Church St.) | 404-377-3311 | www.ragingburrito.com

"If you like burritos without the big corporate spin", this Decatur Cal-Mex "may be the border for you to cross", serving "overflowing" "custom-made" eponymous wraps, "tasty" margaritas and a "great selection of microbrews"; the "hip" staff is a little "slow" but "tourists",

|  | FOOD | DECOR | SERVICE | COST |
|--|------|-------|---------|------|

"business" types and "students on a budget" manage to "chill" in the "grubby-pubby" digs or on one of the "best" patios "on the square."

### Raja Indian  *Indian* ▽ 19 | 10 | 16 | $26

**Buckhead** | 2955 Peachtree Rd. NE (bet. Peachtree Ave. & Pharr Rd.) | 404-237-2661

The naan is "warm and fluffy" and the "spices are right on" in "any of the tandooris, saags" and "adventurous curries" at this "solid" Buckhead Indian "on the Peachtree main drag"; it's "strong" on service (if not on decor) and moderately priced, making it a "dependable" option for "family dining."

### Rare ● *Soul Food* ▽ 24 | 24 | 18 | $35

**Midtown** | 554 Piedmont Ave. NE (North Ave.) | 404-541-0665 | www.rareatl.com

A "diverse crowd" that includes some of the "chicest people you'll ever encounter" comes to "see and be seen" at Lorenzo Wyche's "new concept" in Midtown serving "experimental" but "delicious" "soul food tapas"; there's a "slew of wonderful choices" of small plates, which "you can share" in the "cool", "refreshingly sexy" space where "beds" serve as seats, making this midpriced spot the "perfect social meeting place" in the minds of many.

### ☑ Rathbun's ☒ *American* 28 | 25 | 25 | $48

**Inman Park** | Stove Works | 112 Krog St. NE (bet. Edgewood Ave. NE & Irwin St. NE) | 404-524-8280 | www.rathbunsrestaurant.com

Just "throw a dart at the menu" when ordering, for "you cannot go wrong" at this "superb" Inman Park New American from a "genius" chef, where "everything feels right and tastes fabulous", "from little plates to 'mortgage' plates"; "wonderful wines" and "decadent desserts" also win praise, and a "stellar" staff works the "enormous" "industrial-chic" space with a "high-energy" bar and a "wine room" that offers sanctuary to those who find the scene too "loud"; still, expect to "wait" "even with a reservation."

### Ray's in the City  *Seafood* 22 | 20 | 20 | $36

**Downtown** | 240 Peachtree St. NE (bet. Andrew Young Int'l Blvd. & Harris St.) | 404-524-9224 | www.raysrestaurants.com

This urban sibling of Ray's Killer Creek is "much needed" on the Downtown scene, "pleasantly surprising" nine-to-fivers with a "variety" of "super-fresh" and "beautifully prepared" seafood and sushi; "reasonable prices" and "courteous" "quick" service make it "great for a business lunch" or "quiet dinner", but foes find the "inconsistent" fare a bit fishy.

### Ray's Killer Creek  *Steak* 22 | 23 | 23 | $42
### (fka Killer Creek Chophouse)

**Alpharetta** | 1700 Mansell Rd. (GA 400) | 770-649-0064 | www.raysrestaurants.com

Cronies crow you "could do a lot worse", but "it'd be hard to do much better" in the "'burbs" than this "killer" "high-end" Alpharetta meatery from Ray Schoenbaum (Ray's on the River, Ray's in the City) serving "fantastic steaks", "excellent sides" and an "expansive" wine list to a "swanky OTP set"; a "friendly" staff makes guests feel like they "own the place", and the "chalet"-inspired interior, while a "little loud at times", is "beautiful", making this a "strong" choice for "impressing" "friends", "business guests" or "that certain someone."

### Ray's New York Pizza  *Pizza*
| 18 | 10 | 15 | $15 |

**Alpharetta** | 5230 Windward Pkwy. W. (GA 400) | 770-521-0222
**Sandy Springs** | Sandy Spring Plaza | 6309 Roswell Rd. (Mt. Vernon Rd.) | 404-252-9888
www.raysnypizza.com

"If you're a fan of thick-crust" pizza, the "great variety" of "brick-oven" beauties at this pizzeria duo in Alpharetta and Sandy Springs (new construction sealed the fate of the Buckhead original) can be "addictive"; the service is "hit-or-miss" in the "pleasant, super-casual" setting, and while skeptics scoff that it "wouldn't make it anywhere near Broadway", fans shrug "so it's not NY – this is Atlanta."

### Ray's on the River  *Seafood*
| 23 | 23 | 21 | $42 |

**Sandy Springs** | 6700 Powers Ferry Rd. NW (I-285) | 770-955-1187 | www.raysrestaurants.com

"Heaven on the river" is what admirers call this seafood sibling of Ray's Killer Creek and Ray's in the City for its "new", "New Yorkish" space that's "as pretty on the inside" as the "scenic views of the Chattahoochee River" outside; new chef Tom McEachern adds "a bit of zing" to the "reincarnated" menu of "always delicious" fin fare, the Sunday brunch is one of the "best in town" and the staff is "knowledgeable."

### Real Chow Baby  *American/Asian*
| 20 | 14 | 15 | $18 |

**Westside** | 1016 Howell Mill Rd. NW (10th St.) | 404-815-4900 | www.therealchowbaby.com

This "modernized Mongolian"-American "stir-fry" spot on the Westside attracts "gastronomists" ready for an "all-you-can-eat", "design-it-yourself" meal featuring a "wide variety of ingredients" and "brought to life" by "grill chefs" – insiders advise "some trial and error is in order" unless you "stick to the recipes" given; there's a "young and happening" vibe in the often "noisy" setting, where "interminable lines" are to be expected, and some cynics suspect servers are "hired with no experience necessary."

### Redfish, a Creole Bistro  *Cajun/Creole*
| 22 | 19 | 22 | $32 |

**Grant Park** | 687 Memorial Dr. SE (Cameron St. SE) | 404-475-1200 | www.redfishcreole.com

A "pleasant surprise" in "a reviving part of town" near Oakland Cemetery, this "outstanding" Cajun-Creole offers "yummy" bayou-inspired cuisine at "modest prices", served by "friendly" servers who "seem genuinely glad to have you"; while a "fish tank and a fireplace" are the highlights of decor in need of an "overhaul", the atmosphere is "interesting" and pros insist it's "a place you cannot judge by the cover."

|  | FOOD | DECOR | SERVICE | COST |
|---|---|---|---|---|

### Red Snapper ⓜ *Seafood*     `22` `13` `22` `$28`

**Cheshire Bridge** | 2100 Cheshire Bridge Rd. (Lavista Rd.) | 404-634-8947 | www.redsnapperatlanta.com

The "time-warp" decor may be as "tired as" some of the "older clientele", but "don't let that put you off" this "intown fave" seafooder in a rather "iffy" section of Cheshire Bridge serving "many" "excellent choices" of "divine snapper" and other fin fare that make it a "very good value"; a "friendly staff" waits on an "interesting mix" of "regulars", "old-timers" and the occasional "lost patron of nearby strip bars", making it a "quirky", yet "quality experience."

### 🆕 Relish *Southern*     `23` `20` `21` `$26`

**Roswell** | 590 Mimosa Blvd. (Marietta Hwy.) | 770-650-7877 | www.relishgoodfood.com

Fans are dead certain the masses will "get over the fact" that this "excellent" and "fairly priced" Roswell Southerner (sibling of the Fickle Pickle) is housed in a "converted funeral home", thanks to its "fantastic" "down-home cooking" with a "modern twist", served in a "slightly upscale", yet "kid-friendly" setting; critics blame the "stone walls" and "hardwood floors" for the "deafening noise" levels, which was probably never a problem in its previous incarnation; P.S. regulars recommend the outdoor "terrace tables" "when it's warm enough."

### Repast ⓩ *American*     `24` `23` `23` `$45`

**Midtown** | 620 Glen Iris Dr. NE (North Ave.) | 404-870-8707 | www.repastrestaurant.com

Appealing to an "environmentally conscious crowd", this "vibrant" Midtown New American is "off the beaten path" but very much on track with "earthy", yet "elegant dishes" prepared "with heart" by the "husband-and-wife" chef-owners who "really care about the food", which is served with "unique wine options" by an "informed", "friendly" staff; "posh loft decor" defines the "open" space that also boasts an "intimate" bar and "lovely" outdoor patio, all of which make for an "unpretentious, scrumptious" experience.

### 🄩 Restaurant Eugene *American*     `28` `26` `26` `$59`

**South Buckhead** | The Aramore | 2277 Peachtree Rd. NE (Peachtree Memorial Dr.) | 404-355-0321 | www.restauranteugene.com

"There aren't enough good things to say about" this "magnificent" South Buckhead establishment that draws "locavores" as well as "foodies" with "magical", "world-class" New American cuisine with a "sublime" Southern drawl, including a "fantastic" "Sunday supper" that "warms the heart and soul"; the wine list is "fabulous", and an "enthusiastic" "mixologist" "whips up" "don't-miss drinks", while "point-perfect" servers "pamper" guests in the "elegant", "wonderfully quiet" space; though it's "aggressively priced", most agree it's "worth it" for "absolute perfection" "without a lot of attitude."

### Rexall Grill ⓢⓜ⌀ *Diner*     ▽ `20` `13` `20` `$9`

**Duluth** | 3165 Buford Hwy. (Rte. 120) | 770-623-8569 | www.rexallgrill.com

"They'll know you aren't from these parts if you ask for a menu" at this "classic" "local hangout" in Duluth, basically a "diner in a drug store", but pros promise you "won't be disappointed" with "ample servings" of "Southern-style meat-and-three" fare served up "quick"; it's a "blast from the past" with "authentic memorabilia" and a "small-town" feel, where the "local state representative", "constituents" and folks who have been "customers for almost 20 years" all "socialize."

### Ria's Bluebird  *Diner*

23 | 15 | 17 | $14

**Cabbagetown** | 421 Memorial Dr. SE (Cherokee Ave.) | 404-521-3737 | www.riasbluebird.com

"Meat eaters and vegheads" alike feel "at home" at this "popular" "bohemian" diner in Cabbagetown that offers "fantastic" all-day breakfast fare and "scrumptious" "vegetarian options", served by a "sassy, no-nonsense" staff that's "brusque" – "in a good way"; the "cozy-hippie" spot near "historic" Oakland Cemetery sports a cheery "expanse of floor-to-ceiling windows" that cast light on "great people-watching" and "piercings" and "tattoo" spotting, but "be prepared" to "wait on weekends."

### Rib Ranch  *BBQ*

∇ 18 | 13 | 19 | $17

**Marietta** | 2063 Canton Rd. (Sandy Plains Rd.) | 770-422-5755 | www.theribranch.com

It may be "in the middle of nowhere", but this "friendly" Marietta BBQ is the center of the universe for longtime fans who make the "tender" "saucy" beef and "Texas-style" ribs a "part of all family functions"; while purists complain the "plasma TV" "kills the old roadhouse feel" to some degree, there's still "tons of junk to look at on the walls", such as snakes and license plates.

### ⨀ Rice Thai Cuisine  ⧄ *Thai*

26 | 22 | 24 | $26

**Roswell** | 1104 Canton St. (Woodstock St.) | 770-640-0788 | www.goforthai.com

"Superlatives" abound about this "charming", if "pricey", Thai "in old Roswell" and its "tasty", "incredibly fresh" cuisine that isn't the "run-of-the-mill" fare and features vegetables "grown in the owner's garden"; a "friendly staff" moves through the small rooms of the "awesome house", adorned with "interesting" "artwork" that's "almost as good as the food", and sitting on the "tiny front porch" is a "delight when it's nice out."

### Righteous Room  ☽ *Pub Food*

∇ 22 | 13 | 19 | $14

**Poncey-Highland** | 1051 Ponce de Leon Ave. NE (N. Highland Ave.) | 404-874-0939

Poncey-Highland hipsters report there's "surprisingly good" American pub grub and "friendly" service at this "dive" near the La Font Theater; tunes from a "great jukebox" fill the "smoky" air, and work by "local artists" adorn the walls – if you can see it in the "dark" digs.

### Rising Roll Sandwich Co.  ⧄ *Deli*

20 | 12 | 18 | $11

**Alpharetta** | 11417 Haynes Bridge Rd. (GA 400) | 770-752-8082
**Midtown** | Atlantic Center Plaza Bldg. | 1180 W. Peachtree St. NW (14th St.) | 404-815-6787
**Westside** | 1700 Northside Dr. (I-75) | 404-351-2881

*(continued)*

## Rising Roll Sandwich Co.

**Lawrenceville** | 1812 N. Brown Rd. (Sugarloaf Pkwy. NW) |
678-847-6088
**Norcross** | 5270 Peachtree Pkwy. (Technology Pkwy.) |
770-326-6606
**Hapeville** | 832 Virginia Ave. (Doug Davis Dr.) | 404-669-1170
www.risingroll.com

The "sandwich makers don't mess around" at this chain of deli
"lunchtime favorites" all over town, where "fantastic" "fresh-
baked" breads are "piled" so "high" with "interesting" ingredients
it's "tough to fit them in your mouth"; it's "always busy" with "weekday office crowds" but the service is "friendly", and even though
some wiseacres dub it "Rising Prices", many agree it "blows
away" the competition.

## ☑ Ritz-Carlton Atlanta Grill *Southern*   26 | 24 | 26 | $60

**Downtown** | Ritz-Carlton Atlanta | 181 Peachtree St. NE (Ellis St.) |
404-659-0400 | www.ritzcarlton.com

With "new, hip" chef Bennett Hollberg in the kitchen, this "special-
occasion" hotel spot has locals rejoicing over its "superior"
"Southern cuisine", including a brunch that can "wake the dead",
and "white-glove service" from a "first-class" staff, featuring a "talented sommelier"; it's a "calm oasis" in the hubbub of Downtown,
especially on the "balcony overlooking Peachtree", and the
"cheater's booth" is a "great place for romantic dates" – in sum, it's
"everything you'd expect from the Ritz."

## Ritz-Carlton Buckhead Café *Continental*   24 | 24 | 24 | $55

**Buckhead** | Ritz-Carlton Buckhead | 3434 Peachtree Rd. NE (Lenox Rd.) |
404-237-2700 | www.ritzcarlton.com

You'll feel like a "pampered grown-up" at this "consistent" lobby
cafe in "one of Atlanta's best hotels", where the Buckhead business
set and Ritz-Carlton guests gravitate for "wonderful" Continental
cuisine, an "expansive, inventive brunch" and "excellent" service in
"lovely", "quiet" surroundings with "incredibly comfortable chairs";
a few feel that it "needs a revamp", while others insist you "can't go
wrong" with this "class act."

## ☑ Ritz-Carlton Buckhead   27 | 26 | 28 | $87
## Dining Room ☒ Ⓜ *French/Mediterranean*

**Buckhead** | Ritz-Carlton Buckhead | 3434 Peachtree Rd. NE (Lenox Rd.) |
404-237-2700 | www.ritzcarlton.com

This "crème de la crème" of the Ritz-Carlton Buckhead would be "a
top restaurant anywhere" gush guests who are "blown away" by the
"inventive", "delicious" French-Med cuisine and "awesome wine
pairings", presented by an "extraordinary" staff that "cossets you
from the outset" (maitre d' Claude Guillaume "is a god"); the
"elegant" room is one of the "quietest" "in town", which makes for
"relaxing" "romantic" meals and "celebrations", and while this
"once-in-a-lifetime experience" "does not come cheap", most agree
it's "worth the price tag."

|  | FOOD | DECOR | SERVICE | COST |
|---|---|---|---|---|

### River Room 🗷 American
21 | 21 | 21 | $43

**Vinings** | Riverside by Post | 4403 Northside Pkwy. NW
(bet. Chattahoochee River & Mt. Paran Rd.) | 404-233-5455 |
www.riverroom.com

The signature "crab cakes alone are reason to find" this "tremendous"
Vinings New American where the "revamped menu" is "more interesting" than ever, making it a "solid" choice for "business lunches"
and "first dates", in a location "convenient" for folks "in the 'burbs
to meet friends from the city"; while the service is "inconsistent",
the "town square" setting near the Chattahoochee is "awesome."

### Roasters American
20 | 12 | 20 | $16

**Smyrna** | 2997 Cumberland Blvd. (Cumberland Mall) |
770-333-6222
**Buckhead** | 2770 Lenox Rd. NE (Buford Hwy.) | 404-237-1122
**Sandy Springs** | 6225B Roswell Rd. NE (Johnson Ferry Rd.) | 678-701-1100
www.roastersfresh.com

"Pig out and still feel self righteous" at this American trio praised for
its "healthy" "rotisserie-style" fare, including "succulent" "chicken
any which way" and "excellent homestyle veggies"; "fast", "friendly"
and "easy on the pocketbook", they're "dependable" options for a
"family" meal or a snack after the "gym", so decor that deserves a
"negative" score doesn't deter fans.

### Rolling Bones Premium Pit BBQ BBQ
22 | 12 | 15 | $14

**Downtown** | 377 Edgewood Ave. SE (Jackson St.) | 404-222-2324 |
www.rollingbonesbbq.com

Intowners "in search of real Texas BBQ" are "gaga" over this "clever"
'cue "spot with character" in Downtown serving "terrific" "smoky
meats", including the "best brisket this side of" the Lone Star State;
it's housed in a "nifty" "renovated gas station" space that "beat the
gentrification rush" to an "um . . . 'transitional'" part of town.

### NEW Room at Twelve American/Steak
▽ 22 | 25 | 21 | $50

**Downtown** | TWELVE Centennial Park | 400 W. Peachtree St. NW
(Ivan Allen Blvd.) | 404-418-1250 | www.roomattwelve.com

Chef "Nick Oltarsh has done it again" with this steakhouse at the
TWELVE Centennial Park, compliments of Concentrics Restaurants
(ONE, TWO, Trois and TAP), a "wonderful new addition to the
Downtown dining scene" where people can count on "tremendous"
meats and "mouthwatering" "sushi"; the sleek "Euro" space is "attractive", and the expansive bar at the entrance is often "packed"
with a see-and-be-seen crowd, even at "lunchtime."

### Rosa Mexicano Mexican
19 | 22 | 19 | $32

**Atlantic Station** | 245 18th St. NW (W. District Ave.) | 404-347-4090 |
www.rosamexicano.com

A "mesmerizing" water feature highlights the "resortlike" setting at
this Atlantic Station link of the "spicy" NYC Mexican chain where
the "irresistible", "upscale" cuisine (*fantastico* guacamole "prepared tableside") is "not your typical Tex-Mex"; service ranges from
"flirty" to "arrogant", and enemigos who find the fare "overpriced"

and "overrated" would rather "eat a sombrero" – as long as they could wash it down with an "incredible" pomegranate margarita.

**Rose of India**  *Indian*  ▽ 19 | 11 | 20 | $20

**Chamblee** | 4847 Peachtree Rd. NE (off Ashford Dunwoody Rd.) | 678-330-1525

This "dinky", "seemingly secret" strip-mall Indian in Chamblee blooms with "wonderful" fare and "friendly" service, but a few grouse that it seems "every time you blink the prices are higher"; a "whacked-out pink" color scheme "casts a funeral parlor glow" on the place, but hey, the food is "good" – and they "deliver"; N.B. it now has a liquor license.

**Roy's**  *Hawaiian*  23 | 22 | 23 | $49

**Buckhead** | 3475 Piedmont Rd. NE (Lenox Rd.) | 404-231-3232 | www.roysrestaurant.com

Boosters say "book 'em, Danno" (reservations, that is) for a "delicious" "trip to paradise" at this Buckhead link in Roy Yamaguchi's national chain where "amazing" Hawaiian "fusion" cuisine is so "vibrant" and "well presented" that guests have "brought cameras to dinner"; expect "personalized service" in a "beautiful" room with a "vacation" feel.

**R. Thomas**  19 | 18 | 16 | $17

**Deluxe Grill** ● *American/Vegetarian*

**South Buckhead** | 1812 Peachtree Rd. NW (bet. Collier Rd. & 26th St.) | 404-881-0246 | www.rthomasdeluxegrill.com

It's "like stepping through the looking glass" at this 24/7 South Buckhead "destination for homeopaths and granolaheads" that "caters to anyone's taste" with "tasty" New American and vegetarian fare; "eclectic" waiters blend in with a "bohemian" outdoor scene that also includes "gorgeous" live birds, "psychics" and "lawn ornaments" – "what more could you want late at night?"

**Rumi's Kitchen**  *Persian*  24 | 19 | 19 | $30

**Sandy Springs** | 6152 Roswell Rd. NE (Hilderbrand Dr.) | 404-477-2100 | www.rumiskitchen.com

"Avid" aficionados "highly recommend" this "popular" Sandy Springs Persian for its "major delicious" fare that's a "cut above" the competition; it's "full of personality", the staff is "extremely friendly" and the "intimate" (read: "small"), "trendy"-looking space is "packed every night of the week" so "reservations are a must."

**Ru San's**  *Japanese*  18 | 12 | 16 | $21

**Marietta** | 2313 Windy Hill Rd. SE (Cobb Pkwy.) | 770-933-8315

**Midtown** | Ansley Sq. | 1529 Piedmont Ave. NE (Monroe Dr.) | 404-875-7042

**Buckhead** | Tower Pl. | 3365 Piedmont Rd. NE (Peachtree Rd. NE) | 404-239-9557

This "American-friendly" Japanese trio is "immensely popular" for its "enormous menu" of "sushi with training wheels" (read: "cooked fish"), "cross-cultural rolls" and "super" lunch buffet, served in a "rowdy" setting with a "spirited" staff and the "highest decibels in town"; purists pan the "yard-sale quality" eats, but if you "don't take it too seriously", it's "a riot" – and a "cheap" one at that.

### Ruth's Chris Steak House  *Steak*    | 23 | 20 | 23 | $56 |

**Buckhead** | Embassy Suites Hotel | 3285 Peachtree Rd. NE (Piedmont Rd.) | 404-365-0660
**Downtown** | Embassy Suites Hotel | 267 Marietta St. (Park Ave. W.) | 404-223-6500
**Sandy Springs** | 5788 Roswell Rd. (I-285, exit 25) | 404-255-0035
www.ruthschris.com

"Nothing beats a steak sizzling in butter" at this "special-occasion", New Orleans–based chain where the "melt-in-your-mouth" chops are "cooked to perfection" and presented on "hot plates"; sure, the "decor varies" – from "blah" to "old-fashioned in a good way" – but service is "attentive" and the "off-the-charts" pricing manageable "so long as your boss doesn't care how much you spend."

### Sage on Sycamore  Ⓜ *American*    | 20 | 20 | 20 | $28 |

**Decatur** | 121 Sycamore St. (Church St.) | 404-373-5574 |
www.thebistros.com

For a bit of "laid-back luxury", Decaturites descend on this New American in the historic town square for "delicious" eats at "excellent prices" "balanced by" a "great wine list", served by a "friendly" staff in a "warm", "easy environment"; while some sniff that it "never quite excites", most agree the "whole experience" is "always a good one."

### Sala – Sabor de Mexico  *Mexican*    | 19 | 21 | 20 | $27 |

**Virginia-Highland** | 1186 N. Highland Ave. NE (Amsterdam Ave.) | 404-872-7203 | www.sala-atlanta.com

An "authentic Mexican experience" can be had at this "very cool" Virginia-Highland spot featuring "delicious", "upscale" small plates and entrees, "killer" margaritas "shaken at the table", an "amazing" tequila selection, "big wine list" and "polished" service; textured walls and dark woods accent the rustic interior, while the outdoor patio is a "perfect way to spend a sunny afternoon."

### Sal Grosso  *Brazilian/Steak*    | 21 | 19 | 20 | $48 |

**Cobb** | 1927 Powers Ferry Rd. SE (Windy Hill Rd.) | 770-850-1540 |
www.salgrosso.com

If you "love meat on a sword", you can "eat to your heart's desire" at this "decent" Cobb County "entry in the Brazilian meat wars" that costs "less per head" than some of its competitors; while some beef about "spotty" fare and "inconsistent" service ranging from "excellent" to "surly", others call it a "classy all-you-can-eat" that's "worth the money."

### Salsa  Ⓢ *Cuban*    ▽ | 18 | 17 | 16 | $19 |

**Midtown** | Howell Mill Vill. | 2020 Howell Mill Rd. NW (Collier Rd.) | 404-352-3101
**East Atlanta** | 749 Moreland Ave. SE (Ormewood Ave.) | 404-624-3105

For a "cheap" "night out with friends" or a "family-friendly" meal, fans are "delighted" with this Cuban pair in Midtown and East

| | FOOD | DECOR | SERVICE | COST |
|---|---|---|---|---|

Atlanta serving "impressive" fare with a "slight gourmet edge"; while the service can be "hit-or-miss", the settings are "cheery" and the "prices are perfect"; P.S. the "expanded bar" is a "delightful addition" at the Howell Mill Village location.

## ☒ Sam & Dave's BBQ1 *BBQ*

| | 26 | 8 | 18 | $13 |

**Marietta** | 4944 Lower Roswell Rd. (Richmond Hill Dr. NE) | 770-977-3005

## ☒ Sam & Dave's BBQ2 ☒ *BBQ*

**Marietta** | 660 Whitlock Ave. NW (Lindley Ave. NW) | 770-792-2272
www.lostmountainbbq.com

The "best brisket, buns down", "pulled pork like no other" and other "phenomenal" fare make this Marietta duo Atlanta's smokehouse "champions" (voted No. 1 for BBQ), and the "best choice for funeral drop-off food", where "wonderful" "local owners" "wow" "fans" with their "flavorful, smoky" concoctions; "if you want atmosphere you're in the wrong place", but for "real" 'cue, they're a "must-do."

## Santoor Indian Cuisine *Indian*

| | - | - | - | I |

**Alpharetta** | 3050 Mansell Rd. (Old Alabama Connector) | 770-650-8802

"Off the beaten track", this Alpharetta Indian nonetheless draws a "steady customer base" "attracted by" the "tastiness of the food" and the "kindness of the owners"; "samosas to die for" and "lamb dishes that make you salivate" served in "ok" digs make for a "nice surprise" to those who find it.

## Savage Pizza *Pizza*

| | 20 | 10 | 15 | $14 |

**Little Five Points** | 484 Moreland Ave. NE (bet. Euclid & Mansfield Aves.) | 404-523-0500 | www.savagepizza.com

"Just like Little Five Points", "every" "superb" "exotic pizza" "marches to a different drum" at this "rocker hangout" that "fits" the neighborhood "like a perfect seven-finger glove", and "reasonable prices" strike the right note for the "young grunge" crowd and "upwardly mobile urban families" alike; grown-ups will "feel like kids again" in the "cool" space with "superhero" decor and a "dreamy" patio, but many who report "frustration" with the service opt for "takeout" instead.

## Sawadee - A Taste of Thailand *Thai*

| | - | - | - | I |

**Sandy Springs** | Fountain Oaks Shopping Ctr. | 4920 Roswell Rd. (Long Island Dr.) | 404-303-1668

Pros praise the owner who's also "cook, server and kitchen manager" at this "one-woman operation" in Sandy Springs offering an "extensive menu" of "authentic" Thai cuisine that's "definitely a step above the typical", and "worth being patient"; "linen tablecloths" gussy up the strip-mall space.

## Sawicki's Meat, Seafood & More Ⓜ *Deli*

| | ▽ 26 | 13 | 24 | $14 |

**Decatur** | 250 W. Ponce de Leon Ave. (bet. Commerce Dr. & Ponce de Leon Pl.) | 404-377-0992 | www.sawickismeatsseafoodandmore.com

"Lucky" locals laud this "delightful" Decatur deli for its "perfect" "high-end" sandwiches crafted from "quality meats" and "condiments", and an "eclectic selection" of "goodies to take home" (including "amazing desserts"), but for many the "main attractions" are the "awesome" "fresh seafood" and "specialty" meats carved up by the "best butcher around"; it's "pricey", but the owner and staff "couldn't be nicer"; N.B. there's limited seating amongst the deli and bakery cases.

### ☑ Seasons 52  *American*     22 | 23 | 22 | $33

**Buckhead** | Two Buckhead Plaza | 3050 Peachtree Rd. NW
(W. Paces Ferry Rd.) | 404-846-1552
**Dunwoody** | 90 Perimeter Ctr. W. (Ashford Dunwoody Rd.) |
770-671-0052
www.seasons52.com

"You *can* have your cake and eat it too" – in a "shot glass", that is, at this "healthy" New American duo in Buckhead and Dunwoody that earns "nothing but kudos" from fans who "adore" its "clever menu" of "yummy, guilt-free" fare, "clever, tasty" "mini-desserts" and "exceptional wine list"; add "gorgeous" "Frank Lloyd Wright–inspired decor", "romantic lighting", a "wonderful piano bar" and "helpful" service, and you have a "great date spot" or "ladies'" "lunch" choice, not to mention "long waits" if you don't have a reservation.

### Shaun's Ⓜ  *American*     24 | 22 | 20 | $43

**Inman Park** | 1029 Edgewood Ave. (Hurt St. NE) | 404-577-4358 |
www.shaunsrestaurant.com

"Rub elbows with Inman Park hipsters" at this "fabulous" New American bistro from "home-town favorite" Shaun Doty, whose "creative", "phenomenal" cuisine includes an "amazing brunch", served in a "minimalist", but "inviting" space with a "fantastic patio", "see-and-be-seen bar area" and "long" communal table in front of the open kitchen; "yummy" "specialty drinks" enhance the "expensive" experience, and despite "uneven service" and some "major-league attitude", it's like "a dream" to many.

### Shorty's  *Pizza*     24 | 13 | 18 | $17

**Emory** | 2884 N. Druid Hills Rd. (Clairmont Rd.) | 404-315-6262
**Tucker** | 3701 Lawrenceville Hwy. (Shady Ln.) | 770-414-6999

"Those crazy kids" at this "cheap" pizzeria pair in Emory and Tucker are "reinventing the meal" with their "rock-star" "brick-oven" pizzas that are veritable "festivals of flavors", "large", "tasty" salads and "to-die-for" "freshly smashed guacamole"; the service is "pleasant", if somewhat "ditzy", and there are "lots of TVs to watch the game" in the "kid-friendly", "easygoing" setting; P.S. the newer location is a "welcome addition to the Tucker corridor."

### Shout  *Eclectic*     16 | 19 | 16 | $26

**Midtown** | Colony Sq. | 1197 Peachtree St. NE (14th St.) | 404-846-2000 |
www.heretoserverestaurants.com

This Midtown Eclectic from the "Catherall empire" is a "popular" "gathering place" for its "VIP patio" "overlooking Peachtree" that's "one of the best in Atlanta" and "huge" dining room, where "locals" and a "young crowd" order from a small-plates menu that "has something for everyone" at "good prices"; critics quip "shout is right, this place is loud", while service varies from

| | FOOD | DECOR | SERVICE | COST |
|---|---|---|---|---|

"pleasant" to "inept", but for many, it's all about "the scene and nothing but the scene."

### Sia's 🅱 *American/Asian* | 25 | 23 | 24 | $47 |

**Duluth** | 10305 Medlock Bridge Rd. (Wilson Rd.) | 770-497-9727 | www.siasrestaurant.com

When "something a little more extraordinary and elegant" than usual is in order, fans tout this "fantastic" Duluth sibling of Mitra for its "outstanding presentations" of "excellent", "high-end" New American cuisine with an Asian accent, and lunch specials that are a "great deal"; "friendly", "professional" service adds to the "wonderful ambiance" in the "upscale" space, which includes "lots of dark wood, wine bottles" and "modern light fixtures", as well as a private room with a fireplace.

### Silk *Pan-Asian* | 20 | 22 | 21 | $38 |

**Midtown** | 919 Peachtree St. NE (8th St.) | 678-705-8888 | www.silkrestaurant.com

"Beautiful", "interesting" decor and "cool bathrooms" set the stage at this "elegant" Midtown Pan-Asian (sibling of Hsu's and Pacific Rim) where a "huge, eclectic menu" that includes "incredibly well-prepared fish" and "delicious" Kobe beef is "worth a splurge" for a "special occasion"; "affable bartenders" and a "friendly" staff deliver "great service" to the "business and convention set", but many feel "let down" by fare that doesn't "measure up to fine dining expectations" or "expense-account" tabs.

### Silver Midtown Grill *Southern* | ▽ 16 | 15 | 18 | $13 |

**Midtown** | 900 Monroe Dr. NE (8th St.) | 404-876-8145

"When city living leaves you homesick", regulars recommend "Midtown's favorite meat-and-three", which is "back" with "new owners" but the "same cook" dishing out the "same" "traditional" Southern fare, at "good prices"; the waitresses "know locals by name" and are "happy to have you" in the "tiny", "unassuming" diner space.

### Silver Skillet *Diner* | 18 | 11 | 19 | $12 |

**Midtown** | 200 14th St. NW (I-75) | 404-874-1388 | www.thesilverskillet.com

"Set your watches back 35 years" when you enter this "classic dive" that's seemingly "been there forever" in Midtown, serving up "a little history with your breakfast" of "wonderful" "Southern-style" "comfort food at a comfort price", including "delicious" biscuits, "mighty good" pies and "country ham and red-eye gravy" that's "worth the effort" and "calories"; the "period" staff "sees all and knows all" in the "'60s" space that's "so awful it's good."

### Simpatico 🅱Ⓜ *American* | ▽ 20 | 15 | 18 | $32 |

**Marietta** | 23 N. Park Sq. NE (bet. Cherokee & Church Sts.) | 770-792-9086

At this family-owned Marietta New American, which "shares a space" with sibling Willie Rae's, an "imaginative" menu keeps fans "coming back for more" (signature "egg rolls" are a "favorite" of many), and you can order from either kitchen; "consistently good" performance makes locals "glad" to have it "in the area."

## Six Feet Under  *Seafood*                19 | 16 | 18 | $20

**Westside** | 685 11th St. (bet. Howell Mill Rd. & Northside Dr.) | 404-810-0040
**Grant Park** | 415 Memorial Dr. SE (Oakland Ave.) | 404-523-6664 ●
www.sixfeetunder.net

This "cleverly named" seafood "shack" in Grant Park near Oakland Cemetery and its Westside younger sibling "serve up anything that swims", as well as one of the "best burgers in Atlanta" and a "top-notch beer selection"; at the original, an "eclectic", "competent" staff mans the "friendly bar" and downstairs dining area to the beat of a "rockin' jukebox" or on the rooftop deck overlooking the graveyard, which is "not to be missed on a pretty day."

## Slope's BBQ  *BBQ*                        18 | 12 | 18 | $12

**Roswell** | 34 E. Crossville Rd. (Crabapple Rd.) | 770-518-7000 ⑤
**NEW Cumming** | 436 Canton Hwy. (Chamblee Gap Rd.) | 770-886-1678
**Alpharetta** | 5865 Gateway Dr. (Hwy. 9) | 678-393-1913 ⑤
**Sandy Springs** | The Springs | 200 Johnson Ferry Rd. NE (Sandy Spring Circle) | 404-252-3220 ⑤
www.slopesbbq.com

"Nothin' says luvin' like something from the pit" of this "inexpensive" 'cue quintet that injects a little "personality in the chain-infested suburbs" with "flavorful" BBQ and "excellent" sides "prepared in true Southern style"; "counter service" is delivered with so much "country sarcasm" and "humor" that no one even notices the "bare-bones" decor; N.B. the Cumming location opened post-Survey.

## Smokejack  *BBQ*                          19 | 17 | 19 | $22

**Alpharetta** | 29 S. Main St. (Old Milton Pkwy.) | 770-410-7611 |
www.smokejackbbq.com

Owner "David Filipowicz has a winner" with this "upscale"-"casual" BBQ in a "great location" in historic Downtown Alpharetta where the "chef"-driven menu boasts "delicious" meats and "terrific" sides ("you have to try the fried pickles!"), served by a "friendly" staff in a "tasteful" renovated 1847 building; though foes fume over "exorbitant" prices, it's a "favorite" for the "horse-and-SUV set."

## NEW Social House  *Southern*             - | - | - | I

**Westside** | 1663 Howell Mill Rd. (Chattahoochee Ave. NW) | 404-350-1938 | www.socialhouseatl.com

Lorenzo Wyche (Rare) cracks open an all-day breakfast spot on a restaurant-poor strip of Westside's Howell Mill where blue- and white-collar diners tuck into impeccably sourced Southern fare, with soul food classics and Creole-inspired eats sharing the bill with the basics; classic Americana, from an antique bicycle to jazz- and literature-inspired art and trinkets, accent the renovated house.

| | FOOD | DECOR. | SERVICE | COST |
|---|---|---|---|---|

### SoHo  *Eclectic*
22 | 20 | 22 | $36

**Vinings** | Vinings Jubilee Shopping Ctr. | 4300 Paces Ferry Rd. SE (Paces Mill Rd.) | 770-801-0069 | www.sohoatlanta.com
There's "no pretense to fine dining" at this "intimate" and "memorable" Vinings "hot spot", just an "interesting variety" of Eclectic dishes paired with an "amazing" wine list, and on Wednesday "flight nights", it's the "place to be"; oenophiles "learn a lot" from the "wine savvy" bartenders and appreciate the "energetic" vibe as well as the "good value" it offers.

### So Kong Dong  *Korean*
▽ 20 | 13 | 15 | $17

**Doraville** | 5280 Buford Hwy. (Oakmont Ave.) | 678-205-0555
You may not "understand what you're ordering" at this no-frills Doraville Korean, but pros promise "you'll enjoy" the "huge portions" of "freshly prepared" "traditional" fare (an "adventure for the senses") nonetheless; "attentive" servers "don't speak much English" but "make sure you have more than plenty to eat."

### Soleil Bistro  *French*
18 | 16 | 18 | $33

**Buckhead** | 3081 Maple Dr. NE (E. Paces Ferry Rd.) | 404-467-1790
The "wonderful" French fare is a "darn good value" at this bistro "tucked away" on a "quiet street behind the insanity of Buckhead", a "favorite" of many for Sunday brunch thanks to the "fabulous patio" fronting the "romantic" "old house"; "fantastic" service adds to the "charm", making this a "delightful place" for a "girlie lunch" or "pleasant light dinner."

### Son's Place 🅱️🍽️  *Soul Food*
▽ 19 | 8 | 18 | $11

**Inman Park** | 100 Hurt St. NE (DeKalb Ave.) | 404-581-0530
Boosters of this Inman Park "institution" "don't come for the ambiance", just "true soul food done right", and served up "buffet style" by the "eponymous son" of legendary Deacon Burton, who channels dad through "pan-fried" "chicken" that's among the "best in Atlanta"; an "outgoing" crew mans the spot that oozes "serious character" – aficionados attest there "ain't nothin' like it."

### Sops on Ellis/Loaf & Kettle 🅱️  *Eclectic*
▽ 25 | 14 | 18 | $14

**Downtown** | Carnegie Bldg. | 170 Ellis St. NW (Peachtree St.) | 404-223-7677
Downtowners in search of "something a little different" for lunch head to this "upscale" "hippie-type" Eclectic spot for "fabulous soups" (try their signature corn, crab and spinach chowder), "inventive sandwiches" and "wonderful" bread pudding; you order at the "self-service" counter and then grab a seat in the "cute", if somewhat "crammed", new space.

### 🆉 Sotto Sotto  *Italian*
27 | 21 | 24 | $44

**Inman Park** | 313 N. Highland Ave. NE (Elizabeth St.) | 404-523-6678 | www.sottosottorestaurant.com
Loyalists "all bow" to Riccardo Ullio (Fritti, Beleza and Cuerno) for this "perfection in Inman Park", where "authentic", "stunningly tasty" Northern Italian cuisine ("fabulous wood grilled fish" and

"brilliant pastas") and an "excellent wine list" are served by a "smart", "attentive" staff; there's "high energy" in the "cozy" (read: "cramped") space with an open kitchen and a "great" patio for "romantic evenings", and while it's "expensive", it remains a "keeper" for most.

## Soul Vegetarian
**Restaurant** *Soul Food/Vegetarian*

▽ | 17 | 10 | 19 | $15

**Downtown** | 879 Ralph David Abernathy Blvd. SW (Dunn St.) | 404-752-5194
**Virginia-Highland** | 652 N. Highland Ave. (Ponce de Leon Ave. NE) | 404-875-0145 **M**
www.soulvegetarian.com

"You'd swear it's your mother's home cooking – if her name is Paisley" quip fans of this "super-cheap" "dive" duo in Downtown and Virginia-Highland that delivers a "great breadth of choices" of "succulent" vegetarian soul food, served "without pretenses"; while some huff that "collared greens" sans "bacon" is "against the law", many "non-vegs enjoy" the "interesting" flesh-free options.

## **Z** Souper Jenny ⊅ *Soup*

25 | 14 | 20 | $12

**Buckhead** | Andrews Square Shopping Ctr. | 56 E. Andrews Dr. NW (Roswell Rd.) | 404-237-7687

"Ten dollars gets you a plate of happiness" at this "cafeteria-style" Buckhead soup standout where "health nuts", "soccer moms" and others head for "dazzling" bowls and "'souper' fresh foods", including a "delicious" "new Sunday brunch", that are a "superb value"; expect a "lo-ong line" at the door of the "tiny" "cafe setting", but "singing actors" (aka servers) can "brighten" a "busy day" with "quick" service and a "smile"; P.S. "don't forget your cash" ("no credit cards").

## **Z** South City Kitchen *Southern*

23 | 21 | 22 | $37

**Smyrna** | 1675 Cumberland Pkwy. (Atlanta Rd. SE) | 770-435-0700
**Midtown** | 1144 Crescent Ave. NE (14th St.) | 404-873-7358
www.southcitykitchen.com

"Still clicking on all cylinders", this Midtown "hit" from the Fifth Group (Food Studio, Ecco, La Tavola) now has a new sibling, and some swear Smyrna has "never looked or tasted so chic"; fans are "addicted" to its "delicious", "fresh take on Southern cuisine", which is served by an "attentive", "caring" staff in "comfortable", "cozy" surroundings with a "beautiful" patio at both locations, and while the scene can get "too crowded and loud" at times, it's still an "outstanding value."

## **NEW** Spice Market *SE Asian*

- | - | - | M

**Midtown** | W Atlanta-Midtown | 188 14th St. NE (bet. Juniper St. & Piedmont Ave.) | 404-549-5450 | www.spicemarketatlanta.com

Jean-Georges Vongerichten adds a Southern star to his constellation of restaurants with this new venture at the W Atlanta-Midtown, where the vibrant, complex street food of Southeast Asia is served family-style by a staff clad in Indian-inspired uniforms; islands of seating outfitted with celadon silk pillows, dangling pagoda-inspired structures, heavy ropes adorned with found artifacts and hundreds of candles at night create a sensual, transporting space.

| | FOOD | DECOR | SERVICE | COST |
|---|---|---|---|---|

### Spoon ⊠ *Thai*
▽ 25 | 18 | 20 | $24

**Downtown** | 768 Marietta St. (bet. Bankhead Hwy. & Means St.) |
404-522-5655 | www.spoonatlanta.com

Located in an "up-and-coming neighborhood" on the edge of
Downtown, this "little restaurant that could" is "not to be missed",
dishing out "delicious" Thai eats at prices that "don't break the
bank"; the "friendly owner" "greets you at the door" of the "dark,
swanky spot" where a "hip" crowd shows up at all hours of the day.

### NEW Stats ● *American*
▽ 19 | 26 | 20 | $25

**Downtown** | 300 Marietta St. NW (Thurmond St.) | 404-885-1472 |
www.statsatl.com

"Get here stat" prescribe fans who are "so happy" this "breath of
fresh air" has blown into Downtown, a "perfect combination of
sports bar and gastropub" with "flavorful" American eats and a
"great selection of beers"; "über-yuppies" and the "young and hip"
convene in the "roomy", "upscale" digs with "lots of space for private
parties" and "so-o many flat-screens" (70 to be exact), and "where
else can you get your beer from a tap right at your own table?"

### NEW Steel ⊠ *Pan-Asian*
- | - | - | M

**Midtown** | Plaza Midtown | 950 W. Peachtree St. (Peachtree Pl.) |
404-477-6111 | www.steelatlanta.com

This Dallas-based upscale Indochine brings a dash of spice to a
mushrooming section of Midtown with its signature cocktails, an
award-winning wine list and chef Aaron Norford's diverse Asian offerings bolstered with sushi chef Jeff Voung's creations; shades of
green and orange pop against the rich brown palette in the Johnson
Studio–designed space, which melds elements of fire and wood with
numerous water features, include a mesmerizing rain curtain.

### NEW Stella *Italian*
- | - | - | I

**Grant Park** | 563 Memorial Dr. (Park Ave. SE) | 404-688-4238 |
www.stellaatlanta.com

Celebrate life with a bowl of handmade pasta at this affordable
Italian (sibling of Doc Chey's and Osteria 832) in Grant Park overlooking the quiet residents of Oakland Cemetery, where locavores
are salivating over its responsibly sourced, heavily organic rustic
fare; a somewhat awkward entrance leads into a space accented
with shades of green and rich woods, boasting an open kitchen, bar
area and stellar wraparound patio.

### ⊠ Stoney River Legendary Steaks *Steak*
24 | 22 | 22 | $42

**Cobb** | Cumberland Mall | 1640 Cumberland Mall SE (Cobb Pkwy.) |
678-305-9229
**Roswell** | 10524 Alpharetta Hwy. (E. Crossville Rd.) | 678-461-7900
**Duluth** | 5800 State Bridge Rd. (Medlock Bridge Rd.) | 770-476-0102
www.stoneyriver.com

Groupies "make up special occasions just to go" to this "high-end"
steakhouse trio that's a "legend" for "superb" meat, "top-notch"
sides and "ambrosial" rolls, brought to table by "unobtrusive" servers who are nonetheless "always 'there'" in the "hunting-lodge"

space; the "no-reservations" policy means there's "always a wait", so "arrive early" or use the "call-ahead service."

### NEW Straits *Singaporean* — | — | — | M
**Midtown** | 793 Juniper St. (5th St.) | 404-877-1283 | www.straitsrestaurants.com

Bay-area restaurateur-chef Chris Yeo and Ludacris take center stage in Midtown's former Spice location, showcasing Yeo's vibrant, modern Singaporean cuisine meant for sharing; fire and water elements blend with warm colors and blue LED lighting in the multilevel space, which underwent a $1 million face-lift by the Johnson Studio, while cozy leather-blended seating, a sultry private lounge area, and a lively central bar offer a wide range of wining and dining experiences.

### Strip *Seafood/Steak* 17 | 18 | 16 | $36
**Atlantic Station** | Atlantic Station | 245 18th St. (17th St. NW) | 404-385-2005 | www.heretoserverestaurants.com

For something a "little clubby" with "lots of bubbly", fans tout this seafood-steakhouse sibling of Shout and Twist as "one of the trendiest destinations" in Atlantic Station, where the "big draws" are the "urban vibe" and "see-and-be-seen" scene in the "sexy", "loud" space with a "chic bar" on each level; there's a "broad menu" of "yummy" fare, and while critics sniff it's "not always worth the price", citing "disappointing" eats and "indifferent" service, to others it's a "convenient" "gathering place" with "lots of energy."

### Sultan's *Lebanese/Mediterranean* 21 | 12 | 17 | $24
(fka Cedars)
**Sandy Springs** | 5920 Roswell Rd. (Hammond Dr.) | 404-257-2220

After relocating from Buckhead to Sandy Springs, this "taste of Lebanon" (and the Mediterranean) still offers "excellent value" with its "fresh, well-made" meze from the "awesome" buffet table, "served by gracious folks"; N.B. the move to suburbia occurred post-Survey.

### Z Sun Dial *American* 19 | 24 | 20 | $50
**Downtown** | Westin Peachtree Plaza | 210 Peachtree St., 72st fl. (Andrew Young Int'l Blvd.) | 404-589-7506 | www.sundialrestaurant.com

For a "romantic dinner, anniversary or birthday celebration", this "spinning restaurant on top of the Westin" Downtown offers "spectacular views" from its 72nd-story perch, a "fantastic atmosphere" and "great service", not to mention chef Christian Messier's "tasty" New American offerings from a "seasonal" menu; cynics dismiss it as a "touristy", "overpriced gimmick" that "badly needs renovating", but to "watch the sun set" it "can't" be "beat."

### Sun in My Belly *Diner* 24 | 18 | 15 | $17
**Kirkwood** | 2161 College Ave. NE (Murray Hill Ave.) | 404-370-1088 | www.suninmybelly.com

"For a cheap, plentiful brunch" and other "outstanding" fare "made with care and flair", fans attest this Kirkwood American "cannot be topped", and its "catering side" is also among the "best in Atlanta";

the "former hardware store" looks like a "hole-in-the-wall" on the "outside", but the "quaint" interior is "simple and elegant", and while some raise hell about the "devil-may-care service", most agree this one's "worth the trip."

**Surin of Thailand**  *Thai*  | 23 | 18 | 20 | $23 |

Virginia-Highland | 810 N. Highland Ave. NE (Greenwood Ave.) | 404-892-7789 | www.surinofthailand.com

"Reasonably priced", "generous portions" of "top-notch Thai" fare "keep people coming back" to this "favorite neighborhood spot" in the heart of "trendy" Virginia-Highland ("sister restaurant to Harry & Sons"); the "beautiful floral arrangements" on the "small bar" are "almost worth the trip" by themselves, and the service is "friendly" and "attentive" in the "loud", "see-and-be-seen" milieu that gets "extremely crowded on weekends."

**Sushi Avenue**  *Japanese*  | 24 | 18 | 19 | $22 |

Decatur | 131 Sycamore St. (Church St.) | 404-378-0228
Decatur | Shops of W. Ponce de Leon Pl. | 308 W. Ponce de Leon Ave. (Ponce de Leon Pl.) | 404-378-8448

Advocates of these Decatur raw-fin twins "would lay down in the street to keep these guys in town" since they "can't go wrong" with "amazingly fresh" sushi and "excellent" Japanese eats at "reasonable prices"; the "location on the square is hipper" but the "original" one has been "beautifully remodeled", and both boast "pleasant" staffs and an owner who's "an angel."

**Sushi Huku**  Ⓜ *Japanese*  | 25 | 17 | 23 | $32 |

Sandy Springs | Powers Ferry Landing | 6300 Powers Ferry Rd. NW (Northside Dr.) | 770-956-9559

The "only place with fresher (fish) is the ocean" swear piscophiles about this "family-run" Sandy Springs Japanese "hole-in-the-wall" where "sushi heaven" can be found in the form of "traditional" fare "prepared the way it's supposed to be" and served with "friendly" efficiency; "don't let the (strip mall) location discourage you" – it's a "wonderful experience" inside, complete with "cozy" private rooms.

**Swallow at the Hollow**  Ⓜ *BBQ*  | 23 | 16 | 19 | $20 |

Roswell | 1072 Green St. (Woodstock St.) | 678-352-1975 | www.theswallowatthehollow.com

"Families", folks with "out-of-town guests" and others who "don't mind limited elbow room" "queue up" at this "good old-fashioned dive" in "historic Roswell" for "generous portions" of "dance-on-the-table" "delicious" BBQ, "comfy" sides that include some "incredible" veggies and "must-have" banana pudding; "long neck beers on ice" and "live country music" are fixtures in the "rustic", "barnlike setting" full of "charm" and "lots of noise."

**Swan Coach House**  ⓈZ *Southern*  | 18 | 23 | 21 | $22 |

Buckhead | 3130 Slaton Dr. NW (W. Paces Ferry Rd.) | 404-261-0636 | www.swancoachhouse.com

The "old South still reigns" at this "ultimate chick place" located behind Buckhead's Swan Mansion, where "genteel" "pretty ladies" "gather" for a "leisurely meal" of "quintessential" Southern "tea-room" fare, such as "frozen fruit salad" and "cheese straws", served by a "pleasant" staff; real "men" "never darken" the "foo-foo door" of the "lovely" "dining room" that "hums with feminine power."

### Table 1280 Ⓜ *American*  `20` `22` `19` `$42`
**Midtown** | Woodruff Arts Ctr. | 1280 Peachtree St. NE (bet. 15th & 16th Sts.) | 404-897-1280 | www.table1280.com
You "can't beat" the "convenient" location of this "creative" New American in Midtown's Woodruff Arts Center serving a pre-theater "prix fixe", "tapas at the bar" and a "superb" Sunday brunch in a "spotless modern dining room" that "fits in with the arty surroundings"; critics complain of "overpriced, undersized" fare and service that fluctuates from "attentive" to "oblivious", and declare the "experience is not up to what it should be."

### ☒ Taka Ⓢ *Japanese*  `27` `15` `22` `$38`
**Buckhead** | 375 Pharr Rd. NE (Grandview Ave.) | 404-869-2802
Boosters of this Buckhead Japanese advise "put your trust in" "master" chef-owner Taka Moriuchi and "you won't be disappointed", since he's "fanatically devoted to freshness" and "delivers every time" with "flawless, inventive" sushi and sashimi, but just remember that "top-flight fresh fish costs real money"; the "friendly, quick" staff works the "small, unpretentious" space as well as the "cozy", "nicely landscaped" patio.

### ☒ Tamarind Seed Thai Bistro *Thai*  `27` `21` `23` `$32`
**Midtown** | Colony Sq. | 1197 Peachtree St. NW (14th St.) | 404-873-4888 | www.tamarindseed.com
"Thank God it's back" sigh supporters of Nan's "reserved" sibling (voted Atlanta's No. 1 Thai), which relocated to a "cheery" "new" space in Midtown's Colony Square just "down the street" from its former site; you can "throw a dart at the menu and no matter where it lands", you'll get "superb", "authentic" fare that's "actually worth the prices"; "flawless service" and a "modern" space with "lots of outdoor seating" and "validated" "parking" are also much "appreciated."

### NEW TAP ● *American*  `14` `19` `15` `$25`
**Midtown** | Hines Bldg. | 1180 Peachtree St. NE (14th St.) | 404-347-2220 | www.tapat1180.com
"BlackBerry-toting yuppies" and "scensters" "spill out onto the large patio" at this New American "gastropub" from the Concentrics Group located at "'the' corner" in "the center of everything in Midtown", where "high-quality munchies" complement "extensive" selections of wines and "beers on tap"; while foes report "spotty service" and "surprisingly average" eats, others insist it's "worth going" for the "hot happy-hour scene" in the "fantastic", "trendy" multilevel space.

### ☒ Taqueria del Sol Ⓢ *Mexican/Southwestern*  `24` `14` `14` `$14`
**Westside** | 1200B Howell Mill Rd. NW (Huff Rd.) | 404-352-5811
**Cheshire Bridge** | 2165 Cheshire Bridge Rd. NE (Lavista Rd.) | 404-321-1118

| | FOOD | DECOR | SERVICE | COST |
|---|---|---|---|---|

*(continued)*

### Taqueria del Sol

**Decatur** | 359 W. Ponce de Leon Ave. (bet. Fairview Ave. &
Ponce de Leon Pl.) | 404-377-7668
www.taqueriadelsol.com

"Dirt-cheap", "fast-ish" fare that's "better than most slow food in
town" sets off a veritable "stampede" of sol-jahs to this Mexican-
Southwestern trio where "gourmet tacos" are "made fresh to order"
and you can chase them down with "terrific margaritas"; the lines
are "long" but "fast-moving", the digs "sparse but classy" and while
parents complain of "surly" servers who are so "not family-friendly",
wags insist the staff does "like kids – preferably fried or boiled."

### Tarahumata Mexican Grill *Mexican*    ▽ 23 | 24 | 20 | $18

**Alpharetta** | 6195 Windward Pkwy. (bet. Union Hill Rd. &
Windward Concourse) | 770-772-4540

Alpharettans in search of "something other than 'normal' chain
Mexican" head to this "upscale" option for "fantastic, fresh and up-
lifting" fare "with a twist", "amazing" "tequila choices" and "excellent guacamole" whipped up by a "genuine" staff; the "beautiful
interior" and "wonderful outdoor patio" also make this one
"worth the drive."

### Tasting Room ☒ *Creole/Mediterranean*    22 | 21 | 21 | $37

**NEW Sandy Springs** | 6010 Sandy Springs Circle NE (Hammond Dr.) |
404-252-8170
**East Point** | 3560 Camp Creek Pkwy. (Commerce Dr.) | 404-346-0697
www.atlwines.com/tastingroom

This "promising" pair is a "welcome addition" to East Point and
Sandy Springs alike thanks to "delicious" Mediterranean-Creole fare
"sure to please all comers" and a "superb wine selection" that reflects the "eclectic choices" from its sister wine store; a "beautiful
bar" befits the "grown-up" atmosphere, and while service can vary
from "knowledgeable" to "amateur", most find "everything" "extremely pleasant" – "except the prices."

### Tasty China *Chinese*    ▽ 24 | 7 | 17 | $18

**Marietta** | 585 Franklin Rd. SE (Hwy. 120) | 770-419-9849

"Just feed me" "should be your only attempt at ordering" at this
"truly authentic", "surprisingly inexpensive" BYO Sichuan specialist
in Marietta boasting a "large menu" of "amazing" ("hot!") fare, and
aficionados swear "once you've had" it, "you'll never go back to 'regular' Chinese"; an "attentive" staff lends "help" to those in need ("the
owner won't let you order something you may not like") and makes
it easy to overlook the shrimp-pink walls of the no-frills space.

### Taurus *American/Steak*    23 | 23 | 21 | $38

**South Buckhead** | Brookwood Place Plaza | 1745 Peachtree St. NE, 3rd fl.
(25th St.) | 404-214-0641 | www.taurusrestaurant.com

Fans "never get tired" of "fantastic chef" Gary Mennie's "tasty" New
American chophouse fare at his "delightful" (if somewhat "hard
to find") "haunt" in South Buckhead, where "scrumptious" prix fixe

options and a "reasonable wine list" make it an "amazing deal"; the "solid" service "is a pleasure", as is the "unique, inviting" space with "plush red booths", a "long, spacious" bar and an outdoor patio that provides an "extraordinary view of Midtown and Downtown."

## Taverna Fiorentina  *Italian*          - | - | - | M

**Vinings** | Riverview Village in Vinings | 3324 Cobb Pkwy. | 770-272-9825
Vinings bon vivants and those with romance on their minds are discovering this intimate midpriced newcomer showcasing the Tuscan cuisine of chef Franck Ouvrard, who creates lush pastas, his signature wild boar and other dishes in a tiny open kitchen while providing guests with serious eye candy; a diminutive bar overflows with vino from Italy, and a European vibe fills the surprising strip-mall space.

## Taverna Plaka  *Greek*          17 | 15 | 16 | $27

**Cheshire Bridge** | 2196 Cheshire Bridge Rd. NE (Woodland Ave.) | 404-636-2284 | www.tavernaplakaatlanta.com
"It's perfectly all right to dance on the table" at this "tacky and wacky" Hellenic "dining experience" on Cheshire Bridge where it's "always a party" as "friendly" servers shout *"opa"* and "belly dancers shake their stuff"; "smush your own hummus" and "eat great Mediterranean fare" in the "festive" setting where "conversation is impossible", and while its appeal may be "Greek to" those who prefer "subtle dining", "it's a hoot" for the rest.

## Tavern at Phipps  *American*          18 | 18 | 18 | $30

**Buckhead** | Phipps Plaza | 3500 Peachtree Rd. NE (Lenox Rd.) | 404-814-9640 | www.centrarchy.com
"Even if you're not one of the beautiful people" "you can enjoy watching their antics" at this "clubby" Buckhead American located in "one of the best malls around", where "waitresses in skimpy clothing" and "hot bartenders" "put on a show" in the "dark mahogany" setting that gets "noisy when busy, which is often"; fans rate the pub grub "way above average", but pickier patrons "go for the bar" scene and "eat elsewhere."

## ⓩ Ted's Montana Grill  *American*          19 | 18 | 18 | $23

**Kennesaw** | 2500 Cobb Place Ln. NW (Cobb Place Blvd.) | 678-581-7890
**Marietta** | The Avenues of West Cobb | 3625 Dallas Hwy. SW/Rte. 120 (Casteel Rd.) | 678-594-7242
**Marietta** | Parkaire Landing Shopping Ctr. | 640 Johnson Ferry Rd. (Lower Roswell Rd.) | 770-578-8337
**Midtown** | 1874 Peachtree Rd. NE (Collier Rd.) | 404-355-3897
**Decatur** | 201 W. Ponce de Leon Ave. (Commerce Dr.) | 404-378-1123
**Downtown** | 133 Luckie St. NW (Spring St.) | 404-521-9796
**Buford** | Mill Creek | 1680 Mall of Georgia Blvd. (Buford Dr.) | 678-546-3631
**Norcross** | The Forum | 5165 Peachtree Pkwy. NW/Hwy. 141 (Medlock Bridge Rd.) | 678-405-0305
**Peachtree City** | The Avenue | 314 City Circle (Hwy. 54) | 678-829-0272
www.tedsmontanagrill.com
The "tasty" signature bison burger is "reason enough" to visit Ted Turner's Western-themed American chain even if the "remainder of

the menu is of average quality"; sure, service can be "uneven" and there's "nothing flashy" ambiancewise, yet it's still "good value for the money" – and it makes a point of being environmentally responsible.

### 10 Degrees South ☒ *S African*  | 23 | 21 | 22 | $41 |
**Buckhead** | 4183 Roswell Rd. NE (bet. Piedmont & Wieuca Rds.) | 404-705-8870 | www.10degreessouth.com

"The 'game' is on" at this "unexpectedly good" South African in north Buckhead that "transports you right to Cape Town" with "unique" fare that'll "wow your taste buds" and an "exceptional" selection of that country's wines to match; "knowledgeable" (if sometimes "snotty") waiters man the "ultraelegant" front dining room, while there's a "hip bar scene" in the back with occasional "live music."

### Terra Terroir Grille & Wine Bar ☒ *American*  | 19 | 14 | 18 | $24 |
**Brookhaven** | Brookhaven Shopping Plaza | 3974 Peachtree Rd. NE, Ste. C (N. Druid Hills Rd.) | 404-841-1032 | www.terragrille.com

"Bring the whole family" to this "casual" Brookhaven bistro that "proves healthy can be yummy" with its "interesting menu" of "wholesome" American cuisine complemented by an "excellent wine list", and served by a "friendly" staff; despite the "strip-mall" location, this "non-chain" has "lots of character" and a "great patio" that "provides one of Atlanta's few outdoor dining spots where you don't have to look at a parking lot."

### Thai Chili *Thai*  | 22 | 15 | 19 | $21 |
**Emory** | Briarvista Shopping Ctr. | 2169 Briarcliff Rd. NE (Lavista Rd.) | 404-315-6750 | www.thaichilicuisine.com

"One of Atlanta's oldest Thai" choices and "still one of the best", this "dependable", "moderately priced" Emory stalwart is touted for "high-quality" fare that's "spicy if you like spicy", including "primo" pad Thai; "friendly and helpful" service also helps "students, CDC staff" and others "get past the mall exterior."

### Thaicoon & Sushi Bar *Japanese/Thai*  | ▽ 22 | 19 | 21 | $23 |
**Marietta** | 34 Mill St. NE (N. Marietta Pkwy. NW) | 678-766-0641
Ok, it may have a "stupid name", but this "casual" spot on "historic Marietta Square" boasts a "broad menu" of "reliable", "beautifully presented" Thai cuisine and "boats" of "fresh" sushi (afishionados "love" the Monday and Tuesday dollar sushi specials); the "friendly" "service couldn't be better" in the "small" space "divided into cozy, comfortable rooms" – all in all, it's a "satisfying" and "affordable" experience.

### Thelma's Kitchen ☒ *Southern*  | ▽ 21 | 10 | 22 | $15 |
**Downtown** | 302 Auburn Ave. (Fort St.) | 404-688-5855
If you want to know "how to say yummy in Southern", insiders recommend this Downtown soul food spot where the "par excellence" chef delivers the "real thing"; the digs have been updated but are still no frills, but for the "best food outside my mama's kitchen", it don't matter none, dahlin'.

**Thrive** *American*  | 17 | 19 | 14 | $31 |

**Downtown** | 101 Marietta St. (Spring St.) | 404-389-1000 |
www.thriveatl.com

The Johnson Studio "decor is the standout" at this "chic", "upscale" "addition to the Downtown dining scene", where "sexy" servers deliver Asian-influenced American small plates, including "great sushi", to a "hip" crowd; critics cavil about "inexperienced, inattentive" service and "subpar" fare, but for "pre-show" or "pre-hockey" dining, many consider it the "best" option in "Centennial Tower."

**Thumbs Up** ⏺ *Diner*  | 23 | 14 | 20 | $13 |

**Inman Park** | 573 Edgewood Ave. SE (Boulevard SE) | 404-223-0690
**Airport (East Point)** | 1617 White Way (bet. E. Point & Main Sts.) |
East Point | 404-768-3776
www.thumbsupdiner.com

"If you like big breakfasts" and "can tolerate the crowds", pros promise this "homey" cash-only pair in Edgewood and East Point is "just what the doctor ordered", giving a "thumbs-up" to its "cheap" and "super-yummy" Southern fare (the signature "heap" is "heaven in a skillet"); the "friendly" staff serves you "quick" and "your coffee cup is always full", but if you can't "get up" early enough or "go later in the day" to avoid the rush, regulars recommend "takeout."

**⛉ Tierra** ⓈⓂ *Pan-Latin*  | 26 | 16 | 23 | $36 |

**Midtown** | 1425B Piedmont Ave. NE (Westminster Dr.) |
404-874-5951

"It's all *bueno*" at this "warm and wonderful" Midtown Pan-Latin "hidden between Ansley Park and the Botanical Garden", where an "extremely talented husband/wife team" utilize "new, creative" ingredients "so authentic you have to use the glossary" in their "phenomenal", "ever-changing dishes", which are matched with a "thoughtful wine list"; a "super-friendly" staff mans the "small dining room" and "enclosed" "back patio", enhancing the "excellent experience"; P.S. "save room" for the "killer" tres leches cake.

**Tin Drum Asia Café** *Asian Fusion/Noodle Shop*  | 16 | 11 | 14 | $11 |

**Midtown** | Tech Sq. | 88 Fifth St. (Veterans St.) | 404-881-1368
**Dunwoody** | 4530 Olde Perimeter Way (Ashford Dunwoody Rd.) |
770-393-3006
www.tindrumcafe.net

Midtown and Dunwoody diners "in a hurry" beat it to this "popular" pair for "generous" portions of "fresh", "cheap, fast and tasty" Asian fusion fare and noodles that are a "wonderful option for takeout"; expect "friendly" "counter service" in a "minimalist" setting, and while phos find "nothing that will blow your mind" on the menu, fans swear it's still "better than other fast food."

**tomas** Ⓢ *American*  | ▽ 24 | 19 | 24 | $26 |

**Norcross** | 6025 Peachtree Pkwy. NW (Jay Bird Alley) | 770-447-0005 |
www.cheftomaslee.com

At his midpriced eatery in Norcross, chef-owner Thomas Lee's "fantastic", "inventive" New American fare and nearly "perfect wine list" "exceed the expectations" created by its "dull strip-mall" location; those who "have discovered" this "hidden gem" are also "shocked by how nice it is" inside the doors, further "proof that you can't judge a book by its cover."

**Tomo** Ⓜ *Japanese*                 ▽ 27 | 19 | 22 | $37

**Vinings** | Riverview Shopping Ctr. | 3256 Cobb Pkwy. (Cumberland Blvd.) | 770-690-0555 | www.tomorestaurant.com

Vinings foodies are "glad" "talented" chef Tomohiro Naito "chose" their "little corner of the world" to locate his "outstanding" Japanese, where the "first-rate" sushi crafted from "fish flown in directly from Japan", including "tantalizing" specials, "strikes a balance" between "authentic" and "creative"; the service is "attentive", while the "minimalist urban" decor "reflects" the kitchen's "artistic presentations", and though it's "pricey", as "one of the best sushi experiences in metro Atlanta", it's "still reasonable."

**NEW  Top Flr** ◑Ⓜ *American*        ▽ 25 | 14 | 19 | $28

**Midtown** | 674 Myrtle St. (Ponce de Leon Ave.) | 404-685-3110

"Top-notch technique" is on display in the "tiny kitchen" of this "cool" new Midtown spot where "awe-inspiring" American eats and an "astonishingly good wine list" attract "groovy locals" both "young" and "old"; a staff of "very trendy" types provides "pleasant" but "spacey" service in a "cozy" bi-level space, and though the "scene" can be "hectic" and "cramped", fans insist it's "worth checking out" – "but only a few of you at a time!"

**Top Spice** *Malaysian/Thai*         21 | 20 | 19 | $21

**Midtown** | 1529F Piedmont Ave. NE (Monroe Dr.) | 404-685-9333 | www.topspiceansleypark.com

**Emory** | Toco Hills Shopping Ctr. | 3007 N. Druid Hills Rd. NE (Lavista Rd.) | 404-728-0588

**Vinings** | Akers Mill Shopping Ctr. | 2997 Cobb Pkwy. (Riverwood Pkwy. SE) | 770-988-9007 | www.topspiceatlanta.com

Those who "crave spicy food" laud this trio for its "great mix" of "high-end" Thai and Malaysian fare "so fresh" it "will shock you", served up in "just-right portions" by "courteous" servers; "college students, faculty and hospital staff" "haunt" the "surprisingly" "elegant" Emory original "located in un-glamorous Toco Hills", while the Midtown spot offers "incredible taste for a decent price", and the Vinings branch is located near the performing arts center.

**Toscano & Sons**                     ▽ 23 | 18 | 20 | $9
**Italian Market** ⊠ *Italian*

**Westside** | 1000 Marietta St. NW, Ste. 106 (Howell Mill Rd.) | 404-815-8383 | www.toscanoandsons.com

"You can pick up every must-have for your *cucina Italia*" at this Westside market "hideaway", a "fabulous addition" to an "interesting neighborhood", where "unforgettable" panini is "freshly made in front of you" and the "best collection of sundries anywhere" can be found, including "lots of hard-to-find items"; limited seating is available in the cheery warehouse space.

| | FOOD | DECOR | SERVICE | COST |

### Tossed  *American*                         ▽ 16 | 12 | 14 | $13

**Alpharetta** | Windward Plaza | 5530 Windward Pkwy., Ste. 1070
(GA 400, exit 11) | 678-339-1313
**NEW Decatur** | 201 W. Ponce de Leon Ave. (bet. Clairemont Ave. &
Commerce Dr.) | 404-378-1400
www.tossed.com

Seemingly "thousands" of "make-your-own-and-mix-in options" are
offered at these New American twins in Alpharetta and Decatur,
where the "great selection" of wraps and "fresh salads" are certainly
"healthier than fast food"; "lots of windows" brighten up the otherwise no-frills digs, but critics take a dim view of "outrageous prices"
and "bland" offerings.

### Toulouse  *American*                        21 | 18 | 21 | $32

**South Buckhead** | 2293B Peachtree Rd. NE (Peachtree Memorial Dr.) |
404-351-9533 | www.toulouserestaurant.com

"Once you figure out how to get in", this South Buckhead New
American with a "fine bistro" accent is a "great escape right on
Peachtree", offering "marvelous", "comforting" cuisine paired with
"one of the best wine lists in town", all with an utter "lack of pretension"; oenophiles also appreciate the "superior tastings", and owner
George Tice "makes you feel welcome" in the "wonderful", "romantic" loftlike space decorated with "great" paintings.

### Trader Vic's 🅂 *Pacific Rim*                20 | 21 | 20 | $39

**Downtown** | Hilton Atlanta | 255 Courtland St. NE (Baker St.) |
404-221-6339 | www.tradervicsatlanta.com

When it's time to "scratch your kitschy tiki itch" or just "wear a
Hawaiian shirt", this "old-school Polynesian" chain link in the
Downtown Hilton is a "delightful" choice for a "good, stiff" "retro
cocktail" and "delightful" Pacific Rim eats ("pupu platter", anyone?); service is "good", even for "large groups", and pros promise
a "pleasant experience" amid the "fake palm trees" and bamboo.

### Trattoria La Strada  *Italian*              ▽ 19 | 13 | 19 | $26

**Marietta** | 2930 Johnson Ferry Rd. NE (Freeman Rd.) | 770-640-7008 |
www.lastradainc.com

"You feel like you're in Little Italy" at this "neighborhood trattoria" in
Marietta where a "friendly, efficient" staff serves up "consistently
good and affordable" *mangiare* in a simple room redolent with the
"smell of garlic"; while some feel it's "slipped in recent years", others insist it's still "worth a trip."

### Trilogy  *American*                         ▽ 14 | 16 | 13 | $32

**Marietta** | 4930 Davidson Rd. (Lower Roswell Rd. SE) | 770-971-4770 |
www.trilogydining.net

A "fun addition to East Cobb" for the "older" set, this Marietta dining room/bar/entertainment venue turns out "nice" New American
fare, including "especially good" apps and "respectable" steaks, and
serves as a "singles bar for the divorced" set and "married" folks
who "don't want to go far"; detractors declare it a "disappointment",
however, citing "very average" fare and "rude" service.

|  | FOOD | DECOR | SERVICE | COST |
|--|------|-------|---------|------|

### Tringalis  *Italian*
### (fka Lombardi's)

| - | - | - | M |

**Downtown** | Underground Atlanta | 94 Upper Pryor St. SW
(Martin Luther King Jr. Dr.) | 404-522-6568 | www.tringalisatlanta.com

Its "proximity to the state capitol" makes this Downtown Italian a natural "legislative power-lunch" venue where "lobbyists and politicos" go to "see and be seen"; "hot, fresh" dishes that are "infused with flavor" are served in a Mediterranean-inspired space by a staff that "welcomes you warmly", making it "one of the better options" in the area.

### ☑ Trois  *French*

| 22 | 25 | 21 | $50 |

**Midtown** | 1180 Peachtree St. NE (14th St.) | 404-815-3337 |
www.trois3.com

The "third time's the charm" for Todd Rushing and Bob Amick (ONE. midtown kitchen and TWO urban licks), "dedicated" owners of this "stunning" French in Midtown that "puts a smile" on the faces of its "young and beautiful" clientele; "gorgeous views" serve as backdrop to the "airy", "ultrachic" dining room, setting the stage for chef Jeremy Lieb's "stellar" modern Gallic fare, while "genius" bartenders mix "interesting" libations at the "swanky", "way-cool" bar downstairs, and "helpful" servers make up for "snooty" hostesses.

### ☑ TWO urban licks ◑ *American*

| 23 | 25 | 20 | $38 |

**Poncey-Highland** | 820 Ralph McGill Blvd. NE (Freedom Pkwy.) |
404-522-4622 | www.twourbanlicks.com

A "dramatic" open kitchen and towering "wood-fire rotisserie" highlight the "cavernous", "warehouse" space of this Poncey-Highland New American (sibling of ONE. midtown kitchen and Trois) that attracts a "beautiful" crowd with "stellar" small plates and entrees with "Creole influences", "amazing wines cleverly offered" from "exposed barrels" and an "energizing", "pa-ar-ty" vibe; you "don't go for the service", though, and the noise can be "deafening", so regulars "visit the bocce court out back" for a "welcome break from the din" and "awesome" "views of Downtown."

### Udipi Cafe  *Indian/Vegetarian*

| 22 | 9 | 16 | $16 |

**Decatur** | 1850 Lawrenceville Hwy. (Woodridge Dr.) | 404-325-1933

"No one misses the meat" at this "fantastic" vegetarian BYO Indian in Decatur, an outpost of a national chain offering "cheap", "excellent" fare and a "tasty" buffet; the "bland" decor "leaves a lot to be desired", but it's "always clean" and the staff is "friendly."

### Umezono  *Japanese*

| ▽ 26 | 13 | 18 | $21 |

**Smyrna** | Windy Hill Plaza | 2086 Cobb Pkwy. SE (Windy Hill Rd.) |
770-933-8808 | www.umezono.us

"Unassuming digs" behind a "less-than-flashy exterior" make this Smyrna "favorite" a "tough spot to find", but the "intrepid" are rewarded with "wonderful" Japanese fare, including "addictive" "sushi bar staples" ("nothing too adventurous here") starring "some of the freshest fish in town"; a "variety of choices", "affordable" tabs and a "friendly" atmosphere translate into a "crowded" scene and service that's sometimes "not great", but fans "still go back" for "some of the best" *washoku* "in town."

## Uncle Julio's Casa Grande  *Tex-Mex*      18 | 15 | 17 | $23

**South Buckhead** | 1860 Peachtree Rd. NW (Collier Rd.) | 404-350-6767 | www.unclejulios.com

"Big is the theme" of this South Buckhead link of a Dallas-based chain that's *numero uno* for folks who've "had enough cheap Tex-Mex" and want something "beyond fajitas and tacos", while others can't get their fill of "terrific" "sangria-swirled margaritas"; a "personable" staff "handles" the weekday "happy-hour" crew, a *très chic gay* faction on Fridays and "families" on weekends, and the "neat tortilla machine" helps to "keep kids patient."

## Universal Joint ❶  *Pub Food*      18 | 17 | 13 | $17

**Decatur** | 906 Oakview Rd. NE (E. Lake Dr.) | 404-373-6260 | www.ujointbar.com

It might be "more about the location", "beer" and "welcoming vibe" than the menu of "cheap" "pub food" (or "half-hearted help") at this "solid neighborhood joint" in Decatur, but fans insist you'd "be hard-pressed to find a better burger" elsewhere; the "awesome patio" of the renovated "old gas station" overlooking the "streetscape of the heart of Oakhurst" is "perfect for gatherings", and overflowing with "yuppies" "who have dogs instead of kids" and "parents" who "let the rug rats roam free."

## NEW  Valenza  ⑤  *Italian*      22 | 20 | 21 | $36

**Brookhaven** | 1441 Dresden Dr., Ste. 100 (bet. Appalachee & Camille Drs.) | 404-969-3233 | www.valenzarestaurant.com

This Italian bistro from the "delightful" owners of Haven "really classes up the Brookhaven scene", thanks to chef Matt Swickerath's "well-executed" cuisine and "gracious" service from a "responsive" staff; the "cool" space with a rustic look of weathered oak and dark pine can get a "little noisy", but a "relaxed atmosphere" prevails, prompting pros to profess "we can't rave enough about this place."

## Ⓩ Varsity, The  *American*      17 | 13 | 17 | $9

**Kennesaw** | 2790 Town Center Dr. NW (Mall Blvd.) | 770-795-0802
**Alpharetta** | 11556 Rainwater Dr. (Westside Pkwy.) | 770-777-4004
**Downtown** | 61 North Ave. (Spring St.) | 404-881-1706 ❶
**Norcross** | 6045 Dawson Blvd. (Jimmy Carter Blvd.) | 770-840-8519

## Ⓩ Varsity Jr.  *American*

**Cheshire Bridge** | 1085 Lindbergh Dr. NE (Cheshire Bridge Rd.) | 404-261-5200
www.thevarsity.com

"Fast food can't get any faster" than the American eats at this "iconic" Downtown drive-in where the "carhops are hoppin'" to bring you the "best chili dogs in the universe", "onion rings the size of hubcaps" and other eats, all "covered in good old American grease"; its five branches might not "have the gritty feel of the original", but they're still part of the "Atlanta institution"; N.B. the Cheshire Bridge location also offers curbside service.

|  | FOOD | DECOR | SERVICE | COST |
|---|---|---|---|---|

## Vatica Indian
## Vegetarian Cuisine *Indian/Vegetarian*

▽ 21 | 9 | 19 | $13

**Marietta** | Terrell Mill Junction Shopping Ctr. | 1475 Terrell Mill Rd. SE (Powers Ferry Rd.) | 770-955-3740

"Strict" flesh-free foodies in Marietta report some of the "best vegetarian Indian you can find outside of Bombay" (well, at least "in East Cobb") can be found at this "friendly" "husband-and-wife" BYO spot; there's "no menu", so you get "whatever they serve", but it's "delicious" and "plentiful", and an "especially good bargain for lunch."

## Veni Vidi Vici *Italian*

23 | 22 | 22 | $43

**Midtown** | 41 14th St. NW (bet. Peachtree & Spring Sts.) | 404-875-8424 | www.buckheadrestaurants.com

This "perennial" Italian "favorite" in Midtown from the Buckhead Life Group "continues to surprise and delight" with "phenomenal" cuisine, including "rotisserie specials" that "shouldn't be missed", and "polished service" that "takes the edge off the bustle" and "difficult" parking; its "office-building" location is offset by "one of the handsomest" rooms "in town", with an "elegant" vibe to "impress" your "fiancé's uppity parents", but it can get "loud" and be sure to "bring your inheritance", for it's "expensive."

## Verve *American*

- | - | - | M

**Downtown** | 511 Peachtree St. NE (Renaissance Pkwy. NE) | 404-888-8880 | www.verveatlanta.com

"There's a place for everyone to enjoy" at this "upscale" Downtown restaurant lounge that's "worth visiting" for chef Darryl Evans' "excellent" New American cuisine and a tapas menu to go along with "great drinks and dancing"; regulars "love the three levels" and "diversity" of options, including a rooftop with expansive city views.

## NEW Via Ⓜ *Italian/Mediterranean*

- | - | - | I

**Buckhead** | Eclipse Bldg. | 262 Pharr Rd. (Peachtree Rd.) | 404-214-5404 | www.viarestaurant.net

A "place for the single crowd" that gets "better later at night", this "hip" Buckhead Italian-Mediterranean inhabits a "sleek" multilevel space with a modern European look, highlighted by a floor of white tile and blue glass, granite-topped bar and wood-burning ceramic brick oven; the seasonal menu includes small plates such as the signature shrimp and grits, pizzas and a Sunday brunch, and there are specials such as the half-price bottles of wine on Tuesdays.

## Vickery's *Eclectic/Southern*

19 | 16 | 18 | $23

**Midtown** | 1106 Crescent Ave. NE (12th St.) | 404-881-1106
**Glenwood Park** | 933 Garrett St. (Glenwood Ave.) | 404-627-8818 ◑
www.vickerys.com

"Like the Energizer Bunny", this "easygoing" Midtown venue and its younger sibling "just keep on going" with a "diverse" Southern-Eclectic menu of "comfort food" with "delicious" "twists", "amazing" brunch and "speedy service"; the original location boasts a patio that's "perfect on a sunny day", while the Glenwood Park branch offers sidewalk seating.

### Villa Christina ☒ *Italian*  19 | 22 | 20 | $41
**Dunwoody** | 4000 Summit Blvd. NE (Parkside Pl.) | 404-303-0133 |
www.villachristina.com
"Take a walk in the beautifully landscaped garden" and try your hand
on the "putting green" at this Dunwoody Italian best known for its
"great views" and "romantic" setting, but while some find the
"pricey" menu "disappointing", many others laud the "predictable"
yet "well-executed" fare; the "quiet" atmosphere "makes it great for
business" or a "date", and "warm service" "makes it even more pleasurable"; N.B. Caffe Christina, the take-out section, is located just
inside the entrance.

### Village Tavern *American*  21 | 23 | 21 | $29
**Alpharetta** | 11555 Rainwater Dr. (Haynes Bridge Rd.) | 770-777-6490 |
www.villagetavern.com
You "can't go wrong" with this Alpharetta link in a Denver-based
chain say surveyors who've "never been disappointed" with its
"delicious" New American eats, "excellent Sunday brunch" and
"well-done" wine list; the service is "consistently good", and the
"lodgelike interior" exudes "elegance in moderation", so guests can
celebrate a "special occasion" or "feel comfortable" "with jeans and
a toddler", while an "interesting collection of characters" "social-
izes" in the "large" lounge.

### Vine *American*  21 | 20 | 20 | $36
**Virginia-Highland** | 1190 N. Highland Ave. (Amsterdam Ave.) |
404-892-2393 | www.vinerestaurant.com
"What a comeback" exclaim oenophiles about this "quiet" Virginia-
Highland New American where the new ownership delivers a "spot-
on" experience, with a focus on the "fantastic", "diverse" wine list
(including "half-priced bottles on Mondays") that's paired with
"delicious" Med-accented fare; the staff is "helpful", and the
"romantic" patio is an "attractive" setting for "alfresco dining."

### Vinings Inn ☒ *Southern*  21 | 18 | 21 | $41
**Vinings** | 3011 Paces Mill Rd. SE (Paces Ferry Rd.) | 770-438-2282 |
www.viningsinn.com
Set in an inn from 1853, this "vintage Vinings" Southern set "has just
gone through a complete makeover", and the "new owner and chef"
are "making this old standby much better" say supporters who find
"value" in the "consistent" fare and "quaint" "charm" that lures fans
"again and again"; service "can be a little slow", but it comes "with
a smile" in a "romantic" setting that's "lovely" and "relaxing", and
while critics are "unimpressed" with the "ordinary" fare, defenders
insist it has "improved."

### Vinny's on Windward *Italian*  22 | 22 | 19 | $36
**Alpharetta** | 5355 Windward Pkwy. (GA 400) | 770-772-4644 |
www.sedgwickrestaurantgroup.com
Alpharettans do the "mambo Italiano" at this "great suburban stop"
from the Sedgwick group (Bistro VG, Aspens and Pure) that's "been
around for years", serving "wonderful" Italian eats (try their signa-

| | FOOD | DECOR | SERVICE | COST |
|---|---|---|---|---|

ture "rack of lamb"), "great drinks" and "fairly priced" wines; the high-ceilinged brick space is "upscale but not pretentious", but critics complain the service can be "excellent one day and barely passable the next."

### Vinocity  *American*

▽ | 19 | 21 | 20 | $24 |

Kirkwood | 1963 Hosea Williams Dr. (Howard St.) | 404-870-8886 | www.vinocitywinebar.com

"Kirkwood goes high class" with the relocation of this New American small-plates specialist that was squeezed out of Midtown and is now an "oasis" "in an area with lots of bar food", with an "inviting" lounge that "opens onto a two-story dining room"; fans appreciate its "extensive" list of New World wines, paired with a "menu ranging from small plates" to "real meals of steaks and seafood."

### Vino Libro ❶  *Mediterranean*

▽ | 19 | 23 | 18 | $25 |

Grant Park | 933 Garrett St. SE (Bill Kennedy Way) | 404-624-3643 | www.vinolibro.com

Literati and oenophiles now have a "charming" choice for a "Friday with friends" or a "Saturday night date" with the arrival of this Grant Park wine bar/retailer and book shop, set in an arty space with a "nice ambiance"; you can "lounge", "listen to live jazz" and "taste new wines" (Monday night bottomless wine specials are "fantastic") paired with "good" Mediterranean small plates.

### Violette ☒  *French*

| 21 | 20 | 21 | $28 |

Clairmont | 2948 Clairmont Rd. NE (I-85) | 404-633-3363 | www.violetterestaurant.com

"The pickins' on this side of town are slim", so the "business" set and "budget-minded" *bec fins* appreciate this "approachable", "nicely packaged" Clairmont French bistro between I-75 and Buford Highway for its "fine" "country" fare that might just be "the best value in the South"; the "beautiful candlelit" space is "romantic" and "serene" even with the "wonderful" live entertainment nightly, and the staff "maintains high standards" of service.

### NEW Vita  *Italian*

| - | - | - | M |

South Buckhead | 2110 Peachtree Rd. NW (Bennett St.) | 404-367-8482 | www.vitaatl.com

Restaurateur and leukemia survivor Tony LaRocco (of Fratelli di Napoli fame) is celebrating a new lease on life with his aptly named South Buckhead Italian, which serves the same classic New York red-sauce fare that's made him a family-style favorite; the former Mick's space has been transformed with a cheerful gold interior and exterior, stylized columns, a 70-ft. under-lit bar and huge windows that overlook the bustle of Peachtree.

### Vito Goldberg's Pizza  *Pizza*

| - | - | - | I |

Marietta | 999 Whitlock Ave. (Mayfair Pl. NW) | 770-795-8292 | www.vitogoldbergs.com

Piezani praise the "fantastic thin, NY-style" pizzas at this strip-mall spot in Marietta, where a "pitcher of brew is quite reasonable" and diners of "all ages" "can be entertained" with "karaoke, trivia" or "bands"; the "friendly owner" "stops by to check" on everyone, and the space has a separate room for "special occasions."

### Vortex Bar & Grill ● *Burgers*   | 22 | 19 | 17 | $17 |

**Midtown** | 878 Peachtree St. NE (bet. 7th & 8th Sts.) | 404-875-1667
**Little Five Points** | 438 Moreland Ave. NE (Euclid Ave.) | 404-688-1828
www.thevortexbarandgrill.com

"You may feel nerdy without a tattoo" at these "biker-dude-inspired" joints in "L5P" and Midtown, but "when you want to get away from the Man", these "meat palaces" "rock" with "huge", "crazy good" hamburgers with a "galaxy of topping and sauce options", "great tater tots" and an "extensive single-malt selection"; an "irreverent" crew (but "nice as hell") provides service "on their time, not yours" in a "wild and crazy" setting that's "just this side of preciously wacky"; P.S. "no kids allowed", since "smoking is."

### Vreny's Biergarten 🏞 Ⓜ *German*   | ▽ 22 | 16 | 18 | $22 |

**Duluth** | 4225 River Green Pkwy. (Peachtree Industrial Blvd.) |
770-623-9413 | www.vrenysbiergarten.com

It's like "Oktoberfest all year" at this "traditional" "biergarten" located behind sibling Kurt's in Duluth, where "pretzels, fondue and brats, oh my!" are among the "solid", "authentic" German eats that are "nice on the palate" and complemented by a "great selection" of draft and imported beers; the outside deck is a "nice place in spring or fall", and the "quaint" scene is "friendly" for the "whole family" – "*Oma* and *Opa* would be proud."

### Wahoo! A Decatur Grill *American*   | 22 | 21 | 21 | $29 |

**Decatur** | 1042 W. College Ave. (E. Lake Dr.) | 404-373-3331 |
www.wahoogrilldecatur.com

"Pretend you're on the coast" at this "understated" Decatur American with a "real local vibe" and "terrific" "fresh" fare, including "lots of yumptious fish" (the "namesake grilled Wahoo is excellent"); a "friendly" staff delivers "attentive" service and "you can't beat the romance and aura" of the "glorious" "year-round" "patio", all of which add up to a "pleasurable dining experience."

### Ⓩ Watershed *Southern*   | 25 | 19 | 23 | $34 |

**Decatur** | 406 W. Ponce de Leon Ave. (Commerce Dr.) | 404-378-4900 |
www.watershedrestaurant.com

Choosing this "top performer" in Decatur is a "no-brainer" to fans who tout its "outstanding" Southern cuisine, including "out-of-this-world" veggies, "ethereal chocolate cake" and the "famous" Tuesday "fried chicken night" that leaves many "giddy"; "cool watery pastels" create a "bright, airy" milieu in the "converted gas-station" space, while the staff is "courteous" and "accessible", and though a few find it "over-hyped and overpriced", others consider its laurels "well-deserved."

### White House ∅ *Southern*   | 19 | 11 | 22 | $13 |

**Buckhead** | Peachtree Plaza | 3172 Peachtree Rd. NW (Mathieson Dr.) |
404-237-7601

"See the natives in their habitat" at this Southern "hole-in-the-wall treasure" where "Buckhead boys" "talk bidness without any hassle" over one of the "finest breakfasts in Atlanta" and "meat-and-three" fixin's that "can't be beat"; "tacky" decor and "political memorabilia" take a back seat to "the most genuine staff in Atlanta", and while some find it "overrated", cronies counter "there's a reason it's still going strong" after 60 years.

## Wildfire  *Steak*                           21 | 22 | 20 | $37

**Dunwoody** | Perimeter Mall | 94 Perimeter Ctr. W. (Ashford Dunwoody Rd. NE) | 770-730-9080 | www.wildfirerestaurant.com

"Delectable smells" greet you at the door of this Dunwoody steakhouse from the Chicago-based Lettuce Entertain You group that sizzles with "terrific" meats and "phenomenal desserts", plus an "extensive wine list" and "great martinis" that "keep the fire lit all night"; while the "high-end yet comfortable" '40s-style interior can get "loud", there's a "nice patio", but some who find the fare and service "hit-or-miss" "expect more for the price."

## Williamson Bros. Bar-B-Q  *BBQ*            20 | 13 | 18 | $14

**Marietta** | 1425 Roswell Rd. NE (Powers Ferry Rd.) | 770-971-3201
**Douglasville** | 7040 Concourse Pkwy. (Hwy. 5) | 770-949-5058
www.williamsonbros.com

A "mecca" of the smoke and spit, this family-owned BBQ duo (with a branch in Canton) serves up 'cue "just about any way you want" it, slathered with "your choice" of "tasty" sauce – purportedly "Newt had it flown to Washington when he was speaker"; the "good old-fashioned" fare is "worth the sacrifice of decor", and the "nice" folks running things offer a "conglomerate" of options, including "eat-in", "efficient" call-ahead takeout and retail sales.

## Willie Rae's  🖂 *Cajun/Southwestern*      ▽ 19 | 15 | 18 | $20

**Marietta** | 25 N. Park Sq. NE (bet. Cherokee & Church Sts.) | 770-792-9995

Simpatico's "cool" sibling in Downtown Marietta satisfies suburbanites with "creative", "consistent" Cajun and Southwestern eats, including the "best fish tacos east of the Mississippi" and "shrimp and grits" that are a "credit to the dish"; the "kid-friendly" "staff is always smiling", and "great local art makes things interesting" in the "cute" "joint" where fans "always feel at home."

## Willy's Mexicana Grill  *Mexican*          20 | 11 | 16 | $11

**Marietta** | Delk Spectrum Shopping Ctr. | 2900 Delk Rd. SE (Powers Ferry Rd.) | 770-690-0075
**Midtown** | 1071 Piedmont Ave. NE (12th St.) | 404-249-9054
**Atlantic Station** | 1920 Howell Mill Rd. (I-75) | 404-351-8883
**Buckhead** | 1228 W. Paces Ferry Rd. NW (Northside Pkwy.) | 404-816-2690
**Buckhead** | Roswell Wieuca Shopping Ctr. | 4377 Roswell Rd. NE (Wieuca Rd.) | 404-252-2235
**Decatur** | 2074A N. Decatur Rd. (Clairmont Rd.) | 404-321-6060
**Downtown** | Peachtree Center Food Ct. | 235 Peachtree St. NE (Andrew Young Int'l Blvd.) | 404-524-0821 🖂

*(continued)*

*(continued)*

## Willy's Mexicana Grill

**Dunwoody** | 1100 Hammond Dr. NE (Peachtree Dunwoody Rd.) |
770-512-0555
**South Buckhead** | Peachtree Sq. | 2280 Peachtree Rd. NW
(Peachtree Memorial Dr.) | 404-351-4671
**Virginia-Highland** | 832 Virginia Ave. NE (Doug Davis Dr.) |
404-968-4756 🗷
www.willys.com
Additional locations throughout the Atlanta area

"Lunchers with limited time to spare" and those who "don't want to
cook" appreciate this "cheap and cheerful" Mexican chain deemed
the "best of the bunch" thanks to "better, bigger" burritos made with
"top-notch" fillings and "free salsa" at most locations; "lines move
quickly" through the "nearly self service" drill in "unglamorous" but
"clean" spaces, and the "primo location" of the Midtown outlet
overlooking Piedmont Park makes it a "local favorite."

## Wisteria  *Southern*

24 | 22 | 24 | $40

**Inman Park** | 471 N. Highland Ave. NE (bet. Colquitt Ave. &
Freedom Pkwy.) | 404-525-3363 | www.wisteria-atlanta.com

"For a romantic dinner" or an "evening with friends" "that won't
blow the bank", this Inman Park "keeper" "never fails to deliver", offering "superb" Southern cuisine and "unpretentious" service by a
staff that "really cares", in a "dark", "intimate" space housed in a
"charming old brick building"; although it can get "loud when full",
the ambiance remains "cozy", whether you're "enjoying the banter
at the bar" or snuggling at a "table in the back."

## Wolfgang Puck Express  *Californian*

16 | 13 | 15 | $17

**South Buckhead** | Brookwood Village Shopping Plaza |
1745 Peachtree Rd. NE (25th St.) | 404-815-1500 |
www.wolfgangpuck.com

South Buckheaders brag on their "little bit of Wolfgang at an affordable price" that "fits well in the neighborhood" since "there's a little
something for everyone" from the "fast" "casual" Californian menu
starring "great" "brick-oven pizzas" and "interesting" "short-order"
fare that "beats burgers and chicken tenders by a mile"; while the
decor may be "school cafeteria", the counter service is "quick", but
puckrakers feel the food's "too express" and "barely good."

## Woodfire Grill  Ⓜ *Californian*

25 | 21 | 23 | $43

**Cheshire Bridge** | 1782 Cheshire Bridge Rd. NE (Piedmont Rd.) |
404-347-9055 | www.woodfiregrill.com

At his "mercifully non-trendy" Cheshire Bridge Californian, chef-
owner Michael Tuohy "puts his heart and soul" into the "exquisitely
prepared" and "impeccably sourced" "farm-to-table cuisine" that's
paired with a "top-notch wine list", while the staff "could not be
more helpful or informed"; there's a "welcoming" atmosphere in the
"serene" space highlighted by the "eponymous" oven, and while this
"special-occasion" spot is "pricey", many consider it a "terrific"
"choice to blow the budget" on.

| | FOOD | DECOR | SERVICE | COST |
|---|---|---|---|---|

**YellowFin** Ⓜ *American*  22 | 18 | 21 | $34

Roswell | 1170 Canton St. (Woodstock Rd.) | 678-277-9551 |
www.yellowfinblueroom.com

It "feels like the big city" at this "lovely" New American, a "pleasant
surprise in Roswell" where an "ambitious menu with a wide range of
seafood choices" is served by an "accommodating" staff; the atmosphere's "inviting", and fans find it easy to "celebrate life" on
the "pleasant patio", "nicely designed" dining room or in the "hip,
modern martini room."

**Zab-E-Lee** Ⓢ *Thai*  ▽ 23 | 10 | 22 | $17

Airport (College Park) | 4837 Old National Hwy. (Sullivan Rd.) |
College Park | 404-477-2987

Zealots "want to try the whole menu" "each time" they visit this
"outstanding", "reliable" Thai, an "ideal place for lunch" if you hap-
pen to be "near the airport"; even if you're not, fans insist it's "worth
the trip" – just not "after sundown", according to those who feel the
neighborhood's becoming even iffier.

**Zapata** *Mexican*  22 | 14 | 19 | $21

Norcross | 5975 Peachtree Pkwy. (Jay Bird Alley) | 770-248-0052 |
www.zapata-atl.com

"Not your run-of-the-mill" Mexican, this "wonderful" cantina spices
up Norcross with "authentic" south-of-the-border fare ("i.e. no
tacos") that's a "huge improvement from the usual 'chains'"; service
is "helpful and prompt" in the "casual" space in an "unexpected location", where a "lively, interesting" "crowd" shows up in search of
a "refreshing change."

**NEW Zaya** *Mediterranean*  - | - | - | M

Inman Park | 240 N. Highland Ave., Bldg. 2, Ste. I (Elizabeth St.) |
404-477-0050 | www.zayarestaurant.com

Inman Park gets an infusion of flavor and flair with the opening of this
modern Mediterranean from a New Orleans–based group that's making a name for itself with a menu of traditional regional eats with some
surprises (the signature drunken halloumi and an array of earthy
dips are perfect for sharing) and a moderately priced wine list; warm
sunset colors and dark wood define the modern interior, while the
flower-lined sidewalk patio makes for a pleasant alfresco evening.

**Zesto** *American*  16 | 9 | 12 | $9

Southside (Atlanta) | 1181 E. Confederate Ave. SE (Moreland Ave.) |
404-622-4254
Forest Park | 151 Forest Pkwy. (Old Dixie Hwy.) | 404-366-0564
Lindbergh | 2469 Piedmont Rd. (Lindbergh Way NE) | 404-237-8689
Little Five Points | 377 Moreland Ave. NE (McLendon Ave.) | 404-523-1973
Poncey-Highland | 544 Ponce de Leon Ave. NE (Monroe Dr.) |
404-607-1118
www.zestoatlanta.com

"Hot damn", "you get good stuff" at this family-owned chain of
"throwback burger joints" with "addictive" "fast-food-like"
American fare "actually worth eating" since it's "prepared to order",

including the "best shakes in town" and "tasty" Chubby Decker burger; the "retro decor and counter ladies seem to have traveled back to the '50s" at this "Atlanta mainstay for 50++ years" that's "still going strong."

**Zocalo** *Mexican*

19 | 16 | 16 | $22

**Midtown** | 187 10th St. NE (Piedmont Ave.) | 404-249-7576

**Zocalo Taqueria** *Mexican*

**Grant Park** | 465 Boulevard (I-20) | 404-635-9930

Purists praise this "*muy delicioso*" Midtown Mexican for its "authentic" south-of-the-border cuisine, including "mole to die for" and "sublime enchiladas", as well as "lethal" margaritas that'll "make you forget your name"; "parking is the pits", but the "open-air" patio and "earthy" decor "add even more character" to this "wonderfully relaxed" venue; the taqueria spin-off in Grant Park is closer to a fast-food setting.

**Zola Italian Bistro** 🅼 *Italian*

▽ 25 | 20 | 26 | $29

**Alpharetta** | 14155 Hwy. 9 N. (Bethany Bend) | 770-360-5777

Chef-owner Adriano Baldelli "knows his stuff" affirm aficionados of this Alpharetta Italian where the "outstanding" red-sauce fare is "as good as it gets north of Atlanta" and can be paired with "quality, low-cost wines by the glass"; though he "runs a tight ship" with a staff of "adults", the mood is "relaxed" in this "unpretentious" spot that is still a "secret many do not want discovered."

**Zucca Bar & Pizzeria** ● *Italian*

21 | 17 | 19 | $20

**Smyrna** | 2860 Atlanta Rd. (Spring St.) | 770-803-9990

**NEW** **Kennesaw** | 745 Chastain Rd. (Busbee Dr. NW) | 678-290-9313
www.zuccapizza.com

"Tables heave" with "heavenly pizzas" and other "consistently good" Italian fare at this suburban pair in Smyrna and Kennesaw, where a "friendly staff" waits on "young families" and others dropping in for a "quick bite"; the "casual" environs include patios that are popular in "warm weather", and are additional reasons *amici* give them "two thumbs way up."

**Zyka** 🅼 *Indian*

23 | 5 | 10 | $13

**Decatur** | 1677 Scott Blvd. (bet. DeKalb Industrial Way & N. Decatur Rd.) | 404-728-4444 | www.zyka.com

"It's all about the food" at this "inexpensive" Decatur Indian that's the "first choice" of many who deem its "amazing" fare the "best in Atlanta", including the "divine" "Chicken 65"; on the other hand, "counter service" (from a nonetheless "pleasant" staff), "Styrofoam plates" and "plastic utensils" in a "former church basement" comprise an "almost entertainingly bad environment" (definitely "not a first date place"), but most agree the "good-value" eats are "worth the oddity."

# Savannah

**Atlanta Bread Co.**  *Deli*                    17 | 13 | 15 | $12
**Southside** | 5500 Abercorn St. (Janet Dr.) | 912-691-1949 |
www.atlantabread.com
See review in Atlanta Directory.

**Bonefish Grill**  *Seafood*                   23 | 21 | 21 | $31
**Southside** | 5500 Abercorn St. (E. 73rd St.) | 912-691-2575 |
www.bonefishgrill.com
See review in Atlanta Directory.

🗷 **Carrabba's Italian Grill**  *Italian*       20 | 17 | 19 | $24
**Southside** | 10408 Abercorn St. (Tibet Ave.) | 912-961-7073 |
www.carrabbas.com
See review in Atlanta Directory.

🗷 **Elizabeth on 37th**  *Southern*            25 | 24 | 25 | $55
**Historic District** | 105 E. 37th St. (Drayton St.) | 912-236-5547 |
www.elizabethon37th.net
An "elegant" "showstopper" "dripping with charm", this "can't-be-
missed dining destination" in Savannah's Historic District is "still
the best around these parts" say fans who fete the "impeccable"
service, "fabulous" Southern cuisine, "amazing wine choices" and
"comfortable", "beautifully restored" turn-of-the-century mansion;
while some critics call it "overrated" and "past its prime", others insist "it only gets better with age."

**Garibaldi's**  *Italian*                      25 | 22 | 23 | $42
**Historic District** | 315 W. Congress St. (bet. Jefferson & Montgomery Sts.) |
912-232-7118 | www.garibaldisavannah.com
A "can't-miss if you're in Savannah", this "sophisticated" "old
standby" in the Historic District delivers "excellent" Italian cuisine
from a seafood-centric menu and "personable, competent" service
in a "grand" two-story setting; "plenty of space between tables"
makes an "intimate" meal possible – just "leave the kids at home."

**Il Pasticcio**  *Italian*                     22 | 21 | 20 | $45
**Historic District** | 2 E. Broughton St. (Bull St.) | 912-231-8888 |
www.ilpasticciosavannah.com
At this "excellent" Savannah Italian, "unique combinations" of "fresh
ingredients" highlight an "inventive" menu and the "staff aims to
please – most of the time"; the "swanky" setting gets "noisy" and
"crowded" with tourists thanks to its central location in "the heart of
Bull Street" in the Historic District, and "at 10 it turns into a nightclub",
and while some grouse that it "tries too hard to be NY", right down
to the "annoying attitudes", defenders insist "the food makes up for it."

**Johnny Harris**  🗷 *BBQ/Southern*            19 | 18 | 19 | $27
**Tybee Beach** | 1651 E. Victory Dr. (Wicklow St.) | 912-354-7810 |
www.johnnyharris.com
An "established" "tradition" "beloved by locals", Savannah's oldest
restaurant is not only "historically important", it also serves up "au-

thentic" BBQ and some of the "best fried chicken in the South" that's worth "breaking your diet for"; the service is "consistent", and the atmosphere is "cozy" in the Tybee Beach space that's been around since 1935.

**Lady & Sons** *Southern* | 19 | 15 | 18 | $28 |

**Historic District** | 102 W. Congress St. (Widdicker St.) | 912-233-2600 | www.ladyandsons.com

"Paula (Deen) fans" make a "stop on the 'Hey y'all' tour" at this "Savannah institution" and endure "three-plus hour" "waits" for "wonderful" Southern eats, including an "amazing" all-you-can-eat buffet that "will leave you blissfully stuffed"; the "beautiful" space in the Historic District has a "down-home feel", the "cattle call of tourists" notwithstanding, but some critics would rather "watch the TV show instead", claiming the "food doesn't live up to her reputation."

**Olde Pink House** *American* | 21 | 24 | 22 | $45 |

**Historic District** | 23 Abercorn St. (Bryan St.) | 912-232-4286

"Dripping in romance, candlelight and Southern hospitality", this "classic" "on one of Savannah's picturesque squares" in the Historic District is an "incredible" spot to "bring your sweetheart" for "stately" New American cuisine or "dessert and a drink" in the "cozy" "basement bar", where a pianist performs nightly; it's a "transporting experience" – complete with a resident "ghost" according to legend – but some are more spooked by "bland" fare that "needs a little excitement."

**Pirates' House** *Continental* | 15 | 18 | 16 | $32 |

**Historic District** | 20 E. Broad St. (E. Bay St.) | 912-233-5757 | www.thepirateshouse.com

This "old" "favorite" in Savannah's Historic District has "stood the test of time" (along with the building, which was built in 1753) with its swashbuckling theme, "old pirate tunnels" and "stories" that "make it worth a stop" for some "family fun"; while there's some "first-rate" seafood to be found on the Continental menu, critics keelhaul the "touristy fare", and opt for "a drink at the bar" instead.

**Sapphire Grill** *Eclectic* | 25 | 21 | 23 | $47 |

**Historic District** | 110 W. Congress St. (Whitaker St.) | 912-443-9962 | www.sapphiregrill.com

Pros promise a "delightful experience" at this "top-notch" Eclectic in Savannah's Historic District that has "gotten better with time", delivering "ambitious, delicious" fare (including "amazing choices of fish"), "provocative wine pairings" and "great service"; although some find the setting a bit "cold", others feel the modern treatment of an "old warehouse" lends a "hip contrast" to the "demure historical setting."

# Other Outlying Areas

**Big City Bread Cafe**  *Sandwiches*          ▽ 22 | 13 | 18 | $12
**Athens** | 393 N. Finley St. (Meigs St.) | 706-353-0029 |
www.bigcitybreadcafe.com
Any way you slice it, "the bread alone is worth the trip" to this
American sandwich specialist, a "gem on the edge of Downtown"
Athens lauded by loafers for its "fresh", "interesting salads and
sandwiches", and "fantastic baked goods"; the "casual" interior is
augmented by a "cool" patio that's "fine when the weather is nice",
and the setting is "kid- and dog-friendly."

**Bischero**  *Italian*          ▽ 19 | 23 | 20 | $29
**Athens** | 237 Prince Ave. (Newton St.) | 706-316-1006 |
www.italyinathens.com
Athenians find a "good alternative to the typical college town fare"
at this "authentic" Italian praised for its "fresh pastas" and brick-oven
pizzas that are among "the best in town", and some say "improving"
even more under new management; the "lovely" space featuring
exposed-brick walls graced with large-scale paintings is reportedly
due for a makeover sometime in 2008.

**Z Blue Willow Inn**  *Southern*          22 | 22 | 23 | $24
**Social Circle** | 294 N. Cherokee Rd. (Hightower Trail) | 770-464-2131 |
www.bluewillowinn.com
This "special place" in Social Circle evokes many a "childhood memory", serving up heaping plates of "outstanding" Southern fare ("try
the fried green tomatoes") from a buffet table in a "gorgeous" restored
Victorian mansion that's "decorated to the teeth" at Christmas
time; most agree it's "worth the drive", but warn that the temptation
to "stuff yourself" is high.

**Cargo Portside Grill**  🅂🅼 *Eclectic*          - | - | - | M
**Brunswick** | 1423 Newcastle St. (Gloucester St.) | 912-267-7330 |
www.cargoportsidegrill.com
This "pioneer in fine dining for Brunswick" is a "must when in the
area" according to those in-the-know who praise chef-owner
Kate Buchanan's "fine" Eclectic fare featuring "excellent, creative" seafood; locals and visitors alike "feel welcome" in the "very
cool establishment" located in a renovated century-old building
near the water.

**Z Carrabba's Italian Grill**  *Italian*          20 | 17 | 19 | $24
**Athens** | 3194 Atlanta Hwy. (Athens W. Pkwy.) | 706-546-9938 |
www.carrabbas.com
See review in Atlanta Directory.

**Crab Shack**  *Seafood*          18 | 15 | 17 | $23
**Tybee Island** | 40 Estill Hammock Rd. (Hwy. 80 E.) | 912-786-9857 |
www.thecrabshack.com
It may be "one of the least fancy places" you'll find, but for "Low
Country boil" with "personality galore", this Tybee Island seafood

spot is a "mecca" for many, serving "fresh" seafood in a "laid-back" setting with scenic "marsh views", complete with "live alligators" on display; crabby critics call it an "overrated tourist trap", but many agree it's still a "good bet for out-of-towners."

**Dillard House** *Southern*    21 | 16 | 20 | $23

Dillard | The Dillard House | 768 Franklin St. (Hwy. 441) | 706-746-5348 | www.dillardhouse.com

A "guilty pleasure" in the "foothills of North Georgia", this Dillard landmark offers a "family-style smorgasbord" of "fresh and tasty" Southern fare "at its finest" ("anything cooked with this much butter and lard can't be bad") in a "gorgeous" "lodge" setting with "breathtaking" "mountain views" that help make it "worth the drive"; foes find the fare "bland", but for others the "basic down-home taste" and "endless portions" are "never a disappointment" – just don't forget to "say when."

**D. Morgan's** ⊠Ⓜ *American*    - | - | - | M

Cartersville | 28 W. Main St. (Erwin St.) | 770-383-3535 | www.dmorgans.com

"God bless Derek Morgan" for this "gift to Cartersville" declare devotees of his American serving "delicious", "reasonably priced" cuisine in a renovated circa-1880 building strewn with antiques and boasting a "quaint" downstairs bar; for those "stuck on I-75" or Northwest Georgia residents who just "don't want to drive into Atlanta", it's a real "find."

**Doc Chey's Asian Kitchen** *Noodle Shop*    19 | 12 | 17 | $13

Athens | Michaels Bldg. | 320 E. Clayton St. (Jackson St.) | 706-546-0015 | www.doccheys.com

See review in Atlanta Directory.

**East West Bistro** *American*    21 | 19 | 21 | $27

Athens | 351 E. Broad St. (bet. Jackson & Wall Sts.) | 706-546-9378 | www.eastwestbistro.com

East meets West on the "eclectic" American menu of this "hip" Athens spot where locals and visiting UGA fans rally for "solid" eats in a "laid-back but sophisticated" setting; the "Downtown location" across from the university is "great for a date" or a "business lunch" – but "students" may find it "a bit steep for an everyday meal."

**Farm 255** Ⓜ *Mediterranean/Southern*    20 | 22 | 21 | $26

Athens | 255 W. Washington St. (bet. Hull & Pulaski Sts.) | 706-549-4660 | www.farm255.com

Locavores love this "cool" Athens Med-Southerner, where "modern-day hippies" "grow everything they cook", including mostly "organic" produce, which is "served in a no-frills manner", but "with flair", in a "cozy", "minimalist" setting; you can "stay for dancing" to live music on the patio (caveat: on "home game days", "Dawg fans" can get "rowdy after nine"), and while some sniff the "scene is far better than the food", others insist it's "worth a visit"; N.B. a post-Survey chef change is not reflected in the above Food score.

| | FOOD | DECOR | SERVICE | COST |
|---|---|---|---|---|

## ☒ Five & Ten  *American*    | 28 | 21 | 26 | $44 |

**Athens** | 1653 S. Lumpkin St. (Milledge Ave.) | 706-546-7300 |
www.fiveandten.com

A "must-do" for those "who live to eat", this "superb" Athens American can "compete with any of the big boys in Atlanta" say fans, thanks to "genius" chef Hugh Acheson's "terrific" cuisine that "oozes fresh" with "locally sourced" ingredients, and is paired with "nice wine options"; there's "no pretense" here, just "impeccable" service in a "relaxed", "eclectic" space, all of which leads some Atlantans to lament "can't we get it to move a little closer?"

## Five Star Day  *American/Soul Food*    | 21 | 13 | 17 | $12 |

**Athens** | 2230 Barnett Shoals Rd. (College Station Rd.) | 706-613-1001
**Athens** | 229 E. Broad St. (bet. College & Jackson Sts.) | 706-543-8552
www.fivestardaycafe.com

"They know how to butter a biscuit" at this "eclectic", "inexpensive" Athens duo that gets high marks for its "delicious hippie take" on soul food that's "perfect" for "college kids" in need of "mom's cooking" ("here's where the 'freshman 15' starts"), served by staffs of "mostly townie types"; the original location on East Broad boasts a "tiny" patio, and both branches spotlight "interesting" art.

## Flowery Branch Yacht Club  Ⓜ *American*    | - | - | - | I |

**Flowery Branch** | 5510 Church St. (Pine St.) | 770-967-9060 |
www.fbyachtclub.com

This New American "near Lake Lanier" in historic Downtown Flowery Branch blossoms with "good intentions" say insiders who praise its "inventive", "surprisingly good" eats; the renovated Victorian Queen Anne cottage is on the "small" side and service can be "spotty" but those in-the-know insist it's "worth the drive" (or cruise).

## Grit, The  *Vegetarian*    | 21 | 15 | 17 | $15 |

**Athens** | 199 Prince Ave. (Pulaski St.) | 706-543-6592 | www.thegrit.com

Athens "alts" and anyone else looking for a meal "absent of carnivorous fare" head to this "vegetarian mecca" for its "excellent variety" of "fantastic" meat-free eats featuring "fresh, local ingredients" at "reasonable prices"; the historic building where it's housed is a no-frills, affair and insiders quip there's a good chance your server will be a local "band member."

## H&H Restaurant  ☒ *Southern*    | - | - | - | I |

**Macon** | 807 Forsyth St. (Plum St.) | 478-742-9810 | www.mamalouise.com

"Soul food meets Southern rock" at this "Macon institution" where the "Allman Brothers" used to hang, an "old-school" "meat-and-three" that's "better than its reputation" according to cognoscenti; it's "nothing fancy", but the "down-home" Southern cooking (including "fried chicken that's worth the drive") "will leave you smiling."

## Harry Bissett's Bayou Grill  *Cajun/Creole*    | 21 | 20 | 20 | $35 |

**Athens** | 1155 Mitchell Bridge Rd. (Timothy Rd.) | 706-552-1193 |
www.harrybissetts.net

*(continued)*

*(continued)*

## Harry Bissett's New Orleans Café *Cajun/Creole*

**Athens** | 279 E. Broad St. (Jackson St.) | 706-353-7065 |
www.cafe.harrybissetts.net

Evoking "fond memories of the Crescent City" for many, this "Athens icon" "just across" the UGA campus (and its Westside spin-off) earns accolades for its "classic bayou-style" Cajun-Creole fare with "lots of spice and cream", including a "variety of seafood options"; while space can be "tight" in the Downtown original, the upstairs room is "romantic and rustic", and while some find the fare "hit-or-miss", fans tout it as the place "if you must get a New Orleans fix."

## La Parrilla *Mexican*          22 | 17 | 21 | $16

**Flowery Branch** | 3446 Winder Hwy. (Atlanta Hwy.) | 770-297-0811 |
www.laparrilla.com

See review in Atlanta Directory.

## ☑ Last Resort *Southern*          24 | 19 | 21 | $27

**Athens** | 184 W. Clayton St. (Hull St.) | 706-549-0810 |
www.lastresortgrill.com

The "first choice" of many in Athens, this socially conscious Southerner delivers "wonderful" "nouvelle" cuisine with a Southwestern flair, including an "inventive" "Sunday brunch"; the "bar scene" is "always packed" with a "young, attractive" crowd, while a rotating collection of "fantastic" "local art" in the rustic space "sparks conversation", which may help to fill the "long waits" that are a product of its "no-reservations policy."

## Linger Longer Bar & Grill *American/Steak*     ▽ 27 | 27 | 27 | $41

**Greensboro** | The Ritz-Carlton Lodge, Reynolds Plantation |
1 Lake Oconee Trail (Hwy. 44) | 706-467-0600 | www.ritzcarlton.com

Fans find it easy to linger over a rib-eye steak at this "expensive" Traditional American with an emphasis on beef, the "favorite" dining option of many at the Ritz-Carlton Lodge, Reynolds Plantation at Lake Oconee, where you can watch the golfers from the stone veranda or snuggle by the fire in the rustic space.

## Natalia's ☑ *Italian*          - | - | - | M

**Macon** | Riverside Plaza Shopping Ctr. | 2720 Riverside Dr. (Lee Rd.) |
478-741-1380 | www.natalias.net

"So good you won't believe you're in Macon", this "wonderful" Italian sets the "local standard in fine dining" and "stacks up with any restaurant" say peripatetic pros who "make a point of stopping" here whenever in the area; it's "close to I-75", and the setting is "lovely", graced with an eclectic display of imported treasures.

## NEW National, The ☑ *Mediterranean*     ▽ 28 | 23 | 27 | $34

**Athens** | 232 W. Hancock Ave. (bet. N. Hull & Pulaski Sts.) |
706-549-3450 | www.thenationalrestaurant.com

Hugh Acheson (Five & Ten) "comes up with another winner", this "lovely" Athens Mediterranean serving "imaginative, Spanish-inspired" fare, including "small plates", and an "excellent wine list" with a "multitude" of selections by the glass; the prix fixe menu is a "great deal" (Monday and Tuesday nights it includes a complimentary movie ticket to the theater next door), and the "Downtown" setting is "very hip", with an open kitchen, maps adorning the walls and a bar that stays open until 2 AM every night.

### ☑ Nu-Way Weiners ☒ *Hot Dogs*
| 20 | 11 | 17 | $8 |

**Macon** | 430 Cotton Ave. (1st St.) | 478-743-1368 | www.nu-wayweiners.com

"They've been getting it right since 1916" at this "low-tech" hot dog "icon" that's "worth a stop in Macon" for its "distinctive" "red wieners" and "secret chili sauce"; it's "not the place to go if you're worried about counting calories", but "when you're in the mood" for a "guilty pleasure" at a "bargain" price, fans insist "nothing else will do."

### Palm Beach Restaurant Ⓜ *American*
| - | - | - | I |

**McDonough** | 2180 W. Hwy. 20 (Westridge Pkwy.) | 770-898-6877 | www.palmbeach-restaurant.com

"They go out of their way to make you feel at home" at this McDonough New American, a family-owned option in a neighborhood replete with chains; the decor combines comfortable Caribbean and edgier Miami looks, and the service is "friendly", making it an "easy place to relax and dine."

### Slope's BBQ ☒ *BBQ*
| 18 | 12 | 18 | $12 |

**Cartersville** | 1131 N. Tennessee St. (Felton Rd.) | 770-386-9090 | www.slopesbbq.com
See review in Atlanta Directory.

### ☑ Varsity, The *American*
| 17 | 13 | 17 | $9 |

**Athens** | 1000 W. Broad St. (Milledge Ave.) | 706-548-6325 | www.thevarsity.com
See review in Atlanta Directory.

### Weaver D's ☒ *Soul Food*
| - | - | - | I |

**Athens** | 1016 E. Broad St. (Spring St.) | 706-353-7797
This Athens "destination" is "rightly famous" and worthy of its "reference in R.E.M. songs" on the strength of its "true soul food" that fans call out as "some of the best in the world"; it's a "hole-in-the-wall", but "perfectly clean", and the vibe is strictly "good natured."

### Whistle Stop Cafe *Southern*
| - | - | - | I |

**Juliette** | 443 McCrackin St. (Juliette Rd.) | 478-992-8886 | www.thewhistlestopcafe.com
This "sweet little jewel" in Juliette "requires some searching to find" but "intrepid diners" who veer off US-23 will find it in a former hardware store just a stone's throw from the Ocmulgee River, where "cured ham with all the fixin's" and other sultry Southern fare is served; you may feel like you're on the set of the Jessica Tandy classic *Fried Green Tomatoes*, which was filmed on location.

### Williamson Bros. Bar-B-Q *BBQ*
| 20 | 13 | 18 | $14 |

**Canton** | 1600 Marietta Hwy. (Hwy. 575, exit 16A) | 770-345-9067 | www.williamsonbros.com
See review in Atlanta Directory.

# INDEXES

All places are in the Atlanta area unless otherwise noted (S=Savannah; O=Other Outlying Areas).

vote at ZAGAT.com                                                    137

# Cuisines

Includes restaurant names, locations and Food ratings. ☑ indicates places with the highest ratings, popularity and importance.

## AMERICAN (NEW)

| | |
|---|---|
| Anthony's \| **Buckhead** | 19 |
| ☑ Aria \| **Buckhead** | 27 |
| ☑ Bacchanalia \| **W'side** | 29 |
| ☑ BluePointe \| **Buckhead** | 24 |
| Brooklyn Cafe \| **Sandy Springs** | 18 |
| ☑ Buckhead Diner \| **Buckhead** | 23 |
| Café di Sol \| **Poncey-Highland** | 20 |
| NEW Cakes & Ale \| **Decatur** | – |
| ☑ Canoe \| **Vinings** | 26 |
| City Grill \| **D'town** | 22 |
| Clubhouse \| **Buckhead** | 17 |
| Corner Cafe \| **Buckhead** | 20 |
| D. Morgan's \| **Cartersville/O** | – |
| East West \| **Athens/O** | 21 |
| NEW VIII fifty \| **Roswell** | – |
| Einstein's \| **Midtown** | 18 |
| Farmhouse \| **Palmetto** | 25 |
| Feast \| **Decatur** | 22 |
| Fickle Pickle \| **Roswell** | 23 |
| ☑ Five & Ten \| **Athens/O** | 28 |
| Five Seasons \| **multi.** | 22 |
| Flowery Branch \| **Flowery Branch/O** | – |
| Food 101 \| **multi.** | 20 |
| ☑ Food Studio \| **W'side** | 24 |
| French Am. Brass. \| **D'town** | 24 |
| Fresh/Order \| **multi.** | 21 |
| NEW Glenwood \| **E Atlanta** | – |
| Globe \| **Midtown** | 20 |
| ☑ Grace 17.20 \| **Norcross** | 25 |
| Haven \| **Brookhaven** | 23 |
| NEW Hil \| **Palmetto** | – |
| Hi Life \| **Norcross** | 23 |
| NEW Holeman/Finch \| **S Buckhead** | – |
| ☑ Java Jive \| **Poncey-Highland** | 22 |
| JCT. Kitchen \| **W'side** | 24 |
| Lobby at 12 \| **Atlantic Sta.** | 20 |
| Mitra \| **Midtown** | 20 |
| Muss/Turner's \| **Smyrna** | 25 |
| Nirvana \| **multi.** | 18 |
| Olde Pink \| **Historic Dist/S** | 21 |
| ☑ ONE. midtown \| **Midtown** | 22 |
| Palm Beach Rest. \| **McDonough/O** | – |
| ☑ Park 75 \| **Midtown** | 27 |
| Pleasant \| **Midtown** | 19 |
| ☑ Quinones \| **W'side** | 28 |
| ☑ Rathbun's \| **Inman Pk** | 28 |
| Real Chow Baby \| **W'side** | 20 |
| Repast \| **Midtown** | 24 |
| ☑ Rest. Eugene \| **S Buckhead** | 28 |
| River Room \| **Vinings** | 21 |
| NEW Room at 12 \| **D'town** | 22 |
| R. Thomas \| **S Buckhead** | 19 |
| Sage \| **Decatur** | 20 |
| ☑ Seasons 52 \| **multi.** | 22 |
| Shaun's \| **Inman Pk** | 24 |
| Sia's \| **Duluth** | 25 |
| Simpatico \| **Marietta** | 20 |
| ☑ Sun Dial \| **D'town** | 19 |
| Table 1280 \| **Midtown** | 20 |
| NEW TAP \| **Midtown** | 14 |
| Taurus \| **S Buckhead** | 23 |
| tomas \| **Norcross** | 24 |
| Tossed \| **multi.** | 16 |
| Toulouse \| **S Buckhead** | 21 |
| Trilogy \| **Marietta** | 14 |
| ☑ TWO urban \| **Poncey-Highland** | 23 |
| Verve \| **D'town** | – |
| Village Tavern \| **Alpharetta** | 21 |
| Vine \| **VA-Highland** | 21 |
| Vinocity \| **Kirkwood** | 19 |
| YellowFin \| **Roswell** | 22 |

## AMERICAN (TRADITIONAL)

| | |
|---|---|
| NEW American Girl \| **Alpharetta** | – |
| American Rd. \| **VA-Highland** | 18 |

Ann's Snack | **D'town** _23_

Atkins Park | **multi.** _19_

🅩 Belly General | **VA-Highland** _19_

Blue Ribbon | **Tucker** _20_

Brake Pad | **Airport (College Pk)** _18_

Brickery | **Sandy Springs** _18_

🆕 BrickTop's | **Buckhead** _19_

Brookwood | **Roswell** _20_

🅩 Cheesecake Fac. | **multi.** _19_

Chicago's | **multi.** _18_

Dailey's | **D'town** _21_

Downwind | **DeKalb** _18_

Dressed Salads | **Midtown** _19_

Earl | **E Atlanta** _22_

ESPN Zone | **Buckhead** _10_

Five Star Day | **Athens/O** _21_

Garrison's | **multi.** _19_

George's | **VA-Highland** _22_

Gold Star | **Midtown** _15_

Gordon Biersch | **Midtown** _16_

Greenwoods | **Roswell** _23_

Houston Mill | **Emory** _18_

🅩 Houston's | **multi.** _22_

🆕 Hudson | **Brookhaven** _14_

Joey D's | **Dunwoody** _20_

Johnny Rockets | **multi.** _16_

Linger Longer | **Greensboro/O** _27_

🆕 Luckie | **D'town** _17_

Majestic | **Poncey-Highland** _12_

Manuel's | **Poncey-Highland** _17_

Marlow's | **multi.** _20_

Mick's | **Midtown** _16_

🅩 Murphy's | **VA-Highland** _24_

Norcross | **Norcross** _19_

Paul's | **S Buckhead** _23_

Pub 71 | **Brookhaven** _18_

Righteous Rm. | **Poncey-Highland** _22_

Roasters | **multi.** _20_

🆕 Stats | **D'town** _19_

Sun in Belly | **Kirkwood** _24_

Tavern/Phipps | **Buckhead** _18_

🅩 Ted's Montana | **multi.** _19_

Terra Terroir | **Brookhaven** _19_

Thrive | **D'town** _17_

🆕 Top Flr | **Midtown** _25_

🅩 Varsity | **multi.** _17_

Wahoo! | **Decatur** _22_

Wildfire | **Dunwoody** _21_

Zesto | **multi.** _16_

## ARGENTINEAN

🅩 Pampas Steak | **Alpharetta** _26_

## ASIAN

Harry & Sons | **VA-Highland** _20_

Malaya | **S Buckhead** _17_

Real Chow Baby | **W'side** _20_

Sia's | **Duluth** _25_

## ASIAN FUSION

🆕 Bluefin | **S Buckhead** _-_

Roy's | **Buckhead** _23_

Tin Drum | **multi.** _16_

## BAKERIES

🅩 Alon's | **multi.** _26_

Big City Bread | **Athens/O** _22_

Blue Eyed | **Palmetto** _21_

Bread Gdn. | **Midtown** _26_

Corner Cafe | **Buckhead** _20_

Gabriel's | **Marietta** _24_

Joli Kobe | **Sandy Springs** _23_

La Madeleine | **multi.** _19_

## BANGLADESHI

Panahar | **Buford Hwy. (Atl)** _23_

## BARBECUE

Barbecue Kitchen | **Airport (Atl)** _18_

Bobby/June's | **Midtown** _20_

Daddy D'z | **S'side (Atlanta)** _20_

Dreamland | **multi.** _17_

Dusty's BBQ | **Emory** _16_

Fat Matt's Rib | **VA-Highland** _23_

🆕 Fox Bros. BBQ | **Candler Pk** _-_

Harold's BBQ | **multi.** _23_

Hometown BBQ | **Lawrenceville** _-_

Jim N' Nick's | **multi.** _22_

Johnny Harris | **Tybee Beach/S** _19_

Lowcountry | **Suwanee** _19_

Old South | **Smyrna** _23_

CUISINES

| One Star Ranch | multi. | 20 |
| Pig-N-Chik | multi. | 19 |
| Rib Ranch | Marietta | 18 |
| Rolling Bones | D'town | 22 |
| ∅ Sam & Dave's | Marietta | 26 |
| Slope's BBQ | multi. | 18 |
| Smokejack | Alpharetta | 19 |
| Swallow/Hollow | Roswell | 23 |
| Williamson Bros. | multi. | 20 |

## BRAZILIAN

| NEW Beleza | Midtown | 23 |
| NEW Chima | Buckhead | - |
| Fire/Brazil | multi. | 21 |
| ∅ Fogo de Chão | Buckhead | 24 |
| Sal Grosso | Cobb | 21 |

## BURGERS

| Ann's Snack | D'town | 23 |
| ∅ Five Guys | multi. | 21 |
| Johnny Rockets | multi. | 16 |
| Moe's/Joe's | VA-Highland | 13 |
| Universal | Decatur | 18 |
| Vortex B&G | multi. | 22 |
| Zesto | multi. | 16 |

## CAJUN

| Atkins Park | multi. | 19 |
| Gumbeaux's | Douglasville | 24 |
| Hal's/Old Ivy | Buckhead | 25 |
| Harry Bissett's | Athens/O | 21 |
| Huey's | S Buckhead | 18 |
| McKinnon's | Buckhead | 18 |
| Pappadeaux | multi. | 21 |
| NEW Parish | Inman Pk | - |
| Redfish | Grant Pk | 22 |
| Willie Rae's | Marietta | 19 |

## CALIFORNIAN

| Raging Burrito | Decatur | 18 |
| Wolfgang Puck | S Buckhead | 16 |
| Woodfire Grill | Cheshire Bridge | 25 |

## CARIBBEAN

| Caribe Café | Marietta | - |

## CHINESE

(* dim sum specialist)

| Bamboo Gdn. | multi. | 19 |
| Canton Cooks | Sandy Springs | 23 |
| Canton Hse.* | Buford Hwy. (Cham.) | 20 |
| China Cooks | Sandy Springs | 22 |
| China Delight* | Chamblee | 21 |
| Chin Chin | multi. | 19 |
| Chopstix | Buckhead | 23 |
| East Pearl* | Duluth | - |
| Grand China | Buckhead | 17 |
| Happy Valley* | Buford Hwy. (Atl) | 18 |
| Hong Kong* | Cheshire Bridge | 19 |
| House/Chan | Smyrna | 24 |
| Hsu's | D'town | 21 |
| Lee's Buddha | Buckhead | 19 |
| Little Szechuan | Buford Hwy. (Dora.) | 21 |
| Mu Lan | Midtown | 18 |
| P.F. Chang's | multi. | 20 |
| Pung Mie | Buford Hwy. (Dora.) | 21 |
| Tasty China | Marietta | 24 |

## COFFEEHOUSES

| Cafe Intermezzo | multi. | 21 |

## COFFEE SHOPS/DINERS

| Crescent Moon | multi. | 20 |
| Majestic | Poncey-Highland | 12 |
| OK Cafe | Buckhead | 20 |
| Original Pancake | multi. | 21 |
| Rexall Grill | Duluth | 20 |
| Ria's | Cabbagetown | 23 |
| Silver Skillet | Midtown | 18 |
| Sun in Belly | Kirkwood | 24 |
| Thumbs Up | multi. | 23 |

## CONTINENTAL

| Après Diem | Midtown | 17 |
| ∅ Clark/Schwenk | Vinings | 24 |
| ∅ Ecco | Midtown | 25 |
| Joli Kobe | Sandy Springs | 23 |
| ∅ Nikolai's | D'town | 25 |
| ∅ Pano's/Paul's | Buckhead | 26 |
| Petite Auberge | Emory | 19 |

Pirates' Hse. | **Historic Dist/S**    15

Ritz/Buckhead | **Buckhead**    24

## CREOLE

Hal's/Old Ivy | **Buckhead**    25

Harry Bissett's | **Athens/O**    21

Huey's | **S Buckhead**    18

McKinnon's | **Buckhead**    18

Pappadeaux | **multi.**    21

🆕 Parish | **Inman Pk**    -

Redfish | **Grant Pk**    22

Tasting Room | **multi.**    22

## CUBAN

Coco Loco's | **Buckhead**    19

Fuego | **Midtown**    20

Havana S'wich |    22
   **Buford Hwy. (Atl)**

Las Palmeras | **Midtown**    22

Palomilla's | **Norcross**    23

Salsa | **multi.**    18

## DELIS

Atlanta Bread | **multi.**    17

Goldberg's | **multi.**    20

Jason's Deli | **multi.**    17

Muss/Turner's | **Smyrna**    25

New Yorker | **Buckhead**    22

Oak Grove | **Decatur**    21

Provisions to Go | **W'side**    25

Rising Roll | **multi.**    20

Sawicki's | **Decatur**    26

## DESSERT

🚺 Alon's | **multi.**    26

🚺 Aria | **Buckhead**    27

Atlanta Bread | **multi.**    17

Cafe Intermezzo | **multi.**    21

🚺 Cheesecake Fac. | **multi.**    19

Chocolate Bar | **Decatur**    20

🚺 Chocolate Pink | **Midtown**    25

Dailey's | **D'town**    21

Jake's | **Decatur**    19

La Madeleine | **multi.**    19

Olde Pink | **Historic Dist/S**    21

🚺 Paolo's Gelato | **VA-Highland**    25

## ECLECTIC

Aqua Blue | **Roswell**    21

Cargo | **Brunswick/O**    -

Eats | **Midtown**    18

🆕 Luckie | **D'town**    17

Metrofresh | **Midtown**    22

Sapphire | **Historic Dist/S**    25

Shout | **Midtown**    16

SoHo | **Vinings**    22

Sops on Ellis | **D'town**    25

Vickery's | **multi.**    19

## EUROPEAN

Babette's | **Poncey-Highland**    25

Kurt's | **Duluth**    22

## FONDUE

Dante's Hatch | **Buckhead**    18

Melting Pot | **multi.**    22

## FRENCH

Atmosphere | **Midtown**    25

Au Rendez | **Sandy Springs**    21

Bistro VG | **Roswell**    22

🚺 Floataway | **Emory**    25

🆕 Hil | **Palmetto**    -

🚺 JOËL | **Buckhead**    26

La Madeleine | **multi.**    19

Les Fleurs | **D'town**    27

🚺 Nikolai's | **D'town**    25

🚺 Ritz/Buckhead Din. Rm. |    27
   **Buckhead**

🚺 Trois | **Midtown**    22

## FRENCH (BISTRO)

Anis Bistro | **Buckhead**    22

Cafe Alsace | **Decatur**    22

Le Giverny | **Emory**    20

Pastis | **Roswell**    21

🆕 Peasant Bistro | **D'town**    -

Soleil Bistro | **Buckhead**    18

Violette | **Clairmont**    21

## FRENCH (BRASSERIE)

Au Pied | **Buckhead**    19

French Am. Brass. | **D'town**    24

🆕 La Petite Maison |    -
   **Sandy Springs**

## GASTROPUB

NEW TAP | Amer. | **Midtown** — 14

## GERMAN

Gasthaus | **Cumming** — -
Vreny's Bier | **Duluth** — 22

## GREEK

Athens Pizza | **multi.** — 20
Avra | **Midtown** — 20
Blu Greek | **Marietta** — 20
Z Kyma | **Buckhead** — 25
Taverna Plaka | **Cheshire Bridge** — 17

## HAWAIIAN

Roy's | **Buckhead** — 23

## HEALTH FOOD

(See also Vegetarian)
Terra Terroir | **Brookhaven** — 19

## HOT DOGS

Z Nu-Way Weiners | **Macon/O** — 20
Z Varsity | **multi.** — 17
Zesto | **multi.** — 16

## ICE CREAM PARLORS

Jake's | **Decatur** — 19
Z Paolo's Gelato | **VA-Highland** — 25

## INDIAN

Bhojanic | **Decatur** — 22
Bombay | **Chamblee** — 17
Haveli Indian | **multi.** — 16
Himalayas | **Chamblee** — 21
Madras Chettinaad | **Decatur** — 23
Madras Saravana | **Decatur** — 24
Minerva | **Alpharetta** — 22
Palace | **Norcross** — -
Raja Indian | **Buckhead** — 19
Rose of India | **Chamblee** — 19
Santoor | **Alpharetta** — -
Udipi Cafe | **Decatur** — 22
Vatica | **Marietta** — 21
Zyka | **Decatur** — 23

## IRISH

Meehan's Pub | **multi.** — 18
Pub 71 | **Brookhaven** — 18

## ITALIAN

(N=Northern; S=Southern)
Alfredo's | **Cheshire Bridge** — 22
NEW Allegro | **Midtown** — 20
Amalfi | S | **Roswell** — 23
Z Antica Posta | N | **Buckhead** — 24
Azio | **multi.** — 18
Bambinelli's | S | **Tucker** — 19
Baraonda | S | **Midtown** — 23
Bischero | **Athens/O** — 19
Brio Tuscan | **multi.** — 19
Buca/Beppo | **Alpharetta** — 17
Cafe Prego | **Buckhead** — 19
Z Carrabba's | **multi.** — 20
Z di Paolo | N | **Alpharetta** — 27
Dolce | **Atlantic Sta.** — 18
Dominick's | **multi.** — 23
Enoteca Carbonari | **Midtown** — 22
Figo Pasta | **multi.** — 21
Z Floataway | **Emory** — 25
Fratelli/Napoli | S | **Roswell** — 18
Fritti | **Inman Pk** — 23
Garibaldi's | **Historic Dist/S** — 25
Il Localino | **Inman Pk** — 21
Il Pasticcio | N | **Historic Dist/S** — 22
Ippolito's | **multi.** — 19
Z La Grotta | N | **multi.** — 26
La Tavola | **VA-Highland** — 24
NEW Lola | **Buckhead** — -
Z Maggiano's | **multi.** — 20
Natalia's | N | **Macon/O** — -
Nino's | **Cheshire Bridge** — 22
Oscar's Villa | S | **Dunwoody** — 27
Osteria 832 | **VA-Highland** — 21
Pasta/Pulcinella | N | **Midtown** — 23
Pasta Vino | N | **multi.** — 19
Portofino | **Buckhead** — 21
Pricci | **Buckhead** — 24
Z Sotto Sotto | N | **Inman Pk** — 27
NEW Stella | **Grant Pk** — -
Taverna Fiorentina | N | **Vinings** — -
Toscano | **W'side** — 23
Tratt. La Strada | **Marietta** — 19
Tringalis | **D'town** — -

NEW Valenza | N | **Brookhaven** 22

Veni Vidi Vici | **Midtown** 23

NEW Via | **Buckhead** -

Villa Christina | **Dunwoody** 19

Vinny's | **Alpharetta** 22

NEW Vita | **S Buckhead** -

Zola Italian | **Alpharetta** 25

Zucca | **multi.** 21

## JAPANESE

(* sushi specialist)

Atlantic Sea* | **Alpharetta** 22

Benihana | **multi.** 19

NEW Bluefin* | **S Buckhead** -

Edo | **Decatur** 19

Genki* | **Buckhead** 19

Z Haru Ichiban* | **Duluth** 26

Hashiguchi* | **multi.** 24

Kobe | **Sandy Springs** 20

Lee's Buddha | **Buckhead** 19

Mali* | **VA-Highland** 23

Z NEW MF Buckhead* | 26
  **Buckhead**

Z MF Sushibar* | **Midtown** 27

Mt. Fuji* | **Marietta** 21

Nagoya* | **Roswell** 24

Nakato* | **Cheshire Bridge** 21

Nickiemoto's* | **Midtown** 20

Ru San's* | **multi.** 18

Sushi Ave.* | **Decatur** 24

Sushi Huku* | **Sandy Springs** 25

Z Taka* | **Buckhead** 27

Thaicoon* | **Marietta** 22

Tomo* | **Vinings** 27

Umezono* | **Smyrna** 26

## KOREAN

(* barbecue specialist)

Chosun OK* | **Doraville** -

88 Tofu | **Buford Hwy. (Atl)** 21

Hae Woon* | **Buford Hwy. (Dora.)** 22

So Kong Dong | **Doraville** 20

## LEBANESE

Byblos | **Roswell** 21

Mezza | **Decatur** 24

Nicola's | **Emory** 18

Sultan's | **Sandy Springs** 21

## MALAYSIAN

Penang | **Buford Hwy. (Cham.)** 22

Top Spice | **multi.** 21

## MEDITERRANEAN

Basil's | **Buckhead** 20

Byblos | **Roswell** 21

Café Lily | **Decatur** 23

Carpe Diem | **Decatur** 20

Eno | **Midtown** 23

Farm 255 | **Athens/O** 20

Gilbert's Med. | **Midtown** 20

Grape | **multi.** 16

Ibiza | **S Buckhead** 20

Z Krog Bar | **Inman Pk** 23

Z Little Alley | **Roswell** 26

Lobby at 12 | **Atlantic Sta.** 20

Mosaic | **Buckhead** 22

NEW National | **Athens/O** 28

NEW Peasant Bistro | **D'town** -

Z Ritz/Buckhead Din. Rm. | 27
  **Buckhead**

Sultan's | **Sandy Springs** 21

Tasting Room | **multi.** 22

NEW Via | **Buckhead** -

Vino Libro | **Grant Pk** 19

NEW Zaya | **Inman Pk** -

## MEXICAN

Chipotle | **multi.** 18

El Azteca | **multi.** 16

El Rey de Taco | 24
  **Buford Hwy. (Dora.)**

El Taco | **multi.** 20

Jalisco | **S Buckhead** 21

La Parrilla | **multi.** 22

NEW Lime Taqueria | **Smyrna** -

Mexico City | **Decatur** 16

Nuevo Laredo | **W'side** 24

Pappasito's | **Marietta** 23

Pure Taqueria | **Alpharetta** 23

Raging Burrito | **Decatur** 18

Rosa Mexicano | **Atlantic Sta.** 19

Sala/Sabor | **VA-Highland** _19_

**Taqueria/Sol** | **multi.** _24_

Tarahumata | **Alpharetta** _23_

Willy's Mex. | **multi.** _20_

Zapata | **Norcross** _22_

Zocalo | **multi.** _19_

## MOROCCAN

Imperial Fez | **S Buckhead** _19_

## NOODLE SHOPS

Doc Chey's | **multi.** _19_

Genki | **Buckhead** _19_

Noodle | **multi.** _19_

Tin Drum | **multi.** _16_

## PACIFIC RIM

Trader Vic's | **D'town** _20_

## PAN-ASIAN

Aqua Blue | **Roswell** _21_

Eurasia Bistro | **Decatur** _25_

Nickiemoto's | **Midtown** _20_

Noodle | **multi.** _19_

Pacific Rim | **D'town** _21_

Silk | **Midtown** _20_

**NEW** Steel | **Midtown** _-_

**NEW** Straits | **Midtown** _-_

## PAN-LATIN

La Fonda | **multi.** _20_

Loca Luna | **Midtown** _19_

Pura Vida | **Poncey-Highland** _25_

**Tierra** | **Midtown** _26_

## PERSIAN

Persepolis | **Sandy Springs** _21_

Rumi's | **Sandy Springs** _24_

## PERUVIAN

Machu Picchu | _18_
  **Buford Hwy. (Atl)**

## PIZZA

Athens Pizza | **multi.** _20_

Baraonda | **Midtown** _23_

Bischero | **Athens/O** _19_

Cameli's | **Midtown** _24_

Everybody/Pizza | **multi.** _20_

Fellini's Pizza | **multi.** _20_

Fritti | **Inman Pk** _23_

Grant Pizza | **multi.** _20_

Johnny's | **multi.** _17_

Mellow Mushroom | **multi.** _21_

Osteria 832 | **VA-Highland** _21_

Oz Pizza | **multi.** _19_

Pasta Vino | **multi.** _19_

Ray's Pizza | **multi.** _18_

Savage Pizza | **Little Five Pts** _20_

Shorty's | **multi.** _24_

Vito Goldberg's | **Marietta** _-_

Wolfgang Puck | **S Buckhead** _16_

Zucca | **multi.** _21_

## PUB FOOD

Brick Store | **Decatur** _21_

**NEW** Fadó | **Buckhead** _-_

Gordon Biersch | **Midtown** _16_

Manuel's | **Poncey-Highland** _17_

Marlow's | **multi.** _20_

Meehan's Pub | **multi.** _18_

Moe's/Joe's | **VA-Highland** _13_

Righteous Rm. | **Poncey-Highland** _22_

Universal | **Decatur** _18_

## SANDWICHES

**Alon's** | **multi.** _26_

Atlanta Bread | **multi.** _17_

Big City Bread | **Athens/O** _22_

Blue Eyed | **Palmetto** _21_

Bread Gdn. | **Midtown** _26_

Fickle Pickle | **Roswell** _23_

Goldberg's | **multi.** _20_

Havana S'wich | _22_
  **Buford Hwy. (Atl)**

Jason's Deli | **multi.** _17_

Metrofresh | **Midtown** _22_

New Yorker | **Buckhead** _22_

Rising Roll | **multi.** _20_

Sops on Ellis | **D'town** _25_

Toscano | **W'side** _23_

Tossed | **multi.** _16_

## SEAFOOD

**NEW** AquaKnox | **Buckhead** _-_

**Atlanta Fish** | **Buckhead** _23_

Atlantic Sea | **Alpharetta** 22
Blackstone | **Smyrna** 23
Bonefish Grill | **multi.** 23
Cabernet | **Alpharetta** 24
Chequers | **Dunwoody** 22
Ⓩ Chops/Lobster | **Buckhead** 27
Ⓩ Clark/Schwenk | **Vinings** 24
Crab Shack | **Tybee Is/O** 18
Dantanna's | **Buckhead** 19
Fontaine Oyster | **VA-Highland** 16
Garibaldi's | **Historic Dist/S** 25
Goldfish | **Dunwoody** 21
Ⓩ Kyma | **Buckhead** 25
McCormick/Schmick | **multi.** 20
Oceanaire | **Midtown** 23
Pappadeaux | **multi.** 21
**NEW** Pisces | **Alpharetta** –
Prime | **Buckhead** 23
Ray's/City | **D'town** 22
Ray's/River | **Sandy Springs** 23
Red Snapper | **Cheshire Bridge** 22
Six Feet | **multi.** 19
Strip | **Atlantic Sta.** 17
Wahoo! | **Decatur** 22
YellowFin | **Roswell** 22

## SINGAPOREAN
**NEW** Straits | **Midtown** –

## SMALL PLATES
(See also Spanish tapas specialist)
Bistro VG | French | **Roswell** 22
Ⓩ Ecco | Continental | **Midtown** 25
Enoteca Carbonari | Italian | 22
**Midtown**
Feast | Amer. | **Decatur** 22
Grape | Med. | **multi.** 16
Ibiza | Med. | **S Buckhead** 20
Ⓩ Krog Bar | Med. | **Inman Pk** 23
**NEW** Lime Taqueria | Mex. | –
**Smyrna**
Ⓩ Little Alley | Med. | **Roswell** 26
Mezza | Lebanese | **Decatur** 24
Muss/Turner's | Amer. | 25
**Smyrna**

Noche | SW | **VA-Highland** 20
Pura Vida | Pan-Latin | 25
**Poncey-Highland**
Sala/Sabor | Mex. | **VA-Highland** 19
Shout | Eclectic | **Midtown** 16
Silk | Pan-Asian | **Midtown** 20
Thrive | Amer. | **D'town** 17
Vinocity | Amer. | **Kirkwood** 19

## SOUL FOOD
Busy Bee | **D'town** 27
Carver's | **W'side** 26
Fat Matt's Chicken | 24
**VA-Highland**
Fat Matt's Rib | **VA-Highland** 23
Five Star Day | **Athens/O** 21
Horseradish | **Buckhead** 22
Rare | **Midtown** 24
Son's Place | **Inman Pk** 19
Soul Veg. | **multi.** 17
Thelma's | **D'town** 21
Weaver D's | **Athens/O** –

## SOUP
Metrofresh | **Midtown** 22
Ⓩ Souper Jenny | **Buckhead** 25

## SOUTH AFRICAN
10 Degrees | **Buckhead** 23

## SOUTHEAST ASIAN
**NEW** Spice Market | **Midtown** –

## SOUTHERN
Agnes/Muriel's | **Midtown** 18
Barbecue Kitchen | **Airport (Atl)** 18
Blue Eyed | **Palmetto** 21
Ⓩ Blue Ridge | **Buckhead** 23
Ⓩ Blue Willow | **Social Circle/O** 22
Bobby/June's | **Midtown** 20
Carver's | **W'side** 26
Colonnade | **Cheshire Bridge** 20
Dillard Hse. | **Dillard/O** 21
Ⓩ Elizabeth | **Historic Dist/S** 25
Farm 255 | **Athens/O** 20
Fat Matt's Chicken | 24
**VA-Highland**

| | |
|---|---|
| Fat Matt's Rib | **VA-Highland** | 23 |
| Feed Store | **Airport (College Pk)** | 19 |
| **NEW** Flying Biscuit | **multi.** | 19 |
| Gladys Knight | **multi.** | 18 |
| **NEW** Glenwood | **E Atlanta** | - |
| Greenwoods | **Roswell** | 23 |
| H&H | **Macon/O** | - |
| **NEW** Home | **Buckhead** | - |
| Horseradish | **Buckhead** | 22 |
| JCT. Kitchen | **W'side** | 24 |
| Johnny Harris | **Tybee Beach/S** | 19 |
| Lady & Sons | **Historic Dist/S** | 19 |
| **Z** Last Resort | **Athens/O** | 24 |
| Mary Mac's | **Midtown** | 19 |
| Matthews | **Tucker** | 20 |
| OK Cafe | **Buckhead** | 20 |
| Pittypat's | **D'town** | 15 |
| **NEW** Relish | **Roswell** | 23 |
| **Z** Ritz/Atlanta | **D'town** | 26 |
| Silver Midtown | **Midtown** | 16 |
| Silver Skillet | **Midtown** | 18 |
| Smokejack | **Alpharetta** | 19 |
| **NEW** Social House | **W'side** | - |
| Son's Place | **Inman Pk** | 19 |
| **Z** South City | **multi.** | 23 |
| Swan Coach | **Buckhead** | 18 |
| Thelma's | **D'town** | 21 |
| Thumbs Up | **multi.** | 23 |
| Vickery's | **multi.** | 19 |
| Vinings Inn | **Vinings** | 21 |
| **Z** Watershed | **Decatur** | 25 |
| Whistle Stop | **Juliette/O** | - |
| White House | **Buckhead** | 19 |
| Wisteria | **Inman Pk** | 24 |

## SOUTHWESTERN

| | |
|---|---|
| Agave | **Cabbagetown** | 22 |
| Georgia Grille | **S Buckhead** | 22 |
| Moe's SW | **multi.** | 13 |
| **Z** Nava | **Buckhead** | 23 |
| Noche | **VA-Highland** | 20 |
| **Z** Taqueria/Sol | **multi.** | 24 |
| Willie Rae's | **Marietta** | 19 |

## SPANISH

(* tapas specialist)

| | |
|---|---|
| **NEW** Cuerno* | **Midtown** | - |
| Eclipse* | **Buckhead** | 21 |
| Fuego* | **Midtown** | 20 |
| Loca Luna* | **Midtown** | 19 |

## STEAKHOUSES

| | |
|---|---|
| Aspens/Steak | **Marietta** | 23 |
| Benihana | **multi.** | 19 |
| Blackstone | **Smyrna** | 23 |
| **Z** Bone's | **Buckhead** | 27 |
| Brookwood | **Roswell** | 20 |
| Cabernet | **Alpharetta** | 24 |
| **Z** Capital Grille | **Buckhead** | 24 |
| Chicago's | **multi.** | 18 |
| **Z** Chops/Lobster | **Buckhead** | 27 |
| Cowtippers | **Midtown** | 15 |
| Dantanna's | **Buckhead** | 19 |
| Fire/Brazil | **multi.** | 21 |
| Fleming's/Steak | **Dunwoody** | 23 |
| **Z** Fogo de Chão | **Buckhead** | 24 |
| Garrison's | **multi.** | 19 |
| Hal's/Old Ivy | **Buckhead** | 25 |
| Highland Tap | **VA-Highland** | 20 |
| **Z** Kevin Rathbun | **Inman Pk** | 26 |
| Kobe | **Sandy Springs** | 20 |
| Linger Longer | **Greensboro/O** | 27 |
| **Z** LongHorn | **multi.** | 18 |
| **NEW** Maxim Prime | **D'town** | - |
| McKendrick's | **Dunwoody** | 25 |
| **Z** Morton's | **multi.** | 25 |
| Mt. Fuji | **Marietta** | 21 |
| **Z** New York Prime | **Buckhead** | 25 |
| Outback | **multi.** | 18 |
| Palm | **Buckhead** | 23 |
| **Z** Pampas Steak | **Alpharetta** | 26 |
| Prime | **Buckhead** | 23 |
| Ray's/Killer | **Alpharetta** | 22 |
| **NEW** Room at 12 | **D'town** | 22 |
| Ruth's Chris | **multi.** | 23 |
| Sal Grosso | **Cobb** | 21 |
| **Z** Stoney River | **multi.** | 24 |
| Strip | **Atlantic Sta.** | 17 |

| | |
|---|---|
| Taurus \| **S Buckhead** | 23 |
| Wildfire \| **Dunwoody** | 21 |

**TEX-MEX**

| | |
|---|---|
| Caramba \| **VA-Highland** | 15 |
| Jalisco \| **S Buckhead** | 21 |
| La Paz \| **Vinings** | 19 |
| Uncle Julio's \| **S Buckhead** | 18 |

**THAI**

| | |
|---|---|
| Annie's Thai \| **Buckhead** | 22 |
| Bangkok \| **Midtown** | 21 |
| Jitlada \| **Cheshire Bridge** | 16 |
| King & I \| **Midtown** | 19 |
| Little Bangkok \| **Cheshire Bridge** | 24 |
| Mali \| **VA-Highland** | 23 |
| ⏚ Nan Thai \| **Midtown** | 27 |
| Northlake Thai \| **Tucker** | 24 |
| Penang \| **Buford Hwy. (Cham.)** | 22 |
| Phuket \| **Buford Hwy. (Atl)** | 19 |
| ⏚ Rice Thai \| **Roswell** | 26 |
| Sawadee Thai \| **Sandy Springs** | - |
| Spoon \| **D'town** | 25 |
| Surin \| **VA-Highland** | 23 |

| | |
|---|---|
| ⏚ Tamarind Seed \| **Midtown** | 27 |
| Thai Chili \| **Emory** | 22 |
| Thaicoon \| **Marietta** | 22 |
| Top Spice \| **multi.** | 21 |
| Zab-E-Lee \| **Airport (College Pk)** | 23 |

**VEGETARIAN**

(* vegan)

| | |
|---|---|
| Cafe Sunflower \| **multi.** | 22 |
| ⏚ Flying Biscuit \| **multi.** | 19 |
| Grit \| **Athens/O** | 21 |
| Madras Saravana \| **Decatur** | 24 |
| R. Thomas \| **S Buckhead** | 19 |
| Soul Veg.* \| **multi.** | 17 |
| Udipi Cafe \| **Decatur** | 22 |
| Vatica \| **Marietta** | 21 |

**VIETNAMESE**

| | |
|---|---|
| Com \| **Dunwoody** | 24 |
| Huong Giang \| **Buford Hwy. (Atl)** | - |
| Nam \| **Midtown** | 25 |
| Pho Dai Loi \| **Forest Pk** | 22 |
| Pho Hoa \| **Buford Hwy. (Dora.)** | 19 |
| Pho 79 \| **Buford Hwy. (Dora.)** | 26 |

CUISINES

# Locations

Includes restaurant names, cuisines and Food ratings. ☑ indicates places with the highest ratings, popularity and importance.

## Atlanta

### ACWORTH/COBB/ KENNESAW/MARIETTA/ SMYRNA

| | |
|---|---|
| Aspens/Steak | *Steak* | 23 |
| Atkins Park | *Amer.* | 19 |
| Atlanta Bread | *Deli* | 17 |
| Azio | *Italian* | 18 |
| Blackstone | *Seafood/Steak* | 23 |
| Blu Greek | *Greek* | 20 |
| Caribe Café | *Carib.* | - |
| ☑ Carrabba's | *Italian* | 20 |
| ☑ Cheesecake Fac. | *Amer.* | 19 |
| Chicago's | *Steak* | 18 |
| Chin Chin | *Chinese* | 19 |
| Chipotle | *Mex.* | 18 |
| El Taco | *Mex.* | 20 |
| ☑ Five Guys | *Burgers* | 21 |
| ☑ Flying Biscuit | *Southern* | 19 |
| Gabriel's | *Bakery* | 24 |
| Hashiguchi | *Japanese* | 24 |
| Haveli Indian | *Indian* | 16 |
| House/Chan | *Chinese* | 24 |
| ☑ Houston's | *Amer.* | 22 |
| Ippolito's | *Italian* | 19 |
| Jim N' Nick's | *BBQ* | 22 |
| Johnny Rockets | *Burgers* | 16 |
| Johnny's | *Pizza* | 17 |
| La Madeleine | *Bakery/French* | 19 |
| La Parrilla | *Mex.* | 22 |
| NEW Lime Taqueria | *Mex.* | - |
| ☑ LongHorn | *Steak* | 18 |
| ☑ Maggiano's | *Italian* | 20 |
| Mellow Mushroom | *Pizza* | 21 |
| Melting Pot | *Fondue* | 22 |
| Moe's SW | *SW* | 13 |
| Mt. Fuji | *Japanese/Steak* | 21 |
| Muss/Turner's | *Amer./Deli* | 25 |
| Old South | *BBQ* | 23 |
| Outback | *Steak* | 18 |

| | |
|---|---|
| Pappadeaux | *Cajun/Creole* | 21 |
| Pappasito's | *Mex.* | 23 |
| P.F. Chang's | *Chinese* | 20 |
| Rib Ranch | *BBQ* | 18 |
| Roasters | *Amer.* | 20 |
| Ru San's | *Japanese* | 18 |
| Sal Grosso | *Brazilian/Steak* | 21 |
| ☑ Sam & Dave's | *BBQ* | 26 |
| Simpatico | *Amer.* | 20 |
| ☑ South City | *Southern* | 23 |
| ☑ Stoney River | *Steak* | 24 |
| Tasty China | *Chinese* | 24 |
| ☑ Ted's Montana | *Amer.* | 19 |
| Thaicoon | *Japanese/Thai* | 22 |
| Tratt. La Strada | *Italian* | 19 |
| Trilogy | *Amer.* | 14 |
| Umezono | *Japanese* | 26 |
| ☑ Varsity | *Amer.* | 17 |
| Vatica | *Indian/Veg.* | 21 |
| Vito Goldberg's | *Pizza* | - |
| Williamson Bros. | *BBQ* | 20 |
| Willie Rae's | *Cajun/SW* | 19 |
| Willy's Mex. | *Mex.* | 20 |
| Zucca | *Italian* | 21 |

### AIRPORT/SOUTHSIDE/ COLLEGE PARK

| | |
|---|---|
| Barbecue Kitchen | *Southern* | 18 |
| Brake Pad | *Amer.* | 18 |
| Daddy D'z | *BBQ* | 20 |
| Feed Store | *Southern* | 19 |
| Harold's BBQ | *BBQ* | 23 |
| Noodle | *Noodles* | 19 |
| Zab-E-Lee | *Thai* | 23 |
| Zesto | *Amer.* | 16 |

### ALPHARETTA/ CUMMING/ROSWELL/ STOCKBRIDGE

| | |
|---|---|
| Amalfi | *Italian* | 23 |
| NEW American Girl | *Amer.* | - |
| Aqua Blue | *Eclectic/Pan-Asian* | 21 |

| | | | | |
|---|---|---|---|---|
| Atkins Park | *Amer.* | 19 | Pasta Vino | *Italian* | 19 |
| Atlanta Bread | *Deli* | 17 | Pastis | *French* | 21 |
| Atlantic Sea | *Seafood* | 22 | P.F. Chang's | *Chinese* | 20 |
| Azio | *Italian* | 18 | 🆕 Pisces | *Seafood* | - |
| Benihana | *Japanese* | 19 | Pure Taqueria | *Mex.* | 23 |
| Bistro VG | *French* | 22 | Ray's/Killer | *Steak* | 22 |
| Bonefish Grill | *Seafood* | 23 | Ray's Pizza | *Pizza* | 18 |
| Brookwood | *Amer.* | 20 | 🆕 Relish | *Southern* | 23 |
| Buca/Beppo | *Italian* | 17 | 🇿 Rice Thai | *Thai* | 26 |
| Byblos | *Lebanese/Med.* | 21 | Rising Roll | *Deli* | 20 |
| Cabernet | *Steak* | 24 | Santoor | *Indian* | - |
| 🇿 Cheesecake Fac. | *Amer.* | 19 | Slope's BBQ | *BBQ* | 18 |
| Chicago's | *Steak* | 18 | Smokejack | *BBQ* | 19 |
| Chin Chin | *Chinese* | 19 | 🇿 Stoney River | *Steak* | 24 |
| Chipotle | *Mex.* | 18 | Swallow/Hollow | *BBQ* | 23 |
| 🇿 di Paolo | *Italian* | 27 | Tarahumata | *Mex.* | 23 |
| Dreamland | *BBQ* | 17 | Tossed | *Amer.* | 16 |
| 🆕 VIII fifty | *Amer.* | - | 🇿 Varsity | *Amer.* | 17 |
| El Azteca | *Mex.* | 16 | Village Tavern | *Amer.* | 21 |
| Fickle Pickle | *Amer.* | 23 | Vinny's | *Italian* | 22 |
| Fire/Brazil | *Brazilian/Steak* | 21 | YellowFin | *Amer.* | 22 |
| 🇿 Five Guys | *Burgers* | 21 | Zola Italian | *Italian* | 25 |
| Five Seasons | *Amer.* | 22 | **ANSLEY/INTOWN/** | |
| Fratelli/Napoli | *Italian* | 18 | **MIDTOWN** | |
| Gasthaus | *German* | - | Agnes/Muriel's | *Southern* | 18 |
| Greenwoods | *Southern* | 23 | 🆕 Allegro | *Italian* | 20 |
| Ippolito's | *Italian* | 19 | Après Diem | *Continental* | 17 |
| Jason's Deli | *Deli* | 17 | Atmosphere | *French* | 25 |
| Johnny's | *Pizza* | 17 | Avra | *Greek* | 20 |
| La Parrilla | *Mex.* | 22 | Azio | *Italian* | 18 |
| 🇿 Little Alley | *Med.* | 26 | Bangkok | *Thai* | 21 |
| Marlow's | *Pub* | 20 | Baraonda | *Italian* | 23 |
| Mellow Mushroom | *Pizza* | 21 | 🆕 Beleza | *Brazilian* | 23 |
| Melting Pot | *Fondue* | 22 | Bobby/June's | *Southern* | 20 |
| Minerva | *Indian* | 22 | Bread Gdn. | *Bakery/Sandwiches* | 26 |
| Moe's SW | *SW* | 13 | Cameli's | *Pizza* | 24 |
| Nagoya | *Japanese* | 24 | Chin Chin | *Chinese* | 19 |
| Nirvana | *Amer.* | 18 | Chipotle | *Mex.* | 18 |
| One Star Ranch | *BBQ* | 20 | 🇿 Chocolate Pink | *Dessert* | 25 |
| Original Pancake | *Diner* | 21 | Cowtippers | *Steak* | 15 |
| Outback | *Steak* | 18 | 🆕 Cuerno | *Spanish* | - |
| 🇿 Pampas Steak | *Argent./Steak* | 26 | Dressed Salads | *Amer.* | 19 |
| Pappadeaux | *Cajun/Creole* | 21 | Eats | *Eclectic* | 18 |

LOCATIONS

| | | | | |
|---|---|---|---|
| Ecco \| *Continental* | 25 | Silver Skillet \| *Diner* | 18 |
| Einstein's \| *Amer.* | 18 | **South City** \| *Southern* | 23 |
| El Azteca \| *Mex.* | 16 | **NEW** Spice Market \| *SE Asian* | - |
| Eno \| *Med.* | 23 | **NEW** Steel \| *Pan-Asian* | - |
| Enoteca Carbonari \| *Italian* | 22 | **NEW** Straits \| *Singapor.* | - |
| **Flying Biscuit** \| *Southern* | 19 | Table 1280 \| *Amer.* | 20 |
| Fresh/Order \| *Amer.* | 21 | **Tamarind Seed** \| *Thai* | 27 |
| Fuego \| *Spanish* | 20 | **NEW** TAP \| *Amer.* | 14 |
| Gilbert's Med. \| *Med.* | 20 | **Ted's Montana** \| *Amer.* | 19 |
| Globe \| *Amer.* | 20 | **Tierra** \| *Pan-Latin* | 26 |
| Goldberg's \| *Deli* | 20 | Tin Drum \| *Asian Fusion/Noodles* | 16 |
| Gold Star \| *Amer.* | 15 | **NEW** Top Flr \| *Amer.* | 25 |
| Gordon Biersch \| *Pub* | 16 | Top Spice \| *Malaysian/Thai* | 21 |
| King & I \| *Thai* | 19 | **Trois** \| *French* | 22 |
| Las Palmeras \| *Cuban* | 22 | Veni Vidi Vici \| *Italian* | 23 |
| Loca Luna \| *Pan-Latin* | 19 | Vickery's \| *Eclectic/Southern* | 19 |
| Marlow's \| *Pub* | 20 | Vortex B&G \| *Burgers* | 22 |
| Mary Mac's \| *Southern* | 19 | Willy's Mex. \| *Mex.* | 20 |
| Mellow Mushroom \| *Pizza* | 21 | Zocalo \| *Mex.* | 19 |
| Melting Pot \| *Fondue* | 22 | | |
| Metrofresh \| *Sandwiches/Soup* | 22 | **ATLANTIC STATION/** | |
| **MF Sushibar** \| *Japanese* | 27 | **WESTSIDE** | |
| Mick's \| *Amer.* | 16 | Azio \| *Italian* | 18 |
| Mitra \| *Amer.* | 20 | **Bacchanalia** \| *Amer.* | 29 |
| Moe's SW \| *SW* | 13 | Carver's \| *Soul/Southern* | 26 |
| Mu Lan \| *Chinese* | 18 | Dolce \| *Italian* | 18 |
| Nam \| *Viet.* | 25 | Figo Pasta \| *Italian* | 21 |
| **Nan Thai** \| *Thai* | 27 | **Food Studio** \| *Amer.* | 24 |
| Nickiemoto's \| *Pan-Asian* | 20 | Grape \| *Med.* | 16 |
| Noodle \| *Noodles* | 19 | JCT. Kitchen \| *Southern* | 24 |
| Oceanaire \| *Seafood* | 23 | La Parrilla \| *Mex.* | 22 |
| **ONE. midtown** \| *Amer.* | 22 | Lobby at 12 \| *Amer./Med.* | 20 |
| **Park 75** \| *Amer.* | 27 | Nuevo Laredo \| *Mex.* | 24 |
| Pasta/Pulcinella \| *Italian* | 23 | Provisions to Go \| *Deli* | 25 |
| Pleasant \| *Amer.* | 19 | **Quinones** \| *Amer.* | 28 |
| Rare \| *Soul* | 24 | Real Chow Baby \| *Amer./Asian* | 20 |
| Repast \| *Amer.* | 24 | Rising Roll \| *Deli* | 20 |
| Rising Roll \| *Deli* | 20 | Rosa Mexicano \| *Mex.* | 19 |
| Ru San's \| *Japanese* | 18 | Six Feet \| *Seafood* | 19 |
| Salsa \| *Cuban* | 18 | **NEW** Social House \| *Southern* | - |
| Shout \| *Eclectic* | 16 | Strip \| *Seafood/Steak* | 17 |
| Silk \| *Pan-Asian* | 20 | **Taqueria/Sol** \| *Mex./SW* | 24 |
| Silver Midtown \| *Southern* | 16 | Toscano \| *Italian* | 23 |
| | | Willy's Mex. \| *Mex.* | 20 |

## AUSTELL

🔢 Five Guys | Burgers — 21

## BROOKHAVEN

Chin Chin | Chinese — 19
Haven | Amer. — 23
**NEW** Hudson | Amer. — 14
Pub 71 | Irish — 18
Terra Terroir | Amer. — 19
**NEW** Valenza | Italian — 22

## BUCKHEAD

Anis Bistro | French — 22
Annie's Thai | Thai — 22
Anthony's | Amer. — 19
🔢 Antica Posta | Italian — 24
**NEW** AquaKnox | Seafood — -
🔢 Aria | Amer. — 27
🔢 Atlanta Fish | Seafood — 23
Au Pied | French — 19
Basil's | Med. — 20
🔢 BluePointe | Amer. — 24
🔢 Blue Ridge | Southern — 23
🔢 Bone's | Steak — 27
**NEW** BrickTop's | Amer. — 19
Brio Tuscan | Italian — 19
🔢 Buckhead Diner | Amer. — 23
Cafe Prego | Italian — 19
🔢 Capital Grille | Steak — 24
🔢 Cheesecake Fac. | Amer. — 19
**NEW** Chima | Brazilian — -
Chipotle | Mex. — 18
🔢 Chops/Lobster | Seafood/Steak — 27
Chopstix | Chinese — 23
Clubhouse | Amer. — 17
Coco Loco's | Carib./Cuban — 19
Corner Cafe | Amer. — 20
Dantanna's | Seafood/Steak — 19
Dante's Hatch | Fondue — 18
Eclipse | Spanish — 21
ESPN Zone | Amer. — 10
**NEW** Fadó | Pub — -
Fellini's Pizza | Pizza — 20
🔢 Flying Biscuit | Southern — 19
🔢 Fogo de Chão | Brazilian/Steak — 24

Genki | Japanese — 19
Goldberg's | Deli — 20
Grand China | Chinese — 17
Grape | Med. — 16
Hal's/Old Ivy | Steak — 25
Hashiguchi | Japanese — 24
**NEW** Home | Southern — -
Horseradish | Southern — 22
🔢 Houston's | Amer. — 22
Jason's Deli | Deli — 17
🔢 JOËL | French — 26
Johnny Rockets | Burgers — 16
🔢 Kyma | Greek/Seafood — 25
La Fonda | Pan-Latin — 20
🔢 La Grotta | Italian — 26
Lee's Buddha | Asian — 19
**NEW** Lola | Italian — -
🔢 LongHorn | Steak — 18
🔢 Maggiano's | Italian — 20
McKinnon's | Cajun/Creole — 18
🔢 **NEW** MF Buckhead | Japanese — 26
Moe's SW | SW — 13
🔢 Morton's | Steak — 25
Mosaic | Eclectic — 22
🔢 Nava | SW — 23
New Yorker | Deli — 22
🔢 New York Prime | Steak — 25
OK Cafe | Diner — 20
One Star Ranch | BBQ — 20
Outback | Steak — 18
Palm | Steak — 23
🔢 Pano's/Paul's | Continental — 26
Pasta Vino | Italian — 19
Portofino | Italian — 21
Pricci | Italian — 24
Prime | Seafood/Steak — 23
Raja Indian | Indian — 19
Ritz/Buckhead | Continental — 24
🔢 Ritz/Buckhead Din. Rm. | French/Med. — 27
Roasters | Amer. — 20
Roy's | Hawaiian — 23
Ru San's | Japanese — 18

**LOCATIONS**

| | |
|---|---|
| Ruth's Chris | *Steak* | 23 |
| 🔲 Seasons 52 | *Amer.* | 22 |
| Soleil Bistro | *French* | 18 |
| 🔲 Souper Jenny | *Soup* | 25 |
| Swan Coach | *Southern* | 18 |
| 🔲 Taka | *Japanese* | 27 |
| Tavern/Phipps | *Amer.* | 18 |
| 10 Degrees | *S African* | 23 |
| NEW Via | *Italian/Med.* | - |
| White House | *Southern* | 19 |
| Willy's Mex. | *Mex.* | 20 |

## BUFORD HWY./ CHAMBLEE/DORAVILLE

| | |
|---|---|
| Athens Pizza | *Pizza* | 20 |
| Bombay | *Indian* | 17 |
| Canton Hse. | *Chinese* | 20 |
| China Delight | *Chinese* | 21 |
| Chosun OK | *Korean* | - |
| 88 Tofu | *Korean* | 21 |
| El Rey de Taco | *Mex.* | 24 |
| El Taco | *Mex.* | 20 |
| 🔲 Five Guys | *Burgers* | 21 |
| Hae Woon | *Korean* | 22 |
| Happy Valley | *Chinese* | 18 |
| Havana S'wich | *Cuban/Sandwiches* | 22 |
| Himalayas | *Indian* | 21 |
| Huong Giang | *Viet.* | - |
| Little Szechuan | *Chinese* | 21 |
| Machu Picchu | *Peruvian* | 18 |
| Panahar | *Bangladeshi* | 23 |
| Penang | *Malaysian/Thai* | 22 |
| Pho Hoa | *Viet.* | 19 |
| Pho 79 | *Viet.* | 26 |
| Phuket | *Thai* | 19 |
| Pig-N-Chik | *BBQ* | 19 |
| Pung Mie | *Chinese* | 21 |
| Rose of India | *Indian* | 19 |
| So Kong Dong | *Korean* | 20 |

## CABBAGETOWN/ CANDLER PARK/GRANT PARK/INMAN PARK

| | |
|---|---|
| Agave | *SW* | 22 |
| Fellini's Pizza | *Pizza* | 20 |

| | |
|---|---|
| 🔲 Flying Biscuit | *Southern* | 19 |
| NEW Fox Bros. BBQ | *BBQ* | - |
| Fritti | *Pizza* | 23 |
| Grant Pizza | *Pizza* | 20 |
| Grape | *Med.* | 16 |
| Il Localino | *Italian* | 21 |
| Johnny's | *Pizza* | 17 |
| 🔲 Kevin Rathbun | *Steak* | 26 |
| 🔲 Krog Bar | *Med.* | 23 |
| La Fonda | *Pan-Latin* | 20 |
| NEW Parish | *Cajun/Creole* | - |
| 🔲 Rathbun's | *Amer.* | 28 |
| Redfish | *Cajun/Creole* | 22 |
| Ria's | *Diner* | 23 |
| Shaun's | *Amer.* | 24 |
| Six Feet | *Seafood* | 19 |
| Son's Place | *Soul* | 19 |
| 🔲 Sotto Sotto | *Italian* | 27 |
| NEW Stella | *Italian* | - |
| Thumbs Up | *Diner* | 23 |
| Vino Libro | *Med.* | 19 |
| Wisteria | *Southern* | 24 |
| NEW Zaya | *Med.* | - |
| Zocalo | *Mex.* | 19 |

## CHESHIRE BRIDGE

| | |
|---|---|
| Alfredo's | *Italian* | 22 |
| Colonnade | *Southern* | 20 |
| Hong Kong | *Chinese* | 19 |
| Jitlada | *Thai* | 16 |
| Johnny's | *Pizza* | 17 |
| Little Bangkok | *Thai* | 24 |
| Nakato | *Japanese* | 21 |
| Nino's | *Italian* | 22 |
| Original Pancake | *Diner* | 21 |
| Red Snapper | *Seafood* | 22 |
| 🔲 Taqueria/Sol | *Mex./SW* | 24 |
| Taverna Plaka | *Greek* | 17 |
| 🔲 Varsity | *Amer.* | 17 |
| Woodfire Grill | *Calif.* | 25 |

## CLAIRMONT

| | |
|---|---|
| Violette | *French* | 21 |

## CONYERS

| | |
|---|---|
| Jim N' Nick's | *BBQ* | 22 |

## DECATUR/DEKALB/EMORY

Athens Pizza | *Pizza* — 20
Azio | *Italian* — 18
Bamboo Gdn. | *Chinese* — 19
Bhojanic | *Indian* — 22
Brick Store | *Pub* — 21
Cafe Alsace | *French* — 22
Café Lily | *Med.* — 23
**NEW** Cakes & Ale | *Amer.* — -
Carpe Diem | *Med.* — 20
Chipotle | *Mex.* — 18
Chocolate Bar | *Dessert* — 20
Crescent Moon | *Diner* — 20
Doc Chey's | *Noodles* — 19
Downwind | *Amer.* — 18
Dusty's BBQ | *BBQ* — 16
Edo | *Japanese* — 19
Eurasia Bistro | *Pan-Asian* — 25
Everybody/Pizza | *Pizza* — 20
Feast | *Amer.* — 22
Fellini's Pizza | *Pizza* — 20
Figo Pasta | *Italian* — 21
**Z** Floataway | *French/Italian* — 25
Houston Mill | *Amer.* — 18
Jake's | *Dessert* — 19
Johnny's | *Pizza* — 17
Le Giverny | *French* — 20
**Z** LongHorn | *Steak* — 18
Madras Chettinaad | *Indian* — 23
Madras Saravana | *Indian/Veg.* — 24
Mellow Mushroom | *Pizza* — 21
Mexico City | *Mex.* — 16
Mezza | *Lebanese* — 24
Moe's SW | *SW* — 13
Nicola's | *Lebanese* — 18
Noodle | *Noodles* — 19
Oak Grove | *Deli* — 21
Outback | *Steak* — 18
Petite Auberge | *Continental* — 19
Raging Burrito | *Calif./Mex.* — 18
Sage | *Amer.* — 20
Sawicki's | *Deli* — 26

Shorty's | *Pizza* — 24
Sushi Ave. | *Japanese* — 24
**Z** Taqueria/Sol | *Mex./SW* — 24
**Z** Ted's Montana | *Amer.* — 19
Thai Chili | *Thai* — 22
Top Spice | *Malaysian/Thai* — 21
Tossed | *Amer.* — 16
Udipi Cafe | *Indian/Veg.* — 22
Universal | *Pub* — 18
Wahoo! | *Amer.* — 22
**Z** Watershed | *Southern* — 25
Willy's Mex. | *Mex.* — 20
Zyka | *Indian* — 23

## DOUGLASVILLE

Atlanta Bread | *Deli* — 17
**Z** Carrabba's | *Italian* — 20
Gumbeaux's | *Cajun* — 24
Johnny Rockets | *Burgers* — 16
Outback | *Steak* — 18
Williamson Bros. | *BBQ* — 20

## DOWNTOWN/UNDERGROUND

Ann's Snack | *Amer.* — 23
Azio | *Italian* — 18
Benihana | *Japanese* — 19
Busy Bee | *Soul* — 27
City Grill | *Amer.* — 22
Dailey's | *Amer.* — 21
Fire/Brazil | *Brazilian/Steak* — 21
French Am. Brass. | *Amer./French* — 24
Gladys Knight | *Southern* — 18
Haveli Indian | *Indian* — 16
Hsu's | *Chinese* — 21
Johnny Rockets | *Burgers* — 16
Les Fleurs | *French* — 27
**NEW** Luckie | *Amer./Eclectic* — 17
**NEW** Maxim Prime | *Steak* — -
McCormick/Schmick | *Seafood* — 20
**Z** Morton's | *Steak* — 25
**Z** Nikolai's | *Continental/French* — 25
Pacific Rim | *Pan-Asian* — 21
**NEW** Peasant Bistro | *French/Med.* — -

LOCATIONS

| | | | | |
|---|---|---|---|---|
| Pittypat's | *Southern* | 15 | Kurt's | *Euro.* | 22 |
| Ray's/City | *Seafood* | 22 | La Madeleine | *Bakery/French* | 19 |
| 🛛 Ritz/Atlanta | *Southern* | 26 | 🛛 LongHorn | *Steak* | 18 |
| Rolling Bones | *BBQ* | 22 | Lowcountry | *BBQ* | 19 |
| **NEW** Room at 12 | *Amer./Steak* | 22 | Melting Pot | *Fondue* | 22 |
| Ruth's Chris | *Steak* | 23 | Norcross | *Amer.* | 19 |
| Sops on Ellis | *Eclectic* | 25 | Palace | *Indian* | - |
| Soul Veg. | *Soul/Veg.* | 17 | Palomilla's | *Carib./Cuban* | 23 |
| Spoon | *Thai* | 25 | Pappadeaux | *Cajun/Creole* | 21 |
| **NEW** Stats | *Amer.* | 19 | P.F. Chang's | *Chinese* | 20 |
| 🛛 Sun Dial | *Amer.* | 19 | Rexall Grill | *Diner* | 20 |
| 🛛 Ted's Montana | *Amer.* | 19 | Rising Roll | *Deli* | 20 |
| Thelma's | *Southern* | 21 | Sia's | *Amer./Asian* | 25 |
| Thrive | *Amer.* | 17 | 🛛 Stoney River | *Steak* | 24 |
| Trader Vic's | *Pacific Rim* | 20 | 🛛 Ted's Montana | *Amer.* | 19 |
| Tringalis | *Italian* | - | tomas | *Amer.* | 24 |
| 🛛 Varsity | *Amer.* | 17 | 🛛 Varsity | *Amer.* | 17 |
| Verve | *Amer.* | - | Vreny's Bier | *German* | 22 |
| Willy's Mex. | *Mex.* | 20 | Zapata | *Mex.* | 22 |

## DULUTH/GWINNETT/ NORCROSS

| | | |
|---|---|---|
| Atlanta Bread | *Deli* | 17 |
| Azio | *Italian* | 18 |
| Bamboo Gdn. | *Chinese* | 19 |
| Bonefish Grill | *Seafood* | 23 |
| 🛛 Carrabba's | *Italian* | 20 |
| Chin Chin | *Chinese* | 19 |
| Chipotle | *Mex.* | 18 |
| Dominick's | *Italian* | 23 |
| Dreamland | *BBQ* | 17 |
| East Pearl | *Chinese* | - |
| El Taco | *Mex.* | 20 |
| 🛛 Five Guys | *Burgers* | 21 |
| Fresh/Order | *Amer.* | 21 |
| Garrison's | *Amer.* | 19 |
| 🛛 Grace 17.20 | *Amer.* | 25 |
| Grape | *Med.* | 16 |
| 🛛 Haru Ichiban | *Japanese* | 26 |
| Hi Life | *Amer.* | 23 |
| Hometown BBQ | *BBQ* | - |
| Ippolito's | *Italian* | 19 |
| Jason's Deli | *Deli* | 17 |
| Johnny Rockets | *Burgers* | 16 |

## DUNWOODY/ SANDY SPRINGS

| | | |
|---|---|---|
| 🛛 Alon's | *Bakery* | 26 |
| Au Rendez | *French* | 21 |
| Brickery | *Amer.* | 18 |
| Brio Tuscan | *Italian* | 19 |
| Brooklyn Cafe | *Amer.* | 18 |
| Cafe Intermezzo | *Coffee* | 21 |
| Cafe Sunflower | *Veg.* | 22 |
| Canton Cooks | *Chinese* | 23 |
| 🛛 Carrabba's | *Italian* | 20 |
| 🛛 Cheesecake Fac. | *Amer.* | 19 |
| Chequers | *Seafood* | 22 |
| China Cooks | *Chinese* | 22 |
| Chin Chin | *Chinese* | 19 |
| Chipotle | *Mex.* | 18 |
| Com | *Viet.* | 24 |
| El Azteca | *Mex.* | 16 |
| El Taco | *Mex.* | 20 |
| Fire/Brazil | *Brazilian/Steak* | 21 |
| Five Seasons | *Amer.* | 22 |
| Fleming's/Steak | *Steak* | 23 |
| Food 101 | *Amer.* | 20 |
| Fresh/Order | *Amer.* | 21 |

| | |
|---|---|
| Goldberg's \| *Deli* | 20 |
| Goldfish \| *Seafood* | 21 |
| Grape \| *Med.* | 16 |
| Ippolito's \| *Italian* | 19 |
| Jason's Deli \| *Deli* | 17 |
| Joey D's \| *Amer.* | 20 |
| Joli Kobe \| *Bakery/Continental* | 23 |
| Kobe \| *Japanese/Steak* | 20 |
| **Z** La Grotta \| *Italian* | 26 |
| La Madeleine \| *Bakery/French* | 19 |
| **NEW** La Petite Maison \| *French* | - |
| **Z** LongHorn \| *Steak* | 18 |
| **Z** Maggiano's \| *Italian* | 20 |
| McCormick/Schmick \| *Seafood* | 20 |
| McKendrick's \| *Steak* | 25 |
| Meehan's Pub \| *Pub* | 18 |
| Mellow Mushroom \| *Pizza* | 21 |
| Moe's SW \| *SW* | 13 |
| Oscar's Villa \| *Italian* | 27 |
| Outback \| *Steak* | 18 |
| Persepolis \| *Persian* | 21 |
| P.F. Chang's \| *Chinese* | 20 |
| Pig-N-Chik \| *BBQ* | 19 |
| Ray's Pizza \| *Pizza* | 18 |
| Ray's/River \| *Seafood* | 23 |
| Roasters \| *Amer.* | 20 |
| Rumi's \| *Persian* | 24 |
| Ruth's Chris \| *Steak* | 23 |
| Sawadee Thai \| *Thai* | - |
| **Z** Seasons 52 \| *Amer.* | 22 |
| Slope's BBQ \| *BBQ* | 18 |
| Sultan's \| *Lebanese/Med.* | 21 |
| Sushi Huku \| *Japanese* | 25 |
| Tasting Room \| *Creole/Med.* | 22 |
| Tin Drum \| *Asian Fusion/Noodles* | 16 |
| Villa Christina \| *Italian* | 19 |
| Wildfire \| *Steak* | 21 |
| Willy's Mex. \| *Mex.* | 20 |

## EAST ATLANTA

| | |
|---|---|
| Azio \| *Italian* | 18 |
| Earl \| *Amer.* | 22 |
| Figo Pasta \| *Italian* | 21 |
| **Z** Five Guys \| *Burgers* | 21 |

| | |
|---|---|
| **NEW** Glenwood \| *Southern* | - |
| Grant Pizza \| *Pizza* | 20 |
| Salsa \| *Cuban* | 18 |

## EAST POINT

| | |
|---|---|
| **Z** LongHorn \| *Steak* | 18 |
| Oz Pizza \| *Pizza* | 19 |
| Tasting Room \| *Creole/Med.* | 22 |
| Thumbs Up \| *Diner* | 23 |

## FAIRBURN

| | |
|---|---|
| Oz Pizza \| *Pizza* | 19 |

## FOREST PARK

| | |
|---|---|
| Pho Dai Loi \| *Viet.* | 22 |
| Zesto \| *Amer.* | 16 |

## GAINESVILLE

| | |
|---|---|
| **Z** Five Guys \| *Burgers* | 21 |

## GLENWOOD PARK

| | |
|---|---|
| Vickery's \| *Eclectic/Southern* | 19 |

## HAPEVILLE

| | |
|---|---|
| Rising Roll \| *Deli* | 20 |

## JONESBORO

| | |
|---|---|
| Harold's BBQ \| *BBQ* | 23 |

## KIRKWOOD

| | |
|---|---|
| Sun in Belly \| *Diner* | 24 |
| Vinocity \| *Amer.* | 19 |

## LINDBERGH/ PEACHTREE HILLS/ SOUTH BUCKHEAD

| | |
|---|---|
| Benihana \| *Japanese* | 19 |
| **NEW** Bluefin \| *Asian Fusion/Japanese* | - |
| Cafe Intermezzo \| *Coffee* | 21 |
| Cafe Sunflower \| *Veg.* | 22 |
| Chin Chin \| *Chinese* | 19 |
| El Azteca \| *Mex.* | 16 |
| Fellini's Pizza \| *Pizza* | 20 |
| Figo Pasta \| *Italian* | 21 |
| **Z** Five Guys \| *Burgers* | 21 |
| Georgia Grille \| *SW* | 22 |
| **NEW** Holeman/Finch \| *Amer.* | - |
| **Z** Houston's \| *Amer.* | 22 |
| Huey's \| *Cajun/Creole* | 18 |
| Ibiza \| *Med.* | 20 |

| | |
|---|---|
| Imperial Fez \| *Moroccan* | 19 |
| Jalisco \| *Mex./Tex-Mex* | 21 |
| Malaya \| *Asian* | 17 |
| Moe's SW \| *SW* | 13 |
| Paul's \| *Amer.* | 23 |
| **Z** Rest. Eugene \| *Amer.* | 28 |
| R. Thomas \| *Amer./Veg.* | 19 |
| Taurus \| *Amer./Steak* | 23 |
| Toulouse \| *Amer.* | 21 |
| Uncle Julio's \| *Tex-Mex* | 18 |
| **NEW** Vita \| *Italian* | - |
| Willy's Mex. \| *Mex.* | 20 |
| Wolfgang Puck \| *Calif.* | 16 |
| Zesto \| *Amer.* | 16 |

## LITTLE FIVE POINTS

| | |
|---|---|
| Savage Pizza \| *Pizza* | 20 |
| Vortex B&G \| *Burgers* | 22 |
| Zesto \| *Amer.* | 16 |

## MORNINGSIDE/ PONCEY-HIGHLAND/ VIRGINIA-HIGHLAND

| | |
|---|---|
| **Z** Alon's \| *Bakery* | 26 |
| American Rd. \| *Diner* | 18 |
| Atkins Park \| *Amer.* | 19 |
| Babette's \| *Euro.* | 25 |
| **Z** Belly General \| *Amer.* | 19 |
| Café di Sol \| *Amer.* | 20 |
| Caramba \| *Tex-Mex* | 15 |
| Doc Chey's \| *Noodles* | 19 |
| Everybody/Pizza \| *Pizza* | 20 |
| Fat Matt's Chicken \| *Southern* | 24 |
| Fat Matt's Rib \| *BBQ/Southern* | 23 |
| Fellini's Pizza \| *Pizza* | 20 |
| Fontaine Oyster \| *Seafood* | 16 |
| Food 101 \| *Amer.* | 20 |
| George's \| *Amer.* | 22 |
| Harry & Sons \| *Asian* | 20 |
| Highland Tap \| *Steak* | 20 |
| **Z** Java Jive \| *Amer.* | 22 |
| La Fonda \| *Pan-Latin* | 20 |
| La Tavola \| *Italian* | 24 |
| Majestic \| *Diner* | 12 |
| Mali \| *Thai* | 23 |

| | |
|---|---|
| Manuel's \| *Pub* | 17 |
| Moe's/Joe's \| *Pub* | 13 |
| **Z** Murphy's \| *Amer.* | 24 |
| Noche \| *SW* | 20 |
| Osteria 832 \| *Italian* | 21 |
| **Z** Paolo's Gelato \| *Ice Cream* | 25 |
| Pura Vida \| *Pan-Latin* | 25 |
| Righteous Rm. \| *Pub* | 22 |
| Sala/Sabor \| *Mex.* | 19 |
| Soul Veg. \| *Soul/Veg.* | 17 |
| Surin \| *Thai* | 23 |
| **Z** TWO urban \| *Amer.* | 23 |
| Vine \| *Amer.* | 21 |
| Willy's Mex. \| *Mex.* | 20 |
| Zesto \| *Amer.* | 16 |

## MORROW

| | |
|---|---|
| Atlanta Bread \| *Deli* | 17 |
| **Z** Carrabba's \| *Italian* | 20 |

## NEWNAN/PALMETTO/ PEACHTREE CITY

| | |
|---|---|
| Atlanta Bread \| *Deli* | 17 |
| Blue Eyed \| *Southern* | 21 |
| **Z** Carrabba's \| *Italian* | 20 |
| Chin Chin \| *Chinese* | 19 |
| Farmhouse \| *Amer.* | 25 |
| **NEW** Hil \| *Amer./French* | - |
| La Parrilla \| *Mex.* | 22 |
| Original Pancake \| *Diner* | 21 |
| Outback \| *Steak* | 18 |
| **Z** Ted's Montana \| *Amer.* | 19 |

## SNELLVILLE/ STONE MOUNTAIN/ TUCKER

| | |
|---|---|
| Atlanta Bread \| *Deli* | 17 |
| Bambinelli's \| *Italian* | 19 |
| Blue Ribbon \| *Amer.* | 20 |
| Bonefish Grill \| *Seafood* | 23 |
| Crescent Moon \| *Diner* | 20 |
| Gladys Knight \| *Southern* | 18 |
| Jason's Deli \| *Deli* | 17 |
| Matthews \| *Southern* | 20 |
| Northlake Thai \| *Thai* | 24 |
| Original Pancake \| *Diner* | 21 |

| | |
|---|---|
| Outback | *Steak* | 18 |
| Shorty's | *Pizza* | 24 |

## VININGS

| | |
|---|---|
| 🚫 Canoe | *Amer.* | 26 |
| 🚫 Clark/Schwenk | *Continental/Seafood* | 24 |
| Garrison's | *Amer.* | 19 |
| Grape | *Med.* | 16 |
| La Paz | *Tex-Mex* | 19 |
| Marlow's | *Pub* | 20 |
| Meehan's Pub | *Pub* | 18 |
| Mellow Mushroom | *Pizza* | 21 |
| River Room | *Amer.* | 21 |
| SoHo | *Eclectic* | 22 |
| Taverna Fiorentina | *Italian* | - |
| Tomo | *Japanese* | 27 |
| Top Spice | *Malaysian/Thai* | 21 |
| Vinings Inn | *Southern* | 21 |

## WOODSTOCK

| | |
|---|---|
| Atlanta Bread | *Deli* | 17 |
| Chin Chin | *Chinese* | 19 |
| La Parrilla | *Mex.* | 22 |

# Savannah

## HISTORIC DISTRICT

| | |
|---|---|
| 🚫 Elizabeth | *Southern* | 25 |
| Garibaldi's | *Italian* | 25 |
| Il Pasticcio | *Italian* | 22 |
| Lady & Sons | *Southern* | 19 |
| Olde Pink | *Amer.* | 21 |
| Pirates' Hse. | *Continental* | 15 |
| Sapphire | *Eclectic* | 25 |

## SOUTHSIDE

| | |
|---|---|
| Atlanta Bread | *Deli* | 17 |
| Bonefish Grill | *Seafood* | 23 |
| 🚫 Carrabba's | *Italian* | 20 |

## TYBEE BEACH

| | |
|---|---|
| Johnny Harris | *BBQ/Southern* | 19 |

# Other Outlying Areas

## ATHENS

| | |
|---|---|
| Big City Bread | *Sandwiches* | 22 |
| Bischero | *Italian* | 19 |

| | |
|---|---|
| 🚫 Carrabba's | *Italian* | 20 |
| Doc Chey's | *Noodles* | 19 |
| East West | *Amer.* | 21 |
| Farm 255 | *Med./Southern* | 20 |
| 🚫 Five & Ten | *Amer.* | 28 |
| Five Star Day | *Amer./Soul* | 21 |
| Grit | *Veg.* | 21 |
| Harry Bissett's | *Cajun/Creole* | 21 |
| 🚫 Last Resort | *Southern* | 24 |
| NEW National | *Med.* | 28 |
| 🚫 Varsity | *Amer.* | 17 |
| Weaver D's | *Soul* | - |

## BRUNSWICK

| | |
|---|---|
| Cargo | *Eclectic* | - |

## CANTON

| | |
|---|---|
| Williamson Bros. | *BBQ* | 20 |

## CARTERSVILLE

| | |
|---|---|
| D. Morgan's | *Amer.* | - |
| Slope's BBQ | *BBQ* | 18 |

## DILLARD

| | |
|---|---|
| Dillard Hse. | *Southern* | 21 |

## FLOWERY BRANCH

| | |
|---|---|
| Flowery Branch | *Amer.* | - |
| La Parrilla | *Mex.* | 22 |

## GREENSBORO

| | |
|---|---|
| Linger Longer | *Amer./Steak* | 27 |

## HIRAM

| | |
|---|---|
| Jim N' Nick's | *BBQ* | 22 |

## JULIETTE

| | |
|---|---|
| Whistle Stop | *Southern* | - |

## MACON

| | |
|---|---|
| H&H | *Southern* | - |
| Natalia's | *Italian* | - |
| 🚫 Nu-Way Weiners | *Hot Dogs* | 20 |

## MCDONOUGH

| | |
|---|---|
| Palm Beach Rest. | *Amer.* | - |

## SOCIAL CIRCLE

| | |
|---|---|
| 🚫 Blue Willow | *Southern* | 22 |

## TYBEE ISLAND

| | |
|---|---|
| Crab Shack | *Seafood* | 18 |

LOCATIONS

# Special Features

Listings cover the best in each category and include names, locations and Food ratings. Multi-location restaurants' features may vary by branch.
**Z** indicates places with the highest ratings, popularity and importance.

## BREAKFAST

(See also Hotel Dining)

| | |
|---|---|
| American Rd. | **VA-Highland** | 18 |
| Atlanta Bread | **multi.** | 17 |
| Barbecue Kitchen | **Airport (Atl)** | 18 |
| **Z** Belly General | **VA-Highland** | 19 |
| Bobby/June's | **Midtown** | 20 |
| Corner Cafe | **Buckhead** | 20 |
| Crescent Moon | **Decatur** | 20 |
| **Z** Flying Biscuit | **multi.** | 19 |
| Goldberg's | **multi.** | 20 |
| Gold Star | **Midtown** | 15 |
| Huey's | **S Buckhead** | 18 |
| Jason's Deli | **multi.** | 17 |
| **Z** Java Jive | **Poncey-Highland** | 22 |
| La Madeleine | **multi.** | 19 |
| Majestic | **Poncey-Highland** | 12 |
| Matthews | **Tucker** | 20 |
| New Yorker | **Buckhead** | 22 |
| Oak Grove | **Decatur** | 21 |
| OK Cafe | **Buckhead** | 20 |
| Original Pancake | **multi.** | 21 |
| Ria's | **Cabbagetown** | 23 |
| R. Thomas | **S Buckhead** | 19 |
| Silver Skillet | **Midtown** | 18 |
| **NEW** Social House | **W'side** | – |
| Son's Place | **Inman Pk** | 19 |
| Thumbs Up | **multi.** | 23 |
| White House | **Buckhead** | 19 |
| Willy's Mex. | **D'town** | 20 |

## BRUNCH

| | |
|---|---|
| Agnes/Muriel's | **Midtown** | 18 |
| American Rd. | **VA-Highland** | 18 |
| Après Diem | **Midtown** | 17 |
| Atkins Park | **VA-Highland** | 19 |
| Atmosphere | **Midtown** | 25 |
| Babette's | **Poncey-Highland** | 25 |
| Basil's | **Buckhead** | 20 |

| | |
|---|---|
| **Z** Blue Ridge | **Buckhead** | 23 |
| Brio Tuscan | **multi.** | 19 |
| **Z** Buckhead Diner | **Buckhead** | 23 |
| Cafe Alsace | **Decatur** | 22 |
| Café Lily | **Decatur** | 23 |
| **Z** Canoe | **Vinings** | 26 |
| Carpe Diem | **Decatur** | 20 |
| **Z** Cheesecake Fac. | **multi.** | 19 |
| Chequers | **Dunwoody** | 22 |
| Corner Cafe | **Buckhead** | 20 |
| Einstein's | **Midtown** | 18 |
| **Z** Five & Ten | **Athens/O** | 28 |
| **Z** Flying Biscuit | **multi.** | 19 |
| Food 101 | **Sandy Springs** | 20 |
| Gilbert's Med. | **Midtown** | 20 |
| Himalayas | **Chamblee** | 21 |
| Horseradish | **Buckhead** | 22 |
| **Z** Java Jive | **Poncey-Highland** | 22 |
| La Tavola | **VA-Highland** | 24 |
| Les Fleurs | **D'town** | 27 |
| **NEW** Lime Taqueria | **Smyrna** | – |
| Madras Chettinaad | **Decatur** | 23 |
| Manuel's | **Poncey-Highland** | 17 |
| **Z** Murphy's | **VA-Highland** | 24 |
| OK Cafe | **Buckhead** | 20 |
| **NEW** Parish | **Inman Pk** | – |
| **Z** Park 75 | **Midtown** | 27 |
| Pastis | **Roswell** | 21 |
| **NEW** Pisces | **Alpharetta** | – |
| Pleasant | **Midtown** | 19 |
| Ray's/River | **Sandy Springs** | 23 |
| **Z** Ritz/Atlanta | **D'town** | 26 |
| Ritz/Buckhead | **Buckhead** | 24 |
| R. Thomas | **S Buckhead** | 19 |
| **NEW** Social House | **W'side** | – |
| Soleil Bistro | **Buckhead** | 18 |
| **Z** South City | **Midtown** | 23 |
| Vickery's | **Midtown** | 19 |

Village Tavern | **Alpharetta** 21
Wahoo! | **Decatur** 22
Z Watershed | **Decatur** 25
Zocalo | **multi.** 19

## BUFFET
(Check availability)
Z Blue Willow | **Social Circle/O** 22
Bombay | **Chamblee** 17
Byblos | **Roswell** 21
Chequers | **Dunwoody** 22
Gilbert's Med. | **Midtown** 20
Haveli Indian | **multi.** 16
Himalayas | **Chamblee** 21
Lady & Sons | **Historic Dist/S** 19
Madras Chettinaad | **Decatur** 23
Madras Saravana | **Decatur** 24
Panahar | **Buford Hwy. (Atl)** 23
Pappadeaux | **Alpharetta** 21
Persepolis | **Sandy Springs** 21
NEW Pisces | **Alpharetta** -
Ray's/River | **Sandy Springs** 23
NEW Relish | **Roswell** 23
Z Ritz/Atlanta | **D'town** 26
Ritz/Buckhead | **Buckhead** 24
Santoor | **Alpharetta** -
Sultan's | **Sandy Springs** 21
Udipi Cafe | **Decatur** 22
Wahoo! | **Decatur** 22

## BUSINESS DINING
NEW Allegro | **Midtown** 20
Anthony's | **Buckhead** 19
Z Antica Posta | **Buckhead** 24
NEW AquaKnox | **Buckhead** -
Z Aria | **Buckhead** 27
Z Atlanta Fish | **Buckhead** 23
Z Bacchanalia | **W'side** 29
Z Blue Ridge | **Buckhead** 23
Z Bone's | **Buckhead** 27
Z Buckhead Diner | **Buckhead** 23
Cabernet | **Alpharetta** 24
Cafe Intermezzo | **S Buckhead** 21
Z Canoe | **Vinings** 26

Z Capital Grille | **Buckhead** 24
NEW Chima | **Buckhead** -
Z Chops/Lobster | **Buckhead** 27
City Grill | **D'town** 22
Z Clark/Schwenk | **Vinings** 24
Dailey's | **D'town** 21
Z Elizabeth | **Historic Dist/S** 25
Eno | **Midtown** 23
Fire/Brazil | **multi.** 21
Fleming's/Steak | **Dunwoody** 23
Z Fogo de Chão | **Buckhead** 24
Z Food Studio | **W'side** 24
French Am. Brass. | **D'town** 24
Georgia Grille | **S Buckhead** 22
Horseradish | **Buckhead** 22
Il Pasticcio | **Historic Dist/S** 22
Z JOËL | **Buckhead** 26
Joey D's | **Dunwoody** 20
Z Kevin Rathbun | **Inman Pk** 26
Z Kyma | **Buckhead** 25
Z La Grotta | **Buckhead** 26
Lobby at 12 | **Atlantic Sta.** 20
Z Maggiano's | **Buckhead** 20
NEW Maxim Prime | **D'town** -
McKendrick's | **Dunwoody** 25
Z NEW MF Buckhead | **Buckhead** 26
Z Morton's | **multi.** 25
Z Nan Thai | **Midtown** 27
Z Nava | **Buckhead** 23
Z New York Prime | **Buckhead** 25
Z Nikolai's | **D'town** 25
Oceanaire | **Midtown** 23
Palm | **Buckhead** 23
Z Pano's/Paul's | **Buckhead** 26
Paul's | **S Buckhead** 23
Pirates' Hse. | **Historic Dist/S** 15
Pittypat's | **D'town** 15
Pricci | **Buckhead** 24
Prime | **Buckhead** 23
Z Quinones | **W'side** 28
Z Rest. Eugene | **S Buckhead** 28
Z Ritz/Atlanta | **D'town** 26

SPECIAL FEATURES

| Ritz/Buckhead Din. Rm. \| **Buckhead** | 27 |
| **NEW** Room at 12 \| **D'town** | 22 |
| Rosa Mexicano \| **Atlantic Sta.** | 19 |
| Roy's \| **Buckhead** | 23 |
| Ruth's Chris \| **multi.** | 23 |
| Seasons 52 \| **multi.** | 22 |
| Sia's \| **Duluth** | 25 |
| South City \| **multi.** | 23 |
| **NEW** Spice Market \| **Midtown** | – |
| **NEW** Steel \| **Midtown** | – |
| Table 1280 \| **Midtown** | 20 |
| Tamarind Seed \| **Midtown** | 27 |
| Taurus \| **S Buckhead** | 23 |
| Taverna Fiorentina \| **Vinings** | – |
| Trader Vic's \| **D'town** | 20 |
| Trois \| **Midtown** | 22 |
| Veni Vidi Vici \| **Midtown** | 23 |
| Villa Christina \| **Dunwoody** | 19 |
| Vinings Inn \| **Vinings** | 21 |
| Vinny's \| **Alpharetta** | 22 |

## BYO

| Big City Bread \| **Athens/O** | 22 |
| Blue Willow \| **Social Circle/O** | 22 |
| Chocolate Pink \| **Midtown** | 25 |
| Figo Pasta \| **multi.** | 21 |
| Moe's SW \| **Dunwoody** | 13 |
| Panahar \| **Buford Hwy. (Atl)** | 23 |
| Sops on Ellis \| **D'town** | 25 |
| Sun in Belly \| **Kirkwood** | 24 |
| Tasty China \| **Marietta** | 24 |
| Udipi Cafe \| **Decatur** | 22 |
| Vatica \| **Marietta** | 21 |
| Whistle Stop \| **Juliette/O** | – |
| Zab-E-Lee \| **Airport (College Pk)** | 23 |

## CELEBRITY CHEFS

| Aria \| *Gerry Klaskala* \| **Buckhead** | 27 |
| Atlanta Fish \| *Robert Holley* \| **Buckhead** | 23 |
| Babette's \| *Marla Adams* \| **Poncey-Highland** | 25 |

| Bacchanalia \| *Anne Quatrano, Clifford Harrison* \| **W'side** | 29 |
| **NEW** Beleza \| *Riccardo Ullio* \| **Midtown** | 23 |
| **NEW** Cuerno \| *Riccardo Ullio* \| **Midtown** | – |
| Five & Ten \| *Hugh Acheson, Chuck Ramsey* \| **Athens/O** | 28 |
| Floataway \| *Anne Quatrano, Clifford Harrison* \| **Emory** | 25 |
| Fritti \| *Riccardo Ullio* \| **Inman Pk** | 23 |
| Georgia Grille \| *Karen Hilliard* \| **S Buckhead** | 22 |
| **NEW** Hil \| *Hilary White* \| **Palmetto** | – |
| **NEW** Holeman/Finch \| *Linton Hopkins* \| **S Buckhead** | – |
| **NEW** Home \| *Richard Blais* \| **Buckhead** | – |
| JOËL \| *Joël Antunes* \| **Buckhead** | 26 |
| Kevin Rathbun \| *Kevin Rathbun* \| **Inman Pk** | 26 |
| Krog Bar \| *Kevin Rathbun* \| **Inman Pk** | 23 |
| La Grotta \| *Antonio Abizanda* \| **Buckhead** | 26 |
| Lobby at 12 \| *Nick Oltarsh* \| **Atlantic Sta.** | 20 |
| MF Sushibar \| *Chris Kinjo* \| **Midtown** | 27 |
| Nan Thai \| *Nan Niyomkul* \| **Midtown** | 27 |
| ONE. midtown \| *Tom Harvey* \| **Midtown** | 22 |
| Park 75 \| *Robert Gerstenecker* \| **Midtown** | 27 |
| Paul's \| *Paul Albrecht* \| **S Buckhead** | 23 |
| Provisions to Go \| *Anne Quatrano, Clifford Harrison* \| **W'side** | 25 |
| Quinones \| *Anne Quatrano, Clifford Harrison* \| **W'side** | 28 |
| Rathbun's \| *Kevin Rathbun* \| **Inman Pk** | 28 |
| **NEW** Relish \| *Andy Badgett* \| **Roswell** | 23 |

| 🅩 Rest. Eugene | Linton Hopkins | S Buckhead | 28 |
| 🅩 Ritz/Buckhead Din. Rm. | Arnaud Berthelier | Buckhead | 27 |
| NEW Room at 12 | Nick Oltarsh | D'town | 22 |
| Roy's | Roy Yamaguchi | Buckhead | 23 |
| Shaun's | Shaun Doty | Inman Pk | 24 |
| 🅩 Sotto Sotto | Riccardo Ullio | Inman Pk | 27 |
| NEW Spice Market | Jean-Georges Vongerichten | Midtown | - |
| Taurus | Gary Mennie | S Buckhead | 23 |
| 🅩 Trois | Jeremy Lieb | Midtown | 22 |
| 🅩 TWO urban | Scott Serpas | Poncey-Highland | 23 |
| Veni Vidi Vici | Jamie Adams | Midtown | 23 |
| 🅩 Watershed | Scott Peacock | Decatur | 25 |
| Woodfire Grill | Michael Tuohy | Cheshire Bridge | 25 |

## CHILD-FRIENDLY

(Alternatives to the usual fast-food places; * children's menu available)

| NEW American Girl* | Alpharetta | - |
| American Rd.* | VA-Highland | 18 |
| Athens Pizza* | Decatur | 20 |
| Atkins Park* | multi. | 19 |
| Atlanta Bread* | multi. | 17 |
| 🅩 Atlanta Fish* | Buckhead | 23 |
| Atlantic Sea* | Alpharetta | 22 |
| Babette's* | Poncey-Highland | 25 |
| Bambinelli's* | Tucker | 19 |
| Baraonda | Midtown | 23 |
| Barbecue Kitchen* | Airport (Atl) | 18 |
| Basil's | Buckhead | 20 |
| Blue Ribbon* | Tucker | 20 |
| Bobby/June's | Midtown | 20 |
| Brake Pad | Airport (College Pk) | 18 |
| Brickery* | Sandy Springs | 18 |
| Brio Tuscan* | multi. | 19 |

| Brookwood* | Roswell | 20 |
| 🅩 Buckhead Diner | Buckhead | 23 |
| Byblos* | Roswell | 21 |
| Cafe Sunflower* | multi. | 22 |
| NEW Cakes & Ale | Decatur | - |
| Cameli's* | Midtown | 24 |
| Caramba* | VA-Highland | 15 |
| 🅩 Carrabba's* | multi. | 20 |
| 🅩 Cheesecake Fac. | multi. | 19 |
| Chequers* | Dunwoody | 22 |
| Chin Chin* | multi. | 19 |
| Clubhouse* | Buckhead | 17 |
| Coco Loco's* | Buckhead | 19 |
| Colonnade | Cheshire Bridge | 20 |
| Corner Cafe* | Buckhead | 20 |
| Crescent Moon* | Decatur | 20 |
| Dailey's* | D'town | 21 |
| Doc Chey's* | multi. | 19 |
| Dominick's* | Norcross | 23 |
| Eats | Midtown | 18 |
| Einstein's* | Midtown | 18 |
| El Azteca* | multi. | 16 |
| El Taco* | multi. | 20 |
| ESPN Zone* | Buckhead | 10 |
| Eurasia Bistro | Decatur | 25 |
| Everybody/Pizza | VA-Highland | 20 |
| Fat Matt's Chicken | VA-Highland | 24 |
| Fellini's Pizza | multi. | 20 |
| Fickle Pickle* | Roswell | 23 |
| 🅩 Flying Biscuit* | multi. | 19 |
| Food 101* | Sandy Springs | 20 |
| Fuego | Midtown | 20 |
| Garrison's* | multi. | 19 |
| Goldberg's* | multi. | 20 |
| Gold Star | Midtown | 15 |
| Grand China* | Buckhead | 17 |
| Grant Pizza | Grant Pk | 20 |
| Haven | Brookhaven | 23 |
| Horseradish* | Buckhead | 22 |
| 🅩 Houston's | multi. | 22 |
| Ippolito's* | multi. | 19 |
| Jason's Deli* | multi. | 17 |

| | | |
|---|---|---|
| Ⓩ Java Jive \| **Poncey-Highland** | 22 | |
| Johnny Harris* \| **Tybee Beach/S** | 19 | |
| Johnny Rockets* \| **multi.** | 16 | |
| Johnny's* \| **multi.** | 17 | |
| Lady & Sons \| **Historic Dist/S** | 19 | |
| La Madeleine* \| **multi.** | 19 | |
| La Paz* \| **Vinings** | 19 | |
| Lee's Buddha* \| **Buckhead** | 19 | |
| Linger Longer* \| **Greensboro/O** | 27 | |
| 🆕 Luckie* \| **D'town** | 17 | |
| Madras Saravana* \| **Decatur** | 24 | |
| Ⓩ Maggiano's* \| **multi.** | 20 | |
| Marlow's* \| **multi.** | 20 | |
| Mary Mac's* \| **Midtown** | 19 | |
| Mellow Mushroom \| **multi.** | 21 | |
| Melting Pot \| **Kennesaw** | 22 | |
| Mexico City* \| **Decatur** | 16 | |
| Mick's* \| **Midtown** | 16 | |
| Moe's SW* \| **multi.** | 13 | |
| Ⓩ Murphy's* \| **VA-Highland** | 24 | |
| Nicola's* \| **Emory** | 18 | |
| Nino's \| **Cheshire Bridge** | 22 | |
| Norcross* \| **Norcross** | 19 | |
| Nuevo Laredo* \| **W'side** | 24 | |
| OK Cafe \| **Buckhead** | 20 | |
| Old South* \| **Smyrna** | 23 | |
| Original Pancake* \| **multi.** | 21 | |
| Outback* \| **multi.** | 18 | |
| Pappadeaux* \| **Alpharetta** | 21 | |
| 🆕 Parish \| **Inman Pk** | - | |
| Pasta Vino* \| **Alpharetta** | 19 | |
| Prime* \| **Buckhead** | 23 | |
| Raging Burrito* \| **Decatur** | 18 | |
| Ray's/City* \| **D'town** | 22 | |
| Ria's \| **Cabbagetown** | 23 | |
| Rising Roll* \| **Alpharetta** | 20 | |
| Ritz/Buckhead* \| **Buckhead** | 24 | |
| Roasters* \| **Smyrna** | 20 | |
| R. Thomas* \| **S Buckhead** | 19 | |
| Sage* \| **Decatur** | 20 | |
| Sala/Sabor* \| **VA-Highland** | 19 | |
| Salsa* \| **Midtown** | 18 | |

| | | |
|---|---|---|
| Silver Skillet \| **Midtown** | 18 | |
| Six Feet* \| **Grant Pk** | 19 | |
| Smokejack* \| **Alpharetta** | 19 | |
| 🆕 Social House \| **W'side** | - | |
| Soleil Bistro \| **Buckhead** | 18 | |
| Ⓩ Souper Jenny \| **Buckhead** | 25 | |
| 🆕 Stella* \| **Grant Pk** | - | |
| Ⓩ Stoney River* \| **multi.** | 24 | |
| Sun in Belly* \| **Kirkwood** | 24 | |
| Swallow/Hollow* \| **Roswell** | 23 | |
| Tavern/Phipps* \| **Buckhead** | 18 | |
| Ⓩ Ted's Montana* \| **multi.** | 19 | |
| Terra Terroir* \| **Brookhaven** | 19 | |
| Thumbs Up \| **Inman Pk** | 23 | |
| Tratt. La Strada* \| **Marietta** | 19 | |
| Uncle Julio's* \| **S Buckhead** | 18 | |
| Ⓩ Varsity \| **multi.** | 17 | |
| Village Tavern* \| **Alpharetta** | 21 | |
| Vinny's* \| **Alpharetta** | 22 | |
| 🆕 Vita \| **S Buckhead** | - | |
| Vreny's Bier* \| **Duluth** | 22 | |
| Ⓩ Watershed \| **Decatur** | 25 | |
| Whistle Stop \| **Juliette/O** | - | |
| White House* \| **Buckhead** | 19 | |
| Willie Rae's \| **Marietta** | 19 | |
| Willy's Mex.* \| **multi.** | 20 | |
| Wisteria* \| **Inman Pk** | 24 | |
| Zapata* \| **Norcross** | 22 | |
| 🆕 Zaya \| **Inman Pk** | - | |
| Zesto* \| **multi.** | 16 | |
| Zocalo* \| **Midtown** | 19 | |

## DELIVERY/TAKEOUT

(D=delivery, T=takeout)

| | | |
|---|---|---|
| Agave \| T \| **Cabbagetown** | 22 | |
| Agnes/Muriel's \| T \| **Midtown** | 18 | |
| Alfredo's \| T \| **Cheshire Bridge** | 22 | |
| Amalfi \| T \| **Roswell** | 23 | |
| Anis Bistro \| T \| **Buckhead** | 22 | |
| Ⓩ Antica Posta \| T \| **Buckhead** | 24 | |
| Aqua Blue \| T \| **Roswell** | 21 | |
| Aspens/Steak \| T \| **Marietta** | 23 | |
| Atkins Park \| T \| **multi.** | 19 | |
| Ⓩ Atlanta Fish \| T \| **Buckhead** | 23 | |

| | | |
|---|---|---|
| Atlantic Sea \| T \| **Alpharetta** | 22 | |
| Atmosphere \| T \| **Midtown** | 25 | |
| Au Rendez \| T \| **Sandy Springs** | 21 | |
| Bambinelli's \| T \| **Tucker** | 19 | |
| Basil's \| T \| **Buckhead** | 20 | |
| **Z** Belly General \| D, T \| **VA-Highland** | 19 | |
| Blackstone \| T \| **Smyrna** | 23 | |
| **Z** BluePointe \| T \| **Buckhead** | 24 | |
| **Z** Blue Ridge \| T \| **Buckhead** | 23 | |
| Brio Tuscan \| T \| **multi.** | 19 | |
| Brookwood \| T \| **Roswell** | 20 | |
| **Z** Buckhead Diner \| T \| **Buckhead** | 23 | |
| Byblos \| T \| **Roswell** | 21 | |
| Cabernet \| T \| **Alpharetta** | 24 | |
| Cafe Alsace \| T \| **Decatur** | 22 | |
| Cafe Intermezzo \| T \| **multi.** | 21 | |
| Café Lily \| T \| **Decatur** | 23 | |
| Cafe Sunflower \| T \| **multi.** | 22 | |
| **Z** Canoe \| T \| **Vinings** | 26 | |
| **Z** Cheesecake Fac. \| T \| **multi.** | 19 | |
| Chequers \| T \| **Dunwoody** | 22 | |
| Chicago's \| T \| **multi.** | 18 | |
| **Z** Chops/Lobster \| T \| **Buckhead** | 27 | |
| Chopstix \| T \| **Buckhead** | 23 | |
| City Grill \| T \| **D'town** | 22 | |
| Coco Loco's \| T \| **Buckhead** | 19 | |
| Colonnade \| T \| **Cheshire Bridge** | 20 | |
| Cowtippers \| T \| **Midtown** | 15 | |
| Crab Shack \| T \| **Tybee Is/O** | 18 | |
| Crescent Moon \| T \| **Decatur** | 20 | |
| **Z** di Paolo \| T \| **Alpharetta** | 27 | |
| D. Morgan's \| T \| **Cartersville/O** | - | |
| Eclipse \| T \| **Buckhead** | 21 | |
| Eurasia Bistro \| T \| **Decatur** | 25 | |
| Feed Store \| T \| **Airport (College Pk)** | 19 | |
| **Z** Five & Ten \| T \| **Athens/O** | 28 | |
| Five Seasons \| T \| **Sandy Springs** | 22 | |
| **Z** Flying Biscuit \| T \| **multi.** | 19 | |
| Fontaine Oyster \| T \| **VA-Highland** | 16 | |
| Food 101 \| T \| **Sandy Springs** | 20 | |
| Garrison's \| T \| **multi.** | 19 | |
| Georgia Grille \| T \| **S Buckhead** | 22 | |
| **Z** Grace 17.20 \| T \| **Norcross** | 25 | |
| Greenwoods \| T \| **Roswell** | 23 | |
| Hal's/Old Ivy \| T \| **Buckhead** | 25 | |
| Haven \| T \| **Brookhaven** | 23 | |
| Highland Tap \| T \| **VA-Highland** | 20 | |
| Hi Life \| T \| **Norcross** | 23 | |
| Horseradish \| T \| **Buckhead** | 22 | |
| **Z** Houston's \| T \| **Buckhead** | 22 | |
| Imperial Fez \| T \| **S Buckhead** | 19 | |
| Ippolito's \| T \| **multi.** | 19 | |
| Jalisco \| T \| **S Buckhead** | 21 | |
| **Z** Java Jive \| T \| **Poncey-Highland** | 22 | |
| Joey D's \| T \| **Dunwoody** | 20 | |
| Kurt's \| T \| **Duluth** | 22 | |
| **Z** Kyma \| T \| **Buckhead** | 25 | |
| Lady & Sons \| D, T \| **Historic Dist/S** | 19 | |
| **Z** La Grotta \| T \| **multi.** | 26 | |
| La Tavola \| T \| **VA-Highland** | 24 | |
| Le Giverny \| T \| **Emory** | 20 | |
| Les Fleurs \| T \| **D'town** | 27 | |
| Loca Luna \| T \| **Midtown** | 19 | |
| **Z** LongHorn \| T \| **multi.** | 18 | |
| Madras Chettinaad \| T \| **Decatur** | 23 | |
| Marlow's \| T \| **multi.** | 20 | |
| Mary Mac's \| T \| **Midtown** | 19 | |
| McCormick/Schmick \| T \| **D'town** | 20 | |
| McKinnon's \| T \| **Buckhead** | 18 | |
| Meehan's Pub \| T \| **Vinings** | 18 | |
| Mitra \| T \| **Midtown** | 20 | |
| **Z** Murphy's \| T \| **VA-Highland** | 24 | |
| Muss/Turner's \| T \| **Smyrna** | 25 | |
| **Z** Nava \| T \| **Buckhead** | 23 | |
| Nickiemoto's \| T \| **Midtown** | 20 | |
| Nicola's \| T \| **Emory** | 18 | |
| Nino's \| T \| **Cheshire Bridge** | 22 | |
| Noche \| T \| **VA-Highland** | 20 | |
| Norcross \| T \| **Norcross** | 19 | |
| Original Pancake \| T \| **multi.** | 21 | |
| Oscar's Villa \| T \| **Dunwoody** | 27 | |
| Osteria 832 \| T \| **VA-Highland** | 21 | |

**SPECIAL FEATURES**

| | | |
|---|---|---|
| Outback | T | multi. | 18 |
| Pacific Rim | T | D'town | 21 |
| Palm | T | Buckhead | 23 |
| Z Pampas Steak | T | Alpharetta | 26 |
| Panahar | T | Buford Hwy. (Atl) | 23 |
| Pappadeaux | T | multi. | 21 |
| Pappasito's | T | Marietta | 23 |
| Pastis | T | Roswell | 21 |
| Persepolis | T | Sandy Springs | 21 |
| Petite Auberge | T | Emory | 19 |
| P.F. Chang's | T | multi. | 20 |
| Pleasant | T | Midtown | 19 |
| Portofino | T | Buckhead | 21 |
| Pricci | T | Buckhead | 24 |
| Prime | T | Buckhead | 23 |
| Pura Vida | T | Poncey-Highland | 25 |
| Z Rathbun's | T | Inman Pk | 28 |
| Ray's/City | T | D'town | 22 |
| Ray's/River | T | Sandy Springs | 23 |
| Red Snapper | T | Cheshire Bridge | 22 |
| Ria's | T | Cabbagetown | 23 |
| River Room | T | Vinings | 21 |
| Roy's | T | Buckhead | 23 |
| R. Thomas | T | S Buckhead | 19 |
| Ruth's Chris | T | multi. | 23 |
| Sage | T | Decatur | 20 |
| Sala/Sabor | T | VA-Highland | 19 |
| Sapphire | T | Historic Dist/S | 25 |
| Shout | T | Midtown | 16 |
| Silk | T | Midtown | 20 |
| Silver Skillet | T | Midtown | 18 |
| Simpatico | T | Marietta | 20 |
| Six Feet | T | Grant Pk | 19 |
| Smokejack | T | Alpharetta | 19 |
| Son's Place | T | Inman Pk | 19 |
| Sops on Ellis | T | D'town | 25 |
| Z South City | T | Midtown | 23 |
| Sun in Belly | T | Kirkwood | 24 |
| Swallow/Hollow | T | Roswell | 23 |
| Swan Coach | T | Buckhead | 18 |
| Taverna Plaka | T | Cheshire Bridge | 17 |
| Tavern/Phipps | T | Buckhead | 18 |
| Z Ted's Montana | T | multi. | 19 |
| 10 Degrees | T | Buckhead | 23 |
| Terra Terroir | T | Brookhaven | 19 |
| Thumbs Up | T | multi. | 23 |
| Z Tierra | T | Midtown | 26 |
| Tin Drum | T | Midtown | 16 |
| tomas | T | Norcross | 24 |
| Tratt. La Strada | T | Marietta | 19 |
| Tringalis | T | D'town | - |
| Z TWO urban | T | Poncey-Highland | 23 |
| Universal | T | Decatur | 18 |
| Veni Vidi Vici | T | Midtown | 23 |
| Vickery's | T | Midtown | 19 |
| Villa Christina | T | Dunwoody | 19 |
| Village Tavern | T | Alpharetta | 21 |
| Vinings Inn | T | Vinings | 21 |
| Vinny's | T | Alpharetta | 22 |
| Violette | T | Clairmont | 21 |
| Vreny's Bier | T | Duluth | 22 |
| Wahoo! | T | Decatur | 22 |
| Z Watershed | T | Decatur | 25 |
| Whistle Stop | T | Juliette/O | - |
| White House | T | Buckhead | 19 |
| Willie Rae's | T | Marietta | 19 |
| Zocalo | T | Midtown | 19 |
| Zyka | T | Decatur | 23 |

## DINING ALONE

(Other than hotels and places with counter service)

| | | |
|---|---|---|
| Z Alon's | VA-Highland | 26 |
| Anis Bistro | Buckhead | 22 |
| Ann's Snack | D'town | 23 |
| NEW Beleza | Midtown | 23 |
| Blue Eyed | Palmetto | 21 |
| Blue Ribbon | Tucker | 20 |
| NEW BrickTop's | Buckhead | 19 |
| Busy Bee | D'town | 27 |
| NEW Cakes & Ale | Decatur | - |
| Z Carrabba's | multi. | 20 |
| Chipotle | multi. | 18 |
| Com | Dunwoody | 24 |

| | | | | |
|---|---|---|---|
| Corner Cafe | **Buckhead** | 20 | Thai Chili | **Emory** | 22 |
| Dressed Salads | **Midtown** | 19 | 🗷 Tierra | **Midtown** | 26 |
| Eats | **Midtown** | 18 | Tin Drum | **Midtown** | 16 |
| Everybody/Pizza | **multi.** | 20 | Toscano | **W'side** | 23 |
| Feast | **Decatur** | 22 | Tossed | **Alpharetta** | 16 |
| Figo Pasta | **multi.** | 21 | Uncle Julio's | **S Buckhead** | 18 |
| 🗷 Five Guys | **multi.** | 21 | Zesto | **Lindbergh** | 16 |
| 🗷 Flying Biscuit | **Candler Pk** | 19 | | |

## ENTERTAINMENT

(Call for days and times of performances)

| | |
|---|---|
| Fresh/Order | **multi.** | 21 |
| 🆕 Holeman/Finch | **S Buckhead** | - |
| Aqua Blue | jazz | **Roswell** | 21 |
| 🗷 Houston's | **multi.** | 22 |
| Atkins Park | varies | **Smyrna** | 19 |
| Jake's | **Decatur** | 19 |
| Atmosphere | jazz | **Midtown** | 25 |
| Jason's Deli | **multi.** | 17 |
| Au Pied | jazz | **Buckhead** | 19 |
| 🗷 Java Jive | **Poncey-Highland** | 22 |
| Blackstone | varies | **Smyrna** | 23 |
| La Madeleine | **multi.** | 19 |
| Brookwood | piano | **Roswell** | 20 |
| Les Fleurs | **D'town** | 27 |
| Byblos | belly dancing | **Roswell** | 21 |
| 🆕 Lime Taqueria | **Smyrna** | - |
| 🆕 Luckie | **D'town** | 17 |
| Chicago's | varies | **multi.** | 18 |
| 🗷 MF Sushibar | **Midtown** | 27 |
| Chopstix | piano | **Buckhead** | 23 |
| 🗷 Murphy's | **VA-Highland** | 24 |
| Dailey's | live music | **D'town** | 21 |
| Nicola's | **Emory** | 18 |
| Dante's Hatch | jazz | **Buckhead** | 18 |
| Nino's | **Cheshire Bridge** | 22 |
| Fat Matt's Rib | blues | **VA-Highland** | 23 |
| Nirvana | **multi.** | 18 |
| Noodle | **multi.** | 19 |
| Fuego | Spanish music | **Midtown** | 20 |
| Original Pancake | **Alpharetta** | 21 |
| Goldfish | piano | **Dunwoody** | 21 |
| 🆕 Parish | **Inman Pk** | - |
| Grape | varies | **multi.** | 16 |
| Paul's | **S Buckhead** | 23 |
| Hal's/Old Ivy | piano/vocals | **Buckhead** | 25 |
| 🆕 Peasant Bistro | **D'town** | - |
| R. Thomas | **S Buckhead** | 19 |
| Imperial Fez | belly dancing | **S Buckhead** | 19 |
| Salsa | **Midtown** | 18 |
| Sawicki's | **Decatur** | 26 |
| Lady & Sons | singing waiters | **Historic Dist/S** | 19 |
| Shorty's | **Emory** | 24 |
| Silver Midtown | **Midtown** | 16 |
| Loca Luna | salsa | **Midtown** | 19 |
| 🆕 Social House | **W'side** | - |
| Marlow's | varies | **Alpharetta** | 20 |
| Soleil Bistro | **Buckhead** | 18 |
| McKinnon's | open mic/piano | **Buckhead** | 18 |
| Son's Place | **Inman Pk** | 19 |
| Sops on Ellis | **D'town** | 25 |
| Mexico City | guitar | **Decatur** | 16 |
| Sun in Belly | **Kirkwood** | 24 |
| Nickiemoto's | drag shows | **Midtown** | 20 |
| 🗷 Tamarind Seed | **Midtown** | 27 |
| 🗷 Taqueria/Sol | **multi.** | 24 |
| 🗷 Pampas Steak | piano | **Alpharetta** | 26 |
| 10 Degrees | **Buckhead** | 23 |
| 🗷 Park 75 | piano | **Midtown** | 27 |
| Terra Terroir | **Brookhaven** | 19 |
| Pastis | jazz | **Roswell** | 21 |

**SPECIAL FEATURES**

NEW Pisces | jazz | **Alpharetta** −|

Pura Vida | salsa/merengue | 25|
**Poncey-Highland**

Ray's/River | jazz | 23|
**Sandy Springs**

Z Ritz/Atlanta | jazz | **D'town** 26|

Ritz/Buckhead | jazz | 24|
**Buckhead**

Smokejack | varies | **Alpharetta** 19|

Swallow/Hollow | live music | 23|
**Roswell**

Tavern/Phipps | varies | 18|
**Buckhead**

Z TWO urban | blues | 23|
**Poncey-Highland**

Vinings Inn | varies | **Vinings** 21|

Violette | live music | **Clairmont** 21|

## FAMILY-STYLE

Azio | **multi.** 18|

Bhojanic | **Decatur** 22|

Colonnade | **Cheshire Bridge** 20|

Com | **Dunwoody** 24|

Dillard Hse. | **Dillard/O** 21|

Dreamland | **Norcross** 17|

Dusty's BBQ | **Emory** 16|

Everybody/Pizza | **Decatur** 20|

Fratelli/Napoli | **Roswell** 18|

Greenwoods | **Roswell** 23|

Il Localino | **Inman Pk** 21|

Z Maggiano's | **multi.** 20|

Mary Mac's | **Midtown** 19|

Melting Pot | **multi.** 22|

Nicola's | **Emory** 18|

Z Sam & Dave's | **Marietta** 26|

NEW Vita | **S Buckhead** −|

## FIREPLACES

Agave | **Cabbagetown** 22|

Anthony's | **Buckhead** 19|

Aspens/Steak | **Marietta** 23|

Atkins Park | **multi.** 19|

Basil's | **Buckhead** 20|

Bistro VG | **Roswell** 22|

Z Blue Ridge | **Buckhead** 23|

Z Blue Willow | **Social Circle/O** 22|

Cabernet | **Alpharetta** 24|

Colonnade | **Cheshire Bridge** 20|

Dillard Hse. | **Dillard/O** 21|

NEW VIII fifty | **Roswell** −|

Z Elizabeth | **Historic Dist/S** 25|

Z Fogo de Chão | **Buckhead** 24|

Z Food Studio | **W'side** 24|

Garrison's | **multi.** 19|

Grape | **multi.** 16|

Harold's BBQ | 23|
**S'side (Atlanta)**

Highland Tap | **VA-Highland** 20|

NEW Hil | **Palmetto** −|

Horseradish | **Buckhead** 22|

Houston Mill | **Emory** 18|

Z Houston's | **Buckhead** 22|

NEW Hudson | **Brookhaven** 14|

Ippolito's | **Roswell** 19|

Kurt's | **Duluth** 22|

La Madeleine | **multi.** 19|

Le Giverny | **Emory** 20|

Linger Longer | **Greensboro/O** 27|

Moe's SW | **S Buckhead** 13|

Nirvana | **Roswell** 18|

Olde Pink | **Historic Dist/S** 21|

Pastis | **Roswell** 21|

Persepolis | **Sandy Springs** 21|

Pirates' Hse. | **Historic Dist/S** 15|

NEW Pisces | **Alpharetta** −|

Redfish | **Grant Pk** 22|

Ruth's Chris | **Sandy Springs** 23|

Z Seasons 52 | **Dunwoody** 22|

Z South City | **Midtown** 23|

Z Stoney River | **multi.** 24|

10 Degrees | **Buckhead** 23|

Terra Terroir | **Brookhaven** 19|

Vickery's | **Midtown** 19|

Village Tavern | **Alpharetta** 21|

Vine | **VA-Highland** 21|

Vinings Inn | **Vinings** 21|

Vino Libro | **Grant Pk** 19|

Violette | **Clairmont** 21|

## GRACIOUS HOSTS

Aqua Blue | *John Metz* | **Roswell** 21

Babette's | *Marla Adams* | **Poncey-Highland** 25

Byblos | *Nelly Perez* | **Roswell** 21

Café Lily | *Angelo/Anthony Pitillo* | **Decatur** 23

Chopstix | *Philip Chan* | **Buckhead** 23

Ibiza | *Rita Benjelloun* | **S Buckhead** 20

Imperial Fez | *Rafih/Rita Benjelloun* | **S Buckhead** 19

🄩 La Grotta | *Sergio Favalli* | **Buckhead** 26

McKendrick's | *Doug McKendrick* | **Dunwoody** 25

🄩 Murphy's | *Tom Murphy* | **VA-Highland** 24

🄩 Ritz/Buckhead Din. Rm. | *Claude Guillaume* | **Buckhead** 27

Salsa | *Alexander Palacios* | **Midtown** 18

Sia's | *Sia Moshk* | **Duluth** 25

🄩 Tierra | *Ticha & Dan Krinsky* | **Midtown** 26

## HISTORIC PLACES

(Year opened; * building)

1753 | Pirates' Hse.* | **Historic Dist/S** 15

1771 | Olde Pink* | **Historic Dist/S** 21

1790 | Greenwoods* | **Roswell** 23

1797 | Anthony's* | **Buckhead** 19

1800 | Swan Coach* | **Buckhead** 18

1847 | Smokejack* | **Alpharetta** 19

1850 | Feed Store* | **Airport (College Pk)** 19

1853 | Vinings Inn* | **Vinings** 21

1855 | Pastis* | **Roswell** 21

1880 | D. Morgan's* | **Cartersville/O** –

1890 | Fickle Pickle* | **Roswell** 23

1890 | Parish* | **Inman Pk** –

1890 | Pleasant* | **Midtown** 19

1890 | Rathbun's* | **Inman Pk** 28

1895 | Harry Bissett's* | **Athens/O** 21

1900 | Elizabeth* | **Historic Dist/S** 25

1900 | Manuel's* | **Poncey-Highland** 17

1900 | Mu Lan* | **Midtown** 18

1900 | Sage* | **Decatur** 20

1900 | Toscano* | **W'side** 23

1900 | Wisteria* | **Inman Pk** 24

1902 | Food Studio* | **W'side** 24

1904 | Farmhouse* | **Palmetto** 25

1912 | City Grill* | **D'town** 22

1913 | Les Fleurs* | **D'town** 27

1916 | Nu-Way Weiners | **Macon/O** 20

1917 | Blue Willow* | **Social Circle/O** 22

1917 | Dillard Hse.* | **Dillard/O** 21

1920 | South City* | **Midtown** 23

1922 | Atkins Park | **VA-Highland** 19

1922 | Soleil Bistro* | **Buckhead** 18

1924 | Johnny Harris | **Tybee Beach/S** 19

1927 | Colonnade | **Cheshire Bridge** 20

1927 | Whistle Stop* | **Juliette/O** –

1928 | Varsity | **D'town** 17

1929 | Majestic* | **Poncey-Highland** 12

1930 | Universal* | **Decatur** 18

1945 | Mary Mac's* | **Midtown** 19

1945 | Silver Midtown | **Midtown** 16

1947 | Busy Bee | **D'town** 27

1947 | Harold's BBQ | **S'side (Atlanta)** 23

1947 | Moe's/Joe's | **VA-Highland** 13

1948 | White House | **Buckhead** 19

1949 | Zesto | **multi.** 16

1955 | Matthews | **Tucker** 20

1956 | Silver Skillet | **Midtown** 18

## HOTEL DINING

**Crowne Plaza Ravinia Hotel**
🆉 La Grotta | **Dunwoody** — 26

**Dillard House**
Dillard Hse. | **Dillard/O** — 21

**Embassy Suites Hotel**
Ruth's Chris | **multi.** — 23

**Emory Inn**
Le Giverny | **Emory** — 20

**Four Seasons**
🆉 Park 75 | **Midtown** — 27

**Glenn Hotel**
NEW Maxim Prime | **D'town** — ⌐

**Hilton**
🆉 Nikolai's | **D'town** — 25

**Hilton Atlanta**
Trader Vic's | **D'town** — 20

**Inn at Serenbe**
Farmhouse | **Palmetto** — 25

**InterContinental Buckhead**
Au Pied | **Buckhead** — 19

**Ritz-Carlton Atlanta**
🆉 Ritz/Atlanta | **D'town** — 26

**Ritz-Carlton Buckhead**
Ritz/Buckhead | **Buckhead** — 24
🆉 Ritz/Buckhead Din. Rm. | — 27
**Buckhead**

**Ritz-Carlton Lodge**
Linger Longer | **Greensboro/O** — 27

**Twelve Hotel**
Lobby at 12 | **Atlantic Sta.** — 20

**W Atlanta Midtown**
NEW Spice Market | **Midtown** — ⌐

**Westin Buckhead**
Palm | **Buckhead** — 23

**Westin Peachtree Plaza**
🆉 Sun Dial | **D'town** — 19

## LATE DINING

(Weekday closing hour)
Atkins Park | varies | **multi.** — 19
Au Pied | 24 hrs. | **Buckhead** — 19
NEW Bluefin | 12 AM | — ⌐
**S Buckhead**

Brake Pad | 12 AM | — 18
**Airport (College Pk)**
Brick Store | 12 AM | **Decatur** — 21
🆉 Buckhead Diner | 12 AM | — 23
**Buckhead**
Cafe Intermezzo | varies | **multi.** — 21
China Cooks | 2 AM | — 22
**Sandy Springs**
NEW Cuerno | 12 AM | **Midtown** — ⌐
Dantanna's | 3 AM | **Buckhead** — 19
Earl | 2:30 AM | **E Atlanta** — 22
East Pearl | 12 AM | **Duluth** — ⌐
88 Tofu | 24 hrs. | — 21
**Buford Hwy. (Atl)**
El Rey de Taco | 24 hrs. | — 24
**Buford Hwy. (Dora.)**
El Taco | varies | — 20
**Buford Hwy. (Dora.)**
Fellini's Pizza | 2 AM | **multi.** — 20
Fontaine Oyster | 12 AM | — 16
**VA-Highland**
Hae Woon | 6 AM | — 22
**Buford Hwy. (Dora.)**
Happy Valley | 12 AM | — 18
**Buford Hwy. (Atl)**
Hashiguchi | 12 AM | **Buckhead** — 24
NEW Holeman/Finch | — ⌐
1:30 AM | **S Buckhead**
Hong Kong | 1 AM | — 19
**Cheshire Bridge**
NEW Hudson | 2 AM | — 14
**Brookhaven**
Johnny's | 2:30 AM | **Inman Pk** — 17
🆉 Krog Bar | 12 AM | **Inman Pk** — 23
NEW Luckie | 2 AM | **D'town** — 17
Majestic | 24 hrs. | — 12
**Poncey-Highland**
Manuel's | 1 AM | — 17
**Poncey-Highland**
Marlow's | varies | **multi.** — 20
Meehan's Pub | varies | **multi.** — 18
NEW Parish | 12 AM | **Inman Pk** — ⌐
NEW Pisces | 2 AM | **Alpharetta** — ⌐
Righteous Rm. | 1 AM | — 22
**Poncey-Highland**

| | |
|---|---|
| R. Thomas \| 24 hrs. \| **S Buckhead** | 19 |
| Six Feet \| 1 AM \| **Grant Pk** | 19 |
| **NEW** Stats \| 12 AM \| **D'town** | 19 |
| **NEW** TAP \| varies \| **Midtown** | 14 |
| **NEW** Top Flr \| 1 AM \| **Midtown** | 25 |
| **Z** TWO urban \| 12 AM \| **Poncey-Highland** | 23 |
| Universal \| 12 AM \| **Decatur** | 18 |
| Vickery's \| 12 AM \| **Glenwood Park** | 19 |
| Vino Libro \| 12 AM \| **Grant Pk** | 19 |
| Vortex B&G \| varies \| **multi.** | 22 |
| Zucca \| varies \| **multi.** | 21 |

## MEET FOR A DRINK

| | |
|---|---|
| Après Diem \| **Midtown** | 17 |
| Aqua Blue \| **Roswell** | 21 |
| **NEW** AquaKnox \| **Buckhead** | - |
| **Z** Aria \| **Buckhead** | 27 |
| Atkins Park \| **multi.** | 19 |
| **Z** Atlanta Fish \| **Buckhead** | 23 |
| Atmosphere \| **Midtown** | 25 |
| Au Pied \| **Buckhead** | 19 |
| Avra \| **Midtown** | 20 |
| Basil's \| **Buckhead** | 20 |
| **NEW** Beleza \| **Midtown** | 23 |
| Bistro VG \| **Roswell** | 22 |
| **Z** BluePointe \| **Buckhead** | 24 |
| **Z** Blue Ridge \| **Buckhead** | 23 |
| **Z** Bone's \| **Buckhead** | 27 |
| **NEW** BrickTop's \| **Buckhead** | 19 |
| Brio Tuscan \| **Buckhead** | 19 |
| **Z** Buckhead Diner \| **Buckhead** | 23 |
| Cabernet \| **Alpharetta** | 24 |
| Café di Sol \| **Poncey-Highland** | 20 |
| Cafe Intermezzo \| **multi.** | 21 |
| **NEW** Cakes & Ale \| **Decatur** | - |
| **Z** Capital Grille \| **Buckhead** | 24 |
| Carpe Diem \| **Decatur** | 20 |
| Chocolate Bar \| **Decatur** | 20 |
| **Z** Chops/Lobster \| **Buckhead** | 27 |
| City Grill \| **D'town** | 22 |
| **Z** Clark/Schwenk \| **Vinings** | 24 |
| **NEW** Cuerno \| **Midtown** | - |

| | |
|---|---|
| Dailey's \| **D'town** | 21 |
| Dantanna's \| **Buckhead** | 19 |
| Dante's Hatch \| **Buckhead** | 18 |
| Earl \| **E Atlanta** | 22 |
| East West \| **Athens/O** | 21 |
| Einstein's \| **Midtown** | 18 |
| Eno \| **Midtown** | 23 |
| **NEW** Fadó \| **Buckhead** | - |
| Feast \| **Decatur** | 22 |
| Five Seasons \| **multi.** | 22 |
| Fleming's/Steak \| **Dunwoody** | 23 |
| Fontaine Oyster \| **VA-Highland** | 16 |
| Food 101 \| **Sandy Springs** | 20 |
| **Z** Food Studio \| **W'side** | 24 |
| French Am. Brass. \| **D'town** | 24 |
| Genki \| **Buckhead** | 19 |
| George's \| **VA-Highland** | 22 |
| Goldfish \| **Dunwoody** | 21 |
| Gordon Biersch \| **Midtown** | 16 |
| Grape \| **multi.** | 16 |
| Hal's/Old Ivy \| **Buckhead** | 25 |
| Highland Tap \| **VA-Highland** | 20 |
| **NEW** Hil \| **Palmetto** | - |
| Hi Life \| **Norcross** | 23 |
| **NEW** Holeman/Finch \| **S Buckhead** | - |
| Horseradish \| **Buckhead** | 22 |
| Ibiza \| **S Buckhead** | 20 |
| JCT. Kitchen \| **W'side** | 24 |
| **Z** JOËL \| **Buckhead** | 26 |
| **Z** Kevin Rathbun \| **Inman Pk** | 26 |
| **Z** Krog Bar \| **Inman Pk** | 23 |
| Le Giverny \| **Emory** | 20 |
| **Z** Little Alley \| **Roswell** | 26 |
| Lobby at 12 \| **Atlantic Sta.** | 20 |
| **NEW** Luckie \| **D'town** | 17 |
| Manuel's \| **Poncey-Highland** | 17 |
| McCormick/Schmick \| **D'town** | 20 |
| Meehan's Pub \| **multi.** | 18 |
| **Z NEW** MF Buckhead \| **Buckhead** | 26 |
| Moe's/Joe's \| **VA-Highland** | 13 |
| **Z** Nava \| **Buckhead** | 23 |
| Oceanaire \| **Midtown** | 23 |

**SPECIAL FEATURES**

| | | |
|---|---|---|
| Z ONE. midtown \| **Midtown** | 22 | |
| Paul's \| **S Buckhead** | 23 | |
| Portofino \| **Buckhead** | 21 | |
| Pricci \| **Buckhead** | 24 | |
| Prime \| **Buckhead** | 23 | |
| Pub 71 \| **Brookhaven** | 18 | |
| Pure Taqueria \| **Alpharetta** | 23 | |
| Ray's/Killer \| **Alpharetta** | 22 | |
| Righteous Rm. \| **Poncey-Highland** | 22 | |
| NEW Room at 12 \| **D'town** | 22 | |
| Rosa Mexicano \| **Atlantic Sta.** | 19 | |
| Roy's \| **Buckhead** | 23 | |
| R. Thomas \| **S Buckhead** | 19 | |
| Sala/Sabor \| **VA-Highland** | 19 | |
| Sapphire \| **Historic Dist/S** | 25 | |
| Shaun's \| **Inman Pk** | 24 | |
| Shout \| **Midtown** | 16 | |
| Smokejack \| **Alpharetta** | 19 | |
| SoHo \| **Vinings** | 22 | |
| Soleil Bistro \| **Buckhead** | 18 | |
| Z South City \| **multi.** | 23 | |
| NEW Stats \| **D'town** | 19 | |
| NEW Steel \| **Midtown** | - | |
| Strip \| **Atlantic Sta.** | 17 | |
| Table 1280 \| **Midtown** | 20 | |
| NEW TAP \| **Midtown** | 14 | |
| Z Taqueria/Sol \| **Cheshire Bridge** | 24 | |
| Tasting Room \| **multi.** | 22 | |
| Taurus \| **S Buckhead** | 23 | |
| Tavern/Phipps \| **Buckhead** | 18 | |
| Thrive \| **D'town** | 17 | |
| Tratt. La Strada \| **Marietta** | 19 | |
| Z Trois \| **Midtown** | 22 | |
| Z TWO urban \| **Poncey-Highland** | 23 | |
| Veni Vidi Vici \| **Midtown** | 23 | |
| Verve \| **D'town** | - | |
| NEW Via \| **Buckhead** | - | |
| Vickery's \| **Midtown** | 19 | |
| Villa Christina \| **Dunwoody** | 19 | |
| Village Tavern \| **Alpharetta** | 21 | |
| Vine \| **VA-Highland** | 21 | |
| Vinny's \| **Alpharetta** | 22 | |
| Vinocity \| **Kirkwood** | 19 | |

| | | |
|---|---|---|
| NEW Vita \| **S Buckhead** | - | |
| Vortex B&G \| **multi.** | 22 | |

## MICROBREWERIES

| | | |
|---|---|---|
| Five Seasons \| **Sandy Springs** | 22 | |
| Gordon Biersch \| **Midtown** | 16 | |

## NATURAL/ORGANIC

(These restaurants often or always use organic, local ingredients)

| | | |
|---|---|---|
| Z Aria \| **Buckhead** | 27 | |
| Z Bacchanalia \| **W'side** | 29 | |
| Z Belly General \| **VA-Highland** | 19 | |
| Blue Eyed \| **Palmetto** | 21 | |
| Z Blue Ridge \| **Buckhead** | 23 | |
| NEW Cakes & Ale \| **Decatur** | - | |
| Z Canoe \| **Vinings** | 26 | |
| Carpe Diem \| **Decatur** | 20 | |
| Crescent Moon \| **multi.** | 20 | |
| Z Elizabeth \| **Historic Dist/S** | 25 | |
| Farmhouse \| **Palmetto** | 25 | |
| Farm 255 \| **Athens/O** | 20 | |
| Z Five & Ten \| **Athens/O** | 28 | |
| Five Seasons \| **multi.** | 22 | |
| Z Floataway \| **Emory** | 25 | |
| Z Food Studio \| **W'side** | 24 | |
| Fresh/Order \| **Sandy Springs** | 21 | |
| Globe \| **Midtown** | 20 | |
| Grape \| **Inman Pk** | 16 | |
| NEW Hil \| **Palmetto** | - | |
| NEW Holeman/Finch \| **S Buckhead** | - | |
| NEW Home \| **Buckhead** | - | |
| Z JOËL \| **Buckhead** | 26 | |
| Z ONE. midtown \| **Midtown** | 22 | |
| NEW Parish \| **Inman Pk** | - | |
| Z Park 75 \| **Midtown** | 27 | |
| Provisions to Go \| **W'side** | 25 | |
| Z Quinones \| **W'side** | 28 | |
| Z Rathbun's \| **Inman Pk** | 28 | |
| Z Rest. Eugene \| **S Buckhead** | 28 | |
| R. Thomas \| **S Buckhead** | 19 | |
| Shaun's \| **Inman Pk** | 24 | |
| Sia's \| **Duluth** | 25 | |
| Smokejack \| **Alpharetta** | 19 | |

| | |
|---|---|
| Soul Veg. \| **multi.** | 17 |
| Z South City \| **multi.** | 23 |
| Spoon \| **D'town** | 25 |
| NEW Straits \| **Midtown** | - |
| Table 1280 \| **Midtown** | 20 |
| Terra Terroir \| **Brookhaven** | 19 |
| Z Tierra \| **Midtown** | 26 |
| tomas \| **Norcross** | 24 |
| Z Trois \| **Midtown** | 22 |
| Z Watershed \| **Decatur** | 25 |
| Wolfgang Puck \| **S Buckhead** | 16 |
| Woodfire Grill \| **Cheshire Bridge** | 25 |
| Zola Italian \| **Alpharetta** | 25 |

## NOTEWORTHY NEWCOMERS

| | |
|---|---|
| Allegro \| **Midtown** | 20 |
| American Girl \| **Alpharetta** | - |
| AquaKnox \| **Buckhead** | - |
| Beleza \| **Midtown** | 23 |
| Bluefin \| **S Buckhead** | - |
| BrickTop's \| **Buckhead** | 19 |
| Cakes & Ale \| **Decatur** | - |
| Chima \| **Buckhead** | - |
| Cuerno \| **Midtown** | - |
| VIII fifty \| **Roswell** | - |
| Fadó \| **Buckhead** | - |
| Farmhouse \| **Palmetto** | 25 |
| Fox Bros. BBQ \| **Candler Pk** | - |
| Glenwood \| **E Atlanta** | - |
| Hil \| **Palmetto** | - |
| Holeman/Finch \| **S Buckhead** | - |
| Home \| **Buckhead** | - |
| Hudson \| **Brookhaven** | 14 |
| La Petite Maison \| **Sandy Springs** | - |
| Lime Taqueria \| **Smyrna** | - |
| Lola \| **Buckhead** | - |
| Luckie \| **D'town** | 17 |
| Maxim Prime \| **D'town** | - |
| Z MF Buckhead \| **Buckhead** | 26 |
| National \| **Athens/O** | 28 |
| Parish \| **Inman Pk** | - |
| Peasant Bistro \| **D'town** | - |
| Pisces \| **Alpharetta** | - |
| Relish \| **Roswell** | 23 |
| Room at 12 \| **D'town** | 22 |
| Social House \| **W'side** | - |
| Spice Market \| **Midtown** | - |
| Stats \| **D'town** | 19 |
| Steel \| **Midtown** | - |
| Stella \| **Grant Pk** | - |
| Straits \| **Midtown** | - |
| TAP \| **Midtown** | 14 |
| Top Flr \| **Midtown** | 25 |
| Valenza \| **Brookhaven** | 22 |
| Via \| **Buckhead** | - |
| Vita \| **S Buckhead** | - |
| Zaya \| **Inman Pk** | - |

## OFFBEAT

| | |
|---|---|
| Agave \| **Cabbagetown** | 22 |
| Agnes/Muriel's \| **Midtown** | 18 |
| Après Diem \| **Midtown** | 17 |
| Au Rendez \| **Sandy Springs** | 21 |
| Avra \| **Midtown** | 20 |
| NEW Beleza \| **Midtown** | 23 |
| Benihana \| **multi.** | 19 |
| Blue Eyed \| **Palmetto** | 21 |
| Brake Pad \| **Airport (College Pk)** | 18 |
| Buca/Beppo \| **Alpharetta** | 17 |
| Cafe Sunflower \| **multi.** | 22 |
| Caribe Café \| **Marietta** | - |
| Carpe Diem \| **Decatur** | 20 |
| Z Chocolate Pink \| **Midtown** | 25 |
| Com \| **Dunwoody** | 24 |
| Dante's Hatch \| **Buckhead** | 18 |
| Doc Chey's \| **multi.** | 19 |
| Earl \| **E Atlanta** | 22 |
| Eats \| **Midtown** | 18 |
| Eclipse \| **Buckhead** | 21 |
| Einstein's \| **Midtown** | 18 |
| Farmhouse \| **Palmetto** | 25 |
| Fat Matt's Chicken \| **VA-Highland** | 24 |
| Fat Matt's Rib \| **VA-Highland** | 23 |
| Feast \| **Decatur** | 22 |
| Fellini's Pizza \| **Decatur** | 20 |
| Figo Pasta \| **multi.** | 21 |

| | |
|---|---|
| ℤ Floataway \| Emory | 25 |
| ℤ Flying Biscuit \| Candler Pk | 19 |
| ℤ Food Studio \| W'side | 24 |
| Fritti \| Inman Pk | 23 |
| Gasthaus \| Cumming | – |
| Gladys Knight \| multi. | 18 |
| Grit \| Athens/O | 21 |
| Hae Woon \| Buford Hwy. (Dora.) | 22 |
| Ibiza \| S Buckhead | 20 |
| Imperial Fez \| S Buckhead | 19 |
| ℤ Java Jive \| Poncey-Highland | 22 |
| JCT. Kitchen \| W'side | 24 |
| ℤ Krog Bar \| Inman Pk | 23 |
| La Fonda \| multi. | 20 |
| Loca Luna \| Midtown | 19 |
| Majestic \| Poncey-Highland | 12 |
| Mellow Mushroom \| Sandy Springs | 21 |
| ℤ MF Sushibar \| Midtown | 27 |
| Nicola's \| Emory | 18 |
| Noodle \| multi. | 19 |
| OK Cafe \| Buckhead | 20 |
| Osteria 832 \| VA-Highland | 21 |
| ℤ Paolo's Gelato \| VA-Highland | 25 |
| Pasta/Pulcinella \| Midtown | 23 |
| Pittypat's \| D'town | 15 |
| Pure Taqueria \| Alpharetta | 23 |
| Raging Burrito \| Decatur | 18 |
| Righteous Rm. \| Poncey-Highland | 22 |
| R. Thomas \| S Buckhead | 19 |
| Ru San's \| multi. | 18 |
| Sapphire \| Historic Dist/S | 25 |
| Shorty's \| Emory | 24 |
| Six Feet \| Grant Pk | 19 |
| SoHo \| Vinings | 22 |
| Sops on Ellis \| D'town | 25 |
| ℤ Souper Jenny \| Buckhead | 25 |
| Sun in Belly \| Kirkwood | 24 |
| ℤ Taqueria/Sol \| multi. | 24 |
| Taverna Plaka \| Cheshire Bridge | 17 |
| 10 Degrees \| Buckhead | 23 |
| Thrive \| D'town | 17 |
| ℤ Tierra \| Midtown | 26 |

| | |
|---|---|
| NEW Top Flr \| Midtown | 25 |
| Toscano \| W'side | 23 |
| Universal \| Decatur | 18 |
| ℤ Varsity \| Athens/O | 17 |
| Vortex B&G \| multi. | 22 |
| Zocalo \| Midtown | 19 |
| Zucca \| multi. | 21 |

## OUTDOOR DINING

(G=garden; P=patio; S=sidewalk; T=terrace; W=waterside)

| | |
|---|---|
| Agave \| P \| Cabbagetown | 22 |
| Anis Bistro \| P \| Buckhead | 22 |
| Après Diem \| P \| Midtown | 17 |
| Aqua Blue \| P \| Roswell | 21 |
| ℤ Aria \| P \| Buckhead | 27 |
| Atmosphere \| P \| Midtown | 25 |
| Au Pied \| P \| Buckhead | 19 |
| Babette's \| P \| Poncey-Highland | 25 |
| Bambinelli's \| P \| Tucker | 19 |
| Baraonda \| P \| Midtown | 23 |
| Basil's \| P \| Buckhead | 20 |
| Blue Ribbon \| P \| Tucker | 20 |
| Brake Pad \| P \| Airport (College Pk) | 18 |
| Brick Store \| S \| Decatur | 21 |
| Brio Tuscan \| P, T \| multi. | 19 |
| Brooklyn Cafe \| P, S \| Sandy Springs | 18 |
| Brookwood \| P \| Roswell | 20 |
| Byblos \| P \| Roswell | 21 |
| Cafe Intermezzo \| P, S \| multi. | 21 |
| Café Lily \| P \| Decatur | 23 |
| Cafe Prego \| P \| Buckhead | 19 |
| ℤ Canoe \| P, W \| Vinings | 26 |
| Carpe Diem \| P \| Decatur | 20 |
| ℤ Carrabba's \| P \| Southside/S | 20 |
| ℤ Cheesecake Fac. \| P \| multi. | 19 |
| Chequers \| P \| Dunwoody | 22 |
| Chipotle \| P \| multi. | 18 |
| Cowtippers \| P \| Midtown | 15 |
| Crab Shack \| T, W \| Tybee Is/O | 18 |
| Dantanna's \| P \| Buckhead | 19 |
| Doc Chey's \| P \| multi. | 19 |
| Downwind \| T \| DeKalb | 18 |

subscribe to ZAGAT.com

| | |
|---|---|
| Eclipse \| P \| **Buckhead** | 21 |
| **NEW** VIII fifty \| P \| **Roswell** | - |
| Einstein's \| P \| **Midtown** | 18 |
| El Azteca \| P \| **multi.** | 16 |
| Eno \| S \| **Midtown** | 23 |
| Everybody/Pizza \| P \| **multi.** | 20 |
| **NEW** Fadó \| P \| **Buckhead** | - |
| Fat Matt's Rib \| P \| **VA-Highland** | 23 |
| Fickle Pickle \| G, P \| **Roswell** | 23 |
| Five Seasons \| P \| **Sandy Springs** | 22 |
| 🛛 Floataway \| P \| **Emory** | 25 |
| 🛛 Flying Biscuit \| P \| **multi.** | 19 |
| Fontaine Oyster \| P \| **VA-Highland** | 16 |
| Food 101 \| P \| **Sandy Springs** | 20 |
| 🛛 Food Studio \| P \| **W'side** | 24 |
| Fritti \| P \| **Inman Pk** | 23 |
| Fuego \| P \| **Midtown** | 20 |
| Genki \| P \| **Buckhead** | 19 |
| George's \| P \| **VA-Highland** | 22 |
| Globe \| P \| **Midtown** | 20 |
| Goldfish \| P \| **Dunwoody** | 21 |
| Gordon Biersch \| P \| **Midtown** | 16 |
| 🛛 Grace 17.20 \| P \| **Norcross** | 25 |
| Grape \| P \| **multi.** | 16 |
| Haven \| P \| **Brookhaven** | 23 |
| Hi Life \| P \| **Norcross** | 23 |
| **NEW** Home \| P \| **Buckhead** | - |
| Horseradish \| P \| **Buckhead** | 22 |
| Houston Mill \| T \| **Emory** | 18 |
| 🛛 Houston's \| P \| **Buckhead** | 22 |
| Huey's \| P \| **S Buckhead** | 18 |
| Ibiza \| P \| **S Buckhead** | 20 |
| Jitlada \| P \| **Cheshire Bridge** | 16 |
| 🛛 JOËL \| P \| **Buckhead** | 26 |
| Joey D's \| P \| **Dunwoody** | 20 |
| 🛛 Krog Bar \| P \| **Inman Pk** | 23 |
| La Fonda \| P \| **multi.** | 20 |
| La Tavola \| P \| **VA-Highland** | 24 |
| Linger Longer \| T \| **Greensboro/O** | 27 |
| Loca Luna \| P \| **Midtown** | 19 |
| Madras Chettinaad \| P \| **Decatur** | 23 |
| Mali \| P \| **VA-Highland** | 23 |

| | |
|---|---|
| Marlow's \| P \| **multi.** | 20 |
| McCormick/Schmick \| P, T, W \| **Dunwoody** | 20 |
| Meehan's Pub \| P \| **Vinings** | 18 |
| Mellow Mushroom \| P \| **multi.** | 21 |
| Mitra \| P \| **Midtown** | 20 |
| Moe's/Joe's \| P \| **VA-Highland** | 13 |
| Mosaic \| G, P \| **Buckhead** | 22 |
| Mu Lan \| P \| **Midtown** | 18 |
| 🛛 Murphy's \| P \| **VA-Highland** | 24 |
| Muss/Turner's \| P \| **Smyrna** | 25 |
| 🛛 Nava \| P \| **Buckhead** | 23 |
| Nickiemoto's \| P \| **Midtown** | 20 |
| Nicola's \| P \| **Emory** | 18 |
| Nino's \| P \| **Cheshire Bridge** | 22 |
| Noche \| P \| **VA-Highland** | 20 |
| Noodle \| P \| **Midtown** | 19 |
| Norcross \| P \| **Norcross** | 19 |
| Osteria 832 \| P \| **VA-Highland** | 21 |
| Oz Pizza \| S \| **multi.** | 19 |
| Pacific Rim \| P \| **D'town** | 21 |
| 🛛 Pampas Steak \| P \| **Alpharetta** | 26 |
| 🛛 Paolo's Gelato \| P \| **VA-Highland** | 25 |
| Pappadeaux \| P \| **Norcross** | 21 |
| Pappasito's \| P \| **Marietta** | 23 |
| **NEW** Parish \| P \| **Inman Pk** | - |
| Pasta/Pulcinella \| P \| **Midtown** | 23 |
| Pasta Vino \| P \| **multi.** | 19 |
| Pastis \| T \| **Roswell** | 21 |
| P.F. Chang's \| P \| **multi.** | 20 |
| Portofino \| P \| **Buckhead** | 21 |
| 🛛 Rathbun's \| P \| **Inman Pk** | 28 |
| Ray's/River \| P, W \| **Sandy Springs** | 23 |
| Real Chow Baby \| P \| **W'side** | 20 |
| 🛛 Rice Thai \| P \| **Roswell** | 26 |
| 🛛 Ritz/Atlanta \| T \| **D'town** | 26 |
| Ritz/Buckhead \| P \| **Buckhead** | 24 |
| River Room \| G, P, S \| **Vinings** | 21 |
| Rolling Bones \| P \| **D'town** | 22 |
| Roy's \| P \| **Buckhead** | 23 |
| R. Thomas \| P \| **S Buckhead** | 19 |
| Ruth's Chris \| P \| **D'town** | 23 |

| | | |
|---|---|---|
| Sage \| S \| **Decatur** | 20 | |
| Sala/Sabor \| P \| **VA-Highland** | 19 | |
| Savage Pizza \| P \| **Little Five Pts** | 20 | |
| Shaun's \| P \| **Inman Pk** | 24 | |
| Shout \| T \| **Midtown** | 16 | |
| Silk \| P \| **Midtown** | 20 | |
| Six Feet \| P \| **Grant Pk** | 19 | |
| Smokejack \| P \| **Alpharetta** | 19 | |
| SoHo \| G, P \| **Vinings** | 22 | |
| Soleil Bistro \| P \| **Buckhead** | 18 | |
| **Z** Sotto Sotto \| P \| **Inman Pk** | 27 | |
| **Z** Souper Jenny \| P \| **Buckhead** | 25 | |
| **Z** South City \| P \| **Midtown** | 23 | |
| **NEW** Stella \| P \| **Grant Pk** | - | |
| Sultan's \| P \| **Sandy Springs** | 21 | |
| Sun in Belly \| P \| **Kirkwood** | 24 | |
| Table 1280 \| P \| **Midtown** | 20 | |
| **Z** Taka \| P \| **Buckhead** | 27 | |
| **NEW** TAP \| P \| **Midtown** | 14 | |
| **Z** Taqueria/Sol \| P, T \| **multi.** | 24 | |
| Taverna Plaka \| P \| **Cheshire Bridge** | 17 | |
| Tavern/Phipps \| P \| **Buckhead** | 18 | |
| **Z** Tierra \| T \| **Midtown** | 26 | |
| tomas \| P \| **Norcross** | 24 | |
| **Z** TWO urban \| P \| **Poncey-Highland** | 23 | |
| Uncle Julio's \| P \| **S Buckhead** | 18 | |
| Universal \| P \| **Decatur** | 18 | |
| Veni Vidi Vici \| P \| **Midtown** | 23 | |
| Vickery's \| P \| **Midtown** | 19 | |
| Villa Christina \| G \| **Dunwoody** | 19 | |
| Village Tavern \| P \| **Alpharetta** | 21 | |
| Vinings Inn \| P \| **Vinings** | 21 | |
| Vinny's \| P \| **Alpharetta** | 22 | |
| Vinocity \| T \| **Kirkwood** | 19 | |
| Violette \| P \| **Clairmont** | 21 | |
| Vortex B&G \| P \| **multi.** | 22 | |
| Vreny's Bier \| T \| **Duluth** | 22 | |
| Wahoo! \| P \| **Decatur** | 22 | |
| Woodfire Grill \| T \| **Cheshire Bridge** | 25 | |
| **NEW** Zaya \| P \| **Inman Pk** | - | |
| Zocalo \| P \| **Midtown** | 19 | |

## PEOPLE-WATCHING

| | |
|---|---|
| **NEW** AquaKnox \| **Buckhead** | - |
| **Z** Aria \| **Buckhead** | 27 |
| **Z** Atlanta Fish \| **Buckhead** | 23 |
| Atmosphere \| **Midtown** | 25 |
| Au Pied \| **Buckhead** | 19 |
| Barbecue Kitchen \| **Airport (Atl)** | 18 |
| **NEW** Beleza \| **Midtown** | 23 |
| Bistro VG \| **Roswell** | 22 |
| **Z** BluePointe \| **Buckhead** | 24 |
| **Z** Buckhead Diner \| **Buckhead** | 23 |
| Café di Sol \| **Poncey-Highland** | 20 |
| Cafe Intermezzo \| **S Buckhead** | 21 |
| **NEW** Cakes & Ale \| **Decatur** | - |
| **Z** Canoe \| **Vinings** | 26 |
| **Z** Clark/Schwenk \| **Vinings** | 24 |
| Colonnade \| **Cheshire Bridge** | 20 |
| Cowtippers \| **Midtown** | 15 |
| East West \| **Athens/O** | 21 |
| Eats \| **Midtown** | 18 |
| Einstein's \| **Midtown** | 18 |
| Feast \| **Decatur** | 22 |
| Fellini's Pizza \| **Decatur** | 20 |
| Five Seasons \| **Alpharetta** | 22 |
| **Z** Flying Biscuit \| **Candler Pk** | 19 |
| **Z** Fogo de Chão \| **Buckhead** | 24 |
| Food 101 \| **VA-Highland** | 20 |
| **Z** Food Studio \| **W'side** | 24 |
| French Am. Brass. \| **D'town** | 24 |
| Goldfish \| **Dunwoody** | 21 |
| Grape \| **multi.** | 16 |
| Hal's/Old Ivy \| **Buckhead** | 25 |
| Highland Tap \| **VA-Highland** | 20 |
| Horseradish \| **Buckhead** | 22 |
| Ibiza \| **S Buckhead** | 20 |
| Il Pasticcio \| **Historic Dist/S** | 22 |
| **Z** Java Jive \| **Poncey-Highland** | 22 |
| JCT. Kitchen \| **W'side** | 24 |
| **Z** JOËL \| **Buckhead** | 26 |
| **Z** Kevin Rathbun \| **Inman Pk** | 26 |
| **Z** Krog Bar \| **Inman Pk** | 23 |
| **Z** Kyma \| **Buckhead** | 25 |
| La Fonda \| **multi.** | 20 |

| | | | |
|---|---|---|---|
| ☑ Little Alley | **Roswell** | 26 | |
| Lobby at 12 | **Atlantic Sta.** | 20 | |
| **NEW** Luckie | **D'town** | 17 | |
| ☑ Maggiano's | **Buckhead** | 20 | |
| Majestic | **Poncey-Highland** | 12 | |
| ☑ **NEW** MF Buckhead | **Buckhead** | 26 | |
| ☑ MF Sushibar | **Midtown** | 27 | |
| ☑ Nan Thai | **Midtown** | 27 | |
| ☑ Nava | **Buckhead** | 23 | |
| ☑ New York Prime | **Buckhead** | 25 | |
| Noche | **VA-Highland** | 20 | |
| Oceanaire | **Midtown** | 23 | |
| OK Cafe | **Buckhead** | 20 | |
| ☑ ONE. midtown | **Midtown** | 22 | |
| Palm | **Buckhead** | 23 | |
| Paul's | **S Buckhead** | 23 | |
| Pricci | **Buckhead** | 24 | |
| Prime | **Buckhead** | 23 | |
| ☑ Rathbun's | **Inman Pk** | 28 | |
| Rolling Bones | **D'town** | 22 | |
| **NEW** Room at 12 | **D'town** | 22 | |
| Rosa Mexicano | **Atlantic Sta.** | 19 | |
| R. Thomas | **S Buckhead** | 19 | |
| Sala/Sabor | **VA-Highland** | 19 | |
| Sapphire | **Historic Dist/S** | 25 | |
| Shaun's | **Inman Pk** | 24 | |
| Shout | **Midtown** | 16 | |
| Six Feet | **W'side** | 19 | |
| SoHo | **Vinings** | 22 | |
| ☑ South City | **Midtown** | 23 | |
| **NEW** Steel | **Midtown** | - | |
| Strip | **Atlantic Sta.** | 17 | |
| Table 1280 | **Midtown** | 20 | |
| ☑ Tamarind Seed | **Midtown** | 27 | |
| **NEW** TAP | **Midtown** | 14 | |
| Taurus | **S Buckhead** | 23 | |
| Tavern/Phipps | **Buckhead** | 18 | |
| Thrive | **D'town** | 17 | |
| **NEW** Top Flr | **Midtown** | 25 | |
| ☑ Trois | **Midtown** | 22 | |
| ☑ TWO urban | **Poncey-Highland** | 23 | |
| Veni Vidi Vici | **Midtown** | 23 | |

| | | | |
|---|---|---|---|
| Verve | **D'town** | - | |
| **NEW** Vita | **S Buckhead** | - | |
| Vortex B&G | **multi.** | 22 | |
| White House | **Buckhead** | 19 | |
| Woodfire Grill | **Cheshire Bridge** | 25 | |

## POWER SCENES

| | | | |
|---|---|---|---|
| **NEW** AquaKnox | **Buckhead** | - | |
| ☑ Atlanta Fish | **Buckhead** | 23 | |
| Au Pied | **Buckhead** | 19 | |
| ☑ BluePointe | **Buckhead** | 24 | |
| ☑ Bone's | **Buckhead** | 27 | |
| ☑ Buckhead Diner | **Buckhead** | 23 | |
| ☑ Capital Grille | **Buckhead** | 24 | |
| ☑ Chops/Lobster | **Buckhead** | 27 | |
| Chopstix | **Buckhead** | 23 | |
| City Grill | **D'town** | 22 | |
| ☑ Elizabeth | **Historic Dist/S** | 25 | |
| Fleming's/Steak | **Dunwoody** | 23 | |
| ☑ JOËL | **Buckhead** | 26 | |
| Joey D's | **Dunwoody** | 20 | |
| ☑ Kevin Rathbun | **Inman Pk** | 26 | |
| ☑ Kyma | **Buckhead** | 25 | |
| ☑ La Grotta | **Buckhead** | 26 | |
| Lobby at 12 | **Atlantic Sta.** | 20 | |
| Manuel's | **Poncey-Highland** | 17 | |
| ☑ **NEW** MF Buckhead | **Buckhead** | 26 | |
| ☑ Morton's | **multi.** | 25 | |
| ☑ Nan Thai | **Midtown** | 27 | |
| ☑ Nava | **Buckhead** | 23 | |
| Oceanaire | **Midtown** | 23 | |
| ☑ ONE. midtown | **Midtown** | 22 | |
| Palm | **Buckhead** | 23 | |
| ☑ Pano's/Paul's | **Buckhead** | 26 | |
| Paul's | **S Buckhead** | 23 | |
| Pricci | **Buckhead** | 24 | |
| Prime | **Buckhead** | 23 | |
| ☑ Quinones | **W'side** | 28 | |
| ☑ Rest. Eugene | **S Buckhead** | 28 | |
| ☑ Ritz/Buckhead Din. Rm. | **Buckhead** | 27 | |
| **NEW** Room at 12 | **D'town** | 22 | |
| Ruth's Chris | **multi.** | 23 | |
| ☑ South City | **Midtown** | 23 | |

**SPECIAL FEATURES**

| | | | | |
|---|---|---|---|
| Table 1280 | **Midtown** | 20 | Le Giverny | **Emory** | 20 |
| NEW TAP | **Midtown** | 14 | Madras Chettinaad | **Decatur** | 23 |
| Thrive | **D'town** | 17 | Z Maggiano's | **multi.** | 20 |
| Z Trois | **Midtown** | 22 | Manuel's | **Poncey-Highland** | 17 |
| Veni Vidi Vici | **Midtown** | 23 | McCormick/Schmick | **Dunwoody** | 20 |

## PRIVATE ROOMS

(Restaurants charge less at off times; call for capacity)

| | | | | |
|---|---|---|---|
| Agave | **Cabbagetown** | 22 | McKendrick's | **Dunwoody** | 25 |
| Z Antica Posta | **Buckhead** | 24 | McKinnon's | **Buckhead** | 18 |
| Z Aria | **Buckhead** | 27 | Melting Pot | **multi.** | 22 |
| Z Atlanta Fish | **Buckhead** | 23 | Mitra | **Midtown** | 20 |
| Au Pied | **Buckhead** | 19 | Z Morton's | **multi.** | 25 |
| Bistro VG | **Roswell** | 22 | Mosaic | **Buckhead** | 22 |
| Z BluePointe | **Buckhead** | 24 | Z Nan Thai | **Midtown** | 27 |
| Z Blue Ridge | **Buckhead** | 23 | Z New York Prime | **Buckhead** | 25 |
| Z Bone's | **Buckhead** | 27 | Z Nikolai's | **D'town** | 25 |
| Brio Tuscan | **multi.** | 19 | Nino's | **Cheshire Bridge** | 22 |
| Z Canoe | **Vinings** | 26 | Oceanaire | **Midtown** | 23 |
| Z Capital Grille | **Buckhead** | 24 | Palm | **Buckhead** | 23 |
| Z Chops/Lobster | **Buckhead** | 27 | Z Pampas Steak | **Alpharetta** | 26 |
| Chopstix | **Buckhead** | 23 | Portofino | **Buckhead** | 21 |
| City Grill | **D'town** | 22 | Pricci | **Buckhead** | 24 |
| Z Ecco | **Midtown** | 25 | Prime | **Buckhead** | 23 |
| Eno | **Midtown** | 23 | Ray's/City | **D'town** | 22 |
| Feed Store | **Airport (College Pk)** | 19 | Ray's/River | **Sandy Springs** | 23 |
| Fleming's/Steak | **Dunwoody** | 23 | Z Rest. Eugene | **S Buckhead** | 28 |
| Z Floataway | **Emory** | 25 | Z Ritz/Buckhead Din. Rm. | **Buckhead** | 27 |
| Z Fogo de Chão | **Buckhead** | 24 | | |
| Food 101 | **Sandy Springs** | 20 | River Room | **Vinings** | 21 |
| Z Food Studio | **W'side** | 24 | Roy's | **Buckhead** | 23 |
| Fritti | **Inman Pk** | 23 | Ruth's Chris | **multi.** | 23 |
| Goldfish | **Dunwoody** | 21 | Sage | **Decatur** | 20 |
| Z Grace 17.20 | **Norcross** | 25 | Sal Grosso | **Cobb** | 21 |
| Z Haru Ichiban | **Duluth** | 26 | Shout | **Midtown** | 16 |
| Hashiguchi | **multi.** | 24 | Sia's | **Duluth** | 25 |
| Hi Life | **Norcross** | 23 | Silk | **Midtown** | 20 |
| Horseradish | **Buckhead** | 22 | Soleil Bistro | **Buckhead** | 18 |
| Il Localino | **Inman Pk** | 21 | Z Stoney River | **Duluth** | 24 |
| Ippolito's | **multi.** | 19 | Swan Coach | **Buckhead** | 18 |
| Z JOËL | **Buckhead** | 26 | tomas | **Norcross** | 24 |
| Kobe | **Sandy Springs** | 20 | Toulouse | **S Buckhead** | 21 |
| Kurt's | **Duluth** | 22 | Z TWO urban | **Poncey-Highland** | 23 |
| Z La Grotta | **Dunwoody** | 26 | Veni Vidi Vici | **Midtown** | 23 |
| | | | Villa Christina | **Dunwoody** | 19 |

| | |
|---|---|
| Vinings Inn \| **Vinings** | 21 |
| Violette \| **Clairmont** | 21 |
| Woodfire Grill \| **Cheshire Bridge** | 25 |

## PRIX FIXE MENUS

(Call for prices and times)

| | |
|---|---|
| Au Rendez \| **Sandy Springs** | 21 |
| 🔲 Bacchanalia \| **W'side** | 29 |
| Dillard Hse. \| **Dillard/O** | 21 |
| Fire/Brazil \| **multi.** | 21 |
| 🔲 Fogo de Chão \| **Buckhead** | 24 |
| Imperial Fez \| **S Buckhead** | 19 |
| Little Szechuan \| **Buford Hwy. (Dora.)** | 21 |
| Madras Saravana \| **Decatur** | 24 |
| Nicola's \| **Emory** | 18 |
| 🔲 Pano's/Paul's \| **Buckhead** | 26 |
| 🔲 Park 75 \| **Midtown** | 27 |
| 🔲 Quinones \| **W'side** | 28 |
| 🔲 Ritz/Atlanta \| **D'town** | 26 |
| 🔲 Ritz/Buckhead Din. Rm. \| **Buckhead** | 27 |
| Roy's \| **Buckhead** | 23 |
| Sal Grosso \| **Cobb** | 21 |
| Salsa \| **Midtown** | 18 |

## QUICK BITES

| | |
|---|---|
| 🔲 Alon's \| **multi.** | 26 |
| Baraonda \| **Midtown** | 23 |
| Barbecue Kitchen \| **Airport (Atl)** | 18 |
| 🆕 Beleza \| **Midtown** | 23 |
| Bistro VG \| **Roswell** | 22 |
| Blue Eyed \| **Palmetto** | 21 |
| Bread Gdn. \| **Midtown** | 26 |
| 🆕 BrickTop's \| **Buckhead** | 19 |
| Café di Sol \| **Poncey-Highland** | 20 |
| Cafe Intermezzo \| **S Buckhead** | 21 |
| 🆕 Cakes & Ale \| **Decatur** | - |
| Carver's \| **W'side** | 26 |
| China Cooks \| **Sandy Springs** | 22 |
| Chipotle \| **multi.** | 18 |
| Chocolate Bar \| **Decatur** | 20 |
| 🔲 Chocolate Pink \| **Midtown** | 25 |
| Chopstix \| **Buckhead** | 23 |

| | |
|---|---|
| Coco Loco's \| **Buckhead** | 19 |
| Com \| **Dunwoody** | 24 |
| Corner Cafe \| **Buckhead** | 20 |
| Dressed Salads \| **Midtown** | 19 |
| 88 Tofu \| **Buford Hwy. (Atl)** | 21 |
| El Taco \| **multi.** | 20 |
| Everybody/Pizza \| **VA-Highland** | 20 |
| Fellini's Pizza \| **multi.** | 20 |
| Figo Pasta \| **S Buckhead** | 21 |
| 🔲 Five Guys \| **multi.** | 21 |
| 🆕 Fox Bros. BBQ \| **Candler Pk** | - |
| Fresh/Order \| **multi.** | 21 |
| Gabriel's \| **Marietta** | 24 |
| Goldberg's \| **multi.** | 20 |
| Jason's Deli \| **multi.** | 17 |
| Jim N' Nick's \| **multi.** | 22 |
| Johnny Rockets \| **multi.** | 16 |
| Lobby at 12 \| **Atlantic Sta.** | 20 |
| 🆕 Luckie \| **D'town** | 17 |
| Majestic \| **Poncey-Highland** | 12 |
| Matthews \| **Tucker** | 20 |
| Metrofresh \| **Midtown** | 22 |
| Moe's SW \| **multi.** | 13 |
| New Yorker \| **Buckhead** | 22 |
| Nino's \| **Cheshire Bridge** | 22 |
| Noodle \| **College Pk** | 19 |
| Nuevo Laredo \| **W'side** | 24 |
| Oak Grove \| **Decatur** | 21 |
| OK Cafe \| **Buckhead** | 20 |
| Original Pancake \| **Alpharetta** | 21 |
| Provisions to Go \| **W'side** | 25 |
| Pure Taqueria \| **Alpharetta** | 23 |
| Raging Burrito \| **Decatur** | 18 |
| 🆕 Relish \| **Roswell** | 23 |
| Rising Roll \| **multi.** | 20 |
| Rolling Bones \| **D'town** | 22 |
| Rumi's \| **Sandy Springs** | 24 |
| Ru San's \| **multi.** | 18 |
| Sawicki's \| **Decatur** | 26 |
| Shorty's \| **Emory** | 24 |
| Six Feet \| **W'side** | 19 |
| 🔲 Souper Jenny \| **Buckhead** | 25 |
| Spoon \| **D'town** | 25 |

**SPECIAL FEATURES**

| | | | | |
|---|---|---|---|---|
| Surin \| **VA-Highland** | 23 | Farmhouse \| **Palmetto** | 25 |
| **NEW** TAP \| **Midtown** | 14 | Five Seasons \| **Alpharetta** | 22 |
| ☑ Taqueria/Sol \| **multi.** | 24 | Fleming's/Steak \| **Dunwoody** | 23 |
| Tasty China \| **Marietta** | 24 | ☑ Food Studio \| **W'side** | 24 |
| 10 Degrees \| **Buckhead** | 23 | Georgia Grille \| **S Buckhead** | 22 |
| Tin Drum \| **Midtown** | 16 | Grape \| **multi.** | 16 |
| Toscano \| **W'side** | 23 | Harry & Sons \| **VA-Highland** | 20 |
| Tossed \| **Alpharetta** | 16 | ☑ Haru Ichiban \| **Duluth** | 26 |
| **NEW** Valenza \| **Brookhaven** | 22 | **NEW** Hil \| **Palmetto** | - |
| ☑ Varsity \| **multi.** | 17 | JCT. Kitchen \| **W'side** | 24 |
| **NEW** Via \| **Buckhead** | - | ☑ La Grotta \| **Buckhead** | 26 |
| Willy's Mex. \| **Marietta** | 20 | Le Giverny \| **Emory** | 20 |
| Wolfgang Puck \| **S Buckhead** | 16 | ☑ Little Alley \| **Roswell** | 26 |
| Zesto \| **Lindbergh** | 16 | McCormick/Schmick \| **multi.** | 20 |

## QUIET CONVERSATION

| | | | | |
|---|---|---|---|---|
| | | McKendrick's \| **Dunwoody** | 25 |
| Alfredo's \| **Cheshire Bridge** | 22 | McKinnon's \| **Buckhead** | 18 |
| **NEW** Allegro \| **Midtown** | 20 | Melting Pot \| **multi.** | 22 |
| Anis Bistro \| **Buckhead** | 22 | ☑**NEW** MF Buckhead \| **Buckhead** | 26 |
| Anthony's \| **Buckhead** | 19 | Mosaic \| **Buckhead** | 22 |
| ☑ Antica Posta \| **Buckhead** | 24 | Mu Lan \| **Midtown** | 18 |
| Atmosphere \| **Midtown** | 25 | Nakato \| **Cheshire Bridge** | 21 |
| Babette's \| **Poncey-Highland** | 25 | Nam \| **Midtown** | 25 |
| ☑ Bacchanalia \| **W'side** | 29 | ☑ Nikolai's \| **D'town** | 25 |
| Basil's \| **Buckhead** | 20 | Nino's \| **Cheshire Bridge** | 22 |
| **NEW** Beleza \| **Midtown** | 23 | Palm \| **Buckhead** | 23 |
| Benihana \| **multi.** | 19 | ☑ Pano's/Paul's \| **Buckhead** | 26 |
| Bistro VG \| **Roswell** | 22 | ☑ Park 75 \| **Midtown** | 27 |
| Blackstone \| **Smyrna** | 23 | Petite Auberge \| **Emory** | 19 |
| Blue Eyed \| **Palmetto** | 21 | Portofino \| **Buckhead** | 21 |
| ☑ Blue Ridge \| **Buckhead** | 23 | Prime \| **Buckhead** | 23 |
| ☑ Bone's \| **Buckhead** | 27 | ☑ Quinones \| **W'side** | 28 |
| Cafe Alsace \| **Decatur** | 22 | Redfish \| **Grant Pk** | 22 |
| Café di Sol \| **Poncey-Highland** | 20 | Red Snapper \| **Cheshire Bridge** | 22 |
| Cafe Intermezzo \| **multi.** | 21 | ☑ Rest. Eugene \| **S Buckhead** | 28 |
| Chocolate Bar \| **Decatur** | 20 | ☑ Rice Thai \| **Roswell** | 26 |
| ☑ Chocolate Pink \| **Midtown** | 25 | ☑ Ritz/Buckhead Din. Rm. \| | 27 |
| Chopstix \| **Buckhead** | 23 | **Buckhead** | |
| City Grill \| **D'town** | 22 | Rumi's \| **Sandy Springs** | 24 |
| ☑ Clark/Schwenk \| **Vinings** | 24 | Sapphire \| **Historic Dist/S** | 25 |
| Edo \| **Decatur** | 19 | Sia's \| **Duluth** | 25 |
| ☑ Elizabeth \| **Historic Dist/S** | 25 | Silk \| **Midtown** | 20 |
| Eurasia Bistro \| **Decatur** | 25 | Soleil Bistro \| **Buckhead** | 18 |
| **NEW** Fadó \| **Buckhead** | - | ☑ South City \| **Smyrna** | 23 |

| | |
|---|---|
| NEW Steel \| **Midtown** | - |
| Z Tamarind Seed \| **Midtown** | 27 |
| Taverna Fiorentina \| **Vinings** | - |
| 10 Degrees \| **Buckhead** | 23 |
| Z Tierra \| **Midtown** | 26 |
| Tomo \| **Vinings** | 27 |
| Top Spice \| **Emory** | 21 |
| Toulouse \| **S Buckhead** | 21 |
| Tratt. La Strada \| **Marietta** | 19 |
| NEW Valenza \| **Brookhaven** | 22 |
| Villa Christina \| **Dunwoody** | 19 |
| Vine \| **VA-Highland** | 21 |
| Vinings Inn \| **Vinings** | 21 |
| Violette \| **Clairmont** | 21 |
| Wisteria \| **Inman Pk** | 24 |

## RAW BARS

| | |
|---|---|
| NEW AquaKnox \| **Buckhead** | - |
| Z Atlanta Fish \| **Buckhead** | 23 |
| Au Pied \| **Buckhead** | 19 |
| Benihana \| **D'town** | 19 |
| NEW Bluefin \| **S Buckhead** | - |
| Z Chops/Lobster \| **Buckhead** | 27 |
| Z Clark/Schwenk \| **Vinings** | 24 |
| Edo \| **Decatur** | 19 |
| Fontaine Oyster \| **VA-Highland** | 16 |
| Garrison's \| **Duluth** | 19 |
| Goldfish \| **Dunwoody** | 21 |
| Gumbeaux's \| **Douglasville** | 24 |
| JCT. Kitchen \| **W'side** | 24 |
| McCormick/Schmick \| **Dunwoody** | 20 |
| Oceanaire \| **Midtown** | 23 |
| NEW Parish \| **Inman Pk** | - |
| Ray's/City \| **D'town** | 22 |
| Ray's/River \| **Sandy Springs** | 23 |
| Six Feet \| **Grant Pk** | 19 |

## ROMANTIC PLACES

| | |
|---|---|
| Alfredo's \| **Cheshire Bridge** | 22 |
| NEW Allegro \| **Midtown** | 20 |
| Anis Bistro \| **Buckhead** | 22 |
| Z Antica Posta \| **Buckhead** | 24 |
| Après Diem \| **Midtown** | 17 |

| | |
|---|---|
| NEW AquaKnox \| **Buckhead** | - |
| Z Aria \| **Buckhead** | 27 |
| Atmosphere \| **Midtown** | 25 |
| Babette's \| **Poncey-Highland** | 25 |
| Z Bacchanalia \| **W'side** | 29 |
| Basil's \| **Buckhead** | 20 |
| NEW Beleza \| **Midtown** | 23 |
| Bistro VG \| **Roswell** | 22 |
| Z Blue Ridge \| **Buckhead** | 23 |
| Blu Greek \| **Marietta** | 20 |
| Cabernet \| **Alpharetta** | 24 |
| Café di Sol \| **Poncey-Highland** | 20 |
| Cafe Intermezzo \| **multi.** | 21 |
| Cargo \| **Brunswick/O** | - |
| Chocolate Bar \| **Decatur** | 20 |
| City Grill \| **D'town** | 22 |
| Z Clark/Schwenk \| **Vinings** | 24 |
| NEW Cuerno \| **Midtown** | - |
| Z di Paolo \| **Alpharetta** | 27 |
| Edo \| **Decatur** | 19 |
| Z Elizabeth \| **Historic Dist/S** | 25 |
| Eno \| **Midtown** | 23 |
| Farmhouse \| **Palmetto** | 25 |
| Feast \| **Decatur** | 22 |
| Z Five & Ten \| **Athens/O** | 28 |
| Five Seasons \| **Alpharetta** | 22 |
| Fleming's/Steak \| **Dunwoody** | 23 |
| Food 101 \| **Sandy Springs** | 20 |
| Z Food Studio \| **W'side** | 24 |
| French Am. Brass. \| **D'town** | 24 |
| Georgia Grille \| **S Buckhead** | 22 |
| Haven \| **Brookhaven** | 23 |
| NEW Hil \| **Palmetto** | - |
| NEW Home \| **Buckhead** | - |
| Ibiza \| **S Buckhead** | 20 |
| Imperial Fez \| **S Buckhead** | 19 |
| JCT. Kitchen \| **W'side** | 24 |
| Z JOËL \| **Buckhead** | 26 |
| Z Kyma \| **Buckhead** | 25 |
| Z La Grotta \| **multi.** | 26 |
| Le Giverny \| **Emory** | 20 |
| Z Little Alley \| **Roswell** | 26 |
| McCormick/Schmick \| **Dunwoody** | 20 |

SPECIAL FEATURES

| | |
|---|---|
| McKendrick's \| **Dunwoody** | 25 |
| ∎**NEW** MF Buckhead \| **Buckhead** | 26 |
| Mosaic \| **Buckhead** | 22 |
| Mu Lan \| **Midtown** | 18 |
| **NEW** National \| **Athens/O** | 28 |
| ∎ Nikolai's \| **D'town** | 25 |
| ∎ Pano's/Paul's \| **Buckhead** | 26 |
| ∎ Park 75 \| **Midtown** | 27 |
| Paul's \| **S Buckhead** | 23 |
| Pleasant \| **Midtown** | 19 |
| Portofino \| **Buckhead** | 21 |
| ∎ Quinones \| **W'side** | 28 |
| Repast \| **Midtown** | 24 |
| ∎ Rest. Eugene \| **S Buckhead** | 28 |
| ∎ Rice Thai \| **Roswell** | 26 |
| ∎ Ritz/Atlanta \| **D'town** | 26 |
| ∎ Ritz/Buckhead Din. Rm. \| **Buckhead** | 27 |
| **NEW** Room at 12 \| **D'town** | 22 |
| Sage \| **Decatur** | 20 |
| Sapphire \| **Historic Dist/S** | 25 |
| Sia's \| **Duluth** | 25 |
| Soleil Bistro \| **Buckhead** | 18 |
| ∎ Sotto Sotto \| **Inman Pk** | 27 |
| ∎ South City \| **Smyrna** | 23 |
| **NEW** Spice Market \| **Midtown** | – |
| **NEW** Steel \| **Midtown** | – |
| ∎ Sun Dial \| **D'town** | 19 |
| ∎ Tamarind Seed \| **Midtown** | 27 |
| Taverna Fiorentina \| **Vinings** | – |
| Thrive \| **D'town** | 17 |
| **NEW** Top Flr \| **Midtown** | 25 |
| Top Spice \| **Emory** | 21 |
| Toulouse \| **S Buckhead** | 21 |
| **NEW** Via \| **Buckhead** | – |
| Villa Christina \| **Dunwoody** | 19 |
| Vine \| **VA-Highland** | 21 |
| Vinings Inn \| **Vinings** | 21 |
| Vinocity \| **Kirkwood** | 19 |
| Violette \| **Clairmont** | 21 |
| Wisteria \| **Inman Pk** | 24 |
| Woodfire Grill \| **Cheshire Bridge** | 25 |

## SENIOR APPEAL

| | |
|---|---|
| Alfredo's \| **Cheshire Bridge** | 22 |
| **NEW** Allegro \| **Midtown** | 20 |
| ∎ Atlanta Fish \| **Buckhead** | 23 |
| Au Pied \| **Buckhead** | 19 |
| Au Rendez \| **Sandy Springs** | 21 |
| Babette's \| **Poncey-Highland** | 25 |
| ∎ Bacchanalia \| **W'side** | 29 |
| Blackstone \| **Smyrna** | 23 |
| Blue Ribbon \| **Tucker** | 20 |
| ∎ Blue Willow \| **Social Circle/O** | 22 |
| Bobby/June's \| **Midtown** | 20 |
| Bonefish Grill \| **Alpharetta** | 23 |
| Brickery \| **Sandy Springs** | 18 |
| Brio Tuscan \| **Buckhead** | 19 |
| Cabernet \| **Alpharetta** | 24 |
| ∎ Cheesecake Fac. \| **Marietta** | 19 |
| ∎ Clark/Schwenk \| **Vinings** | 24 |
| Colonnade \| **Cheshire Bridge** | 20 |
| Dillard Hse. \| **Dillard/O** | 21 |
| ∎ di Paolo \| **Alpharetta** | 27 |
| Fleming's/Steak \| **Dunwoody** | 23 |
| Food 101 \| **VA-Highland** | 20 |
| Georgia Grille \| **S Buckhead** | 22 |
| Goldberg's \| **Midtown** | 20 |
| Greenwoods \| **Roswell** | 23 |
| Hal's/Old Ivy \| **Buckhead** | 25 |
| JCT. Kitchen \| **W'side** | 24 |
| ∎ La Grotta \| **multi.** | 26 |
| ∎ LongHorn \| **Buckhead** | 18 |
| Mary Mac's \| **Midtown** | 19 |
| McKinnon's \| **Buckhead** | 18 |
| ∎ Morton's \| **multi.** | 25 |
| ∎ Nikolai's \| **D'town** | 25 |
| OK Cafe \| **Buckhead** | 20 |
| Olde Pink \| **Historic Dist/S** | 21 |
| Original Pancake \| **multi.** | 21 |
| ∎ Pano's/Paul's \| **Buckhead** | 26 |
| Paul's \| **S Buckhead** | 23 |
| Petite Auberge \| **Emory** | 19 |
| Pittypat's \| **D'town** | 15 |
| Pleasant \| **Midtown** | 19 |
| Portofino \| **Buckhead** | 21 |

| | |
|---|---|
| Ray's/River \| **Sandy Springs** | 23 |
| Red Snapper \| **Cheshire Bridge** | 22 |
| Silver Skillet \| **Midtown** | 18 |
| Son's Place \| **Inman Pk** | 19 |
| **Z** South City \| **Smyrna** | 23 |
| Swan Coach \| **Buckhead** | 18 |
| Tratt. La Strada \| **Marietta** | 19 |
| Village Tavern \| **Alpharetta** | 21 |
| Vinings Inn \| **Vinings** | 21 |
| Violette \| **Clairmont** | 21 |

## SINGLES SCENES

| | |
|---|---|
| Agave \| **Cabbagetown** | 22 |
| Après Diem \| **Midtown** | 17 |
| Athens Pizza \| **Chamblee** | 20 |
| Atkins Park \| **VA-Highland** | 19 |
| Azio \| **D'town** | 18 |
| **Z** BluePointe \| **Buckhead** | 24 |
| **NEW** Cakes & Ale \| **Decatur** | - |
| **Z** Capital Grille \| **Buckhead** | 24 |
| Doc Chey's \| **VA-Highland** | 19 |
| Dolce \| **Atlantic Sta.** | 18 |
| East West \| **Athens/O** | 21 |
| Eats \| **Midtown** | 18 |
| Einstein's \| **Midtown** | 18 |
| Everybody/Pizza \| **multi.** | 20 |
| **NEW** Fadó \| **Buckhead** | - |
| Fat Matt's Rib \| **VA-Highland** | 23 |
| Fellini's Pizza \| **multi.** | 20 |
| Fleming's/Steak \| **Dunwoody** | 23 |
| **Z** Flying Biscuit \| **Candler Pk** | 19 |
| Fritti \| **Inman Pk** | 23 |
| Genki \| **Buckhead** | 19 |
| Grape \| **multi.** | 16 |
| Hal's/Old Ivy \| **Buckhead** | 25 |
| Haven \| **Brookhaven** | 23 |
| Highland Tap \| **VA-Highland** | 20 |
| La Fonda \| **multi.** | 20 |
| Lobby at 12 \| **Atlantic Sta.** | 20 |
| **Z** LongHorn \| **multi.** | 18 |
| **NEW** Luckie \| **D'town** | 17 |
| Majestic \| **Poncey-Highland** | 12 |
| Mellow Mushroom \| **Sandy Springs** | 21 |

| | |
|---|---|
| **Z** Murphy's \| **VA-Highland** | 24 |
| **NEW** National \| **Athens/O** | 28 |
| Nickiemoto's \| **Midtown** | 20 |
| Noodle \| **Midtown** | 19 |
| **Z** ONE. midtown \| **Midtown** | 22 |
| Pricci \| **Buckhead** | 24 |
| Pub 71 \| **Brookhaven** | 18 |
| Pure Taqueria \| **Alpharetta** | 23 |
| Repast \| **Midtown** | 24 |
| Rosa Mexicano \| **Atlantic Sta.** | 19 |
| R. Thomas \| **S Buckhead** | 19 |
| Ru San's \| **Midtown** | 18 |
| Savage Pizza \| **Little Five Pts** | 20 |
| Shaun's \| **Inman Pk** | 24 |
| **NEW** Stats \| **D'town** | 19 |
| Strip \| **Atlantic Sta.** | 17 |
| Surin \| **VA-Highland** | 23 |
| **NEW** TAP \| **Midtown** | 14 |
| Tavern/Phipps \| **Buckhead** | 18 |
| Thrive \| **D'town** | 17 |
| **Z** Trois \| **Midtown** | 22 |
| **Z** TWO urban \| **Poncey-Highland** | 23 |
| **NEW** Via \| **Buckhead** | - |
| Vickery's \| **Midtown** | 19 |

## SLEEPERS

(Good to excellent food, but little known)

| | |
|---|---|
| Amalfi \| **Roswell** | 23 |
| Ann's Snack \| **D'town** | 23 |
| **NEW** Beleza \| **Midtown** | 23 |
| Big City Bread \| **Athens/O** | 22 |
| **Z** Blue Willow \| **Social Circle/O** | 22 |
| Bread Gdn. \| **Midtown** | 26 |
| Busy Bee \| **D'town** | 27 |
| Cameli's \| **Midtown** | 24 |
| Carver's \| **W'side** | 26 |
| China Cooks \| **Sandy Springs** | 22 |
| Earl \| **E Atlanta** | 22 |
| El Rey de Taco \| **Buford Hwy. (Dora.)** | 24 |
| Farmhouse \| **Palmetto** | 25 |
| Fat Matt's Chicken \| **VA-Highland** | 24 |
| Gabriel's \| **Marietta** | 24 |

Garibaldi's | **Historic Dist/S** | 25
Gumbeaux's | **Douglasville** | 24
Hae Woon | **Buford Hwy. (Dora.)** | 22
🇿 Haru Ichiban | **Duluth** | 26
Hi Life | **Norcross** | 23
House/Chan | **Smyrna** | 24
Il Pasticcio | **Historic Dist/S** | 22
🇿 Java Jive | **Poncey-Highland** | 22
Kurt's | **Duluth** | 22
🇿 Last Resort | **Athens/O** | 24
Les Fleurs | **D'town** | 27
Linger Longer | **Greensboro/O** | 27
🇿 Little Alley | **Roswell** | 26
Madras Chettinaad | **Decatur** | 23
Minerva | **Alpharetta** | 22
Nagoya | **Roswell** | 24
**NEW** National | **Athens/O** | 28
New Yorker | **Buckhead** | 22
Northlake Thai | **Tucker** | 24
Old South | **Smyrna** | 23
Oscar's Villa | **Dunwoody** | 27
Palomilla's | **Norcross** | 23
Pho Dai Loi | **Forest Pk** | 22
Pho 79 | **Buford Hwy. (Dora.)** | 26
Provisions to Go | **W'side** | 25
Rare | **Midtown** | 24
Red Snapper | **Cheshire Bridge** | 22
Righteous Rm. | **Poncey-Highland** | 22
**NEW** Room at 12 | **D'town** | 22
Sapphire | **Historic Dist/S** | 25
Sawicki's | **Decatur** | 26
Sops on Ellis | **D'town** | 25
Spoon | **D'town** | 25
Sun in Belly | **Kirkwood** | 24
Tarahumata | **Alpharetta** | 23
Tasting Room | **multi.** | 22
Tasty China | **Marietta** | 24
Thaicoon | **Marietta** | 22
tomas | **Norcross** | 24
Tomo | **Vinings** | 27
**NEW** Top Flr | **Midtown** | 25
Toscano | **W'side** | 23
Udipi Cafe | **Decatur** | 22

Umezono | **Smyrna** | 26
Vreny's Bier | **Duluth** | 22
YellowFin | **Roswell** | 22
Zab-E-Lee | **Airport (College Pk)** | 23
Zapata | **Norcross** | 22
Zola Italian | **Alpharetta** | 25

## SPECIAL OCCASIONS

**NEW** Allegro | **Midtown** | 20
Anthony's | **Buckhead** | 19
**NEW** AquaKnox | **Buckhead** | -
🇿 Aria | **Buckhead** | 27
Au Pied | **Buckhead** | 19
🇿 Bacchanalia | **W'side** | 29
🇿 BluePointe | **Buckhead** | 24
🇿 Canoe | **Vinings** | 26
Cargo | **Brunswick/O** | -
🇿 Chops/Lobster | **Buckhead** | 27
🇿 di Paolo | **Alpharetta** | 27
D. Morgan's | **Cartersville/O** | -
🇿 Elizabeth | **Historic Dist/S** | 25
Eno | **Midtown** | 23
Farmhouse | **Palmetto** | 25
Fleming's/Steak | **Dunwoody** | 23
🇿 Food Studio | **W'side** | 24
Horseradish | **Buckhead** | 22
Imperial Fez | **S Buckhead** | 19
🇿 JOËL | **Buckhead** | 26
Kurt's | **Duluth** | 22
🇿 La Grotta | **multi.** | 26
Linger Longer | **Greensboro/O** | 27
🇿 Morton's | **multi.** | 25
🇿 Nan Thai | **Midtown** | 27
🇿 New York Prime | **Buckhead** | 25
🇿 Nikolai's | **D'town** | 25
Oceanaire | **Midtown** | 23
Olde Pink | **Historic Dist/S** | 21
🇿 Pano's/Paul's | **Buckhead** | 26
🇿 Park 75 | **Midtown** | 27
Prime | **Buckhead** | 23
🇿 Quinones | **W'side** | 28
🇿 Rest. Eugene | **S Buckhead** | 28
🇿 Ritz/Atlanta | **D'town** | 26

| | |
|---|---|
| ☑ Ritz/Buckhead Din. Rm. \| **Buckhead** | 27 |
| Roy's \| **Buckhead** | 23 |
| Sapphire \| **Historic Dist/S** | 25 |
| Sia's \| **Duluth** | 25 |
| ☑ Sotto Sotto \| **Inman Pk** | 27 |
| Table 1280 \| **Midtown** | 20 |
| ☑ Trois \| **Midtown** | 22 |
| Villa Christina \| **Dunwoody** | 19 |

## TEEN APPEAL

| | |
|---|---|
| Athens Pizza \| **Decatur** | 20 |
| Benihana \| **multi.** | 19 |
| Brickery \| **Sandy Springs** | 18 |
| NEW BrickTop's \| **Buckhead** | 19 |
| Buca/Beppo \| **Alpharetta** | 17 |
| ☑ Cheesecake Fac. \| **multi.** | 19 |
| Chipotle \| **multi.** | 18 |
| Dante's Hatch \| **Buckhead** | 18 |
| Downwind \| **DeKalb** | 18 |
| Einstein's \| **Midtown** | 18 |
| ESPN Zone \| **Buckhead** | 10 |
| Everybody/Pizza \| **multi.** | 20 |
| Fellini's Pizza \| **Decatur** | 20 |
| ☑ Five Guys \| **multi.** | 21 |
| Ippolito's \| **multi.** | 19 |
| Jake's \| **Decatur** | 19 |
| Johnny Rockets \| **multi.** | 16 |
| La Paz \| **Vinings** | 19 |
| ☑ LongHorn \| **multi.** | 18 |
| Madras Chettinaad \| **Decatur** | 23 |
| Mellow Mushroom \| **Sandy Springs** | 21 |
| Mexico City \| **Decatur** | 16 |
| Nirvana \| **multi.** | 18 |
| Noodle \| **College Pk** | 19 |
| Outback \| **multi.** | 18 |
| Pappadeaux \| **Alpharetta** | 21 |
| Pasta Vino \| **Alpharetta** | 19 |
| ☑ Varsity \| **multi.** | 17 |
| Zesto \| **multi.** | 16 |

## THEME RESTAURANTS

| | |
|---|---|
| Avra \| **Midtown** | 20 |
| Benihana \| **multi.** | 19 |

| | |
|---|---|
| Buca/Beppo \| **Alpharetta** | 17 |
| ☑ Cheesecake Fac. \| **multi.** | 19 |
| Dante's Hatch \| **Buckhead** | 18 |
| ESPN Zone \| **Buckhead** | 10 |
| NEW Fadó \| **Buckhead** | - |
| Fire/Brazil \| **multi.** | 21 |
| ☑ Fogo de Chão \| **Buckhead** | 24 |
| Gladys Knight \| **multi.** | 18 |
| Ibiza \| **S Buckhead** | 20 |
| Johnny Rockets \| **multi.** | 16 |
| Kobe \| **Sandy Springs** | 20 |
| Madras Chettinaad \| **Decatur** | 23 |
| Melting Pot \| **multi.** | 22 |
| ☑ Pampas Steak \| **Alpharetta** | 26 |
| Pub 71 \| **Brookhaven** | 18 |
| Sal Grosso \| **Cobb** | 21 |
| ☑ Seasons 52 \| **Buckhead** | 22 |
| Taverna Plaka \| **Cheshire Bridge** | 17 |
| ☑ Ted's Montana \| **multi.** | 19 |
| ☑ Varsity \| **multi.** | 17 |
| NEW Vita \| **S Buckhead** | - |

## TRANSPORTING EXPERIENCES

| | |
|---|---|
| Alfredo's \| **Cheshire Bridge** | 22 |
| ☑ Bacchanalia \| **W'side** | 29 |
| ☑ BluePointe \| **Buckhead** | 24 |
| Blu Greek \| **Marietta** | 20 |
| Byblos \| **Roswell** | 21 |
| Com \| **Dunwoody** | 24 |
| ☑ Elizabeth \| **Historic Dist/S** | 25 |
| NEW Fadó \| **Buckhead** | - |
| Farmhouse \| **Palmetto** | 25 |
| Hae Woon \| **Buford Hwy. (Dora.)** | 22 |
| Hashiguchi \| **multi.** | 24 |
| Ibiza \| **S Buckhead** | 20 |
| Imperial Fez \| **S Buckhead** | 19 |
| ☑ JOËL \| **Buckhead** | 26 |
| Madras Chettinaad \| **Decatur** | 23 |
| ☑ NEW MF Buckhead \| **Buckhead** | 26 |
| ☑ MF Sushibar \| **Midtown** | 27 |
| ☑ Nan Thai \| **Midtown** | 27 |
| NEW Parish \| **Inman Pk** | - |
| Pittypat's \| **D'town** | 15 |

Ⓩ Quinones | **W'side** — 28

**NEW** Spice Market | **Midtown** — -

Tarahumata | **Alpharetta** — 23

## TRENDY

Anis Bistro | **Buckhead** — 22

**NEW** AquaKnox | **Buckhead** — -

Ⓩ Aria | **Buckhead** — 27

Au Pied | **Buckhead** — 19

Ⓩ Bacchanalia | **W'side** — 29

**NEW** Beleza | **Midtown** — 23

Bistro VG | **Roswell** — 22

Ⓩ BluePointe | **Buckhead** — 24

Ⓩ Buckhead Diner | **Buckhead** — 23

Café di Sol | **Poncey-Highland** — 20

**NEW** Cakes & Ale | **Decatur** — -

Ⓩ Canoe | **Vinings** — 26

Ⓩ Capital Grille | **Buckhead** — 24

Cargo | **Brunswick/O** — -

Chocolate Bar | **Decatur** — 20

Ⓩ Chops/Lobster | **Buckhead** — 27

**NEW** Cuerno | **Midtown** — -

Dolce | **Atlantic Sta.** — 18

East West | **Athens/O** — 21

Ⓩ Ecco | **Midtown** — 25

Einstein's | **Midtown** — 18

Eno | **Midtown** — 23

**NEW** Fadó | **Buckhead** — -

Farmhouse | **Palmetto** — 25

Farm 255 | **Athens/O** — 20

Ⓩ Five & Ten | **Athens/O** — 28

Five Seasons | **Alpharetta** — 22

Ⓩ Floataway | **Emory** — 25

Ⓩ Flying Biscuit | **Candler Pk** — 19

Ⓩ Fogo de Chão | **Buckhead** — 24

Food 101 | **multi.** — 20

Ⓩ Food Studio | **W'side** — 24

French Am. Brass. | **D'town** — 24

Fritti | **Inman Pk** — 23

Highland Tap | **VA-Highland** — 20

**NEW** Hil | **Palmetto** — -

Hi Life | **Norcross** — 23

Horseradish | **Buckhead** — 22

Ibiza | **S Buckhead** — 20

Il Pasticcio | **Historic Dist/S** — 22

JCT. Kitchen | **W'side** — 24

Ⓩ JOËL | **Buckhead** — 26

Ⓩ Kevin Rathbun | **Inman Pk** — 26

Ⓩ Krog Bar | **Inman Pk** — 23

Ⓩ Kyma | **Buckhead** — 25

La Tavola | **VA-Highland** — 24

Ⓩ Little Alley | **Roswell** — 26

Lobby at 12 | **Atlantic Sta.** — 20

Ⓩ Maggiano's | **Buckhead** — 20

Ⓩ**NEW** MF Buckhead | **Buckhead** — 26

Ⓩ MF Sushibar | **Midtown** — 27

Nam | **Midtown** — 25

Ⓩ Nan Thai | **Midtown** — 27

**NEW** National | **Athens/O** — 28

Ⓩ Nava | **Buckhead** — 23

Noche | **VA-Highland** — 20

Ⓩ ONE. midtown | **Midtown** — 22

Palm | **Buckhead** — 23

Pricci | **Buckhead** — 24

Prime | **Buckhead** — 23

Pure Taqueria | **Alpharetta** — 23

Ⓩ Rathbun's | **Inman Pk** — 28

Ray's/Killer | **Alpharetta** — 22

Repast | **Midtown** — 24

**NEW** Room at 12 | **D'town** — 22

Rosa Mexicano | **Atlantic Sta.** — 19

Roy's | **Buckhead** — 23

Ru San's | **multi.** — 18

Sala/Sabor | **VA-Highland** — 19

Sapphire | **Historic Dist/S** — 25

Ⓩ Seasons 52 | **multi.** — 22

Shaun's | **Inman Pk** — 24

Shout | **Midtown** — 16

Sia's | **Duluth** — 25

Six Feet | **W'side** — 19

SoHo | **Vinings** — 22

Ⓩ Sotto Sotto | **Inman Pk** — 27

Ⓩ South City | **multi.** — 23

**NEW** Steel | **Midtown** — -

Ⓩ Stoney River | **Duluth** — 24

Strip | **Atlantic Sta.** — 17

| | |
|---|---|
| Surin \| **VA-Highland** | 23 |
| Table 1280 \| **Midtown** | 20 |
| **NEW** TAP \| **Midtown** | 14 |
| **Z** Taqueria/Sol \| **Decatur** | 24 |
| Taurus \| **S Buckhead** | 23 |
| Thrive \| **D'town** | 17 |
| **NEW** Top Flr \| **Midtown** | 25 |
| **Z** Trois \| **Midtown** | 22 |
| **Z** TWO urban \| **Poncey-Highland** | 23 |
| Veni Vidi Vici \| **Midtown** | 23 |
| Village Tavern \| **Alpharetta** | 21 |
| Vinocity \| **Kirkwood** | 19 |
| **NEW** Vita \| **S Buckhead** | - |
| Woodfire Grill \| **Cheshire Bridge** | 25 |

## VIEWS

| | |
|---|---|
| Agave \| **Cabbagetown** | 22 |
| **Z** Canoe \| **Vinings** | 26 |
| **Z** Capital Grille \| **Buckhead** | 24 |
| Dillard Hse. \| **Dillard/O** | 21 |
| Downwind \| **DeKalb** | 18 |
| **Z** Ecco \| **Midtown** | 25 |
| **NEW** VIII fifty \| **Roswell** | - |
| **NEW** Fadó \| **Buckhead** | - |
| French Am. Brass. \| **D'town** | 24 |
| Horseradish \| **Buckhead** | 22 |
| Ibiza \| **S Buckhead** | 20 |
| JCT. Kitchen \| **W'side** | 24 |
| Linger Longer \| **Greensboro/O** | 27 |
| **Z** Nikolai's \| **D'town** | 25 |
| **Z** ONE. midtown \| **Midtown** | 22 |
| Pappadeaux \| **Alpharetta** | 21 |
| Ray's/River \| **Sandy Springs** | 23 |
| River Room \| **Vinings** | 21 |
| Ruth's Chris \| **D'town** | 23 |
| Six Feet \| **Grant Pk** | 19 |
| **NEW** Stats \| **D'town** | 19 |
| **NEW** Stella \| **Grant Pk** | - |
| **Z** Sun Dial \| **D'town** | 19 |
| Taurus \| **S Buckhead** | 23 |
| **NEW** Top Flr \| **Midtown** | 25 |
| **Z** TWO urban \| **Poncey-Highland** | 23 |
| Verve \| **D'town** | - |
| Villa Christina \| **Dunwoody** | 19 |

## VISITORS ON EXPENSE ACCOUNT

| | |
|---|---|
| **NEW** Allegro \| **Midtown** | 20 |
| **NEW** AquaKnox \| **Buckhead** | - |
| Au Pied \| **Buckhead** | 19 |
| **Z** Bacchanalia \| **W'side** | 29 |
| **Z** BluePointe \| **Buckhead** | 24 |
| **Z** Blue Ridge \| **Buckhead** | 23 |
| **Z** Bone's \| **Buckhead** | 27 |
| **Z** Canoe \| **Vinings** | 26 |
| **Z** Chops/Lobster \| **Buckhead** | 27 |
| Chopstix \| **Buckhead** | 23 |
| City Grill \| **D'town** | 22 |
| **Z** Elizabeth \| **Historic Dist/S** | 25 |
| Fire/Brazil \| **D'town** | 21 |
| Fleming's/Steak \| **Dunwoody** | 23 |
| **Z** Fogo de Chão \| **Buckhead** | 24 |
| **Z** Food Studio \| **W'side** | 24 |
| French Am. Brass. \| **D'town** | 24 |
| **Z** Kyma \| **Buckhead** | 25 |
| **Z** La Grotta \| **multi.** | 26 |
| McKendrick's \| **Dunwoody** | 25 |
| **Z NEW** MF Buckhead \| **Buckhead** | 26 |
| **Z** Morton's \| **multi.** | 25 |
| **Z** Nava \| **Buckhead** | 23 |
| **Z** Nikolai's \| **D'town** | 25 |
| Oceanaire \| **Midtown** | 23 |
| Palm \| **Buckhead** | 23 |
| **Z** Pano's/Paul's \| **Buckhead** | 26 |
| **Z** Park 75 \| **Midtown** | 27 |
| Pirates' Hse. \| **Historic Dist/S** | 15 |
| **Z** Pricci \| **Buckhead** | 24 |
| Prime \| **Buckhead** | 23 |
| **Z** Quinones \| **W'side** | 28 |
| **Z** Ritz/Atlanta \| **D'town** | 26 |
| **Z** Ritz/Buckhead Din. Rm. \| **Buckhead** | 27 |
| Roy's \| **Buckhead** | 23 |
| Ruth's Chris \| **multi.** | 23 |
| **Z** South City \| **Midtown** | 23 |
| **Z** Sun Dial \| **D'town** | 19 |
| Table 1280 \| **Midtown** | 20 |
| Tratt. La Strada \| **Marietta** | 19 |
| **Z** Trois \| **Midtown** | 22 |

**SPECIAL FEATURES**

Veni Vidi Vici | **Midtown** 23

VIlla Christina | **Dunwoody** 19

## WINE BARS

D. Morgan's | **Cartersville/O** –

Eno | **Midtown** 23

Enoteca Carbonari | **Midtown** 22

Fuego | **Midtown** 20

Grape | **multi.** 16

**Z** Krog Bar | **Inman Pk** 23

**Z** Murphy's | **VA-Highland** 24

Pura Vida | **Poncey-Highland** 25

SoHo | **Vinings** 22

Tasting Room | **multi.** 22

Terra Terroir | **Brookhaven** 19

Vinocity | **Kirkwood** 19

Vino Libro | **Grant Pk** 19

## WINNING WINE LISTS

**NEW** Allegro | **Midtown** 20

**Z** Antica Posta | **Buckhead** 24

**NEW** AquaKnox | **Buckhead** –

**Z** Aria | **Buckhead** 27

**Z** Atlanta Fish | **Buckhead** 23

**Z** Bacchanalia | **W'side** 29

Bistro VG | **Roswell** 22

**Z** Blue Ridge | **Buckhead** 23

**Z** Bone's | **Buckhead** 27

**Z** Buckhead Diner | **Buckhead** 23

**Z** Canoe | **Vinings** 26

Cargo | **Brunswick/O** –

**Z** Chops/Lobster | **Buckhead** 27

City Grill | **D'town** 22

**Z** Clark/Schwenk | **Vinings** 24

**NEW** Cuerno | **Midtown** –

**Z** Ecco | **Midtown** 25

**Z** Elizabeth | **Historic Dist/S** 25

Eno | **Midtown** 23

Five Seasons | **Alpharetta** 22

Fleming's/Steak | **Dunwoody** 23

**Z** Floataway | **Emory** 25

Food 101 | **VA-Highland** 20

**Z** Food Studio | **W'side** 24

**Z** Grace 17.20 | **Norcross** 25

Grape | **multi.** 16

Horseradish | **Buckhead** 22

Il Pasticcio | **Historic Dist/S** 22

**Z** JOËL | **Buckhead** 26

**Z** Kevin Rathbun | **Inman Pk** 26

**Z** Kyma | **Buckhead** 25

**Z** La Grotta | **Buckhead** 26

Lobby at 12 | **Atlantic Sta.** 20

**NEW** Luckie | **D'town** 17

McKendrick's | **Dunwoody** 25

**Z** Morton's | **multi.** 25

**Z** Murphy's | **VA-Highland** 24

**NEW** National | **Athens/O** 28

**Z** Nava | **Buckhead** 23

**Z** Nikolai's | **D'town** 25

**Z** ONE. midtown | **Midtown** 22

**Z** Pano's/Paul's | **Buckhead** 26

Park 75 | **Midtown** 27

Portofino | **Buckhead** 21

Pricci | **Buckhead** 24

Prime | **Buckhead** 23

**Z** Quinones | **W'side** 28

**Z** Rathbun's | **Inman Pk** 28

**Z** Ritz/Atlanta | **D'town** 26

**Z** Ritz/Buckhead Din. Rm. | **Buckhead** 27

Ruth's Chris | **D'town** 23

**Z** Seasons 52 | **multi.** 22

Shaun's | **Inman Pk** 24

Sia's | **Duluth** 25

SoHo | **Vinings** 22

**Z** South City | **multi.** 23

Table 1280 | **Midtown** 20

Toulouse | **S Buckhead** 21

Tratt. La Strada | **Marietta** 19

**Z** Trois | **Midtown** 22

**Z** TWO urban | **Poncey-Highland** 23

Veni Vidi Vici | **Midtown** 23

Villa Christina | **Dunwoody** 19

Vine | **VA-Highland** 21

Vinings Inn | **Vinings** 21

Vinocity | **Kirkwood** 19

Woodfire Grill | **Cheshire Bridge** 25

## WORTH A TRIP

**Athens**
| | |
|---|---|
| East West | 21 |
| Farmhouse | 25 |
| ◲ Five & Ten | 28 |

**Brunswick**
| | |
|---|---|
| Cargo | – |

**Cartersville**
| | |
|---|---|
| D. Morgan's | – |

**Dillard**
| | |
|---|---|
| Dillard Hse. | 21 |

**Greensboro**
| | |
|---|---|
| Linger Longer | 27 |

**Norcross**
| | |
|---|---|
| ◲ Grace 17.20 | 25 |

**Palmetto**
| | |
|---|---|
| Blue Eyed | 21 |
| Farm 255 | 20 |

**Savannah**
| | |
|---|---|
| ◲ Elizabeth | 25 |
| Il Pasticcio | 22 |
| Olde Pink | 21 |
| Pirates' Hse. | 15 |

**Social Circle**
| | |
|---|---|
| ◲ Blue Willow | 22 |

SPECIAL FEATURES

# Wine Vintage Chart

This chart, based on our 0 to 30 scale, is designed to help you select wine. The ratings (by **Howard Stravitz,** a law professor at the University of South Carolina) reflect the vintage quality and the wine's readiness to drink. We exclude the 1991–1993 vintages because they are not that good. A dash indicates the wine is either past its peak or too young to rate. Loire ratings are for dry white wines.

| Whites | 88 | 89 | 90 | 94 | 95 | 96 | 97 | 98 | 99 | 00 | 01 | 02 | 03 | 04 | 05 | 06 |
|---|---|---|---|---|---|---|---|---|---|---|---|---|---|---|---|---|
| **French:** | | | | | | | | | | | | | | | | |
| Alsace | - | 25 | 25 | 24 | 23 | 23 | 22 | 25 | 23 | 25 | 27 | 25 | 22 | 24 | 25 | - |
| Burgundy | - | 23 | 22 | - | 28 | 27 | 24 | 22 | 26 | 25 | 24 | 27 | 23 | 27 | 26 | 24 |
| Loire Valley | - | - | - | - | - | - | - | - | 24 | 25 | 26 | 23 | 24 | 27 | 24 | |
| Champagne | 24 | 26 | 29 | - | 26 | 27 | 24 | 23 | 24 | 24 | 22 | 26 | - | - | - | - |
| Sauternes | 29 | 25 | 28 | - | 21 | 23 | 25 | 23 | 24 | 24 | 28 | 25 | 26 | 21 | 26 | 23 |
| **California:** | | | | | | | | | | | | | | | | |
| Chardonnay | - | - | - | - | - | - | - | 24 | 23 | 26 | 26 | 25 | 27 | 29 | 25 | |
| Sauvignon Blanc | - | - | - | - | - | - | - | - | - | - | 27 | 28 | 26 | 27 | 26 | 27 |
| **Austrian:** | | | | | | | | | | | | | | | | |
| Grüner Velt./ Riesling | - | - | - | 25 | 21 | 26 | 26 | 25 | 22 | 23 | 25 | 26 | 25 | 26 | | - |
| **German:** | 25 | 26 | 27 | 24 | 23 | 26 | 25 | 26 | 23 | 21 | 29 | 27 | 24 | 26 | 28 | - |

| Reds | 88 | 89 | 90 | 94 | 95 | 96 | 97 | 98 | 99 | 00 | 01 | 02 | 03 | 04 | 05 | 06 |
|---|---|---|---|---|---|---|---|---|---|---|---|---|---|---|---|---|
| **French:** | | | | | | | | | | | | | | | | |
| Bordeaux | 23 | 25 | 29 | 22 | 26 | 25 | 23 | 25 | 24 | 29 | 26 | 24 | 25 | 24 | 27 | 25 |
| Burgundy | - | 24 | 26 | - | 26 | 27 | 25 | 22 | 27 | 22 | 24 | 27 | 25 | 25 | 27 | 25 |
| Rhône | 26 | 28 | 28 | 24 | 26 | 22 | 25 | 27 | 26 | 27 | 26 | - | 25 | 24 | 25 | - |
| Beaujolais | - | - | - | - | - | - | - | - | 24 | - | 23 | 25 | 22 | 28 | 26 | |
| **California:** | | | | | | | | | | | | | | | | |
| Cab./Merlot | - | - | 28 | 29 | 27 | 25 | 28 | 23 | 26 | 22 | 27 | 26 | 25 | 24 | 24 | 23 |
| Pinot Noir | - | - | - | - | - | - | 24 | 23 | 24 | 23 | 27 | 28 | 26 | 25 | 24 | - |
| Zinfandel | - | - | - | - | - | - | - | - | - | 25 | 23 | 27 | 24 | 23 | - | |
| **Oregon:** | | | | | | | | | | | | | | | | |
| Pinot Noir | - | - | - | - | - | - | - | - | - | - | 27 | 25 | 26 | 27 | - | |
| **Italian:** | | | | | | | | | | | | | | | | |
| Tuscany | - | - | 25 | 22 | 24 | 20 | 29 | 24 | 27 | 24 | 27 | 20 | 25 | 25 | 22 | 24 |
| Piedmont | - | 27 | 27 | - | 23 | 26 | 27 | 26 | 25 | 28 | 27 | 20 | 24 | 25 | 26 | - |
| **Spanish:** | | | | | | | | | | | | | | | | |
| Rioja | - | - | - | 26 | 26 | 24 | 25 | 22 | 25 | 24 | 27 | 20 | 24 | 25 | 26 | 24 |
| Ribera del Duero/Priorat | - | - | - | 26 | 26 | 27 | 25 | 24 | 25 | 24 | 27 | 20 | 24 | 26 | 26 | 24 |
| **Australian:** | | | | | | | | | | | | | | | | |
| Shiraz/Cab. | - | - | - | 24 | 26 | 23 | 26 | 28 | 24 | 24 | 27 | 27 | 25 | 26 | 24 | - |
| **Chilean:** | - | - | - | - | - | 24 | - | 25 | 23 | 26 | 24 | 25 | 24 | 26 | - | |

# Zagat Products

## RESTAURANTS & MAPS

America's Top Restaurants
Atlanta
Beijing
Boston
Brooklyn
California Wine Country
Cape Cod & The Islands
Chicago
Connecticut
Europe's Top Restaurants
Hamptons (incl. wineries)
Hong Kong
Las Vegas
London
Long Island (incl. wineries)
Los Angeles I So. California
(guide & map)
Miami Beach
Miami I So. Florida
Montréal
New Jersey
New Jersey Shore
New Orleans
New York City (guide & map)
Palm Beach
Paris
Philadelphia
San Diego
San Francisco (guide & map)
Seattle
Shanghai
Texas
Tokyo
Toronto
Vancouver
Washington, DC I Baltimore
Westchester I Hudson Valley
World's Top Restaurants

## LIFESTYLE GUIDES

America's Top Golf Courses
Movie Guide
Music Guide
NYC Gourmet Shop./Entertaining
NYC Shopping

## NIGHTLIFE GUIDES

Los Angeles
New York City
San Francisco

## HOTEL & TRAVEL GUIDES

Beijing
Hong Kong
Las Vegas
London
New Orleans
Montréal
Shanghai
Top U.S. Hotels, Resorts & Spas
Toronto
U.S. Family Travel
Vancouver
Walt Disney World Insider's Guide
World's Top Hotels, Resorts & Spas

## WEB & WIRELESS SERVICES

ZAGAT TO GO[SM] for handhelds
ZAGAT.com[SM] • ZAGAT.mobi[SM]

**Available wherever books are sold or at ZAGAT.com. To customize
Zagat guides as gifts or marketing tools, call 800-540-9609.**

0  20613 06978  2